Dimitrios Kanellakis
Aristophanes and the Poetics of Surprise

Trends in Classics – Supplementary Volumes

Edited by
Franco Montanari and Antonios Rengakos

Associate Editors
Stavros Frangoulidis · Fausto Montana · Lara Pagani
Serena Perrone · Evina Sistakou · Christos Tsagalis

Scientific Committee
Alberto Bernabé · Margarethe Billerbeck
Claude Calame · Jonas Grethlein · Philip R. Hardie
Stephen J. Harrison · Stephen Hinds · Richard Hunter
Christina Kraus · Giuseppe Mastromarco
Gregory Nagy · Theodore D. Papanghelis
Giusto Picone · Tim Whitmarsh
Bernhard Zimmermann

Volume 96

Dimitrios Kanellakis

Aristophanes and the Poetics of Surprise

DE GRUYTER

ISBN 978-3-11-077808-3
e-ISBN (PDF) 978-3-11-067703-4
e-ISBN (EPUB) 978-3-11-067716-4
ISSN 1868-4785

Library of Congress Control Number: 2019956254

Bibliographic information published by the Deutsche Nationalbibliothek
The Deutsche Nationalbibliothek lists this publication in the Deutsche Nationalbibliografie;
detailed bibliographic data are available on the Internet at http://dnb.dnb.de.

© 2021 Walter de Gruyter GmbH, Berlin/Boston
This volume is text- and page-identical with the hardback published in 2020.
Editorial Office: Alessia Ferreccio and Katerina Zianna
Logo: Christopher Schneider, Laufen
Printing and binding: CPI books GmbH, Leck

www.degruyter.com

He has a great future behind him

Contents

Acknowledgments — IX
List of Figures — XI
List of Tables — XIII
Texts and Abbreviations — XV

Introduction — 1
Surprise — 1
Poetics — 8
Aristophanes — 17

1 **Verbal Surprise: *Para Prosdokian* Jokes** — 23
1.1 The Term — 27
1.2 The Concept — 33
1.3 Non-Standard Uses — 41
1.4 Three Common Types of *Para Prosdokian* — 57
1.5 Tracing the Norms (A Comparative Analysis) — 68
1.6 And What About Oxymoron? — 85

2 **Thematic Surprise: Appropriating Myths** — 88
2.1 *Acharnians* — 91
2.2 *Knights* — 94
2.3 *Clouds* — 95
2.4 *Wasps* — 98
2.5 *Peace* — 102
2.6 *Birds* — 104
2.7 *Lysistrata* — 109
2.8 *Thesmophoriazusae* — 114
2.9 *Frogs* — 117
2.10 *Ecclesiazusae* — 120
2.11 *Wealth* — 122
2.12 The Intra-Dramatic Functions of Appropriated Myths — 124
2.13 A Comparison with Tragedy — 125

3 **Theatrical Surprise** — 129
3.1 Actions Contradictory to Words — 133
3.2 Breaching Theatrical Conventions — 138
3.3 Consulting Modern Performances — 153

4 Brekekekex, Surprise! Surprise! —— 175
4.1 Prologue —— 177
4.2 First Episode —— 186
4.3 Second Episode —— 189
4.4 Third Episode —— 190
4.5 Fourth Episode —— 192

Afterword —— 198

Appendices —— 201

Bibliography —— 219
Index Locorum —— 237
Index Nominum et Rerum —— 243

Acknowledgments

This book arises from my doctoral thesis at the University of Oxford (2016–2019). Special thanks are due to The Faculty of Classics and The Queen's College, both as institutions and as lively communities, for having offered the most supportive and inspiring environment for this project; to my former *alma mater*, the Faculty of Philology of the University of Athens, for preparing me for this path; and to A.S. Onassis Foundation, A.G. Leventis Foundation, and L. Voudouri Foundation, for their generous scholarships during various stages of my graduate studies.

My primary debt is owed to my academic supervisor Professor Armand D' Angour, as well as to my supervisor for my master's degree Professor Angus Bowie, who have provided me with invaluable guidance, suggestions, and corrections, and have displayed admirable patience with my endless drafts and clumsy English. I have also been benefited from the feedback of Professors Ioannis Konstantakos, Fiona Macintosh, Bruno Currie, Evert Boas, Felix Budelmann, Nick Lowe, Constanze Güthenke, Dr Almut Fries, and the reviewers of De Gruyter.

Warm thanks are also due to Professors Michael Fontaine and Javier Bilbao Ruiz for offering me bibliographical assistance at the very beginning of my research; to Professor Kaiti Diamantakou for providing me access to the DVD archive of the Theatre Studies Department, University of Athens; to Ms Sofia Mbouga, Mr Fabian Saupe, and Ms Nabila Mu for scanning some unpublished dissertations from abroad; and to Anne Hiller and Katerina Zianna of De Gruyter for dealing wonderfully with my quite complicated manuscript.

This is also the appropriate place to thank Professors Anne Sheppard, Mary Giossi, Peggy Karpouzou, and Katerina Carvounis, who have supported me with academic references – not to mention inspiring lectures – and my Greek teacher in middle-school, Ms Maria Nikolopoulou, who introduced me to Aristophanes and equipped me, like another Hoopoe-Tereus, with the feathers of imagination.

I wish to dedicate the fruits of my labour to my family, my parents Titos and Ioanna and my siblings Elias and Elina, who have always been an inexhaustible source of love, support, and motivation.

Oxford, September 2019

List of Figures

Fig. 1: 'Emperor' herm decorating the fence outside the Sheldonian Theatre, Oxford. Photograph by Alice Brown —— 16

Fig. 2: Sketch of the fifth and the sixth metope of the pronaos, Temple of Zeus at Olympia. Drawing by Max Kühnert, in E. Curtius/F. Adler (eds.), *Olympia: Die Ergebnisse der von dem Deutschen Reich veranstalteten Ausgrabung*, vol. 3, Berlin 1894, pl. xlv —— 101

Fig. 3: A schematic comparison of Aristophanes' cosmogony (left frame) and Hesiod's *Theogony* (right frame) —— 108

Fig. 4: The Persephone Painter (Greek, Attic), *Bell Krater; Front: Helen fleeing from Menelaos*, 440–430 BC, earthware. H: 32.5 cm; Diam (lip): 37.5 cm; Diam (foot): 18 cm. The Toledo Museum of Art. Purchased with funds from the Libbey Endowment, Gift of Edward Drummond Libbey, 1967.154 —— 110

Fig. 5: Christoforos Nezer as Trygaeus on the dung-beetle in *Peace* directed by A. Solomos for the Greek National Theatre, 1964. Photograph by Dimitris Harissiadis, Benaki Museum —— 149

Fig. 6a–b: Mary Aroni as Lysistrata and Anna Kyriakou as Calonice in *Lysistrata* directed by A. Solomos, 1972. Screenshots from the video-recording of the performance —— 155

Fig. 7: Cover illustration by John Taylor. Biles/Olson 2015. Oxford Publishing Limited. Reproduced with permission of the Licensor through PLSclear —— 159

Fig. 8: Gianna Kourou as the cheese-grater in *Wasps* directed by N. Giannopoulos, 1977. Screenshot from the video-recording of the performance —— 159

Fig. 9: Cinesias, the baby, and a nurse in *Lysistrata* directed by A. Solomos, 1972. Photograph from the Archive of the Greek National Theatre —— 161

Fig. 10: Cinesias, the baby, and Myrrhine in *Lysistrata* directed by K. Tsianos, 2004. Photograph from the Archive of the Greek National Theatre —— 161

Fig. 11: A sleeping nurse, the toddler, and Myrrhine in *Lysistrata* directed by D. Chronopoulos, 1997. Screenshot from the video-recording of the performance —— 161

Fig. 12 a–c: Nikos Mbousdoukos as Cinesias, dealing with a phallus prop collapsing, in *Lysistrata* directed by D. Chronopoulos, 1997. Screenshot from the video-recording of the performance —— 163

Fig. 13: Zoe Konstantopoulou on 27 January 2015. Photograph from *thetoc.gr* —— 167

Fig. 14: Giannis Mbezos as Praxagora in *Ecclesiazusae* directed by himself, 2015. Photograph by Marilena Stafylidou —— 167

Fig. 15: Apulian red-figured bell krater 375–350 BC (formerly Berlin F3046). M. Bieber, *Die Denkmaler zum Theaterwesen im Altertum*, Berlin/Leipzig 1920, pl. 80 —— 179

Fig. 16: Giannis Mbezos as Dionysus and Petros Philippidis as Xanthias in *Frogs* directed by K. Tsianos, 1998. Photograph from the Archive of the Greek National Theatre —— 179

Fig. 17: Portrait masks of David Cameron and Nick Clegg as the Empousa in *Frogs* directed by H. Eastman, 2013. Screenshot from the video-recording of the performance —— 185

Fig. 18–20: Apulian frog gutti, 4th century BC. Left: Cleveland Museum of Art 1985.176, Ohio. Middle: Museo Jatta 1458, Ruvo. Right: Leo Mildenberg Collection II 76, Zurich. Drawings by D. Kanellakis —— 193

List of Tables

Tab. 1: J. Robson's classification of speech (2006) —— 12
Tab. 2: A selection of modern productions of Aristophanic plays —— 153
Tab. 3: Two modern productions of *Frogs* —— 175
Tab. 4: Proposed *Para Prosdokian* - Acharnians —— 201
Tab. 5: Proposed *Para Prosdokian* - Peace —— 203
Tab. 6: Proposed *Para Prosdokian* - Thesmophoriazusae —— 205
Tab. 7: Proposed *Para Prosdokian* - Wealth —— 206
Tab. 8: Norms in *Para Prosdokian* - Acharnians —— 208
Tab. 9: Norms in *Para Prosdokian* - Peace —— 210
Tab. 10: Norms in *Para Prosdokian* - Thesmophoriazusae —— 212
Tab. 11: Norms in *Para Prosdokian* - Wealth —— 214
Tab. 12: The Intra-Dramatic Functions of Appropriated Myths —— 216

Texts and Abbreviations

In quoting from, and citing, Greek and Latin texts I follow the latest *OCT* editions for most authors. Where I deviate from N.G. Wilson's edition of Aristophanes (2007), this is made explicit. I use R. Kassel and C. Austin, *Poetae Comici Graeci* (1983 –) for comic fragments; B. Snell, R. Kannicht, and S. Radt, *Tragicorum Graecorum Fragmenta* (1986 –) for tragic fragments; M.L. West, *Iambi et Elegi Graeci* (1989–1992), D.L. Page, *Poetae Melici Graeci* (1962), and E. Lobe and D.L. Page, *Poetarum Lesbiorum Fragmenta* (1955) for the respective categories of lyric poetry. The translations are from Loeb (thus J. Henderson for Aristophanes), or of my own when necessary, unless otherwise stated in the footnotes. The names of ancient authors and the titles of their works are abbreviated according to the *OCD* (thus Aesch. instead of A. for Aeschylus, or *Eccl.* instead of *Ec.* for *Ecclesiazusae*), unless they are not included there and except for the Greek Anthology, in which cases I follow the abbreviations of *LSJ* (thus *AP* instead of *Anth. Pal.*, or Hippon. for Hipponax). Journals are abbreviated according to *L'Année philologique* (thus *TAPhA* instead of *TAPA*, or *AJPh* instead of *AJP*).

Introduction

The purpose of this book is to examine the variety, the mechanisms, and the poetological intention of the effect of surprise in Aristophanic comedy, addressing the phenomenon not as a self-evident or unselfconscious element of comedy as a genre, but as an elaborate system which characterises the poetic idiolect of the specific dramatist. More precisely, the book analyses Aristophanes' most prominent *verbal*, *thematic*, and *theatrical* modes of surprise from a typological perspective, and interprets them as comprising the key area in which the playwright claims and demonstrates his artistic superiority over rival genres and individual poets. In line with this purpose, two parallel aims of the book are to provide an original commentary on the passages under examination, and to promote the study of modern performances – a practice which has so far been either restricted to Classical Reception or only theoretically acknowledged (if at all) by mainstream philological scholarship. To delimit the scope and methodology of the book, I explain the three terms appearing in its title in reverse order, i.e. from the broader to the narrower subject area.

Surprise

As a topic of intellectual discourse in the modern world, surprise passed from the field of philosophy (with Aristotle's *Poetics*, Descartes' *The Passions of the Soul*, and Kant's *Anthrophony from a Pragmatic Point of View* being the most decisive contributions) to that of psychology (with Darwin's *The Expression of Emotions in Man and Animals*) and more recently to neuroscience,[1] while also finding crucial applications in economics and marketing.[2] Surprise is one of the six emotions which Paul Ekman identified as 'basic', along with anger, disgust, fear, happiness, and sadness. He associated these feelings with facial displays which are universally recognised (e.g. open mouth and bulging eyes show surprise), as well as with reactions of the autonomic nervous system (e.g. a high heart rate indicates anger when accompanied by high skin temperature, but fear or sadness

---

[1] That turn is marked by the simultaneous appearance of Squires *et al.* 1975 on auditory stimuli, and Courchesne *et al.* 1975 on visual stimuli.
[2] E.g. Shackle 1938; 1949; 1970; Vanhamme 2000; Alden *et al.* 2000.

when accompanied by low skin temperature).[3] Recent psychologists have now dropped surprise from the list of basic emotions,[4] and have reappraised it more as a cognitive state, i.e. as an attempt to explain the occurrence of an abnormal event, with emotion coming as a side-effect of this understanding process.[5] There is still evidence, however, that there is an interplay of cognitive and emotional elements both during and in response to surprising events.[6] Along with this general debate, there have been important discoveries recently on particular issues: according to research, surprising events interrupt cognition (short-term memory in particular) via the same brain mechanism that interrupts skeletomotor activity in a stop-signal task.[7] During visual replays, i.e. alternating appearances and disappearances of a visual target, pupil dilation scales with the level of surprise about the timing of switches.[8] When presented with a sequence of visual stimuli, our neural responses differ for the frequent and the infrequent stimuli, but whether this difference is due to an enhancement of neural response for the surprising presentations, or to a reduction of neural response for the repetitive presentations depends on the nature of the stimulus, i.e. whether it is an object, a person, a letter etc.[9] As for behavioural responses, we initiate a movement (of approach or avoidance) to a threat-related surprising stimulus faster than to a pleasant surprising stimulus.[10] When it comes to reading jokes, most pertinently for this book, the readers who display bigger surprise, comprehension, and amusement to jokes are those who elicit larger neural deflections at the respective sub-stage of humour processing: incongruity detection, incongruity resolution, and elaboration.[11]

Although this research did not involve any experiments – which theoretically could range from measuring spectators' heart rate and skin temperature to eye

---

[3] Ekman 1972; 1980; 1983. Plutchik 1980 raised the number of such emotions to eight and grouped them into pairs of opposites (joy–sadness, anger–fear, trust–distrust, surprise–anticipation).
[4] In a survey conducted by Ekman himself (2016, 32), surprise is endorsed by 40–50% of the specialists.
[5] Foster/Keane 2013.
[6] Foster/Keane 2015.
[7] Wessel *et al.* 2016.
[8] Kloosterman *et al.* 2015.
[9] Amado/Kovács 2016.
[10] Schützwohl 2018.
[11] Ku *et al.* 2017.

tracking and brain scanning[12] – the physiological aspect has been taken into account as much as realistically possible. For example, Chapter 1 acknowledges that the capability of an audience to decode jokes in the context of performed/oral speech is less than that of readers, who can revisit a line as many times as they wish. In Chapters 3 and 4 I consider video-recorded modern performances of Aristophanes' plays and examine when and how the audience laughs: the volume, duration, and consistency of laughter is telling for the quality of the joke. Even though laughter is not a necessary or sufficient result of surprise, it remains a very plausible indicator of it. For Vladimir Propp, 'laughter is caused not only by the presence of flaws, but by their sudden and unexpected revelation'; or in Immanuel Kant's more abstract formulation, 'laughter is an affect that arises if a tense expectation is transformed into nothing'.[13] The hypothesis is tested on a case-by-case basis through the analysis of the drama itself.

Drama both incorporates and evokes surprise in both the *dramatis personae* and in the audience (more precisely the intended audience). The present book is almost exclusively concerned with the latter category, i.e. with the 'reception-perspective' rather than the 'figure-perspective' of surprise.[14] In the field of communication theory, Burgoon proposed the *Expectancy Violations Theory* (EVT): surprise arises from the violation of the social behaviour that is expected between two communicators according to their characteristics, to the context of their communication, and to social norms; such violations either cause positive surprise, which increases the attraction of the violator, or negative, which decreases the attraction.[15] In trying to transfer this model to drama, the restrictions appear to be significantly more than the benefits. Watching or reading a play is a communication between a real participant and a fictional one, the former having artistic expectations from the latter, rather than social ones. The context of the communication is one that allows or even demands from the fictional participant to be offensive; to call someone a 'drunkard', a 'gambler', or a 'poofter' in public, pointing at them, would be a negative violation in reality, but the characters of a comedy are positive violators when doing so with members of their audience (*Vesp.* 73–84). Moreover, while EVT is founded on the study of proxemics, i.e. how one reacts when someone else violates his/her personal space, in theatre the audience and the characters stand away from each other, in fixed places. Even in

---

[12] For the neural basis of humour processing, see Vrticka *et al.* 2013; Campbell *et al.* 2015; Chen *et al.* 2017.
[13] Propp 2009, 36. Kant 1987, 203.
[14] For these terms, see Pfister 1988, 57–9.
[15] Burgoon/Jones 1976.

cases of physical interaction, such as actors invading the cavea or spectators being brought on stage, EVT can only explain what the spectators and *actors* expect from each other (e.g. that the spectator shall not impede the actor from doing his job, or that the actor shall not hurt the spectator with props) and not what the *dramatis personae* expect or are expected to do. EVT seems more functional for the interactions within the play, i.e. for the surprises between the *dramatis personae*, since they share equal status (they are all fictional), equal relation to the context (they are all within the plot), and measurable proxemics. In terms of usefulness, however, to judge the expectations of fictional characters would be as fruitful as early psychoanalytic criticism.

Like most emotions and literary tropes, surprise is anything but simple and unified; there are many varieties, as reflected in the vocabulary. *Surprise, paradox*, and *the unexpected* are synonyms which are used more or less interchangeably in this book, but they all carry nuances which make them 'problematic' as labels. *Surprise* sometimes implies a physical response (e.g. laughter or goggling) to a visual stimulus; *paradox* in English means 'the self-contradictory in terms of logic',[16] which is much narrower than the Greek παράδοξος ('contrary to expectation, incredible' *LSJ*); and *the unexpected* may imply that there is something *expected* in the first place, which is eventually reversed, but this excludes anything 'coming out of the blue', i.e. with no previous expectation at all. *Surprise* is the preferred term here for convenience, as an umbrella term to include mental and/or physical reactions to unpredictable textual and/or visual stimuli. Specific definitions of verbal, thematic, and theatrical surprise are presented in detail in the introductory sections of the respective chapters, but the underlying condition is common: the audience's range of anticipation – be that intratextually, intertextually, or extratextually built up – needs to be violated through cognitively-processed mechanisms, such as incongruity, opposition, and contradiction. However, not every incongruity, opposition, or contradiction lead to surprise effect, but only insofar as they violate expectations; for example, a joke that involves contradiction is not surprising the tenth time we listen to it, or when said by a friend who tells similar jokes all the time. It thus appears that a combination of violation with novelty (of content or context) is required. This model only covers 'the unexpected' while leaving 'the sudden' outside; this is reasonable, because everything unexpected is surprising (a tautology) but not everything sudden is surprising (e.g. the sudden start of a rainfall that has been announced by the weather forecast), even though it causes some sort of astonishment. Despite

---

16 Consider the so-called Socratic 'paradox' *I know one thing, that I know nothing* – hence how can he know this *one* thing?

not being a necessary condition for surprise, suddenness is certainly an intensifying catalyst, which explains for example the short length of *para prosdokian* jokes, or the fast response of actors when accidents happen on stage.

The problem with defining surprise is also reflected in the ancient Greek lexicon of surprise-terms, not the least because there is no word there to mean *surprise* exactly as in modern English, or even ἔκπληξη as in modern Greek. The ancient ἔκπληξις is much narrower, denoting consternation or astonishment caused by terror or misfortunes, since the verb ἐκπλήσσω means to physically or emotionally strike someone by a sudden shock (e.g. for a thunderbolt or a panic-attack).[17] This linguistic interweaving of surprise with fear is not accidental at all; emotion-scientists are still trying to define the limits between the two: 'the difficulty in recognising fear could be attributed to the similar visual configuration with surprise. In effect, they share more muscle movements than they possess distinctive ones.'[18] Aristotle was the first to have used a derivative of this word as a poetic term: a poem becomes ἐκπληκτικώτερον (more thrilling) when it contains some ἀδύνατα (impossibilities).[19] Even though ἐκπληκτικώτερον here has a different nuance from the initial sense of the word (terrifying > thrilling), it retains its basic function: it describes the emotional impact on the receiver.

Contrary to ἔκπληξις, which was linked with 'the sudden', the vocabulary for 'the unexpected' was focussed on the stimulus causing the surprise, rather than on its emotional impact. An unexpected event or spectacle was characterised as θαῦμα (a wonder), νέον τί, καινόν τί (something new or strange), or with the compounds ἀδόξαστος, ἀδόκητος, ἀνεπιδόκητος, ἀπροσδόκητος (unthought-of) and ἀελπής, ἄελπτος (unhoped-for). It would be tempting, according to the latter two groups of adjectives, to distinguish between cognitive-based expectations (δόξα) and emotional-based expectations (ἐλπίς), but in practice there was no such rigid distinction. For example, Archilochus (fr. 122) refers to a solar eclipse as an ἄελπτον phenomenon, meaning an 'unimaginable' one, and conversely Thucydides (7.30.1) refers to the slaughter of children by the Thracians in Mycalessus as an ἀδόκητος disaster, meaning an 'undesired' one. Like with ἔκπληξις, literary criticism appropriated some of these terms too, e.g. τὸ θαυμαστόν (a sense of awe;

---

[17] In a similar way, 'derived from the Old French *surprendre* (to attack or, more literally, overtake), the English word "surprise" first denoted military assault, seizure, rape, or disturbance', Miller 2012, 3; this book offers a highly recommended introduction to the intellectual history of surprise as an aesthetic term.
[18] Roy-Charland *et al.* 2014. In pursuing that distinction, scientists resort into eye-tracking (see *ibid.*) or neural responses (see Zhao *et al.* 2017; Chamberland *et al.* 2017).
[19] Arist. *Poet.* 1460b.

Arist. *Poet.* 1460a), νέος (modernistic; cf. names of genres such as 'New Music' and 'New Comedy'), and of course παρὰ προσδοκίαν.

Surprise has many aspects, and one can find surprise in any of several dramaturgical components.[20] This book is concerned with verbal (Chapter 1), thematic (Chapter 2), and theatrical surprise (Chapter 3), as well as with their intersection (Chapter 4). There are, however, other important aspects, such as plot structure, characterisation, or even the 'ideology' of the plays, which brim with surprising elements but have been excluded due to limitations of space and their more extensive treatment in previous scholarship. A few examples regarding plot structure may be given. In *Knights*, 'one of the most paradoxical aspects of the play has always seemed to be the political alliance between the Knights, representing the richest Athenian class, and the low-born and scoundrel Sausage-Seller'.[21] In *Clouds*, 'the Sophists and their ways are presented as something that no true Athenian should have anything to do with, but at the same time, the way to destroy them appears to be to involve oneself with them'.[22] There is also the striking paradox of the ἥττων defeating the κρείττων argument, which 'neatly reflects Aristophanes' feeling of astonishment that his own exceptional play was ranked behind those of run-of-the-mill competitors (524)'.[23] As for *Wasps*, 'whereas usually a wild son is checked by a severe father, in this case a wild father is checked by a severe son. So throughout 1352-9 there is a comic paradox: υἱός appears where we should normally expect πατήρ, and vice versa'.[24] In *Birds*, Nephelokokkygia is 'a world of paradoxes: like Athens but also suffering from Athens, human and non-human, anti-imperialist and imperialist'.[25] In *Lysistrata*, 'war has paradoxically forced the women to "declare war" in order to make peace',[26] let alone that 'the calling of a sex-strike against men who are away at war is a paradox'.[27] In *Frogs*, κρίνας παρὰ προσδοκίαν ὁ Διόνυσος τὸν Αἰσχύλον νικᾶν, [...] ἀνέρχεται (hypothesis 1) / παρὰ προσδοκίαν τοῦτον λαβὼν ἀλλ' οὐκ Εὐριπίδην, αὖθις ἐς τοὺς ζῶντας ἀνέρχεται (hypothesis 4; παρὰ προσδοκίαν is not used in a technical sense

---

20 Zimmermann 2011, 705-7 distinguishes between verbal, musical/metrical, structural and scenic *aprosdokēta*, and provides examples from Aristophanes and, where possible, from other comic poets. In my discussion, 'structural' surprises have to do with plot construction, whereas Zimmermann uses the term in reference to the κατὰ τὸ ποσὸν parts of a play.
21 Sidwell 2009, 160; also Brock 1986, 20 and Landfester 1967, 44.
22 Bowie 1993, 131.
23 Biles 2011, 204; Sommerstein 2009, 178 n. 5.
24 MacDowell 1971, 308.
25 Ruffell 2014, 212.
26 Bowie 1993, 183.
27 Bowie 1993, 188.

here). Apart from Dionysus' final decision, the contest itself has some surprising features.[28] Moreover, 'the whole quest is paradoxical – to journey into death to find a life-giving poet, and to find the vivifying cultural principle in a voice which had been silent for fifty years'.[29] Regarding the scatology in the play, one cannot omit 'the evident paradox that Aristophanes' own play (half-)exploits the routines which Xanthias suggests are typical of inferior playwrights (13 f.)'.[30] In these examples scholars use the word 'surprise' or 'paradox' with different nuances but the underlying model in most cases is common. Semantic oppositions are presented in pragmatic reversal, i.e. comedies cede temporal, causative, or qualitative precedence to terms which, pragmatically, would follow their opposites (sons>fathers, low class>upper class, bad arguments> strong arguments, death>life, war>peace).

On the level of characterisation, Whitman has emphasised the 'heroic paradox' of the 'comic hero'. The latter is filled with urge towards divinity but also with the necessity of remaining mortal; he is an individual hero alienated from the city but he also emblematises the 'mythic shape of humanity as individual'.[31] As for the 'ideology' or 'agenda' of Aristophanic comedy, most plays are characterised by surprising ambiguity. It is rarely clear whether the poet embraces or lampoons the comic idea which is put forward by the plot; whether he pictures a utopia or a dystopia. Dikaiopolis makes peace but only for himself; Paphlagon is overthrown but only by someone similar to, or worse than him; Peace is rescued but Theoria is left to be abused by the *Boulē*; Peisetairos evangelises for an apolitical society but ends up as a demagogue and a tyrant; Praxagora's communism intends to conquer unfairness but it legalises rape and promotes opportunism; Wealth is redistributed but in a way that promotes idleness and unproductivity. Optimistic or pessimistic? Conservative or radical? Elitist or populist? Aristophanic comedy does not fit in such clear-cut ideological categories. The main reason for this is not simply pragmatic, i.e. that the poet sought to please as many spectators as possible, hence needed to remain ambiguous. Rather, Aristophanes seems to reject the idea of a fixed truth or ethic; since life is full of surprises, so is his poetry.

---

28 See Dover 1993, 7.
29 Whitman 1964, 257.
30 Halliwell 2014, 191.
31 Whitman 1982, 20, 151–3.

Poetics

The meaning of the term is twofold: it refers, on the one hand, to the analysis of different techniques for deriving a typology of poetry and, on the other hand, to the self-awareness and self-referentiality of an artistic creation.

My analysis of poetics is informed by Humour Theory and Performance Theory. Versions of these have been applied to Aristophanes by Robson (2006) and Revermann (2006) respectively. Compared to these treatments the present book might seem undertheorised, but my priority is to comment on the plays rather than to validate an external model. This is a deliberate choice made in view of my personal taste and, more importantly, in view of the biases that theory often involves. For example, in his *Theory and Analysis of Drama*, Pfister says that:

> dramatic productions have been restricted almost exclusively to texts employing acoustic and visual codes alone. Exceptions to this are *more recent developments* such as happenings or ritualist theatre, which also experiment with haptic (physical contact between actors and audience), olfactory and even gustatory effects. [...] The remaining senses of smell, touch and taste have been activated extremely sporadically, and then almost exclusively in the *modern theatre* of the avant-garde.

and:

> in *modern theatre*, particularly in happenings and documentary theatre, [...performances...] strive, from the producer's perspective, to abolish the socially accepted consensus on the categorical distinction between real and fictional dramatic situations. By subverting the audience's expectations, they attempt to make it aware of – and adopt a critical attitude towards – fictionality as a conventional coding procedure.[32]

Such generalisations underestimate ancient drama and especially Aristophanes, whose comedy is soaked in metatheatricality – Slater (2002) emphasises precisely how it instils the audience with a critical attitude – and whose characters in *Peace*, for example, are roasting on stage (1040 f. : smell), dispensing savouries to the audience (962–7 : taste), and even passing mute female characters to the *prohedria* for the officials' entertainment (882 f. : touch). As far as surprise in particular is concerned, the most problematic prejudice of theory is that discrepancy between text and stage action is 'a more recent development... in the context of the innovatory tendencies prevalent in modern drama', which Revermann rather

---

[32] Pfister 1988, 7–8, 35. Italicisation is my own.

uncritically takes from Pfister.[33] It will be argued here that this technique was well familiar to Aristophanes.

Apart from various misconceptions, the main *methodological* problem is that as long as Theatre Semiotics struggles to define discrete theatrical semiotic units (to put it simply, we analyse a text line-by-line but how do we 'chop up' a performance?),[34] it avoids 'getting down to business' and analysing performances even in less formalistic terms. This is not to say that theoretical issues are negligible, but sometimes experience suggests the most appropriate tools. For example, in my experience of video-recorded performances (Chapter 3.3), a practical 'theatrical semiotic unit' for Greek comedy is the duration between two moments where the audience laughs, and everything in between – all the signs involved – lead to this effect, linearly or with fluctuation, and in collaboration or in conflict with each other.[35] As for the 'width of analysis', Fischer-Lichte proposed that the theatrical code ought to be analysed on three different levels: on a 'systemic level' one examines all the repertoire of signs that is theoretically available; on a 'normative level' the focus moves to the signs available according to the conventions of a specific era, place, and genre; and finally, on the 'level of speech' one examines the signs employed in an individual performance.[36] Our analysis in Chapter 3.3 moves between the two latter levels, resorting to specific performances in order to draw information about the genre, but in an unconventional way: *modern* performances are consulted in order to illuminate the possibilities of *ancient* performances, in that they may be though to use analogous (rather than identical) signs.

At the same time, Performance Theory has offered some truly insightful concepts for our analysis, such as 'the collective nature of production and reception' and 'the social psychology of collective reception'.[37] The former refers to the multiple intentions and (re)actions of the members of the production team and of the audience. In the course of this book I attempt to cover as many perspectives as possible: surprise on the part of the audience (what is received), on the part of the director (what is intended), or even on the part of the actors (e.g. when acci-

---

33 Pfister 1988, 48–9, followed by Revermann 2006, 47–8 for the case of Aristophanes.
34 See Elam 2002, 41–4; Fischer-Lichte 1992, 131–4.
35 Even in cases of collaboration, there is always a 'hierarchy' among the theatrical signs, i.e. the predominance of one sign (e.g. of the costume) over the other signs (e.g. language, movements, lighting). This concept was introduced by Mukařovský 1982=1931, the seminal work for Theatre Semiotics.
36 Fischer-Lichte 1992, 10–12.
37 Pfister 1988, 11, 37–8.

dents happen during a performance). The second concept refers to how the numerous individual reactions of the audience may harmonise with each other to produce a relatively homogeneous collective reaction. For example, individual spectators may repress their laughter when the majority is not laughing, or may pretend laughter when the majority is laughing – unconsciously or otherwise. At other times, the fact that laughter is contagious means we may laugh not at the spectacle or the joke itself, but along with our fellow-spectators' laughter. The latter observation can explain, for example, the very common technique of accumulation: the poet presents consecutive surprising stimuli (as will be shown) so that, even if only a part of the audience 'gets the joke' the first time, everyone will eventually be dragged into the vortex of laughter.

Humour studies became a unified academic discourse only in 1989 with the foundation of *Humor: International Journal of Humor Research*, founding editor of which was Raskin. Despite its overall contribution, the journal has surprisingly few articles on surprise; even though these are narrow case-studies, they still offer useful insights. In one empirical research, products with visual-tactual incongruities (e.g. an inflexible rubber ducky), visual-auditory incongruities (e.g. a bell-sounding rubber ducky), and visual-olfactory incongruities (e.g. a malodorous deodorant) were evaluated by the participants as surprising as well as confusing.[38] Such findings – and most of the papers in this journal in general – are of much interest but too far from the realm of literature to adopt them unconditionally. For example, the various incongruities in a 'serious comedy' or a 'funny tragedy' can be surprising for the audience but hardly confusing, because art is not bound by the pragmatic rules that apply to the market: an 'incongruity' in a product is a deal-breaker for the purchase, whereas artists are *a priori* granted with 'poetic licence'.

Leaving aside theories about the psychosocial function of humour (*what it does*) – the most influential being those by Bergson (laughter as a means of social conformity) and Freud (laughter as a means of liberating our repressed instincts) – this book, and particularly Chapter 1, draws on theories about the verbal construction of humour (*how it is*). The similar concepts of 'bisociation' proposed by Koestler (i.e. an idea or situation being associated with two incompatible matrices) and 'isotopy disjunction' proposed by Greimas (i.e. the transition from one 'isotopy' – the background story – to an opposing 'isotopy' in the dramatised story) provided the basis for Raskin's *Semantic-Script Theory of Humour* (SSTH), the first coherent theory on the matter.[39] According to SSTH, a text is a joke when

---

[38] Ludden *et al.* 2012.
[39] Koestler 1964; Greimas 1983; Raskin 1985.

it is compatible with two different 'scripts' which are 'opposite'. A script is 'a large chunk of semantic information surrounding the word or evoked by it' and it is opposite to another script when they fall into binary categories such as 'real/unreal', 'good/bad', 'life/death', 'obscene/non-obscene'.[40] A crucial disadvantage of SSTH is that it does not differentiate between puns and non-pun humour, which is a consequence of its examining only the semantic aspect and not the morphology of the jokes.

Such a distinction is drawn in Attardo and Raskin's *General Theory of Verbal Humour* (GTVH), which revises and extends SSTH and remains the most widely accepted model today. Apart from 'script oppositions', this model takes into consideration the characters involved, the target, the narrative format, and the language of the joke, as well as its logical resolution. In our analysis of *para prosdokian* jokes, 'script oppositions' and 'logical resolutions' are addressed in the commentary on each passage, whereas the other parameters are addressed aggregately in Chapter 1.5 ('Tracing the Norms'), without however adopting GTVH's terminology and categorisations. In fact, as Attardo admits, GTVH has little to say about stylistic humour because the type of texts analysed for the construction of that model (individual jokes, short stories, novellas etc.) were not the type of texts that depend *heavily* on stylistic humour.[41] This 'fixation on the individual joke rather than the construction of complex extended comic performances' as well as the 'related tendency to underestimate the complexity of individual jokes' make GTVH 'rather poorer with more Aristophanic kinds of surrealism'.[42]

Robson puts forward and applies to Aristophanes a pragmatics-based classification of speech according to how a listener (audience) judges the utterance of a speaker (character) in connection to the latter's capability of speaking coherently. Simplifying his complex terminology, the proposed classification is:

---

40 Raskin 1985, 81, 113–4. That definition of 'script' draws on Schank/Abelson 1977, 41, for whom 'a script is a predetermined, stereotyped sequence of actions that define a well-known situation'.
41 Attardo 2017, 129.
42 Lowe 2008, 10.

Tab. 1: J. Robson's classification of speech (2006)

	If utterance is coherent	If utterance is incoherent
If speaker is considered capable of speaking coherently	Serious Speech	Humorous Speech
If speaker is considered incapable of speaking coherently (e.g. he is mentally disabled or sleeping)	Paradox Speech[43]	Nonsense Speech

Robson himself articulates the main problem with this model: how does a listener gauge whether a speaker is or is not capable of coherent discourse when that speaker is a non-realist Aristophanic creation?[44] In trying to overcome this objection, he arbitrarily transfers the focus from the characters to the poet himself:

> Text is judged to be humorous by the audience member – 'the listener' – when *the playwright*, whilst being perceived as capable of having his characters maintain unitary discourse [= coherent speech], is perceived as having his characters fail to maintain unitary discourse.[45]

Whether 'the playwright' here means Aristophanes as a real person or the 'implied author' of his plays, the proposed model of classification is *de facto* negated if 'the playwright will no doubt generally be judged by the audience member to be capable of unitary discourse'.[46] Most important, the model is challenged by the admission of 'recreative moments [which] inhabit a grey area, not quite humour but *like* humour'.[47]

In principle, however, pragmatics (the context) is certainly as important as semantics in understanding and studying humour. Consider, for instance, the joke in the epigraph of this book, which is reported by Freud in his *Wit and its Relation to the Unconscious* as having been made about a not-so-promising politician.[48] At first glance, the humour only lies on a verbal level, i.e. on the contrast between 'future' and 'behind'. What enables, however, this verbal antithesis to

---

43 Not to be confused with our use of 'paradox' as a synonym of 'surprise' on a semantic level. See Robson's reservations about his use of the term (2006, 24–5).
44 Robson 2006, 27, 39.
45 Robson 2006, 43. Italicisation is my own.
46 Robson 2006, 43.
47 Robson 2006, 46.
48 Freud 1905, 16, 185.

work as a joke is the context, i.e. the very fact that it is said for a 'futureless' individual. If, on the other hand, the person concerned came from an old distinguished family, had a prestigious degree from an ancient university, or was a palaeontologist, then the assertion that 'he has a great future behind him' would be a witty compliment rather than an insult. In fact, context is so important that it can even make jokes out of phrases which entail no verbal signs of humour. Think for example of the stereotypical proverb 'all men are pigs': it bears no antithesis, accumulation, rhyme, alliteration, or any emphatic figure of speech to make it funny; but what if this statement were uttered by Circe? It would automatically become an ironic surprise.

Even though plot construction is not an aspect to concern us in this book, it is useful to discuss the relevance of some ideas from recent narratological work on surprise to our subject-matter. For Mark Currie, surprise depends on 'the already-there-ness of the future' in a narrative:

> The basic structure of narrative is one that blends what has not yet happened with what has already taken place, or which fuses together two apparently incompatible ideas of the future – the future which is to come and the future which is already there. [...] narrative gives access to a future which is already written in the present, in so far as it can be visited out of turn, or known in the present, and the existence of the future in narrative is, in this sense, not hypothetical and inaccessible, but actual and objective.[49]

Under this premise, surprise 'becomes a question not of unforeseeable happenings, but of unforeseen disclosures'.[50] While this is true of most genres, there are certainly some exceptions. A reader can turn directly to the final pages of a novel and read its 'surprising' closure, and a spectator or reader of a Greek tragedy also knows its structure in advance; but stand-up comedy, experimental theatre, or fanfiction often have non-prescribed structure and rely on improvisation and the audience's participation, in a way that the future is truly unforeseeable. While Greek comedy is a case of the former kind when studied as a text, to watch a comic performance without having read the play before certainly presents the spectator with 'unforeseeable happenings'. Quite similarly to Currie, Vera Tobin argues that a 'well-made' surprise plot is one that looks credible in retrospect, i.e. makes the reader reinterpret the events and feel that the evidence was already there; the reader of a novel is oriented by the deceptive viewpoint of a character (which pre-

---

49 Currie 2013, 13.
50 *ibid.* 44.

sents false, partial, or misleading information) and is 'anchored' in one set of persuasive assumptions, which are suddenly overturned later on.[51] Again, while this understanding of surprise is self-evident for genres such as mystery fiction and coming-of-age stories, genres that invest in the absurd, such as Aristophanic comedy, fairy-tales, and nonsense literature do not require 'well-made' surprises in order to be satisfying, nor do they particularly invite the reader into retrospective thinking. Moreover, the concept of 'anchoring' as an intratextual procedure is very restrictive with categories other than plot, such as verbal and scenic surprise, where most of the expectations come externally (from the grammatical rules and the theatrical conventions).

Finally, it is worth noting the recent emergence of mathematical theory on surprise. Most important for our discussion is the distinction between *surprise* and *novelty* made by Günther Palm: 'Usually novelty will be much larger than surprise. [...] Novelty measures how much a piece of information is new and interesting for you. Surprise is provided by an event that is *comparatively improbable*; if everything is equally improbable, nothing is surprising. [...] The idea here is to consider the surprise of one particular outcome in comparison to all the other (usual) outcomes'.[52] This principle of comparability finds a prominent application here in Chapter 3, in which different staging options are discussed. Even though all of them are feasible and the reader is expected – and encouraged – to have his subjective criteria of what he/she considers to be 'funnier', to examine which options are more 'surprising' is largely an objective task.

Humour is largely a matter of personal taste, as we know well from our own experience as spectators, but at the same time, there is a cultural tradition about what is considered funny or not. British humour, for example, is largely based on

---

51 Tobin 2018, 14–36, 88–105.
52 Palm 2012, 26, 28, 19. This also works as a response to Ermida 2018, who speaking of surprising endings in narratives, identifies surprise with *informativeness* (95, 172) and prescribes that 'the passage from the least to the most informative element has to be "abrupt" and sudden, in such a way as to cause surprise' (226). Even though it is true that, statistically speaking, the more informative (i.e. specified in detail) something is, the less probable and predictable it is within a set, this does not explain why more information is necessarily surprising information. A given person is a very specific ('informative') member among the 7.7 billion of global population, but this hardly makes him/her surprising. Moreover, this definition ignores the most obvious kind of surprise, i.e. importing members of one set to another set (e.g. a cow among humans). Ermida draws on Giora 1991, but the latter only says that 'informativeness is *often* assigned surprise value' (469). Italicisation is my own.

'one-liners' which is not at all Aristophanes' kind of humour.[53] Conversely, Aristophanes' plays are full of scatological jokes, a kind of humour which a British audience may not particularly embrace.[54] As spectators or readers, we are certainly allowed to dislike different kinds of humour, but as scholars we must appreciate different standards of humour. In an era when toilet hygiene was not a major concern, when the division between public and private space was not so strict as today, when the physical needs of the people were not stigmatised, and when economy was based on agriculture (hence on dung), the embrace of scatological humour is understandable.

Aside from the various mechanisms of surprise that are analysed in each chapter, attention should be drawn here to a common feature which occurs very often, and which seems surprising in itself. This is *deixis*, i.e. that the dramatist explicitly points towards a joke, theme, or spectacle as being surprising, in a way of prefiguring the response of the audience or the reader. One might suppose that this tactic undermines the intended effect, but in fact it intensifies it. Many examples in the course of the book will illustrate this paradox, but for now the following personal experience shall suffice. To get to the Sheldonian Theatre from Broad Street, in Oxford, one has to pass through a fence which is adorned with a series of carved stone heads (commonly called 'The Emperors'). Only recently I took a step behind to notice this sculpture and I was amazed at how grotesque, almost funny, they looked like (Fig. 1); I wondered why the architect would allow such a sculpture in front of a 'dignified' ceremonial building. A moment afterwards, in my attempt to grasp the feeling that the sculptor wanted to capture, I caught myself imitating the expression of the hems, looking no less ridiculous than them. The 'Emperors' had essentially forced me to stare with wide-open eyes and mouth at what lies behind them, i.e. at the Sheldonian Theatre itself. The concept of 'poetological intention' should now be clear; beyond or regardless of the intentions of artists as real persons, artefacts may have their own intentions, inscribed into their poetics.

---

53 Aside jokes are different in that they are not supposed to be heard by the target of the mockery.
54 For example, in Helen Eastman's *Frogs* 2013, line 308 (Xanthias to Dionysus about the Empousa) was translated in the surtitles as: *It made your pants go brown (Sorry, tasteless we know. Blame Aristophanes)*.

Fig. 1: 'Emperor' herm decorating the fence outside the Sheldonian Theatre, Oxford. Note that the pupils of the eyes are not looking straight forward but lower, to the level of the pedestrians' eyes, thus 'inviting' them to stare back at them. Photograph by Alice Brown.

Aristophanes

Although our focus is on Aristophanes, surprise is a feature of many literary genres. To appreciate fully Aristophanes' mastery of the trope, one has to bear in mind its cross-generic nature, and especially its prevalence in tragedy. In the last section of Chapter 1, for example, I examine how Aristophanic *para prosdokian* differs from Euripidean oxymorons, and in the last section of Chapter 2, how comedy differs from tragedy in appropriating myths for surprise effect. That surprise holds a significant place also in tragedy is illustrated by the longstanding scholarly disputes it has generated. For example, 'the paradox of *Prometheus Vinctus*',[55] i.e. the contrast between the evil Zeus of this play and the all-just Zeus of other plays by Aeschylus, was the main reason for arguing that the tragedy is pseudo-Aeschylean, before Mark Griffith turned the focus on questions of metre and style. In Sophocles' *Ajax*, the unexpected becomes the central theme of the so-called 'deception speech' (646–92). Appearing to have overcome his madness, Ajax says that οὐκ ἔστ' ἄελπτον οὐδέν ('nothing is unexpected' 648), a statement which the chorus interprets in a positive way, i.e. that contrary to expectations Ajax has regained his good sense. But is this truly the case or is he just pretending in front of the chorus? Is he even addressing the chorus or is he speaking to himself? The ambiguity and the scholarly debate over the hero's intentions and mental state are endless.[56] What is definite in the play, however, is that the axiom 'nothing is unexpected' is *de facto* defeated – most emblematically through the hero's on-stage suicide.

As for Euripides, the everlasting debate over his 'tragicomic' style is due to the surprising insertion of comic elements into his dramas: elements verbal (jokes), structural (happy endings), scenic (rags for costumes), and characterological (foolish kings). A verbal surprise for example is found in *Trojan Women*, when Menelaus comes to take Helen to Greece to stone her; Hecuba warns him to

---

55 Farnell 1933.
56 See Crane 1990. Bednarowski 2015 argues that Aeschylus' *Agamemnon* is also full of characterological ambiguities that create *suspense* and *surprise* – e.g. the presentation of Clytaemnestra as a capable ruler and a wronged mother and wife, apart from an adulteress and a regicide. Even though I agree with the term 'suspense', I am sceptical about the 'surprise' effect, because as Bednarowski himself admits in a footnote (183 n. 17), the 'scanty evidence for poetic and visual treatments of the myth between Homer and Aeschylus makes claims of this sort [= about Aeschylus' departure from the earlier tradition] difficult to prove or disprove'. In a second footnote (197 n. 67), he admits that 'This [characterological ambiguity] is not to say that spectators would not have been suspicious of Clytemnestra before now'; it is therefore difficult to speak of 'surprise' in this occasion.

not board on the same ship with her and he gives her the following answer (1049–50):

EK. Μή νυν νεώς σοὶ ταὐτὸν ἐσβήτω σκάφος.
MEN. Τί δ' ἔστι; Μεῖζον βρῖθος ἢ πάροιθ' ἔχει;

HEC. Well, then, do not let her embark on the same vessel as you.
MEN. What is wrong? Is she heavier than she was?

Even though the point of Menelaus is only to be ironic towards Hecuba, the image presented to our minds, i.e. that of a Helen so fat that the ship would sink, is hilarious. The unexpected in Euripides, however, is not limited to 'tragicomic' moments. Arnott offers a brief analysis of some techniques employed by the tragedian to achieve a surprise effect: reversing conventions of tragedy (e.g. the spatial separation of chorus and actors), presenting the audience with 'red herrings' (e.g. the messenger's speech about the murder of Aegisthus in *Electra* 762 f. reaches its conclusion only after three false clues), postponing emotional exaggerations (e.g. when Medea first appears on stage she is totally in control of herself, rather than in hysteria as the nurse had informed us), and so on.[57]

An important approach, were it possible, might be to draw comparisons with other comic poets of the classical era. Even if one identifies some *para prosdokian* jokes in the mass of the comic fragments, or some surprising developments in the plots recorded, there is no way to reconstruct the network of humour of any playwright to such a degree as to be comparable with that of Aristophanes. Statements such as 'it is likely that Epicharmus introduced *para prosdokian* in literature'[58] can only be speculative. As for Aristophanes' rivals, Platonius' treatise Περὶ διαφορᾶς χαρακτήρων informs us that Cratinus was too bitter and vulgar, Eupolis was the most gracious with his mockery, and Aristophanes' style was somewhat in the middle, allowing charm to pervade mockery (75). Insofar as one can trust a testimony from the 9th century AD, and bearing in mind that Alexandrian annotators associate *para prosdokian* with *charis* (as we shall see), then Eupolis and Aristophanes *might* have employed this figure more than Cratinus; but this can only remain a very vague hypothesis.

Another genre which is deeply characterised by surprise – and very often by *para prosdokian* specifically – is Hellenistic epigram. Having to show their mas-

---

57 Arnott 1973.
58 Berk 1946, 54.

tery in very few lines, i.e. in a form which does not facilitate climactic constructions, the epigrammatists turned to sudden twists for concluding their poems.[59] In one of them, Callimachus praises the beauty of his boyfriend (*AP* 12. 51.3–4):

> καλὸς ὁ παῖς, Ἀχελῷε, λίην καλός, εἰ δέ τις οὐχὶ
> φησίν – ἐπισταίμην μοῦνος ἐγὼ τὰ καλά.

> Handsome, so handsome is the boy, O Achelous!
> And if anyone denies it – may I alone know his beauties.

One would expect 'if anyone denies it, go check with your eyes', but Callimachus presents himself as too jealous to share the evidence.[60] Love epigram is indeed a favourable genre for surprise, not only as a figure but also as a theme. Rufinus explains how he unexpectedly turned from homosexuality to heterosexuality and concludes that, if this happened, then nothing is impossible anymore (*AP* 5.19.5–6):

> βοσκήσει δελφῖνας ὁ δενδροκόμης Ἐρύμανθος
> καὶ πολιὸν πόντου κῦμα θοὰς ἐλάφους.

> Dolphins will feed on tree-crowned Erymanthus,
> and swift deer in the foaming wave of the sea![61]

Comparing the *aprosdokēta* in comedy and in epigram, Napolitano makes the case for a key difference: in the former genre *aprosdokēton* becomes part of a broader and more complex context, whereas in the latter genre it is part of a circumscribed context. Thus, in comedy it contributes to the argumentative process (at least for the more critically thinking audience), whereas in epigram it is an end in itself.[62]

The same could be said for the jokes of *Philogelos*, the oldest existing collection of jokes dating to the 4th century AD, which is attributed to Hierocles and Philagrius (of whom we know nothing).[63] In contrast to Hellenistic epigram, however, there is nothing truly witty here. The 'humour' of these 265 jokes is based

---

59 See Garson 1980; 1981. For the Roman paradox epigram, see Feeney 2009.
60 Cf. [Tibullus] 3.19, who reaches such a level of insecurity that he prays *displiceas aliis* (6): 'May you not attract others' instead of 'May others not attract you'.
61 The imagery comes from Archil. 122 (δελφῖσι θῆρες ἀνταμείψωνται νομὸν ἐνάλιον) and survives up to modern Greek Folksong: Ποιὸς εἶδε ψάρι 'ς τὸ βουνὸ καὶ θάλασσα σπαρμένη, ποιὸς εἶδε κόρη λυγερὴ 'ς κλέφτικα ντυμένη; (Politis 1914, 72 B).
62 Napolitano 2007, 47–9.
63 See Andreassi 2004; Beard 2014; West 2017.

on stereotypes about stock characters and they are as original and surprising as modern jokes about blondes. Even in the best instances, the poor technique betrays the supposedly unexpected conclusion:

> 244. Νεανίσκος πρὸς τὴν γυναῖκα οὖσαν ἀσελγῆ εἶπε· Κυρία, τί ποιοῦμεν; ἀριστοῦμεν ἢ ἀφροδισιάζομεν; κἀκείνη πρὸς αὐτὸν ἔφη· Ὡς θέλεις· ψωμὶν οὐκ ἔστιν.
>
> A young man said to his lascivious woman: 'Lady, what shall we do? Have lunch or have sex?' And she replied: 'As you like... only there isn't any food'.

This would be a genuinely funny exchange if it were performed on stage; but with an omniscient narrator disclosing *a priori* that the woman is lascivious, half of its potential is lost.

To return to Aristophanes, this book is concerned with his eleven extant comedies. Even though the study of comic fragments has been a major trend in classical scholarship during the last two decades, our approach requires the examination of certain passages within their narrow and wider, textual and theatrical context, hence the fragments are not suitable by definition. As for the 'distribution' of the eleven plays throughout the book, Chapter 1 deals with *Acharnians*, *Peace*, *Thesmophoriazusae* and *Wealth*; this selection of plays aims at a fair representation of Aristophanes' employment of *para prosdokian* across his career, examining his first and his last play, and two plays from between, with a sufficient temporal distance between them: a decade separates *Peace* from *Thesmophoriazusae*; it has also been taken into account that *Acharnians* and *Peace* have the most occurrences of *para prosdokian* in their scholia. Chapter 2 deals with all the extant comedies; Chapter 3 with *Wasps*, *Lysistrata*, and *Ecclesiazusae*; and Chapter 4 with *Frogs*. *Knights*, *Clouds*, and *Birds* are relatively underrepresented due to limitations in space but also on specific grounds: *Birds* remains the most studied comedy from the perspective of the categories of 'innovation' and 'fantasy', which naturally overlap with 'surprise' to some extent, hence it seemed appropriate to prioritise other plays. *Clouds* was not performed in the version we have, hence the information about staging can be misleading (e.g. the arson in the finale *is* a surprise when compared to other Aristophanic exoduses but can we count it as such when we know that the original version did not include it?). As for *Knights*, it relies so heavily on Cleon as a historical individual,[64] that our scanty historical knowledge about him hinders us from perceiving a large part of the surprising elements of the satire. For example, we cannot know whether the

---

[64] As opposed to Socrates in *Clouds*, for example, who is perceived more as an archetypical sophist than as an individual.

employment of a Sausage-Seller in particular, as a subduer of Paphlagon, was intended as a sexual mockery against Cleon, because we know nothing about the latter's sexuality in reality.[65] Also, his recent litigation with Aristophanes had certainly attracted the public attention, but we cannot know whether the details of this alleged trial have been comically embodied in the contest between Paphlagon and the Sausage-Seller. None of the other comedies present us with gaps of historical information that is essential to appreciating the plot and the protagonists.

*

Chapter 1 presents the history of the term *para prosdokian*, which was initially characterised by ambiguity (verbal *vs* situational surprise), and draws a conceptual and methodological frame on how to identify the figure. Resorting to componential analysis, a linguistic method of the Prague School, the chapter offers a commentary on the *para prosdokian* passages from *Acharnians*, *Peace*, *Thesmophoriazusae* and *Wealth*, supporting or questioning the proposals by other commentators and identifying some new cases. Consequently, it traces the norms in the use of the figure. What is its typology? What characters use it most? In what contexts is it employed? It is argued that, typologically speaking, Aristophanes uses *para prosdokian* less strictly and less effectively in his later plays, but at the same time he avoids oxymoron or only uses it in paratragic contexts.

Chapter 2 offers a play-by-play commentary on the surprising appropriation of myths in the eleven extant comedies, placing special emphasis on the poetological implications of this process. Furthermore, it proposes a scheme of five intra-dramatic functions for appropriated myths in comedy (persuasive, aetiological, antiphonal, abusive, and structural myths) and argues that Aristophanes consciously avoids poetological-only myths. Finally, the chapter explains how tragedy differs from comedy in appropriating myths, as far as surprise effect is concerned.

Chapter 3 is devoted to theatrical surprise. First, it refutes the common assumption that every stage action was necessarily commented on in the play by the characters; even though stage action is usually 'complementary' to the text, there is strong evidence that 'contradiction' was also a very plausible option for the dramatist. Second, it argues that even though comedy uses the same scenic effects as tragedy (the platform and the crane) and knows the same technical restrictions (male casting and masks), comedy exploits them in a very surprising

---

65 λακαταπύγων in *Ach.* 664 is only a formulaic assault and therefore not elaborated.

way. What is also surprising is the way in which Aristophanes mocks public figures and appropriates popular songs to gain publicity and raise political questions. This is better understood when we study analogous cases in modern performances, within the contemporary musical or political context. Thus, the chapter resorts to evidence of video-recorded modern performances of Aristophanes' comedies in order to understand the dynamics of surprise, gauged from the laughter of the audience.

Chapter 4 offers a close reading of *Frogs*, considering verbal, thematic, and theatrical surprises simultaneously – without however repeating the particular categories analysed in the previous chapters. It highlights the role of accumulation, proposes new interpretations of issues such as the Empousa scene and the ληκύθιον joke, and argues that the play ends with a sense of futility.

A book on the typology of surprise could hardly omit tables. Representing compilations of the relevant data, the Appendices have been the starting point for the analysis in the main body of the book, rather than a summary, and therefore should ideally be consulted before reading the respective sections.

1 Verbal Surprise: *Para Prosdokian* Jokes

Aristophanes' poetic arsenal comprises a plethora of techniques of verbal humour. Their scope expands over all levels of language. Phonologically, we encounter comic onomatopoeias (ἀνὴρ παφλάζει – παῦε παῦ', *Eq.* 919; δωριστὶ – δωροδοκιστί, *Eq.* 230–3),[66] alliterations (τίς ἡ πτέρωσις; τίς ὁ τρόπος τῆς τριλοφίας; *Av.* 94), rhymes (ὑμῶν μὲν αὐτῶν οὐχὶ δεξιώτερον, / κωμῳδίας δὲ φορτικῆς σοφώτερον, *Vesp.* 65–6),[67] and consolidations (Διὸς καταιβάτου, *Pax* 42), among other features. Morphologically, we find in abundance multi-word compounds (ὦ σπερμαγοραιολεκιθολαχανοπώλιδες, ὦ σκοροδοπανδοκευτριαρτοπώλιδες, *Lys.* 457–8),[68] diminutives with various endings (κοτυλίσκιον, *Ach.* 459; Σωκρατίδιον, *Nub.* 223; μελύδριον, *Eccl.* 883; καὶ κῳδάριον καὶ ληκύθιον καὶ θυλάκιον, *Ran.* 1201),[69] and as for augmentatives, for which there are only few suffixes in ancient Greek (κατωφαγᾶς, *Av.* 288; γάστρων, *Ran.* 200),[70] Aristophanes compensates with imaginative superlatives (παμμίαρε καὶ μιαρώτατε, *Pax* 183; παροινικώτατος, *Vesp.* 1300; μονοφαγίστατον, *Vesp.* 923; αὐτότατος, *Plut.* 83).[71] On vocabulary, the most discussed categories have been comic or 'speaking' names (Προξενίδης ὁ Κομπασεύς, 'Proxenides of Boaston', *Av.* 1126)[72] and obscenity: sexual terms, scatology, and abusive addresses (ὦ θερμόβουλον πρωκτὸν ἐξυρημένε, *Ach.* 119, comprises them all).[73] A comprehensive study in Aristophanic *hapax legomena* is still missing. Syntactically, long catalogues are maybe Aristophanes' favourite application of the accumulation technique, appearing both in *asyndeton* and *polysyndeton*:[74]

---

[66] See Haury 1960; Horowski 1966; Allen 1968.
[67] See Robson 2006, 123–9.
[68] See Meyer 1923, 119–32; Ramalho 1952.
[69] See Peppler 1910; Schmid 1954; Mikolajczyk 1979; Meluzzi 2017.
[70] γάστρις is also attested (*Av.* 1604) but γάστρων is more likely to mean 'paunchy', in light of πόσθων (presumably 'hung', *Pax* 1330).
[71] On both degrees of comparison, see López Eire 1996, 137–45.
[72] transl. Dunbar 1995. See Olson 1992; Kanavou 2011a. On names of individual characters, see Kapp 1928; Marzullo 1953; Paganelli 1978-1979; Panagl 1983; Bowie 1988.
[73] See Müller 1913; Wit-Tak 1968; Marston 1973; Moulton 1979; Edwards 1991; Henderson 1991; Halliwell 1991; Robson 2006, 70–94.
[74] On lists, see Spyropoulos 1974; on accumulation, more generally, see López Eire 1996, 159–64; Silk 2000, 126–36.

Ran. 112–5:

τούτους φράσον μοι, λιμένας, ἀρτοπώλια,
πορνεῖ', ἀναπαύλας, ἐκτροπάς, κρήνας, ὁδούς, πόλεις, διαίτας,
πανδοκευτρίας, ὅπου
κόρεις ὀλίγιστοι.

Tell me about them, about the harbors, bakeries, whorehouses, rest areas, directions, springs, roads, cities, places to stay, the landladies with the fewest bedbugs.

Av. 881–8:

καὶ ἥρωσιν ὄρνισι καὶ ἡρώων παισί, πορφυρίωνι καὶ
πελεκᾶντι καὶ πελεκίνῳ καὶ φλέξιδι καὶ τέτρακι καὶ
ταῶνι καὶ ἐλεᾷ καὶ βασκᾷ καὶ ἐλασᾷ καὶ ἐδωλίῳ καὶ
καταρράκτῃ καὶ μελαγκορύφῳ καὶ αἰγιθάλλῳ

[Grant to] the Avian heroes and the Heroes' children, Porphyrion and White Pelican and Grey Pelican and Red Hawk and Grouse and Peacock and Reed Warbler and Teal and Harrier and Heron and Tern and Black Tit and Blue Tit...

On semantics level, comedy loves suggestive language, like metaphors (ὁ πλακοῦς πέπεπται, σησαμῆ ξυμπλάττεται, *Pax* 869), similes (ὡς ἐλαπρός, ὥσπερ ψύλλο κατὰ τὸ κῴδιο, *Thesm.* 1180), personifications (καὶ πίθος πληγεὶς ὑπ' ὀργῆς ἀντελάκτισεν πίθῳ, *Pax* 613), and euphemisms (λάμποντι μετώπῳ instead of 'bald', *Eq.* 550);[75] but comedy also loves raw realism (γυμναὶ παρίοιμεν δέλτα παρατετιλμέναι, / στύοιντο δ' ἄνδρες κἀπιθυμοῖεν σπλεκοῦν, *Lys.* 151–2). Finally, on pragmatics level, one could make a long list of metatheatrical references, addressed to the audience or even to the technicians of the theatre (ὦ μηχανοποιέ, πρόσεχε τὸν νοῦν, *Pax* 174; ἄγε δή, θεαταί, δεῦρο συσπλαγχνεύετε | μετὰ νῷν, *Pax* 1115–6), and aside jokes (*Plut.* 1032–7):[76]

ΓΡ.   ἀλλ' οὐδέποτέ με ζῶσαν ἀπολείψειν ἔφη.
ΧΡ.   ὀρθῶς γε· νῦν δέ γ' οὐκέτι σε ζῆν οἴεται.
ΓΡ.   ὑπὸ τοῦ γὰρ ἄλγους κατατέτηκ', ὦ φίλτατε.
ΧΡ.   οὔκ, ἀλλὰ κατασέσηπας, ὥς γ' ἐμοὶ δοκεῖς.
ΓΡ.   διὰ δακτυλίου μὲν οὖν ἐμέ γ' ἂν διελκύσαις.
ΧΡ.   εἰ τυγχάνοι γ' ὁ δακτύλιος ὢν τηλίας.

---

[75] See Lever 1952–1953; Newiger 1957; Taillardat 1965; Komornicka 1964; Müller 1974; López Eire 1996, 177–57. On euphemism, see Sommerstein 2009, 70–103.
[76] See Bain 1977, 87–99.

HAG	But he promised he'd never leave me as long as I live.
CHR.	Quite rightly; but now he considers you no longer alive.
HAG	In fact I'm pining away with grief, my dear man.
CHR.	No, you're rotting away, if you ask me.
HAG	Why, you could pull me right through a ring.
CHR.	Provided the ring were the size of a barrel hoop.

The moods, or modes, or tropes of Aristophanes' verbal techniques, i.e. the functions for which he uses the figures above, are equally abundant. Antithesis, accumulation, ambiguity, irony, satire, parody, and surprise are only some of those. Now, if we consider any possible combination of the aforementioned linguistic levels and modes (e.g. phonological ambiguities, morphological accumulations, lexical obscenities, semantic surprises etc.), we realise what a complex system verbal humour is and what a sizeable task it would be to attempt to map it fully, or to write a 'grammar' of comic language – if such a thing were even possible. As Willi notes, 'the comic use of figures and tropes other than metaphors and personifications is much less well studied', and therefore the present chapter can only aim at filling a small part of this gap.[77]

By focussing on the mode of 'verbal surprise' and sketching a conceptual outline, we can say that this mode comprises any kind of surprising sequence of linguistic units (phonemes, morphemes, lexemes etc). Here we can include nonsense, i.e. meaningless sequence (as with Pseudartabas in *Acharnians* and the Triballian in *Aves*); *para prosdokian*, i.e. unexpected sequence (ἐγὼ δ' ἔκλεπτον ἐπ' ἀγαθῷ γε τῇ πόλει, *Eq.* 1226; νυνὶ δὲ δημαγωγεῖ / ἐν τοῖς ἄνω νεκροῖσι, *Ran.* 419–20); and oxymoron, i.e. contradictory sequence (οὐκ ἔνδον ἔνδον ἐστίν, *Ach.* 395). Dialectic variation, i.e. intralingual sequence, is also surprising when found in one and the same character (e.g. the Spartan Lampito uses the Attic form φροῦδος instead of *φρῶδος, *Lys.* 106).[78] Last but not least, we may have surprising variations in tone, i.e. intergeneric sequence of linguistic units, mixing comic style with epic (e.g. the solemn dactylic hexametre tinged with Homeric *Kunstsprache* in *Pax* 1063–1114),[79] lyric (ὦ θύμ' ἄνευ σκάνδικος ἐμπορευτέα, *Ach.* 480), or preferably tragic style.

---

[77] Willi 2002, 17. A short chapter on that volume, Slings 2002, deals with anaphora, chiasmus, and antithesis. Since then, only few papers on Aristophanes' figures of speech have been published.
[78] As Colvin 1999, 297–300 shows, there are few cases of 'bad dialect' among the non-Attic Greek characters; Boeotean dialect is represented less carefully than Laconian and Megarian.
[79] Revermann 2013a, 123.

Such dividing lines are theoretical and in practice co-operation and overlapping usually occurs. It is also important to emphasise that these techniques (may) exceed the verbal sphere. Parody, to take the most characteristic example, usually also entails scenic surprises (disguises, gestures, songs etc). It is clear that verbal and non-verbal aspects may be intertwined (i.e. a funny theme will probably be expressed with funny words) but this *is not binding* on language. A comic theme may be conveyed with very serious words or with no words at all (comic silence), and can occur through plot and characterisation instead. This chapter is concerned with non-verbal aspects only insofar as they accompany verbally expressed surprises.

In his criticism of James Robson's *Humour, Obscenity and Aristophanes*, Ian Storey rejects the theorising of humour by saying that: 'To explain a joke is to kill a joke, and I would argue that the same applies to analyses of humour on a larger scale'.[80] Ian Ruffell discards *para prosdokian* in particular, by maintaining that: 'The categories used, such as the *para prosdokian* or "surprise" joke or the classification of comic characters into quasi-Aristotelian types, have passed into the common language of Aristophanic criticism, but this approach is no longer particularly fashionable'.[81] In answer to the latter view, it should go without saying that being 'particularly fashionable' is not a *sine qua non* of scholarship, especially in a discipline called 'Classics'. The first dogma requires addressing more seriously, since it is often evoked.[82] Leaving aside that 'not killing the joke' should be the concern of the comedian rather than of the scholar of comedy, one could answer that, in most cases, philology is not concerned with explaining whether a passage is funny, but rather how a passage, recognised as funny, (co)operates within a larger textual and non-textual context; in other words, to explain the system of humour, rather than its obvious expressions. At the same time, however, when engaging with temporally or spatially distant texts such as Aristophanic comedies, there are also some linguistically or culturally obscured jokes which demand explanation *per se*. On such occasions, to explain a joke is not to 'kill it' but to perceive its existence as such. To understand *para prosdokian* we first need to know what the *prosdokia* was for the audience of classical Athens.

The present chapter is devoted to this very figure of speech. Owing to the scholarly discrepancy and vagueness over *para prosdokian*, the following sections offer a theoretical frame, surveying the history of the term from ancient

---

80 Robson 2006; Storey 2007.
81 Ruffell 2011, 56.
82 E.g. 'Comedy is notoriously difficult to study and analyse. The creation of taxonomies of jokes or comic techniques risks destroying the very subject it studies', Slater 2002, 4.

sources to modern dictionaries, and its content, with emphasis on its linguistic structure.[83] Subsequently, there is detailed examination of *para prosdokian* jokes in *Acharnians*, *Peace*, *Thesmophoriazusae*, and *Wealth*. For ease of reading, instead of examining the *para prosdokian* jokes which have been proposed by scholars (or are being proposed in this book) in a play-by-play arrangement, a thematic arrangement has been followed. The two final sections of the chapter offer a comparative review of *para prosdokian* in the four comedies and a comparison of *para prosdokian* with oxymoron, respectively. After tracing some norms about the typology, the context, and the characters who use *para prosdokian* jokes, it is argued that Aristophanes elaborates this figure of speech less consistently in his later plays, but still insists on avoiding oxymoron on purpose. There is also an attempt to observe Aristophanes' development in using the figure over time, although the temporal distance between the plays prevents a fair representation: four years lie between *Ach.* and *Pax* (425 – 421 BC); ten years between *Pax* and *Thesm.* (421 – 411 BC); and twenty-three years between *Thesm.* and *Plut.* (411 – 388 BC); inevitably, the differences in *Plut.* are much more noticeable.

Tables 4–7 in the Appendices collect the cases of *para prosdokian* jokes that have been proposed by the scholia and modern commentators,[84] and incorporates suggestions for some additional cases (marked with +). The proposed cases coloured in grey are those entailing a non-standard use of the term. What the *prosdokia* would be for each case (according to the commentators or me) is placed parallel to the original text. Tables 8–11 present the key data about the traceable norms (on typology, context, and characters), in order to facilitate the comparative analysis in the end.

1.1 The Term

In Hellenistic and Roman rhetorical manuals, the term *para prosdokian* appears first in Demetrius Rhet. (1st century BC), Hermogenes (2nd to 3rd century AD) and Tiberius (3rd to 4th century AD). The former cites examples from the *Odyssey* and

---

[83] The surprisingly scarce bibliography on this figure tends to follow the scholia in an uncritical manner and/or to simply compile and translate individual jokes. A first taxonomy was made in Michael 1981 but not inductively, and on the expense of interpretation. See Filippo 2001–2002; Bilbao Ruiz 2005; Napolitano 2007. The inclusion of the term in Sommerstein 2019 marks a positive turn.

[84] Hereafter, when I refer to their proposals, I mean *ad loc.* in their commentaries, except for Starkie 1909, whose introductory pages lxvii–lxviii I mainly draw upon.

Aristophanes' *Clouds*, whereas the latter two directly quote passages from Demosthenes' Περὶ τοῦ στεφάνου and Περὶ Ἁλοννήσου respectively.

Demetr. *Eloc.* 152:

> Ἔστι δέ τις καὶ ἡ παρὰ προσδοκίαν χάρις, ὡς ἡ τοῦ Κύκλωπος, ὅτι «ὕστατον ἔδομαι Οὖτιν». οὐ γὰρ προσεδόκα τοιοῦτο ξένιον οὔτε Ὀδυσσεὺς οὔτε ὁ ἀναγινώσκων. καὶ ὁ Ἀριστοφάνης ἐπὶ τοῦ Σωκράτους, «κηρὸν διατήξας», φησίν, «εἶτα διαβήτην λαβών, ἐκ τῆς παλαίστρας ἱμάτιον ὑφείλετο».

There is also the charm from the unexpected, as in the Cyclops' words: 'No-man I will eat last.' [*Od.* 9. 369] Neither Odysseus nor the reader was expecting such a strange thing. So Aristophanes says of Socrates: 'He first melted some wax, then grabbed a pair of compasses, and from the wrestling school – he stole a coat.' [*Nub.* 149, 179]

Hermog. *Meth.* 34 (sel.):

> Τὸ δὲ παρὰ προσδοκίαν τοῦτο «βδελυρὸν μὲν οὖν τὸ πρᾶγμα καὶ οὐκ ἂν ἐβουλόμην λαχεῖν, ἐπειδὴ δὲ ἔλαχον»· προσδοκᾷ μὲν ὁ ἀκροατὴς ἀκοῦσαι 'ὑπομενῶ', φησὶ δὲ «οὐκ ἂν ἐβουλόμην».
> [...]
> Τούτοις πᾶσι χρῆται Δημοσθένης ἐν τῷ Περὶ τοῦ στεφάνου· ὅθεν δηλοῦται, ὅτι κωμῳδεῖν ἐπίσταται·[...] τῷ δὲ παρὰ προσδοκίαν οὕτω περὶ Αἰσχίνου λέγων «οὐδὲ γὰρ ὧν ἔτυχεν ἦν, ἀλλ' οἷς ὁ δῆμος καταρᾶται».

An example of contrary to expectation (*para prosdokian*) is this: 'Now the thing is disgusting, and I would not want to get it, but since I did...' The hearer expects to hear 'I put up with getting it' but he says 'I would not want' [adesp. fr. 260].
[...]
Demosthenes uses all of these in *On the Crown*, from which it is clear that he knew how to speak in a comic style. [...] He uses *para prosdokia* when speaking about Aeschines [18.130], thus: 'He was not whatever he happened to be but what the people curse'.[85]

Tib. *Fig. Demosth.* 16:

> Παρὰ προσδοκίαν δ' ἐστὶν ὅταν, ἄλλο τοῦ ἀκροατοῦ προσδεχομένου, ἄλλο μετά τινος χάριτος ἐπενέγκῃ, οἷον·«τὰ μέντοι Φιλίππου εὐεργετήματα τοιαῦτα ἔσται·οὔτε τὰ ὑμέτερα ὑμῖν αὐτοῖς ἀποδώσει, οὔτε ἐν τῇ οἰκουμένῃ αἱ τιμαὶ ἔσονται».

---

[85] transl. Kennedy 2005.

Para prosdokian is when, despite the hearer expecting one thing, something different is emerging, with some charm, like this: 'Such will be the benefactions of Philip: he will neither restore your possessions, nor will he bring glory to the world' [7.35].

The common elements in these definitions are the unexpectedness and the playfulness. Both Demetrius and Tiberius call this unexpectedness a χάρις, a witty trick, and indeed the former cites Aristophanes. Hermogenes too makes a direct connection with comedy (κωμῳδεῖν ἐπίσταται). One difference is that the latter two speak of a listener (ἀκροατὴς) being surprised, whereas Demetrius speaks of a reader (ἀναγινώσκων). This discrepancy is not the result of confusion: Demetrius speaks from his own perspective, as a contemporary reader in a Hellenistic library, whereas Tiberius and Hermogenes are interested in the original performance of the speeches in the Athenian agora or the court. A more important detail is that Demetrius aptly mentions the unexpectedness from Odysseus' perspective: it is not only the 'extradiegetic' listeners/readers that perceive the *para prosdokian*, but also the 'diegetic' characters.

The term also appears in the anonymous *Tractatus Coislinianus*, surviving in a tenth-century manuscript, but without a definition or examples given. This treatise reconstructs a counter-theory for comedy on the model of the surviving part of the *Poetics*. Nesselrath strongly opposed Janko's suggestion that this treatise commentated directly on the *Poetics II*,[86] yet Aristotle was certainly familiar with the concept of *para prosdokian* in the context of oratory and tragedy:

Poet. 1452a:

> Ἐπεὶ δὲ οὐ μόνον τελείας ἐστὶ πράξεως ἡ μίμησις ἀλλὰ καὶ φοβερῶν καὶ ἐλεεινῶν, ταῦτα δὲ γίνεται καὶ μάλιστα [καὶ μᾶλλον] ὅταν γένηται παρὰ τὴν δόξαν δι' ἄλληλα·

> Given that the mimesis is not only of a complete action but also of fearful and pitiable matters, the latter arise above all when events occur contrary to expectation yet on account of one another.

Rhet. 3.1412a:

> ἔστιν δὲ καὶ τὰ ἀστεῖα τὰ πλεῖστα διὰ μεταφορᾶς καὶ ἐκ τοῦ προσεξαπατᾶν: μᾶλλον γὰρ γίγνεται δῆλον ὅ τι ἔμαθε παρὰ τὸ ἐναντίως ἔχειν, καὶ ἔοικεν λέγειν ἡ ψυχὴ "ὡς ἀληθῶς, ἐγὼ δὲ ἥμαρτον". [...] καὶ τὰ εὖ ᾐνιγμένα διὰ τὸ αὐτὸ ἡδέα (μάθησις γάρ ἐστι καὶ μεταφορά), καὶ (ὃ λέγει Θεόδωρος) τὸ καινὰ λέγειν. γίγνεται δὲ ὅταν παράδοξον ᾖ, καὶ μή, ὡς ἐκεῖνος λέγει, πρὸς τὴν ἔμπροσθεν δόξαν, ἀλλ' ὥσπερ ἐν τοῖς γελοίοις τὰ παραπεποιημένα (ὅπερ δύναται καὶ τὰ παρὰ γράμμα σκώμματα· ἐξαπατᾷ γάρ)

---

86 Janko 1984; Nesselrath 1990.

Most smart sayings are derived from metaphor, and also from misleading the hearer beforehand. For it becomes more evident to him that he has learnt something, when the conclusion turns out contrary to his expectation, and the mind seems to say, 'How true it is! But I missed it.' [...] And clever riddles are agreeable for the same reason; for something is learnt, and the expression is also metaphorical. And what Theodorus calls 'novel expressions' arise when what follows is paradoxical, and, as he puts it, not in accordance with our previous expectation; just as humorists make use of slight changes in words. The same effect is produced by jokes that turn on a change of letter; for they are deceptive.

Rhet. 2.1379a:

τέρπει τὸ πολὺ παρὰ δόξαν, ἐὰν γένηται ὃ βούλεται.

Men are overjoyed if, contrary to expectation, what they desire comes to pass.

In the passages above we can locate an early formulation of the term (παρὰ τὴν δόξαν),[87] a connection with comic style (ἐν τοῖς γελοίοις, σκώμματα, τέρπει), and a cognitive-behavioural explanation of how the figure works (ἔοικεν λέγειν ἡ ψυχὴ, μάθησις). However, the unexpectedness of which Aristotle speaks is primarily a situational one (i.e. referring to events) rather than a verbal one.[88] The verbal aspect comes merely as a parenthetical comment. Following the Aristotelian tradition, *Tractatus Coislinianus* puts *para prosdokian* under the category ἐκ τῶν πραγμάτων γέλως rather than ἀπὸ τῆς λέξεως.

In Latin, the term appears as *praeter exspectationem* and the figure is extensively discussed in Cicero's *De oratore*, through the persona of Julius Caesar Strabo. Apart from a definition, the rhetorician gives an Aristotelian explanation on how the figure becomes funny, and assesses this kind of joke as the most successful:[89]

---

[87] παρὰ δόξαν· παρ' ἐλπίδα, παρὰ προσδοκίαν (Hsch).
[88] With the same meaning, a fragment attributing some proverb to Aristotle, links *para prosdokian* to actions, not to words: διὸ ἐπεκράτησεν ἡ παροιμία ἐπὶ τῶν παρὰ προσδοκίαν τι πραττόντων (Arist. *Fragmenta varia* 8.44.571). This is the scholiast's comment (schol. on Ap. Rhod. 1.188) rather than Aristotle's own words, but it still reflects the Aristotelian conception of situational irony.
[89] Cf. Quint. 6.3.84, who characterises it *vel venustissima*, 'the most elegant device'. It is particularly used in Plautine comedy (see Duckworth 1994, 356–9; Fontaine 2010, 7 f.), epigram (see n. 59), and historiography in Imperial Rome (see Plass 1988, 58–62, with the note that the figure appears 'wherever political irrationality is to be found').

Cic. *De or.* 2.63.255; 2.70.284:

> Sed scitis esse notissimum ridiculi genus, cum aliud exspectamus, aliud dicitur: hic nobismet ipsis noster error risum movet. [...] ex his omnibus nihil magis ridetur, quam quod est praeter exspectationem.
>
> But you already know that the most familiar category is when we expect to hear one thing, but another is said. When this happens, our own error makes us laugh. [...] But of all these kinds of humour, none provokes more laughter than the unexpected turn.[90]

Hermogenes and Tiberius follow Cicero, since their *para prosdokian* refers to oratory, rather than Demetrius who applies it to poetry.

In the Alexandrian and medieval scholia, the term *para prosdokian* is applied to the Aristophanic corpus above all, and indeed more times than for all other authors cumulatively.[91] It thus appears that identifying this figure had become a trend for Aristophanic scholarship, presumably an ostentatious desire on the part of grammarians to demonstrate that they mastered the rhetorical manuals. In practice, however, such a mastery is not confirmed: editing the scholia on Aristophanes preserved in the Ravenna manuscript alone, William Rutherford correctly pointed out the terminological inconsistency of the annotators, who sometimes use *para prosdokian* and *par' hyponoian* (which normally means an allusion or metaphor) indistinguishably.[92] More important, not all of them use *para prosdokian* in the same sense. Statistically speaking, however, there is a clear prevalence of the Hermogenean model, which is the most narrow and technical, and which prevails until today.

Moving from secondary sources to literature, one notes that *para prosdokian* occurs as a set phrase repeatedly in Polybius, Diodorus Siculus, and Plutarch,

---

[90] transl. May/Wisse 2001.
[91] TLG gives twenty occurrences of the term in the scholia on Aristophanes and nineteen occurrences in the scholia on all other authors for whom *para prosdokian* is attested (scholia on Epicharmus, Pindar, Sophocles, Euripides, Thucydides, Aristotle, Demosthenes, Aeschines, Apollonius of Rhodes and Lucian). Note that in fr. 98 of Ὀδυσσεὺς αὐτόμολος the scholia are blended with Epicharmus' text, unlike the marginal scholia on fr. 97. In all cases, *para prosdokian* is written by the annotator. For *para prosdokian* in this comedy, see Berk 1964, 54, 137–8.
[92] Rutherford 1905, 449–51. In my *Appendices*, I only include those *par' hyponoian* proposals that modern scholars have identified with *para prosdokian*.

denoting an unexpected historical event.[93] In the latter author, it appears once as a poetic *terminus technicus*, with reference to Homer.

Plut. *De tranq. anim.* 475a:

> εὖ δὲ καὶ ὁ ποιητὴς οἷόν ἐστι τὸ παρὰ προσδοκίαν ἐδίδαξεν· ὁ γὰρ Ὀδυσσεὺς τοῦ μὲν κυνὸς σαίνοντος ἐξεδάκρυσε, τῇ δὲ γυναικὶ κλαιούσῃ παρακαθήμενος οὐδὲν ἔπαθε τοιοῦτον·

> And well has the Poet taught us how strong the effect of an unexpected happening is: Odysseus, for instance, shed a tear when his dog fawned upon him [17.302, 304], yet when he sat beside his weeping wife, gave way to no such emotion [19.211].

In contrast to the rhetorical manuals, Plutarch's conception follows the Aristotelian line: here *para prosdokian* is understood as an ironic, situational surprise. Thus, he compares the content of two scenes of the *Odyssey*, rather than two verbal forms (the expected and the given one) of a single passage.

The only hint at the concept of verbal *para prosdokian* as a recognisable figure before the Hellenistic period occurs in Aesch. *Supp.* 712, where *aprosdokētos* is especially used for *logoi*, among the various fifth-century occurrences of the adjective.

ΔΑ. ὑμεῖς δὲ μὴ τρέσητ' ἀκούσασαι πατρὸς
ἀπροσδοκήτους τούσδε καὶ νέους λόγους.

DA. Do not be afraid when you hear from your father
these unexpected and untoward news.

Given the absence of any other evidence in authors until the end of the Classical period, however, this reference is just a coincidence. Moreover, this kind of verbal unexpectedness has nothing to do with the particular *para prosdokian* figure, since νέους λόγους in the specific context means 'untoward news' (i.e. that the Egyptians are coming to abduct the Danaids), rather than 'strange words', and the anticipated emotional response is negative (terror), rather than positive (laughter).

To sum up, the term *para prosdokian* appears in the Hellenistic period both as a general set phrase about unexpected facts (first attested in Polybius) and as

---

[93] 'Hellenistic historians reflected on the different temporal modes and rhythms of change. Polybius approached this subject with the intention to construct models for knowing and controlling the future by especially drawing attention to how things turn out παρὰ τὴν προσδοκίαν, contrary to expectation', Lianeri 2016, 4–5; see McGing 2013, 189 n. 26.

a verbal *terminus technicus* (first attested in Demetrius). Inspired by the Aristotelian concept of tragic irony (παρὰ τὴν δόξαν), the historians introduced the term *para prosdokian* to denote situational unexpectedness, and rhetoricians appropriated the term, as a stylistic one, for poetry (Demetrius) and oratory (Cicero, Hermogenes, Tiberius). The term was established with the latter, verbal meaning, and became popular among the Alexandrian and medieval scholiasts, with Hermogenes' model becoming the most influential.

1.2 The Concept

After tracing the historical development of the term, this chapter will be confined to the concept of *para prosdokian* as it was eventually established: 'a «straight» sequence interrupted by a sudden explosive joke'.[94] In a narrow sense, it is perceived as a figure of speech in which the latter part of an idiom, proverb, or well-known expression or formula of words is altered to make an unexpected and humorous ending, as in 'If I understand you correctly – it will be the first time ever'.[95] But more commonly, and in the following discussion, this rule applies to any verbal sequence with potential for logical and stylistic cohesion, without necessarily being an idiom, proverb etc. *Para prosdokian* is the verbal version of surprise, or more precisely, one version of it. Oxymorons and 'garden-path' sentences are similar figures.[96]

To identify *para prosdokian* jokes within a text requires that we first know what the *prosdokia* is – what the receiver (reader/listener/spectator, diegetic or extradiegetic) would normally expect to encounter. However, the horizon of expectations of an ancient audience is only partially retrievable. *Para prosdokian* jokes reverse oral tradition (idioms, tales, fables, proverbs and proverbial expressions, everyday gossip), literary tradition (any genre, with tragedy being the main

---

[94] Silk 2000, 137.
[95] Macquarie Dictionary 2013; this is the first, and thus far only, entry of the term in an English dictionary, appearing as a single word. Generally, the first identified occurrence of the term in print, in English, is Anstey 1891, 69.
[96] An example of garden-path sentence is: *The old man the boat*. The first part (*the old man*) gives the impression of being an adjective-noun phrase, working as subject of a forthcoming verb, but eventually it turns out that *old* alone is the subject, and that *man* is a verb (to handle, to manage), having *the boat* as its object. See Sanz *et al.* 2013. To my knowledge, there are no such instances in Aristophanes, with the possible exception of *Pax* 153 discussed below (p. 51). Contrary to garden-path sentences, *para prosdokian* includes only semantic reversals, not syntactical ones.

interlocutor of Aristophanic comedy) and logical sequences. Of these sources, only the latter is fully accessible. Literary tradition is known to us insofar as the surviving texts permit; oral tradition and everyday life are known even less, indeed only to the degree that they are embodied (or assumed to be embodied) in the surviving texts. The Hellenistic and medieval scholia offer important help in bridging this gap but are full of ostentatiousness, anachronisms, and inaccuracies. Therefore, we need to content ourselves with the fact that we can only restore *some* of the jokes and mostly on the basis of logic, as in the following example.

Plut. 27. Chremylus admits his preference for Carion over his other servants: τῶν ἐμῶν γὰρ οἰκετῶν / πιστότατον ἡγοῦμαί σε καὶ κλεπτίστατον. The last word appears *para prosdokian* (a 'comically wry insertion' according to Sommerstein) instead of a positive quality expected after πιστότατον, which would probably be εὐνούστατον (cf. Lys. 13.18.6).[97]

Linguistically, the figure occurs when the semantic value of the second part of a structure (word, phrase, or sentence) contradicts the semantic value of the first part, motivating the reader/listener to reframe, i.e. to reinterpret the first part in the direction of the latter part. To give an example using semantic markers (*componential analysis*),[98] consider what Meton says in *Av.* 995:

γεωμετρῆσαι βούλομαι τὸν ἀέρα
I wish to landscape the sky[99]

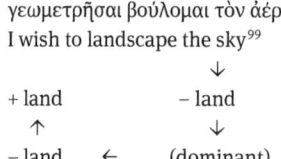

Meton's geometry is thus equated to 'airometry' and he is an ἀερολέσχης, 'a man of big empty words' (Hsch). This example confirms Berk's suggestion that, for a *para prosdokian* not to be degraded into mere nonsense, it should retain some link with reality,[100] whatever the dramatic 'reality' of a play is – in this case, that Meton is a failed geometer, not least because he claims to square the circle (1005).

Ching uses almost the same linguistic model for oxymoron: 'Because the direction of *erasure and replacement* is from the modifier to the head-word (it is the

---

97 For slaves stealing from their masters, cf. *Eq.* 101–2, 109–11; *Vesp.* 449–50; *Plut.* 1139.
98 This method originates from the Prague School. See Katz 1972, 37–42; Nida 1975.
99 Hereafter in this chapter I avoid translating the quoted jokes, because the position of words in English would confuse the reader in locating *para prosdokian*. Even in this example, where 'sky' correctly comes at the end, 'landscape' does not stand out at the start of the line to make a sharp contrast, as in Greek.
100 Berk 1964, 138.

modifier that does the erasing and the replacing), readers feel an emphasis of meaning placed upon the modifier'.[101] Oxymoron and *para prosdokian* indeed work in the same way, since the former can be considered to be a subcategory of the latter: oxymoron is a *para prosdokian* to logic, where the two parts are not just conceptually contradictory (e.g. a living-dead), but pragmatically irreconcilable (a non-dead dead). The difference is sometimes vague: the previous example from *Birds* is an oxymoron for Kakridis, since land is 'completely incompatible' with air,[102] but I consider it a *para prosdokian* joke, because to survey the air as if it were land is something imaginatively possible.[103] What would be inconceivable, i.e. an oxymoron, is an 'airless sky' *vel sim*. In the case of both figures, 'rather than rejecting such odd examples of language, the human mind often reacts by trying to make sense of them'.[104]

That *para prosdokian* should be sought in the second/last part of a structure is not a dogma, but a statistical observation. In fact, there are some exceptions in this scheme. For example, when the first part of a well-known idiom is changed, one perceives the *para prosdokian* of the whole structure in retrospect, soon after, as in 'meowing up the wrong tree'. In *Birds* 1477, the chorus mock Cleonymus as δειλὸν καὶ μέγα, instead of the formulaic δεινὸν καὶ μέγα.[105] In most cases, however, it is a matter of common sense that in order to unexpectedly reverse something, that something, the point of reference, needs to be known in advance. In light of this, we can reassess some identifications of the figure, or more accurately, of its core-component.

Pax 1116. The cleruch Hierokles invokes a series of animal-themed oracles, as well as the famous prophets Bacis and Sibyl, to reprove Trygaeus for making peace. The protagonist refuses to give a share of the roast sacrifices to the cleruch who, tempted by the sight and smell, eventually begs:

TP.   ἄγε δή, θεαταί, δεῦρο συσπλαγχνεύετε
        μετὰ νῷν.
IE.   τί δαὶ 'γώ;
TP.   τὴν Σίβυλλαν ἔσθιε.

---

101 Ching 1980, 181. Note that he uses the umbrella term 'verbal paradox' in the title of his article. On oxymoron, also see Hughes 1984; Shen 1987; Lederer 1990.
102 Kakridis 1982 *ad loc*. Translation is my own.
103 Nowadays, in an era of national airspaces and mapped airlines, the joke loses much of its effect. But for the ancient audience it was certainly something surrealistic.
104 Ross 1998, 31.
105 Cf. *Pax* 403; *Thesm*. 581; Hom. *Il*. 11.10; *Od*. 3.322; Hes. *Theog*. 299; Soph. *Aj*. 205; Isoc. *Paneg*. 52.2.

Trygaeus' reply as a whole is a resentful, ironic *para prosdokian* (Starkie). But on a microscopic level, even though Σίβυλλαν is the tonically emphasised word being placed at the beginning of the *antilabē*, it is not the unexpected one. No one would have expected σπλάγχνα ἔσθιε, because Trygaeus would never invite Hierokles to share. It is the second term, ἔσθιε, which makes the whole phrase a *para prosdokian* – in place of Σίβυλλαν αἰτοῦ, 'ask your Sibyl (for food)'.

Plut. 277–8. Carion mocks the chorus for their old age:

ἐν τῇ σορῷ νυνὶ λαχὸν τὸ γράμμα σου δικάζει,
σὺ δ' οὐ βαδίζεις, ὁ δὲ Χάρων τὸ ξύμβολον δίδωσιν.

The imagery comes from the judicial system, according to which the citizens over thirty years of age registered as potential jurors by being assigned a letter from α to κ, and sat in court when their letter-class was summoned by lot, receiving a token for their service.[106] It is clear that ἐν τῇ σορῷ has replaced ἐν τῷ δικαστηρίῳ and Χάρων has replaced ἄρχων (the nine magistrates who presided over the jury-courts). These replacements are obviously done τοῦ γελοίου χάριν (scholia) but, technically speaking, the *para prosdokian* can only be perceived as such when judicial vocabulary (coming last) interrupts the deathly imagery, rather than vice versa. After hearing ἐν τῇ σορῷ, one would expect something like ὁ Χάρων σε καλεῖ (*Lys.* 606), and Charon would be expected to give a pomegranate, if anything, rather than a ξύμβολον.[107]

There is a second, less frequent group of *para prosdokian* jokes, which do not display a semantic contradiction between two successive verbal units, but between the word given and the word expected. For instance, the invocation πρὸς τῶν κρεῶν (*Pax* 378) is a *para prosdokian* for πρὸς τῶν θεῶν, exploiting the phonological resemblance of the two words. But even in this case, πρὸς τῶν θεῶν itself appears two lines earlier, in order for the pun to be clear.

---

106 MacDowell 1978, 38–6; cf. *Eccl.* 681–5.
107 Pomegranates were considered the fruit of the dead: a certain number of grave statues of *korai* hold a pomegranate, and a series of 4th-century-BC *Totenmahl* reliefs depict the fruit in the funerary context. Most pertinently to our passage, Hades gave this fruit to seduce Persephone and take her to the underworld (*Hymn Dem.* 372–4; see Myres 1938). As Hades' ferryman, Charon could reasonably (synecdochically) be expected here to use the same lure for the chorus. The judicial system is also appropriated in *Plut.* 972, where the chorus addresses the old-woman: ἀλλ' οὐ λαχοῦσ' ἔπινες ἐν τῷ γράμματι; with ἔπινες appearing *para prosdokian* for ἐδίκαζες, after the juror-signifying word λαχοῦσ(α).

Despite the technicality of *para prosdokian*, and in order to blur somehow its distinction from situational surprise, it is important to acknowledge that all figures have a morphological *and* a conceptual aspect, and that their classification by grammarians as either σχήματα λέξεως or σχήματα διανοίας is an arbitrary convention. Irony for example, the σχῆμα διανοίας *par excellence*, does have a typology;[108] and conversely, 'hard-core' σχήματα λέξεως do have a hermeneutic purpose.[109] *Para prosdokian*, in turn, is usually coordinated with situational surprise but it is the textual markers that make it a figure. As Berk aptly identifies, the figure emerges more as a *side effect* in episodes which contain constant change;[110] it comes to 'formalise' a dramatic shift. Let us see two examples.

Pax 300. Trygaeus summons the chorus of farmers to help him rescue Peace:

ὡς τάχιστ' ἅμας λαβόντες καὶ μοχλοὺς καὶ σχοινία·
νῦν γὰρ ἡμῖν αὖ σπάσαι πάρεστιν ἀγαθοῦ δαίμονος.

Whether the correct emendation is σπάσαι (to draw) or van Herwerden's ἁρπάσαι (to grab), both verbs are initially understood as pulling the ropes, or the rocks, or Peace herself, in light of the preceding line. Thus ἀγαθοῦ δαίμονος, which refers to Dionysus and metonymically to wine, is a *para prosdokian* conclusion (Sharpley; cf. the English 'to hit…the bottle'). The joke is dramatically justified: the restoration of Peace *will* be celebrated with abundant wine drinking.[111]

Plut. 765. When Carion announces the cure of Wealth, Chremylus' wife greets him thus:

νὴ τὴν Ἑκάτην, κἀγὼ δ' ἀναδῆσαι βούλομαι
εὐαγγέλιά σε κριβανωτῶν ὁρμαθῷ
τοιαῦτ' ἀπαγγείλαντα.

Here κριβανωτῶν ὁρμαθῷ appears *para prosdokian* for στεφάνῳ. The scholiast is wrong in claiming that the intention is that he διαβάλλει δὲ αὐτὸν [i.e. Carion] ὡς λαίμαργον, because Carion's direct reaction (μή νυν μέλλ' ἔτι, 766) suggests that he is not a glutton, at least on this occasion (cf. 672 –95). More importantly, one can see how this *para prosdokian* joke, too, is dramatically justified in light of the preceding reassurance by Carion that from now on bread will exist in abundance (οὐδεὶς γὰρ ὑμῖν εἰσιοῦσιν ἀγγελεῖ, / ὡς ἄλφιτ' οὐκ ἔνεστιν ἐν τῷ θυλάκῳ. 762–3).

---

108 See Kapogianni 2013; Burgers/Van Mulken 2017.
109 E.g. for the famous alliteration in Soph. *OT* 371, Dawe alone (*ad loc.*) insists that there is no emphatic effect – even though this does not have to be a foreshadowing of Oedipus' blinding.
110 Berk 1964, 138. Translation is my own.
111 Cf. 1323, 1351–2.

In both examples, and almost in all other cases, there is a 'dramatic change' (the cure of Wealth, the restoration of Peace) or at least a 'dramatic reality' in the context of which *para prosdokian* jokes emerge, and are thus explained. Therefore, one also needs to consider the context of the potentially *para prosdokian* passages, apart from their linguistic microstructure, in order to analyse and assess them. Consider the following four examples.

Ach. 1026. A farmer comes to beg Dikaiopolis for peace, because some Boeotians have stolen his cattle. The farmer wears a white tunic, which makes Dikaiopolis wonder:

ΔΙΚ.	τί δ' ἔπαθες;	
ΓΕΩ.	ἐπετρίβην ἀπολέσας τὼ βόε.	
ΔΙΚ.	πόθεν;	
ΓΕΩ.	ἀπὸ Φυλῆς ἔλαβον οἱ Βοιώτιοι.	
ΔΙΚ.	ὦ τρισκακόδαιμον εἶτα λευκὸν ἀμπέχει;	
ΓΕΩ.	καὶ ταῦτα μέντοι νὴ Δί' ὥπερ μ' ἐτρεφέτην	1025
	ἐν πᾶσι βολίτοις.	

Dikaiopolis was expecting the farmer to wear black, the colour of mourning, for the loss of his flock. Rennie and Olson suggest that ἐν πᾶσι βολίτοις is a bathetic surprise for ἐν πᾶσιν ἀγαθοῖς, since the white tunic would normally accompany the farmer in all his joys, not all his defecations. Be that as it may, the only existing semantic contradiction here is between βολίτοις and λευκὸν.[112] An imaginative scenic surprise may be suggested here: the farmer appears in white, which justifies Dikaiopolis' wondering, but the very next moment he turns round and the all-white tunic is revealed to be soiled (with the metrical pause working as a *deixis* for the audience, presumably accompanied by a gesture).[113]

Pax 708; 711. Hermes invites Trygaeus to marry Opora, with the exhortation ταύτῃ ξυνοικῶν ἐκποιοῦ σαυτῷ βότρυς. According to Paley, Sharpley, and Olson, the last word stands *para prosdokian* for παῖδας or τέκνα. Even though the meaning of Opora's name and the ἐν τοῖς ἀγροῖς of the preceding line justify βότρυς as a conclusion, the spontaneous expectation is that a man and a woman – Opora is perceived as such as long as she is on stage – would give birth to children, not to

---

[112] Cf. λευκοπρώκτους (Callias fr. 14).
[113] Cf. Dionysus' soaking and the *para prosdokian* use of the sponge he asks from Xanthias (*Ran.* 479–90).

grapes. In fact, this is the first apparent mixing of sexual and agricultural vocabulary in the play,[114] which proliferates from this point on.[115] For a moment, Trygaeus seems hesitant and asks Hermes:

ἆρ' ἂν βλαβῆναι διὰ χρόνου τί σοι δοκῶ,
ὦ δέσποθ' Ἑρμῆ, τῆς Ὀπώρας κατελάσας;

The implication is very clear ('Is it safe for me to fuck her hard after years of abstinence?') and there is no reason to take κατελάσας as *para prosdokian* for καταφαγών *vel sim.* (as Olson) because Opora is primarily perceived as a woman and not as a fruit.[116]

Plut. 180. Throughout 170–9 Chremylus and Carion accumulate negative rhetorical questions (which work as affirmations) about the power of Wealth:

ΚΑ.	μέγας δὲ βασιλεὺς οὐχὶ διὰ τοῦτον κομᾷ;	170
	ἠκκλησία δ' οὐχὶ διὰ τοῦτον γίγνεται;	
ΧΡ.	τί δαὶ τριήρεις; οὐ σὺ πληροῖς; εἰπέ μοι.	
ΚΑ.	τὸ δ' ἐν Κορίνθῳ ξενικὸν οὐχ οὗτος τρέφει;	
	ὁ Πάμφιλος δ' οὐχὶ διὰ τοῦτον κλαύσεται;	
ΧΡ.	ὁ βελονοπώλης δ' οὐχὶ μετὰ τοῦ Παμφίλου;	175
ΚΑ.	Ἀγύρριος δ' οὐχὶ διὰ τοῦτον πέρδεται;	
ΧΡ.	Φιλέψιος δ' οὐχ ἕνεκα σοῦ μύθους λέγει;	
	ἡ ξυμμαχία δ' οὐ διὰ σὲ τοῖς Αἰγυπτίοις;	
	ἐρᾷ δὲ Ναῒς οὐ διὰ σὲ Φιλωνίδου;	
ΚΑ.	ὁ Τιμοθέου δὲ πύργος—	
ΧΡ.	ἐμπέσοι γέ σοι.	180

Timotheus, son of the famous admiral Conon, inherited an estate from his father and built a mansion.[117] Chremylus' *antilabē* 'may it fall upon you' can be considered a *para prosdokian* as it interrupts the flow; according to the context, we would expect οὐχὶ διὰ τοῦτον ἐγένετο; (cf. 171, 173, 176.) The joke is rather banal and arbitrary on a dramatic level: in their attempt to placate Wealth, Chremylus and Carion are behaving as true allies, answering each other's pretend questions

---

114 556–9 is allusive.
115 Thus, when Trygaeus praises Theoria's αἰδοῖον saying τουτὶ δ' ὁρᾶτε τοὐπτάνιον (891 with schol.), the replacement is no more a surprise; instead of *para prosdokian*, ὀπτάνιον is a readable metonymy for 'cunt'. Besides, the preceding lines say: ἄραντας ὑμᾶς τῷ σκέλει / ταύτης μετεώρῳ (889–90). Cf. Hdt. 5.92.8.
116 The same principle does not apply to Peace, because the role was allocated to a statue (Eup. fr. 62; Plato Com. fr. 86; schol. on Pl. *Ap.* 19c). For κατελάσας, literally 'to go down', as 'to fuck', cf. *Eccl.* 1028; Theoc. 5.116.
117 Lys. 19.40.

(132–8) and accumulating examples (163 f., 190–2); so there is no reason why Chremylus here attacks Carion, unless the meaning is that the former as the protagonist demands to 'have the last word' himself.

Plut. 963. Having been betrayed by her young lover, an old woman comes to Chremylus to complain. The chorus addresses her with ὦ μειρακίσκη, either as an ironic response to her addressing them as γέροντες four lines earlier (van Leeuwen), or more likely, as a reference to her intonation and voice quality (Sommerstein; cf. the chorus' explanation πυνθάνει γὰρ ὡρικῶς). This address is not a verbally marked *para prosdokian*, in the sense of μειρακίσκη contradicting a preceding word. That the woman is old becomes evident from the moment she enters and the audience sees her mask. It is the incongruity between her appearance and the chorus' address that signifies the *para prosdokian* on this occasion.

The meta-dramatic or extra-dramatic context is also employed in some cases, such as in *Pax* 1022. To celebrate the restoration of peace, Trygaeus asks his slave to sacrifice a ship on stage:

OI. οὐχ ἥδεται δήπουθεν Εἰρήνη σφαγαῖς,
οὐδ' αἱματοῦται βωμός.
TP. ἀλλ' εἴσω φέρων
θύσας τὰ μηρί' ἐξελὼν δεῦρ' ἔκφερε,
χοὕτω τὸ πρόβατον τῷ χορηγῷ σῴζεται.

The justification that Peace is not happy with sacrifices on her altar is merely poetic licence for the sake of economy (cf. *Av.* 1056–7; *Lys.* 189–90), given that the real cult of Peace did indeed feature sacrifices.[118] Even though Aristophanes compromises with this solution, he does not miss the opportunity to mock his own χορηγός for his strict budgeting. Χορηγία was a public service (λειτουργία) which was compulsorily assigned to citizens who had the appropriate means to hire, train, and costume the actors and the chorus, as well as to offer them a dinner after the performance. Thus, to 'save food for the funder' is a sharp, embarrassing, metatheatrical *para prosdokian* (Starkie, Rogers).

To sum up, in order to identify *para prosdokian*, one needs to look for semantic contradictions in the later part of verbal structures (words, phrases, or sentences). But in order to estimate the semantic contradictions, one also needs to take into account dramatic (verbal and scenic) and extra-dramatic information.

---

[118] See Parker 1996, 227–37; Stafford 2000, 173–7.

1.3 Non-Standard Uses

The above theoretical discussion of an otherwise simple figure would seem unnecessary, if there were a degree of consensus in practice. Scholarly criticism of Aristophanic comedy, however, displays an inconsistent and sometimes arbitrary usage of the term *para prosdokian*. This section traces the most common non-standard usages of the term and questions the respective proposals by commentators (these cases are coloured in grey in tables 4–7 of the Appendices). The distinction here between 'standard' and 'non-standard' uses is made upon an inductively derived model, that is, the statistically dominant model among the listed proposals, rather than a preconstructed definition. This also justifies the 'rejection' of some (five) cases where the scholia themselves use the term *para prosdokian*.[119] It should also go without saying that the purpose of this 'negative section' is to offer a converse proof of the method outlined above, rather than to indiscriminately discredit previous scholarship.

A) Many non-standard uses overlook the verbal context. Consider the following cases.

Ach. 17–18. Enumerating the happiest and saddest experiences of his life, Dikaiopolis asserts that the Athenians' indifference towards restoring peace is the worst by far:

ἀλλ' οὐδεπώποτ' ἐξ ὅτου 'γὼ ῥύπτομαι
οὕτως ἐδήχθην ὑπὸ κονίας τὰς ὀφρῦς

The suggestion by the scholia and Olson that the expected phrase was ὑπ' ὀδύνης τὴν καρδίαν ignores that ῥύπτομαι ('wash oneself') of the previous line introduces bath-relating vocabulary. Thus, the image of the shampoo (*LSJ* s.v. κονία II.1–2) burning the eyes (metonymy from ὀφρῦς) is anything but unexpected. Furthermore, δάκνω (here ἐδήχθην) is a typical verb for eye-pain: τὠφθαλμὼ δάκνει...τὸ πῦρ (*Lys.* 298–300); ὁ καπνός...ἔδακνε γὰρ τὰ βλέφαρά μου (*Plut.* 821–2); dry winds τὰ ὄμματα δάκνουσι (Hp. *Aph*.3.17).

Ach. 81–3. Dikaiopolis mocks the corrupt ambassador about his alleged mission to meet the Persian king, who eventually had left to 'take a shit':

ΠΡ.   ἀλλ' εἰς ἀπόπατον ᾤχετο στρατιὰν λαβών,
      κἄχεζεν ὀκτὼ μῆνας ἐπὶ χρυσῶν ὀρῶν.
ΔΙΚ. πόσου δὲ τὸν πρωκτὸν χρόνου ξυνήγαγεν;

---

119 To automatically accept all ancient uses as 'standard' would reveal the absurd assumption that ancient scholiasts (including students and copyists) were more systematic than modern ones.

The scholia suggest that instead of πρωκτὸν, the poet should have said στρατὸν, presumably influenced by στρατιὰν in 81. The scatological element, however, has been already introduced (ἀπόπατον, κἄχεζεν). The other possibility, which Olson accepts, is that the scholiast expects στρατὸν because of ξυνήγαγεν; but in the classical period, as Olson himself notes, the verb is not regularly used in the military sense. Moreover, πρωκτὸν is in the first part of the sentence, hence it is unlikely to appear *para prosdokian*. The passage will be discussed again later, for it does contain a *para prosdokian* but not in πρωκτὸν.[120]

Pax 95. When Trygaeus is about to take off for Olympus, riding his giant beetle, one of his servants asks him: τί πέτει; τί μάτην οὐχ ὑγιαίνεις; The scholiast notes that the first question appears *para prosdokian* for τί κάμνεις; But 'why are you flying?' is not an unexpected question at all, given that Trygaeus says ὑπὲρ Ἑλλήνων πάντων πέτομαι just two lines above. In fact, it is the most obvious question to follow. At the same time, τί πέτει also means 'why are you delusional?' which perfectly fits with the following τί μάτην οὐχ ὑγιαίνεις;[121] The option τί κάμνεις is rare (only exists in *Nub.* 707) and closer to medieval Greek.

Thesm. 158. The in-law offers to help Agathon compose a satyr play:

ὅταν σατύρους τοίνυν ποιῇς, καλεῖν ἐμέ,
ἵνα συμποιῶ σοὔπισθεν ἐστυκὼς ἐγώ.

Prato, and with some reservation Austin/Olson, suggest that ἐστυκὼς is put *para prosdokian* for ἐστηκώς. First, ἐστηκὼς could not have been expected because the idiom for 'I help you' is 'to stand by your side', rather than 'to stand behind you' (σοὔπισθεν). Secondly, in the context of a satyr play, an erection can hardly be taken as a surprising concept. When discussing Agathon in particular, anal intercourse is anything but unexpected. Similarly, in Trygaeus' assertion that many people ποθοῦντες ὑμᾶς [sc. Peace, Opora, and Theoria] ἀναμένουσ' ἐστυκότες (*Pax* 728), ἐστυκότες is not put *para prosdokian* for ἐστηκότες (Sharpley); first, because of the preceding ποθοῦντες, and secondly, because the people longing were not ἐστηκότες at all – they actively participated in rescuing the goddesses.

Thesm. 1025. A Scythian soldier undertakes to enchain and guard the in-law, who in turn pretends to be Andromeda waiting for Perseus (Euripides) to free 'her'. In his lament during this waiting, the in-law mentions:

---

[120] pp. 73–4.
[121] Cf. Eur. *Bacch.* 332: νῦν γὰρ πέτῃ τε καὶ φρονῶν οὐδὲν φρονεῖς.

μόλις δὲ γραῖαν ἀποφυγὼν
σαπρὰν ἀπωλόμην ὅμως.

The in-law never escaped the old woman (Critylla) who merely left the stage when the Scythian assumed his role. Thus, ἀποφυγών means that the in-law 'got rid of her' rather than 'escaped'. Note that γραῖα ('grey' and, by extension, 'old') is tragic vocabulary and is only attested in comedy here.[122] In the next line, according to the scholia δέον εἰπεῖν ἐσώθην, ἀπωλόμην εἶπε χάριν γέλωτος. On this basis, Austin/Olson speak of *para prosdokian*. However, given that the in-law says ὅμως, we need an antithesis and ἀποφυγών... ἐσώθην ὅμως would not make much sense. As it stands, the line has a very clear and non-paradoxical meaning, 'I got rid of her *but still* I am doomed', which the in-law explains right afterwards: ὅδε γὰρ ὁ Σκύθης πάλαι <δὴ> φύλαξ / ἐφέστηκε κωλοὸν ἄφιλον ἐκρέμα/σέ <με> κόρακι δεῖπνον (1026–8).

B) Overlooking the wider literary context is another non-standard practice. Consider the following cases.

Ach. 121. Dikaiopolis unmasks the corrupt ambassadors, recognises one of them as Cleisthenes, and exclaims: you really came here εὐνοῦχος ἐσκευασμένος? For Rennie, it is an outrageous *para prosdokian* that 'the height of Cleisthenes' aspirations is – to pass for a eunuch!' He assumes that one would have expected a deed of 'derring-do and insolent hardihood', on the basis of the tragic beginning of 119 (ὦ θερμόβουλον...) and the Aesopic intertext of 120 (both lines will be discussed later).[123] Leaving aside that εὐνοῦχος does not semantically contradict any preceding word, the fundamental objection is: who would ever expect Cleisthenes to do something positive in a play by Aristophanes? *This* would be *para prosdokian*. Secondly, the bathos has already begun in 119, so there is no sudden stylistic shift in 121. Furthermore, εὐνοῦχος here does not literally mean a eunuch but someone who has dressed in a Persian robe. Last but not least, Dikaiopolis is not *actually* asking Cleisthenes about his outfit because he is surprised; his question is a rhetorical one, expressing his indignation.

Ach. 500. Taplin argues that in τὸ γὰρ δίκαιον οἶδε καὶ τρυγῳδία we have Aristophanes' answer to a contemporary tragedy which was praising itself for its ethical agenda.[124] Even if one accepts this idea (I am sceptical about such a self-reference by tragedy), it is hard to accept Olson's suggestion that the line parodies a specific verse from the supposed tragedy, with τρυγῳδία appearing *para*

---

122 Aesch. *Eum.* 69; Soph. *Trach.* 870; Eur. *Heracl.* 584; *Hel.* 441.
123 pp. 58–9.
124 Taplin 1983.

prosdokian for the 'original' πένης ἀνήρ *vel sim.*[125] First of all, if it were a parody it should be somehow funny; τὸ γὰρ δίκαιον οἶδε καὶ τρυγῳδία seems a very sober statement. Second and most important, such ethical self-references are inherent in *Acharnians* (ἀλλ' ὑμεῖς τοι μή ποτ' ἀφῆσθ' ὡς κωμῳδήσει τὰ δίκαια, 655), so there is no need to 'unexpectedly borrow' from a tragedy.

Ach. 684. The chorus of old Acharnians reproach the judicial system of the day: οὐχ ὁρῶντες οὐδὲν εἰ μὴ τῆς δίκης τὴν ἠλύγην. The scholia suggest that τῆς δίκης appears *para prosdokian* for τῶν ἀνθρώπων, presumably because only physical beings can have a shadow; abstract ideas cannot. However, τῶν ἀνθρώπων τὴν ἠλύγην would not fit the context, which does not say that people do not attend the law courts anymore. The context speaks of corrupted trials, and thus, reading τῆς δίκης τὴν ἠλύγην as 'the murkiness of the lawsuit' is preferable (rather than the vague 'the shadow of justice'), and it *is* an expected phrase. Since *para prosdokian* normally occurs in the later part of sentences, here a *para prosdokian* could only lie in τὴν ἠλύγην. Indeed, as Starkie, Rogers, and Olson note, this line could be a play on the tragic image of 'the light of justice'.[126] Yet, the concept of judicial corruption has already been introduced (679 f.), so once again there is no *para prosdokian*.

Ach. 950. Dikaiopolis 'packs' the sycophant Nicarchus as 'takeaway' for the Boeotian (like vessels were packed to be shipped with security; 905, 928). The chorus and Dikaiopolis explain how such a 'gift' can be useful:

ΧΟ.	ἀλλ', ὦ ξένων βέλτιστε, συνθέριζε καὶ πρόσβαλλ' ὅποι	
	βούλει φέρων πρὸς πάντα συκοφάντην.	950
ΔΙΚ.	[...] πάντως μὲν οἴσεις οὐδὲν ὑγιές, ἀλλ' ὅμως·	956
	κἂν τοῦτο κερδάνῃς ἄγων τὸ φορτίον,	
	εὐδαιμονήσεις συκοφαντῶν γ' οὕνεκα.	

For Olson, the last line ('you'll be a lucky man – as far as sycophants are concerned') is a thoroughly ambiguous promise, but in light of the chorus' words the meaning becomes clear: 'take this sycophant and throw him against any opponent; sue them and enjoy your life'. Note the accumulation of explicit (ἄγων) and implicit (πρόσβαλλ[ε], κερδάνῃς) juridical vocabulary. In this sense, the sycophant *is* useful – a sycophant for all purposes, even though οὐδὲν ὑγιές – and not a *para prosdokian* substitute for χρήσιμον (Rogers, Olson).[127]

---

125 Cf. Eur. *Supp.* 863.
126 Cf. Aesch. *Ag.* 773; Eur. *Supp.* 564.
127 Cf. τὸ χρήσιμον καλόν ἐστι πρὸς ὃ ἂν ᾗ χρήσιμον (Xen. *Mem.* 4.6.9).

Pax 235. Trygaeus is scared by the noise of Polemos' mortar: καὶ γὰρ ὥσπερ ἠσθόμην / καὐτὸς θυείας φθέγμα πολεμιστηρίας. Platnauer calls θυείας a *para prosdokian* for σάλπιγγος but the mortar imagery as a metaphor for war is introduced just in the preceding lines (228–31).

Pax 279. When the servant of Polemos goes away to fetch him a pestle, Trygaeus swears: ἀποστραφῆναι τοῦ μετιόντος τὼ πόδε ('may the ankles of the goer be twisted'), which for Sharpley and Olson is *para prosdokian* for ἀποστραφῆναι τὸν κίνδυνον ἡμῖν ('may the danger be averted for our sake'). However, given that the servant has been running from the beginning of the episode (τρέχων, 259) and given Trygaeus' earlier curse against him (ἀπόλοιτο, 267), the current curse for him to twist his ankle is very much an expected rephrasing.

Pax 864. When Trygaeus prides himself on taking Opora as his wife, the chorus responds by mocking the family of the tragedian Carcinus: εὐδαιμονέστερος φανεῖ τῶν Καρκίνου στροβίλων. Carcinus' sons were dancers, so στροβίλων (spins, pirouettes) is a metonymy for παίδων rather than a *para prosdokian* replacement as Rogers and Platnauer suggest. Rogers' comment is indicative of the misappropriation of the term; he writes: 'στροβίλων [...] is here used *para prosdokian* for παίδων, in allusion to the twirls and contortions, or the strange figures of the sons of Carcinus.' In fact, 'in allusion' corresponds to the term *par' hyponoian* ('the implicit') rather than to *para prosdokian*. In *Wasps*, performed a year before *Peace*, Carcinus' sons appeared on stage as dancing crabs and were ridiculed for their appearance and dancing skills (1501 f.). Therefore, στροβίλων here is exactly what the audience would have expected after Carcinus' name. The surprise in this line exists in the whole τῶν Καρκίνου στροβίλων; firstly because it interrupts a potential proverb.[128] Secondly, because according to 781–90 Carcinus and his sons are anything but εὐδαίμονες; they look like ὄρτυγας οἰκογενεῖς, γυλιαύχενας ὀρχηστὰς / νανοφυεῖς, σφυράδων ἀποκνίσματα, μηχανοδίφας. Thus, to say 'εὐδαιμονέστερος φανεῖ than *them*' is not an actual compliment to Trygaeus, but an ironic euphemism: '*At least* you'll look better than Carcinus' pirouettes'. The expected words for a proper compliment would be εὐδαιμονέστερος φανεῖ πάντων τῶν ἀνθρώπων/θνητῶν (Sommerstein).

Thesm. 24. In the prologue of the play, the in-law asks Euripides to teach him how to act as if he were crippled:

```
ΚΗ.                      πῶς ἂν οὖν
         πρὸς τοῖς ἀγαθοῖς τούτοισιν ἐξεύροιμ' ὅπως
         ἔτι προσμάθοιμι χωλὸς εἶναι τὼ σκέλει;           24
```

---

[128] See Robson 2006, 170–1.

For Rogers, the phrase χωλὸς εἶναι τὼ σκέλει is added *para prosdokian*, as a mere piece of impertinence on the part of the in-law. He does not explain what the impertinence is exactly, or what we should expect instead, but one may assume that he reads the line as an ironic intimation of Euripides' crippled characters. There is certainly a semantic discrepancy between ἀγαθοῖς and being χωλός. When the context is taken into account, however, we see that there is no surprise: having just been told that he ought to be both blind and deaf (19), the in-law notes that his problems would all be solved if he could only find a way to be crippled *as well* – and thus spared the need to walk any further (Austin/Olson).

Thesm. 335–7. In a faithful parody of the Athenian Council, the assembly of the Thesmophorian women opens with the herald cursing the traitors:

εἴ τις ἐπιβουλεύει τι τῷ δήμῳ κακὸν   335
τῷ τῶν γυναικῶν, ἢ 'πικηρυκεύεται
Εὐριπίδῃ Μήδοις τ' ἐπὶ βλάβῃ τινὶ

That τῷ τῶν γυναικῶν has taken the place of τῷ τῶν Ἀθηναίων and that Euripides comically appears as a civil enemy alongside the Persians is a fact.[129] But can one say that they appear *para prosdokian*, as Austin/Olson suggest? That the assembly would consist of women had already been announced in 83, and more importantly, this is the scenic 'reality' now: women are addressing each other as women. That Euripides is hostile to women and vice versa is explicitly said already in 82–5 and 181–2. Therefore, there is nothing surprising in the passage when seen within its dramatic context.

Thesm. 346. The list of the 'traitors' continues for quite some time, and includes any old woman who offers gifts to an adulterous lover ἣ καὶ δέχεται προδιδοῦσ' ἑταίρα τὸν φίλον ('or any other woman who receives gifts [δῶρα is implied from the previous line] and yet betrays her lover'). According to Austin/Olson φίλον appears *para prosdokian* for τὴν πόλιν, the actual curse referring to individuals who had been bribed to betray their city. Even though this is the implied intertext, φίλον appears in tandem with the adulterous lover (μοιχῷ) of the previous line, and hence cannot be a *para prosdokian*. More generally, the herald's curse has already introduced in the previous lines examples of 'relationship betrayals', such as fake pregnancies and slaves revealing their masters' secrets (339–45).

Thesm. 1051. The in-law, impersonating Andromeda, is mourning his fate and, in the peak of the paratragic crescendo, he exclaims:

---

[129] For the actual curse, cf. Plut. *Arist.* 10.6; Isoc. *Paneg.* 4.157.

εἴθε με πυρφόρος αἰθέρος ἀστὴρ —
τὸν βάρβαρον ἐξολέσειεν.

That the in-law's voice immediately corrects Andromeda's voice is indeed 'an elaborate literary and social manoeuvre' (Austin/Olson). However, one can hardly consider it a *para prosdokian*, as Prato does, because the in-law's identities (both real and paratragic) interrupt one another already in the preceding lines; in 1022–38 alone: τὸν πολυστονώτατον βροτῶν... κώλοὸν ἄφιλον... / ἕστηκ' ἔχουσ(α)... ἐμπεπλεγμένη / ος, ὦ τάλας ἐγώ, τάλας. Therefore, what we have in 1051 is only the peak of the climax, not its reversal.

Thesm. 1226. In the exodus, the chorus dismisses the Scythian soldier: τρέχε νυν κατ' αὐτοὺς <ἐς> κόρακας ἐπουρίσας. For Prato, ἐς κόρακας is put *para prosdokian* for ἐς αὐτόν, i.e. for Euripides. However, this cannot be what one would have expected, because the chorus is no longer (since 1170) on the Scythian's side in pursuing Euripides; they are now on Euripides' side, pretending that he is indeed an old bawd (1217). It is therefore to be expected that the chorus dismisses the Scythian ἐς κόρακας – a stereotypical curse.[130] The only semantic discrepancy lies between the curse and the wish ἐπουρίσας ('with a good wind') but since both terms come from an avian imagery, this discrepancy is hardly a *para prosdokian*.

C) Other proposals are non-standard due to overlooking the scenic context.

Thesm. 242. When Euripides uses a torch to singe his in-law's arse in order to transform him into a woman, the latter exclaims:

οἴμοι τάλας. ὕδωρ ὕδωρ, ὦ γείτονες,
πρὶν ἀντιλαβέσθαι πρωκτὸν ἕτερον τῆς φλογός.

Prato and Austin/Olson suggest that πρωκτὸν is put *para prosdokian* for οἰκίαν, as a parody of one's appeal, when a house is burning, to fight the fire before it leaps to the next buildings.[131] What happens on stage, however, is an arse singeing rather than a house burning, hence the reference to arses is anything but surprising. In fact, what *is* surprising here (but not a *para prosdokian*) is the concept of *spreading* (ἀντιλαβέσθαι) the fire from arse to arse, as if they were torches or burning houses.

---

130 Cf. *Ach.* 864; *Eq.* 892, 1314; *Nub.* 123, 133, 646, 789, 871; *Vesp.* 51, 458, 835, 852, 982; *Pax* 19, 117, 500, 1221; *Av.* 28, 889, 990; *Thesm.* 1079; *Ran.* 189, 607; *Plut.* 394, 604, 782.
131 οἴμοι τάλας emerges thirty times in the Aristophanic corpus; for ὕδωρ ὕδωρ cf. *Ach.* 1175; for appealing to neighbours for help, cf. *Nub.* 1322–3, *Pax* 79.

Thesm. 288–90. After dressing up, the in-law is ready to join the Thesmophoria and invokes Demeter and Persephone:

δέσποινα πολυτίμητε Δήμητερ φίλη
καὶ Φερρέφαττα, πολλὰ πολλάκις μέ σοι
θύειν ἔχουσαν, εἰ δὲ μή, ἀλλὰ νῦν λαθεῖν.
καὶ τὴν θυγατέρα Χοιρίον ἀνδρός μοι τυχεῖν
πλουτοῦντος, ἄλλως δ' ἠλιθίου κἀβελτέρου,   290

According to Austin/Olson, the in-law's real concern not to be recognised by the women slips into his prayer, and thus λαθεῖν appears *para prosdokian* for θύειν (in which case one would read: 'I shall sacrifice to you many times or, at all events, I shall sacrifice today'). However, 'I shall conceal myself' would be surprising only if the in-law was speaking in front of the chorus, who should not hear that. At this point, just before confronting the chorus, the in-law's wish not to be revealed is most reasonable and with no element of humour. This wish does not 'slip' through into an otherwise hypocritical prayer to the goddesses, but is the very core of his honest invocation. The *para prosdokian* of the passage lies in the in-law's subsequent prayer for his daughter (comically called Χοιρίον, 'Little Pussy') to find a rich but stupid husband, instead of the expected wish to find someone πενιχρὸν μέν, ἄλλως δ' εὐπρόσωπον καὶ καλὸν καὶ χρηστόν (*Plut.* 976–7). The semantic contradiction results from the conjunction to μοι τυχεῖν (+good luck, –good luck).

D) In some cases, the commentaries have failed to read the idioms preserved, misattributing the wording to some *para prosdokian*. The scholia claim a *para prosdokian* in *Ach.* 615, ὑπ' ἐράνων τε καὶ χρεῶν, and *Ach.* 974, τὰ δ' αὖ πρέπει χλιαρὰ κατεσθίειν (χρεῶν and χλιαρὰ are the supposedly surprising words). However, the scholia do not provide any explanation and later commentators have not noticed anything unexpected here. At least in the first case, it is clear that the line contains a set phrase as it stands (cf. τὰ χρέα καὶ τοὺς ἐράνους, Hyp. 3.9.2). Holden,[132] Starkie, and Rogers propose that in *Ach.* 967, ἀλλ' ἐπὶ ταρίχει τοὺς λόφους κραδαινέτω, the word κραδαινέτω appears *para prosdokian* for φαγέτω. This line also preserves an idiom, as Olson has shown (cf. 835: παίειν ἐφ' ἁλὶ τὰν μᾶδδαν). In the opening of *Wealth*, Carion complains that Chremylus does not inform him about the situation, saying οὐδὲ γρῦ (*Plut.* 17); the latter word is onomatopoeia for a grunt. Filippo lists this line as a *para prosdokian*,[133] misreading

---

[132] Holden 1868 *ad loc.* [894 in his numbering].
[133] Filippo 2001–2002, 121.

the scholia which call it a *par' hyponoian* (an allusion) and ignoring that it is a well-attested idiom (*Vesp.* 741; *Ran.* 913; Dem. 19.39.3).

On the other hand, there are cases in which commentators have imagined an underlying idiom that Aristophanes supposedly distorts. *Pax* 868: Opora has been rescued and has taken her bath: ἡ παῖς λέλουται καὶ τὰ τῆς πυγῆς καλά. Sharpley (indeed, with 'no doubt') and Olson take τῆς πυγῆς as *para prosdokian* for τύχης, on the basis of some 'similia' which nevertheless do not prove that there is an underlying formula being distorted.[134] In fact, neither is τὰ τῆς <τύχης> καλά attested, nor is ἡ παῖς λέλουται predisposed to such a construction. Moreover, the idea that Opora took a bath and her 'butt' is beautiful – with the implication that she is now prepared for intercourse – contains nothing surprising; it merely follows on from the reference to her 'boobies' a few lines earlier (863).

E) Overlooking the cultural context seems to be the case with the proposal of *Thesm.* 515–6. In order to expose the knavery of women, the in-law narrates the story of an old woman who became an accomplice to a pretend parturition. The woman would compliment the supposed father about the baby's supposed resemblance to him, in a rather grotesque way:

τά τ' ἄλλ' ἀπαξάπαντα καὶ τὸ πόσθιον
τῷ σῷ προσόμοιον, στρεβλὸν ὥσπερ κύτταρος.

According to Austin/Olson, πόσθιον (they print *ποσθίον) appears *para prosdokian* for ῥινίον *vel sim*. The latter word, in the majority of the few instances it is attested, is a diminutive of ῥίνη (small file)[135] rather than of ῥίς (nostrils).[136] The primary objection, however, is that it is a common practice for parents and nurses to inspect and remark on new-borns' genitalia, both for medical reasons (to check physical integrity) and for social ones (to attribute gender).[137] The only surprising thing in this reference is that the old woman seems too familiar with

---

134 They cite Phryn. Com. fr. 9 (ἀνὴρ χορεύει καὶ τὰ τοῦ θεοῦ καλά); Eur. *Phoen.* 1202 (καλῶς τὰ τῶν θεῶν καὶ τὰ τῆς τύχης ἔχει); Eur. *IA* 1403 (τὸ τῆς τύχης δὲ καὶ τὸ τῆς θεοῦ νοσεῖ). None of these has a sufficient verbal overlap with *Pax* 868, or with each another.
135 Gal. 12.871.17; Hdn. *Epim.* 119.
136 Arist. [*Phgn.*] 808a.34.
137 Cf. Sor. *Gyn.* 2.10 (just after parturition). In *Amphidromia*, a ceremony on the fifth or the seventh day after the birth of a child, the midwives or male runners run around the hearth holding the (naked?) infant; Hsch. 2400 as emended by Kirk 1981, 58. See Hamilton 1984. 'Whereas baby boys are frequently represented in Greek art, baby girls are more difficult to identify. No images of nude babies display female genitalia', Lee 2015, 44. In depictions of children on classical Attic funerary monuments, gender does not seem to have been a concern, 'since the babies are either heavily swaddled or held so that their genitalia are covered', Grossman 2007, 312.

the father's penis, but this is not a verbal issue. The highlighted phrase in this passage is the simile ὥσπερ κύτταρος, and thus is reserved for the end of the period (whereas τὸ πόσθιον falls within an enjambment).

F) While overlooking some kind of context is the common element of all the cases above, another non-standard conception of *para prosdokian* is its confusion with other figures.

Ach. 88–89: The corrupt ambassadors make up a story about how the Persian king supposedly welcomed them:

καὶ ναὶ μὰ Δί' ὄρνιν τριπλάσιον Κλεωνύμου
παρέθηκεν ἡμῖν·

Starkie suggests, though without explanation, that Κλεωνύμου constitutes *para prosdokian*. Cleonymus was a physically large person,[138] so his name is a metonymy for bodily volume. Therefore, his standing after τριπλάσιον might be a hyperbole but hardly a *para prosdokian*, since the semantic marker of both words for the quality of 'bigness' is positive (+). Something like σμικρός, ἡλίκος Μόλων (*Ran*. 55) is a *para prosdokian*; the actor Molon was another big man, so his name is a surprising ending for σμικρός.[139]

The same confusion is found in Olson's proposals (i) that in σκέψασθε παῖδες τὴν ἀρίστην ἔγχελυν (889), the eel appears *para prosdokian* for παρθένον, a young virgin. The context repeatedly and knowingly blends sexual and gastronomic vocabulary, all of which refer to that eel: φιλτάτη, ποθουμένη, ποθεινὴ, φίλη – ἐσχάραν, ῥιπίδα, ἄνθρακας, ἐντετευτλανωμένης (885–94). Thus, this eel becomes simultaneously the object of Dikaiopolis' gastronomic *and* sexual lust,[140] and therefore it is a symbol, metonymy, or metaphor for a girl, but not a *para prosdokian*; (ii) that in ἀσκὸν Κτησιφῶντος λήψεται (1002), the man's name appears *para prosdokian* for the name of some good regional wine. The problem is that we do not have any other testimonies for this person, but if he were a famous guzzler as Olson accepts, then his name is a metonymy for wine and fits perfectly with ἀσκόν; (iii) that in μέτρησον εἰρήνης τί μοι, κἂν πέντ' ἔτη (1021), ἔτη is a *para prosdokian* for κοτύλας *vel sim*. But a 'year' *is* a proper measurement unit for peace, counting its duration.

---

138 Cf. *Eq*. 956–8, 1290–9; *Av*. 288–9.
139 Cf. *Plut*. 210: Chremylus promises Wealth to make him see ὀξύτερον τοῦ Λυγκέως; given that Lynceus had the sharpest sight on earth (Pind. *Nem*. 10.63), to make Wealth's sight even sharper is a hyperbole, not a paradox. A paradox would be to say 'I will make you see better than... Oedipus'.
140 Cf. Trygaeus' ambiguous desire over Opora (*Pax* 706–12).

Ach. 984–5. The chorus reports an incident with a man, Harmodius, misbehaving in a symposium to which he had been invited:

τὰς χάρακας ἦπτε πολὺ μᾶλλον ἐν τῷ πυρί,
ἐξέχει θ' ἡμῶν βίᾳ τὸν οἶνον ἐκ τῶν ἀμπέλων.

Starkie and Olson suggest that ἀμπέλων comes *para prosdokian* for πίθων/ ἀμφορέων/κρατήρων/κυλίκων. Probably, the reasoning is that one can pour the wine out of a vase, not out of a vine, and that in the context of a symposium, the wine is stored in some kind of pot. But ἀμπέλων is by no means a surprising verbal sequel to οἶνον, for their semantic value is similar. Here we have a metonymic rather than a paradoxical substitution.

Pax 34. Trygaeus' servant says that the dung-beetle is devouring its food ὥσπερ παλαιστής, παραβαλὼν τοὺς γομφίους. Paley and Sharpley take the last word as a *para prosdokian* for τοὺς βραχίονας or τοὺς ὀφθαλμούς, the idea being that a wrestler must be on the alert. However, the figure here is a simile (ὥσπερ παλαιστής) and, as such, does not claim a literal reading. Indeed, the commas placed before and after the simile indicate that τοὺς γομφίους refers to the dung-beetle rather than the wrestler. The point of the simile is to emphasise the vigour, not the technique of eating.

Pax 153. Do not fart and do not shit, otherwise the dung-beetle will smell it and κατωκάρα ῥίψας με βουκολήσεται, Trygaeus warns the audience. For Sharpley βουκολήσεται is a neat *para prosdokian* (what for he does not explain), remote from the Aeschylean metaphor 'to beguile one's sufferings' (*Ag.* 669). However, either in its literal sense (the dung-beetle will throw his rider and will 'go to graze') or in its metaphorical sense (the dung-beetle will 'cheat' Trygaeus), βουκολήσεται involves no surprise. In fact, it seems that the ambiguity of the verb is precisely what the poet wants to emphasise, putting με in an ambiguous syntactical position: is it ῥίψας με + intransitive βουκολήσεται, or με βουκολήσεται (transitive)? This is possibly a 'garden-path' sentence, but not a *para prosdokian*.

Pax 199. Hermes informs Trygaeus that the gods have moved far away, towards τοὐρανοῦ τὸν κύτταρον. According to Sharpley, κύτταρον (the cell of a honeycomb) comes *para prosdokian* for μυχόν or ἁψῖδα. In fact, it is only a poetic metaphor, as the scholia acknowledge – even the proposed τοὐρανοῦ μυχόν or ἁψῖδα (+ hollow) is an equivalent poetic metaphor.[141] The only (conceptual) surprise in this line is that Hermes intends to speak ἀτεχνῶς and then resorts to a poetic metaphor.

---

[141] Cf. Eur. *Hel.* 866; *AP* 15. 24.11; οὐρανοῦ ἁψῖδα is first attested in the 1st century AD.

Pax 249. Trygaeus is lamenting the manner in which Polemos is treating the Megarians:

βαβαὶ βαβαιάξ, ὡς μεγάλα καὶ δριμέα
τοῖσιν Μεγαρεῦσιν ἐνέβαλεν τὰ κλαύματα.

According to Paley and Sharpley, κλαύματα is *para prosdokian* for κρόμμυα, presumably on the basis that Polemos in the previous line threatens to smash Megara into garlic sauce. However, (a) it is 'the onions' rather than 'the tears' that belong to comic vocabulary, and therefore only the former could stand *para prosdokian*; (b) 'tears' acts as a metonymy or better a euphemism for 'onions'; and (c) 'tears' fits perfectly with the preceding mourning vocabulary: ἰώ... πολυτλήμονες (236), ἰώ... ἄθλιαι (242).

Pax 627. Hermes says that the Athenian navy has seized the livelihood (metaphorically suggested with a fig-tree) of innocent people:[142]

αἱ γὰρ ἐνθένδ' αὖ τριήρεις ἀντιτιμωρούμεναι
οὐδὲν αἰτίων ἂν ἀνδρῶν τὰς κράδας κατήσθιον.

For Olson, κατέκοπτον *vel sim.* would have been expected instead of κατήσθιον. Indeed, literally speaking, one can eat the figs or chop down the fig-tree, but cannot eat the fig-tree. The idea of 'ruining', however, is well conveyed by κατήσθιον. This is a clear case of *synecdochē*, rather than *para prosdokian*: to eat the fig-tree means to eat *all* the figs.

Pax 669. 'Back then, our mind was only concerned with...leathers', Trygaeus regretfully says to Hermes; according to Sharpley, 'leathers' appears *para prosdokian* for 'battles'. But in light of the preceding 647–8 (ταῦτα δ' ἦν ὁ δρῶν / βυρσοπώλης), 'leathers' can only be an (expected) metaphor for Cleon.

Pax 1186. The chorus renounces the generals who call for war, and conclude:

ταῦτα δ' ἡμᾶς τοὺς ἀγροίκους δρῶσι, τοὺς δ' ἐξ ἄστεως
ἧττον, οἱ θεοῖσιν οὗτοι κἀνδράσι ῥιψάσπιδες.

Some commentators maintain that ῥιψάσπιδες appears *para prosdokian* for ἐχθροί (Platnauer, Sommerstein) while others call it a *par' hyponoian* (scholia, Rogers, Olson). In many cases, the two terms were used indistinguishably in the

---

[142] A fleet of a hundred ships was sent against the Peloponnesians in response to their ravaging the seaboard of Attica in 431 (Thuc. 2.19). The 'innocent people' must refer to the average Spartans, since it was only the elite who decided to wage war; cf. 622.

scholia, as mentioned earlier. On this occasion, however, the ancient commentator was right – either knowingly or by coincidence – not to call it a *para prosdokian*. The charge of desertion is introduced a few lines ago (1177: φεύγει πρῶτος ὥσπερ ξουθὸς ἱππαλεκτρυών), so there is nothing surprising here. Desertion is, after all, a kind of enmity against the city, hence ἐχθροί and ῥιψάσπιδες are equivalent.

Thesm. 53–7. Agathon's servant announces to Euripides and his in-law that his master is inside the house, preparing a new tragedy:

ΘΕ.   δρυόχους τιθέναι δράματος ἀρχάς.
      κάμπτει δὲ νέας ἁψῖδας ἐπῶν,
      τὰ δὲ τορνεύει, τὰ δὲ κολλομελεῖ,
      καὶ γνωμοτυπεῖ κἀντονομάζει   55
      καὶ κηροχυτεῖ καὶ γογγύλλει
      καὶ χοανεύει.
ΚΗ.   καὶ λαικάζει.

The composition of a drama is paralleled to shipbuilding (δρυόχους), to woodcraft or pottery-making or architecture (ἁψῖδας), and metalsmithing (τορνεύει, κηροχυτεῖ, χοανεύει and probably the *hapax* γογγύλλει). Given that all these are forms of art, it seems excessive to say that ἐπῶν appears *para prosdokian* for τροχῶν (Austin/Olson). It is rather a metaphor: *like* artisans, Agathon elaborates his works.[143] That there is nothing surprising in this parallelism is also indicated by the coinage κολλομελεῖ, which stands both for poetry ('to glue songs together') and for plastic arts ('to glue parts/limbs together'). Instead, the humour of these lines lies in the accumulation technique: the *polysyndeton* and the multiple rhymes (τορνεύει – χοανεύει; κολλομελεῖ – γνωμοτυπεῖ – κηροχυτεῖ). Moreover, what *is* a *para prosdokian* is the in-law's *antilabē*, also highlighted through rhyme (κἀντονομάζει – καὶ λαικάζει): 'and he gives blow-jobs'.[144] This aside joke is analogous to what has been said before: Agathon is an artisan-like poet and an equally skilful 'cocksucker'.[145]

G) While decontextualisation and confusion with other figures are the most common non-standard usages, the most problematic identifications of *para prosdokian* are those entailing logical errors, i.e. when the proposed passages contain no contradiction, or at least antithesis. Consider the cases below.

---

143   Cf. κυκλίων τε χορῶν ᾀσματοκάμπτας, *Nub.* 333; στοματουργός, *Ran.* 826.
144   Jocelyn 1980, 12–66; Bain 1991, 74–7; Suda: 'to deceive'.
145   Napolitano 2007, 49–50.

Ach. 118. In Κλεισθένης ὁ Σιβυρτίου, there is certainly a contrast between Cleisthenes' rumoured femininity and Siburtios' masculinity (the latter owned a *palaistra*); the genitive could be a patronymic (Starkie), or denote an active sexual partner (Olson). In any case, the contradicting qualities (+ feminine, – feminine) are not *both* attributed to Cleisthenes himself, who could well have an impressively manly father, teacher, or lover. This antithesis cannot therefore be considered a *para prosdokian*.

Ach. 756. The Megarian blames the local government for a cruel policy. All commentators agree that ὅπως τάχιστα καὶ κάκιστ' ἀπολοίμεθα is a *para prosdokian* for the expected ὅπως τάχιστα καὶ ἄριστα σωθείημεν/σωθῶμεν *vel sim*. Even though this is a rare case of general agreement, its validity is weak. First of all, there is no contradiction within the line itself, since the qualities of speed (τάχιστα) and misfortune (κάκιστ' ἀπολοίμεθα) are not mutually exclusive, as it would be in the case of ἄριστα ἀπολοίμεθα or κάκιστα σωθείημεν or ἄριστα κάκιστα (oxymoron) or ἀπολοίμεθα σωθείημεν (oxymoron). Nor is there a set phrase being disturbed here.[146] Secondly, seen within its context, the line is just another reminder by the Megarian of his troubles (evident from 731), so there is no surprise here. The line could be intended as a reminder of Dikaiopolis' κάκιστ' ἀπολοίμην (151).

Pax 505. It takes a lot of effort for Trygaeus to motivate and synchronise the chorus to pull the rocks together, with some members (grouped by city of origin) being disobedient or obstructing the work. When it comes to the Athenians, Trygaeus complains: οὐδὲν γὰρ ἄλλο δρᾶτε πλὴν δικάζετε. Both the scholia and modern commentators maintain that δικάζετε is put *para prosdokian* for φωνεῖτε/ἐμποδίζετε/κωλύετε *vel sim*. 'You do nothing but yelling/disturbing' would be a legitimate alternative, but 'you do nothing but judging' also contains no semantic contradiction, and the Athenians' obsession with trials was a commonplace.[147] The phrase could mean that they are sitting aside and criticising the other members of the chorus, without themselves helping to pull the rocks; or that they have no manual skills and they only know how to speak to law courts; or that they are haggling like pettifogging lawyers over the terms of peace (Rogers). Given that Pericles had introduced a two-obol daily compensation for farmers to sit as jurors, the phrase could also imply that the Athenian group of the chorus (who are farmers) refuse to offer their services without payment.

---

[146] τάχιστα καὶ ἄριστα as a pair is attested only in Pl. *Leg.* 710b, six (at least) decades after the *Ach*.
[147] *Vesp. passim*; *Ach.* 829; *Eq.* 1317; *Nub.* 208; *Av.* 40–1, 1422–4.

Pax 795. In the first stasimon, the chorus renounces the tragic poet Carcinus and his sons. They mock his alleged poetic idleness, putting cheap excuses in his mouth:

καὶ γὰρ ἔφασχ' ὁ πατὴρ ὃ παρ' ἐλπίδας
εἶχε τὸ δρᾶμα γαλῆν τῆς ἑσπέρας ἀπάγξαι.

Platnauer suggests that ἀπάγξαι may appear *para prosdokian* for κλέψαι, given the thievish character of the weasel.[148] However, it is more expected of a weasel to throttle its victims than merely to steal them without eating them. Platnauer is also deceived in accepting 'the scholiast's *bona fides*', i.e. the constructed information that Carcinus had a play called *The Mice*. As Olson points out, this could not have been the title of a tragedy and Carcinus could not have composed comedies. Besides, the purpose of the weasel-joke is to present a strikingly unbelievable excuse, and a weasel that eats mice, even of a written variety, is comically believable. The actual surprise in the passage – which is not verbal – is clearly indicated: Carcinus had παρ' ἐλπίδας completed a tragedy, at last!

Thesm. 804. In the parabasis, the chorus of women uses the following argument for the supremacy of their sex:

σκεψώμεθα δὴ κἀντιτιθῶμεν πρὸς ἕκαστον,
παραβάλλουσαι τῆς τε γυναικὸς καὶ τἀνδρὸς τοὔνομ' ἑκάστου.
Ναυσιμάχης μέν <γ'> ἥττων ἐστὶν Χαρμῖνος· δῆλα δὲ τἄργα.

For Prato, τἄργα appears *para prosdokian* for τὰ ὀνόματα. It is true that the chorus intends to comment on τοὔνομ' ἑκάστου of the sexes, but it is also true that in practice, neither Charminus (as a word) denotes inferiority,[149] nor Nausimache (as a word) denotes superiority. It is precisely τἄργα of Charminus – not his name – that give sense to the comparison: Charminus was an Athenian general who was defeated that year by Sparta in a naval battle,[150] here personified by Nausimache.

Plut. 219. Chremylus promises Wealth that they will have ὅσοις δικαίοις οὖσιν οὐκ ἦν ἄλφιτα as allies in their plan. Rogers claims that ἄλφιτα is introduced *para prosdokian* and Chremylus was expected to say 'men who have not a grain of fear'. In fact, not having bread to eat is a metonymy (perhaps an exaggerated one) for not having money, and it is indeed the poor (rather than 'the fearless') who

---

[148] He was probably misled by the occurrence of *para prosdokian* in schol. on 793 (which is not used as a *terminus technicus* in that occasion).
[149] On the contrary, there might be a link with χαίρω; see Kanavou 2011a, 38–9.
[150] Thuc. 8.41.3–43.1.

will support Chremylus. Who else would fight for the redistribution of wealth if not the hungry? Secondly, the proposed 'grain of fear' is rather a cheap pun inspired by ἄλφιτα. The Greeks did not have such an idiom.

H) Finally, lexical and grammatical slips are sometimes a 'false alarm' for *para prosdokian* jokes. Again, the context helps to restore the meaning, as with the cases below.

Pax 554. Once Peace has been rescued, Trygaeus reassures the farmers that ἅπαντ' ἤδη 'στὶ μεστὰ τἀνθάδ' εἰρήνης σαπρᾶς. According to *LSJ* the use of σαπρᾶς ('rotted') here is a *para prosdokian* but Platnauer explains why the word actually fits: peace is not 'rotted' but 'mellow', like over-ripe wine.[151] Indeed, a few lines later a lot of emphasis is placed upon wine imagery, in connection to 'the past' (571–9):

ἀλλ' ἀναμνησθέντες, ὦνδρες,
τῆς διαίτης τῆς παλαιᾶς,
ἣν παρεῖχ' αὕτη ποθ' ἡμῖν,
τῶν τε παλασίων ἐκείνων,
τῶν τε σύκων, τῶν τε μύρτων,
τῆς τρυγός τε τῆς γλυκείας,
τῆς ἰωνιᾶς τε τῆς πρὸς
τῷ φρέατι τῶν τ' ἐλαῶν
ὧν ποθοῦμεν

Whose emotions does this recollection, and this vivid visual and olfactory imagery, try to arouse? In other words, who are the ὦνδρες to whom this passage is addressed? Peace as a *dramatis persona* is now free, so there is no reason for Trygaeus to evoke the nostalgia of the chorus. The actual addressee is the audience, for *their* peace is still unfulfilled. The metrical shift in 571 (trochaic dimetres) enhances this metadramatic reading. The Peace of Nicias was signed in March 421 BC, soon after the City Dionysia in which *Peace* was performed, but the script was submitted for approval earlier in the year.[152]

Pax 874. When Trygaeus suggests handing over Theoria to the *Boulē*, his servant asks whether she is the girl whom the two of them had raped at the Brauron festival:[153]

αὕτη Θεωρία 'στίν, ἣν ἡμεῖς ποτε
ἐπαίομεν Βραυρωνάδ' ὑποπεπωκότες;

---

151 Hermipp. fr. 82, 6–10: ἔστι δέ τις οἶνος, τὸν δὴ σαπρίαν καλέουσιν… ὀσμὴ θεσπεσίη… ἀμβροσία καὶ νέκταρ ὁμοῦ τοῦτ' ἐστὶ τὸ νέκταρ.
152 Arist. *Ath. Pol.* 56.3.
153 That is, a quadrennial procession of girls in honour of Artemis, on the east coast of Attica.

There is no reason to take ἐπαίομεν as a *para prosdokian*. Neither ἐπέμπομεν would fit (Platnauer, Olson), because the proper construction is πέμπω εἰς θεωρίαν and not πέμπω θεωρίαν; nor would ἐποιοῦμεν/ἐποιούμεθα (Olson, Sommerstein), because θεωρίαν ποιοῦμαι and ποιῶ (rare) mean 'to philosophise', not 'to go to a festival'. After all, Trygaeus and his servant are talking about Theoria as a person (who as such may have been raped) rather than as an abstract idea.

To sum up, the (statistically) non-standard identifications of *para prosdokian*, as emerging in the commentaries on the four comedies under examination, entail: overlooking the verbal, literary, scenic, or cultural context; confusing the figure with other figures; making logical or grammatical errors. Whether the aforementioned criteria for supporting, and questioning, *para prosdokian* jokes could be widely accepted or not is a secondary concern of this book (which of course does not aim to dictate what the 'correct' and 'wrong' usage of the term is). Its priority has been to set a specific methodology (based on componential analysis) applicable to all cases, which claims its validity through its consistency. What the transhistorical lack of such consistency in Aristophanic scholarship tells us is not that *para prosdokian* never actually meant anything very useful, in which case the term would eventually have disappeared (as *par' hyponoian* did), but that the slight differences found in the rhetorical manuals have been amplified by scholiasts over time, either due to uncritical usage or to deliberate expansion to the Aristotelian conception of surprise.

1.4 Three Common Types of *Para Prosdokian*

Having explained what a non-standard *para prosdokian* is, and most importantly *why*, it is now time to turn to the standard cases, proposing some reinterpretations where necessary. This section compiles and comments on passages comprising paratragic, para-proverbial, and 'magnifying' *para prosdokian* jokes. The first two categories refer to the underlying material that is being comically reversed (tragedies and proverbs respectively), whereas the third group refers to a specific function of the figure, that is, exaggeration.

1.4.1 Paratragic *Para Prosdokian*

From injecting little paratragic hints 'on the spur of the moment' to composing entire collages of paratragedies, Aristophanes is fond of appropriating comedy's sibling-genre. As the following examples demonstrate, *para prosdokian* appears to be a preferential field for expressing this fondness. Of course, not every verbal substitution in a parody of a tragic line is automatically a *para prosdokian*, but it is so when the underlying material is a trademark of tragic style, i.e. a formula or a famous quote.

Ach. 119–20. When Dikaiopolis finds out that Cleisthenes is one of the corrupt ambassadors, he addresses him:

ὦ θερμόβουλον πρωκτὸν ἐξυρημένε
τοιόνδε γ' ὦ πίθηκε τὸν πώγων' ἔχων

As the ancient scholiast noticed, in line 119 παρῳδίᾳ χρῆται. ἔστι γὰρ ἐν Τημενίδαις Εὐριπίδου 'ὦ θερμόβουλον σπλάγχνον' [fr. 858]. οὗτος οὖν σκώπτων Εὐριπίδην προσέθηκε 'πρωκτὸν' παρὰ προσδοκίαν. In this case, there is no logical contradiction and the recognition of the figure depends on the audience's knowledge of the intertext. Even for the less educated spectators, however, who would not have the specific reference, the exclamatory structure ὦ + two nouns ending in -ον, placed at the start of a line, suffices to indicate paratragic style.[154] Semantic markers in that case would be:

ὦ θερμόβουλον   πρωκτὸν
+tragic   −tragic

Of course, θερμόβουλον πρωκτὸν is funny regardless of whether it is recognised as a *para prosdokian*, because it attributes βουλή to an arse, because of the obscene word itself, and because of the sexual/gay element (ἐξυρημένε). Olson maintains that, unlike the American 'hot', θερμός lacks any sexual overtones, and thus the joke comes only from the following πρωκτὸν. That θερμός is a non-sexual word is certainly wrong; apart from the Hellenistic instances θερμός πόθος (*AP* 5.115 = Phld.) and θερμὸς ἔρως (Theoc. *Id.* 7.56), Plato offers a very explicit erotic imagery based on this word (*Phdr.* 253e):

ὅταν δ' οὖν ὁ ἡνίοχος ἰδὼν τὸ ἐρωτικὸν ὄμμα, πᾶσαν αἰσθήσει διαθερμήνας τὴν ψυχήν, γαργαλισμοῦ τε καὶ πόθου κέντρων ὑποπλησθῇ,

When the charioteer beholds the love-inspiring vision, and his whole soul is warmed by the sight, and is full of the tickling and prickings of yearning...

---

154 Cf. ὦ πανδάκρυτον ἁμόν..., Aesch. *Sept.* 654; ὦ κοινὸν αὐτάδελφον..., Soph. *Ant.* 1; ὦ πληρέστατον αὔλιον, Soph. *Phil.* 1087; ὦ πέδον Τροζήνιον, Eur. *Hipp.* 1095; ὦ φίλον γένειον, Eur. *Hec.* 286.

Thus, θερμόβουλον πρωκτὸν is rather clearly an 'arse which desires sex'. Even though we miss the initial tragic context, θερμόβουλον σπλάγχνον obviously meant something like 'irascible heart'. So Aristophanes does not only alter the second part of a tragic line, replacing σπλάγχνον with πρωκτὸν, but he also appropriates semantically the first part of it, replacing the non-sexual θερμόβουλον with a sexual θερμόβουλον. Therefore, it is true that the *para prosdokian* lies in πρωκτὸν, but not that the comic effect arises *only* from this word. This elaborate example confirms Berk's aforementioned theory that a successful *para prosdokian* retains some link with (the contextual) reality.

In the same passage, the scholia identified line 120 as a parody of Archil. 187 (τοιήνδε δ', ὦ πίθηκε, τὴν πυγὴν ἔχων), which in turn depends on oral tradition (Aesop. 81 Perry). In the Aristophanic version, the replacement of πυγὴν by πώγωνα ('beard') can by regarded a literary *para prosdokian*, given the iambic poet's popularity in Old Comedy.[155] Even though the Archilochean πυγὴν would perfectly fit the preceding πρωκτὸν, since they are synonyms, Aristophanes here seems to suggest that Cleisthenes' face (πώγωνα is a *synecdochē* for face) is like an arse.

Ach. 396. When Dikaiopolis visits Euripides to borrow some rags, Euripides' servant responds enigmatically:

ΔΙΚ.   ἔνδον ἔστ' Εὐριπίδης;   395
ΘΕ.   οὐκ ἔνδον ἔνδον ἐστίν, εἰ γνώμην ἔχεις.

Such oxymorons are common in Euripides and their parody in Aristophanes is frequent.[156] As mentioned earlier, a *para prosdokian* is something surrealistic, i.e. imaginatively possible; but 'not inside and inside' is inconceivable – until it is explained, surrealistically, that οὐκ ἔνδον applies to the tragedian's mind and ἔνδον to his body (398–9).[157] The absurdity is emphasised through the anadiplosis of ἔνδον. As for εἰ γνώμην ἔχεις, it is rather ironic: 'if you are smart enough to understand Euripides'... nonsense'.

Ach. 464. Euripides appears, hears, and succumbs to Dikaiopolis' increasing demands, until he gets irritated: ἀφαιρήσει με τὴν τραγῳδίαν, he moans. However, what Dikaiopolis has asked for is some rags, a hat, a cane, a basket, a jug and a pot. Thus, the expected exclamation would rather be ἀφαιρήσει με τὴν

---

155 E.g. *Pax* 1298–9; Cratinus' *Archilochoi*. See Rosen 1988.
156 See pp. 85–7.
157 Kronauer 1954, 43 notes that the surrealistic explanation here furthers the parody: whereas in tragedy oxymorons make sense and are not further discussed, comedy has to illuminate them in a playful way.

οὐσίαν/τὰ χρήματα (my property), which is a well attested phrase.[158] This *para prosdokian* epitomises the central, parodic concept of the scene, i.e. that Euripides' poetry is just a filthy, trivial mishmash.[159] Significantly, it is 'Euripides' who utters this *para prosdokian*, admitting thus to the charge.

Ach. 732–3. The Megarian enters the stage with his two daughters, with the intention to sell them as pigs to Dikaiopolis, and addresses them:

ἀλλ' ὦ πόνηρα κώρι' ἀθλίω πατρός,   731
ἄμβατε ποττὰν μᾶδδαν, αἴ χ' εὑρητέ πᾶ.
ἀκούετε δή, ποτέχετ' ἐμὶν τὰν γαστέρα·

As all commentators agree, τὰν γαστέρα appears *para prosdokian* for τὸν νοῦν, appropriating the rhetorical formula ἀκούσητέ μου προσέχοντες τὸν νοῦν (Isoc. 8.17.5–6). The comic poets often use this formula as it is,[160] but here Aristophanes remodels it to fit the context: the plan of the Megarian is not well thought out and is only driven by their starvation. Olson suggests that μᾶδδαν, too, is perhaps *para prosdokian* for θύραν *vel sim*. The verb ἄμβατε of 732 (Attic ἀνάβητε), a cognate of which is indeed attested near θύραν,[161] and the paratragic tone of the passage (cf. the exclamation in 731 and ὦ φίλα πεσήματ' ἄθλι' ἀθλίου πατρός, Eur. *Phoen.* 1071) strengthen this suggestion.

Thesm. 857. The in-law, impersonating Helen, describes the Egyptians as μελανοσυρμαῖον λεών ('black and purge-plant people'). The blending of these

---

158 οὐσίαν (real property): Xen. *Cyn.* 13.11.1; Pl. *Resp.* 565a.7; Dem. 40.48.5; Arist. *Metaph.* 1229a.16; *Pol.* 1297b.8; *Top.* 140b.5 / χρήματα (belongings): Hdt. 1.89; Ar. *Thesm.* 484; Xen. *Hell.* 2.3.43.7, 7.3.8.9; Pl. *Gorg.* 466c1; Dem. 21.100.1. Even though Euripides' stuff is not real property, οὐσίαν would fit better than χρήματα, since (a) Dikaiopolis is here paying a visit to Euripides' house and therefore stealing his belongings would reasonably make the tragedian worry about losing the house itself, and (b) οὐσία also means the 'essence' and Dikaiopolis *is* stealing the essence of Euripides' plays.
159 Cf. *Ran.* 840–2, 1063 (rags); 941–3 (chard, porridge); 1199 f. (crock).
160 ἄκουε δὴ νυν καὶ πρόσεχε τὸν νοῦν ἐμοί (*Eq.* 1014); ὦ σοφώτατοι θεαταὶ δεῦρο τὸν νοῦν προσέχετε (*Nub.* 575); ἄκουε, σίγα, πρόσεχε τὸν νοῦν (Cratinus fr. 315); πρόσεχε τὸν νοῦν κἀκροῶ (Pherecr. 163.3).
161 ἐπ' αὐτὸν ἥκεις τὸν βατῆρα τῆς θύρας (Amips. fr. 25). For summoning children to exit the scene-building, cf. ὦ τέκνα τέκνα, δεῦτε, λείπετε στέγας, / ἐξέλθετ' (Eur. *Med.* 894–5); for exiting from the θύραν in particular, cf. τίν' αὖ σὺ τήνδε πρὸς θυρῶνος ἐξόδοις / ἐλθοῦσα φωνεῖς (Soph. *El.* 328–9).

two qualities is a comic compound, but not a *para prosdokian* as Robson suggests,[162] firstly because there is no semantic contradiction between them and secondly because both are well known with reference to the Egyptians.[163] What *is para prosdokian*, instead, is the sudden interruption of the Euripidean intertext in the middle of the line, and the contrast between the whiteness of the land and its black people. Euripides in fact only speaks of the whiteness of the snow in Egypt.

> Νείλου μὲν αἵδε καλλιπάρθενοι ῥοαί,
> ὃς ἀντὶ δίας ψακάδος Αἰγύπτου πέδον
> λευκῆς λευκῆς τακείσης χιόνος ὑγραίνει γύας. (Eur. *Hel.* 1–3)

> Νείλου μὲν αἵδε καλλιπάρθενοι ῥοαί,
> ὃς ἀντὶ δίας ψακάδος Αἰγύπτου πέδον
> λευκῆς νοτίζει μελανοσυρμαῖον λεών. (Ar. *Thesm.* 855–7)

***Thesm.* 935.** Critylla, an old and prominent woman within the assembly, reports to the Prytanis that the in-law attempted to escape with the aid of a stranger, who is no other than Euripides:

> νὴ Δί', ὡς νυνδή γ' ἀνὴρ
> ὀλίγου μ' ἀφείλετ' αὐτὸν ἱστιορράφος.

The *hapax* ἱστιορράφος ('sail-stitcher') appears *para prosdokian* for μηχανορράφος (cf. Eur. *Andr.* 447, 1116; Soph. *OT* 387), and as Austin/Olson note, it alludes to the disguise of the Aristophanic Euripides as Menelaus – who indeed sewed his rugs out of sailcloth in *Helen* (421–2). It is an instance of poetic licence that the Aristophanic Euripides, who left the stage at 279 and came back at 871, knew that the in-law would pretend to be Helen (867, 901, 910) so that he could dress up accordingly as Menelaus.

***Thesm.* 1201.** Euripides becomes a bawd in order to finally unchain his in-law, and offers a young girl to the Scythian to put him out of the way. The Scythian asks the bawd's name, so that he can pay 'her' later:[164]

---

162 Robson 2006, 51–2.
163 For their colour, cf. Aesch. *Supp.* 154, 719–20, 745; Hdt. 2.57.2; 2.104.2. For their fondness for purges, cf. *Pax* 1253–4; Hdt. 2.77.4; 2.88.2; 2.125.6.
164 Wilson's text omits to distribute the first part of the *antilabē* on the Scythian, leaving it to Euripides – which makes no sense. The average price for a hired *hetaira* in that time ranged from three obols to a drachma (*Thesm.* 1195; Antiph. 293.3; Plato Com. 188.17), with the most expensive ones charging a stater (four drachmas, Theopomp. Com. 22) or more (like the Corinthian Lais

    ΤΟ.   ὄνομα δέ σοι τί ἐστιν;
    ΕΥ.   Ἀρτεμισία.
    ΤΟ.   μεμνῆσι τοίνυν τοὔνομ'· Ἀρταμουξία.

Ἀρταμουξία appears *para prosdokian* – not so much for its juxtaposition with the proper Ἀρτεμισία, as for its contradiction with the preceding assertion μεμνῆσι τοίνυν τοὔνομ(α). The Scythian returns and seeks for the bawd, running around the stage and calling her insistently with the wrong name (1213, 1216, 1222). This game with the fake identities and names alludes to Odysseus introducing himself as 'Mr. Nobody' to Polyphemus. Given that *Thesmophoriazusae* is a collage of parodies of Euripidean plays (*Telephus, Palamedes, Helen, Andromeda*), this final parody possibly draws on *Cyclops* (esp. 675–88) – and therefore we may take 411 BC as a *terminus ante quem* for the satyr play.[165] Imitating tragedians' trilogies, Aristophanes ends his own play with an embedded satyr-play.[166]

Plut. 600. Chremylus' *agōn* against Poverty reaches an impasse, with the former not being actually able to address the latter's arguments, and therefore resorting to abuse in order to get rid of her. In fact, Chremylus even admits that he approves of one of her arguments (571). Having no more counterarguments, he abruptly concludes: οὐ γὰρ πείσεις, οὐδ' ἢν πείσῃς, which is an oxymoron (the extreme end of the *para prosdokian* spectrum), instead of οὐδ' ἢν θέλῃ (Soph. *Phil.* 982) *vel sim*. The oxymoron here is probably inspired by Eur. *Phoen.* 272-3, where Polyneices mistrusts his mother, i.e. an old woman like Poverty:

πέποιθα μέντοι μητρὶ κοὐ πέποιθ' ἅμα,
ἥτις μ' ἔπεισε δεῦρ' ὑπόσπονδον μολεῖν.

Para prosdokian is employed for the parody of other high-register genres too, such as epic and elegiac poetry. Consider the following examples.

Pax 1065. Hierokles was assigned a cleruch at northern Euboea (which Pericles colonised in 446 BC) but was also politically active in Athens. In the third

---

in her prime; Epicr. 3.10-9). At the other end, common street *pornai* costed only an obol (one sixth of a drachma, Philem. 3.13). See Loomis 1998, 166-85.

165 Ussher 1978, 24, who also noted the similarity, does not claim an influence. Austin/Olson 2004, lxiv are more acquiescent. Wright 2006 dates *Cyclops* to 412 BC. On the other hand, Dale 1969, 129 and Seaford 1984, 49–50 take 408 BC as *terminus post quem* – despite the fact that Seaford 1982, 161-8 had initially proposed the late 410s.

166 Equally plausibly, Bowie 1993, 224-5 sees this final act as a comic coda, in the way of a comedy being performed after a tragic trilogy and a satyr play. For the City Dionysia being structured like this, see Pickard-Cambridge 1988, 66.

episode, Aristophanes makes him come uninvited – and in sacred guise – to appropriate Trygaeus' sacrifices. Hierokles blames Trygaeus and his fellows because συνθήκας πεποίησθ' ἄνδρες χαροποῖσι πιθήκοις. The word χαροπός ('fierce' or 'grey-eyed') is an epic adjective applicable to lions or dogs,[167] thus πιθήκοις is put here *para prosdokian* and refers to the 'monkey-tricksters' Spartans (*LSJ*).[168] Trygaeus biases the audience's reaction to the joke: αἰβοιβοῖ [...] ἥσθην χαροποῖσι πιθήκοις (1066).[169]

Ach. 480. After many concessions, Euripides refuses to provide Dikaiopolis with the chervil he asks for, and shuts him out of the house. Paratragically resigned, Dikaiopolis mourns: ὦ θύμ' ἄνευ σκάνδικος ἐμπορευτέα. The *para prosdokian* mixing of 'high' and 'low' vocabulary is probably the most typical means of parody in Aristophanes (cf. *Ran.* 1331 f.). The underlying verse could be Thgn. 1.1029, τόλμα, θυμέ, κακοῖσιν ὅμως ἄτλητα πεπονθώς, in which case the lack of cabbages is equated with 'unbearable sufferings'. The wider passage (480–9) seems to appropriate Archil. 128 (θυμέ, θύμ', ἀμηχάνοισι κήδεσιν κυκώμενε...).

1.4.2 Para-Proverbial *Para Prosdokian*

Appropriating proverbs and proverbial expressions is another common source for *para prosdokian* jokes. As mentioned earlier, our knowledge of such oral material is limited and filtered through the surviving literary tradition; moreover, the scholiasts' testimonies need to be read with suspicion. Indeed, we have already seen cases (*Ach.* 967; 615) where the ignorance of a proverb has led to misidentifying the figure – in the sense of claiming a *para prosdokian* at passages which actually preserve some proverb, and are therefore anything but surprising to listen to. Let us now turn to the reverse situation: truly *para prosdokian* cases, where idioms have been reversed for comic effect (*Ach.* 732 and *Pax* 864 have already been discussed).[170]

---

167 Cf. *Od.* 11.611; Hes. *Theog.* 321; [*Sc.*] 177; *Hymn Ven.* 70; *Hymn Merc.* 569, 194.
168 For monkeys as tricksters, cf. *Ach.* 120–1, 907; *Eq.* 887; *Vesp.* 1290–1; *Ran.* 1085–6.
169 In the next line, Hierokles repeats the charge, using another animal metaphor: κέπφοι τρήρωνες ἀλωπεκιδεῦσι πέπεισθε. The epic idiom was πέλειαι τρήρωνες (timorous doves; *Il.* 23.853; *Od.* 12.63) but I do not see a *para prosdokian* here (as Platnauer does), because κέπφοι (storm-petrels) comes before the adjective (in contrast to χαροποῖσι πιθήκοις) and also because the word is used for 'stupid' (cf. schol.; *Plut.* 912; Hsch.) and there is no semantic contradiction between +stupid and +fearful.
170 p. 60 and p. 45 respectively.

Ach. 909. When Nicarchus the sycophant approaches Dikaiopolis' territory, the latter and his Boeotian friend describe the unwanted visitor as follows:

ΔΙΚ. καὶ μὴν ὁδὶ Νίκαρχος ἔρχεται φανῶν.   908
ΒΟΙ. μικκός γα μᾶκος οὗτος.
ΔΙΚ.   ἀλλ' ἅπαν κακόν.

Although characterising someone as 'entirely bad' is commonplace,[171] the μικκός here has not prepared us for such a conclusion. Olson aptly noted that κακόν is a *para prosdokian* which reverses the 'normal' claim that a thing is small but *good* ('the best/good things come in small packages'). However, he did not give evidence that such a proverbial expression existed in classical antiquity. The evidence can be found in Eur. *El.* 1003 (σμικρὸν γέρας, καλὸν δὲ κέκτημαι δόμοις) and *AP* 4.1.6 (Σαπφοῦς βαιὰ μέν, ἀλλὰ ῥόδα).

Pax 898. Sexual imagery has manifested itself in the play since v.708, and the lines just before 899 also have clear sexual connotations: τετραποδηδὸν (896), ὑπαλειψαμένοις (898). Therefore, Trygaeus' current inducement of the *Boulē* members to παίειν, ὀρύττειν, πὺξ ὁμοῦ καὶ τῷ πέει Theoria is a reasonable sequel. Even though not surprising on a conceptual level, πέει is a *para prosdokian* since it disrupts the set phrase (according to the scholia) πὺξ ὁμοῦ καὶ τῷ σκέλει, which was used for *pankration*. Cf. Philemon fr. 41.6: τῶι σ[κ]έλει παίει τε λὰξ πύξ.

Thesm. 530. During the assembly, the chorus of the Thesmophoriazusae express their lack of confidence in the disguised in-law by remarking:

τὴν παροιμίαν δ' ἐπαινῶ τὴν παλαιάν·
ὑπὸ λίθῳ γὰρ παντί που χρὴ
μὴ δάκῃ ῥήτωρ ἀθρεῖν.   530

The women here appropriate a known proverb, putting 'orator' (i.e. the in-law who had spoken before) *para prosdokian* for 'scorpion'.[172] That they have recourse to a παλαιὰν παροιμίαν is a doubly misleading statement which intensifies the surprise effect: their saying, as it ends up being, is neither a true proverb nor an old one; 'be careful of the politicians' reflects rather contemporary worries.

Thesm. 531–2. Immediately after the previous joke – for the sake of accumulation – the chorus' leader exclaims the aphorism:

---

[171] E.g. πᾶσα βλάβη (Soph. *El.* 301 = *Phil.* 622).
[172] For the proverb, cf. ὑπὸ παντὶ λίθωι σκορπίον ὦ ἑταῖρε φυλάσσεο (Praxill. 4); ἐν παντὶ γάρ τοι σκορπίος φρουρεῖ λίθῳ (Soph. fr. 37); ὑπὸ παντὶ λίθῳ σκορπίος, ὦ ἑταῖρ', ὑποδύεται (Ath. 15.695d). A similar joke is made in *Plut.* 885: συκοφάντου δήγματος, and Eup. fr. 245: Τῆνος αὕτη, πολλοὺς ἔχουσα σκορπίους ἔχεις τε συκοφάντας.

> ἀλλ' οὐ γάρ ἐστι τῶν ἀναισχύντων φύσει γυναικῶν
> οὐδὲν κάκιον εἰς ἅπαντα—πλὴν ἄρ' εἰ γυναῖκες.

That women are the worst creatures of all is not a novel concept.[173] Here however, women are not compared to other creatures but to women: they are so shameless that they are proven worse than even themselves. The *para prosdokian* is technically located in the conclusion πλὴν ἄρ' εἰ γυναῖκες, but it has been prepared from the previous line: according to the underlying 'proverb', it is *the first* part of the comparison which should refer to (all) other creatures (τῶν ἀναισχύντων φύσει θεμμάτων/θηρίων *vel sim*). Menander uses this kind of *para prosdokian* as well: οὐκ ἂν γένοιτ' ἐρῶντος ἀθλιώτερον / οὐδὲν γέροντος πλὴν ἕτερος γέρων ἐρῶν (fr. 400.1–2). For Prato, an important aspect of the surprise in this aphorism against women is the fact that a woman utters it,[174] but one should not forget that the actor was after all a man.

Plut. 737. Carion concludes his narration about the incidents in the Asclepieion by saying:

> καὶ πρίν σε κοτύλας ἐκπιεῖν οἴνου δέκα,
> ὁ Πλοῦτος, ὦ δέσποιν', ἀνειστήκει βλέπων·

According to the scholia, the proverbial expression equivalent to 'in the blink of an eye' was πρὶν εἰπεῖν σε λόγον ἕνα/πρὶν πτύσαι (cf. Men. *Pk.* 392). The *para prosdokian* lies not only in the distortion of a known formula but also in the distortion of its diminutive intention; it is not just that 'a word/a spit' has been replaced by 'bottles of wine', but '*one* word/*one* spit' has been replaced by '*ten* bottles of wine'. Ten κοτύλας of wine is about 2.7 litres or five pints, which is a rather extreme quantity for drinking at once (one can suppose that Chremylus' wife starts drinking at 645). That women are alcoholics is a commonplace in Aristophanes.[175]

---

173 Cf. *Lys.* 369 οὐδὲν γὰρ ὧδε θρέμμ' ἀναιδές ἐστιν ὡς γυναῖκες. 1014–5 οὐδέν ἐστι θηρίον γυναικὸς ἀμαχώτερον, / οὐδὲ πῦρ, οὐδ' ὧδ' ἀναιδὴς οὐδεμία πάρδαλις. Soph. fr. 189.2–3 κάκιον ἀλλ' οὐκ ἔστιν οὐδ' ἔσται ποτὲ / γυναικός. Eur. fr. 494. 1–2 τῆς μὲν κακῆς κάκιον οὐδὲν γίγνεται / γυναικός.
174 Prato 2001 *ad loc.*
175 Cf. *Lys.* 194–239, 466; *Thesm.* 374–8, 393, 628–32, 733–57; *Eccl.* 132–57, 227, 1118–24.

1.4.3 'Magnifying' *Para Prosdokian*

The last group of *para prosdokian* jokes to be discussed in this section may be called 'magnifying', as they express a hyperbole. In terms of form, they are distinguished by their structure: 'not X but... XX'.

Pax 7. In the prologue of the play, a servant of Trygaeus is moulding excrement-balls and another servant is feeding them to the dung-beetle. The first servant asks:

OIK_A   οὐ κατέφαγεν;
OIK_B   μὰ τὸν Δί', ἀλλ' ἐξαρπάσας
       ὅλην ἐνέκαψε περικυλίσας τοῖν ποδοῖν.

Whether one accepts the manuscripts' οὐ κατέφαγεν; ('Didn't it eat them?') or Bentley's ἦ κατέφαγεν; ('Did it truly eat them?'), as Wilson does, μὰ τὸν Δί(α) remains a negative response ('By Zeus, no, it did not eat them').[176] The following ἀλλ[ά]... ἐνέκαψε ('instead it swallowed them at once') is a 'magnifying' *para prosdokian* because the preceding part is rejected (– eat) only to return in an exaggerated form in the second half (+ + eat). After 'By Zeus, no, it did not', one would expect something like 'but it threw them away' (ἀπέρριψε instead of ἐνέκαψε).

Pax 363. When Trygaeus approaches the cave where Peace is imprisoned, Hermes furiously asks him:

ΕΡ.   ὦ μιαρὲ καὶ τόλμηρε, τί ποιεῖν διανοεῖ;
ΤΡ.   οὐδὲν πονηρόν, ἀλλ' ὅπερ καὶ Κιλλικῶν.

After οὐδὲν πονηρόν, ἀλλ(ά)... we would expect something like πᾶν ἀγαθὸν, or ὅπερ καί followed by the name of a benefactor ('just something similar to that great man'). Instead, Trygaeus mentions Cillicon, a notorious traitor of his city who yet had the audacity to say πάντα οὖν ἀγαθὰ ποιῶ.[177] Thus Trygaeus' reply means 'I have nothing bad in mind – just treason' (cf. σμικρός, ἡλίκος Μόλων, *Ran.* 55). This very sharp *para prosdokian* makes sense to us, only because we happen to know who Cillicon was; the cases which we cannot decode are many more.

---

[176] See Wilson 2007, 99.
[177] Cf. Σ *ad loc*. Cillicon was so often made a target of the comedians that his name became a verb: εἴ γ' ἐγκιλικίσαιμ', ἐξολοίμην, φαθὶ λέγων ('Go and say: If I ever Cilliconise myself [i.e. act like Cillicon], may I die' Ar. fr. 107), ἀεί ποθ' ἡμῖν ἐγκιλικίζουσ' οἱ θεοί ('Since always the gods Cilliconise us [i.e. mistreat us]' Pherecr. fr. 176).

Pax 823. When Trygaeus returns from Olympus, his servant asks him about his experience in the sky:

TP.   ...ἔμοιγέ τοι
ἀπὸ τοὐρανοῦ 'φαίνεσθε κακοήθεις πάνυ,
ἐντευθενὶ δὲ πολύ τι κακοηθέστεροι.

'From above you look wicked, but from here...even more wicked!' For Paley, κακοήθεις is *para prosdokian* for φαῦλοι, which makes no sense because these words are clearly synonyms. For Platnauer, κακοήθεις is *para prosdokian* for μικροί ('from above you look small'), but κακοήθεις is not surprising at all in the context; Trygaeus observed the people's behaviour from above and now is judging them in moral terms. The text itself indicates that the emphasis is placed upon the relation of the pair κακοήθεις – κακοηθέστεροι, the latter being a 'magnifying' *para prosdokian*. One would expect 'From above, you look wicked, but from here you look decent'.

Plut. 372. The peasant Blepsidemus is very suspicious about Chremylus' rumoured enrichment, which in terms of plot is a *prōthysteron*, since Wealth has not yet been cured from his blindness. This can be attributed either to the unrealism of comedy or to the very realistic fact that rumours spread fast, sometimes even before something has actually happened. Blepsidemus, in a rather overstretched joke (352–89), repeatedly blames Chremylus that he must have stolen something, if he became rich so suddenly. Despite Chremylus' denial, Blepsidemus insists:

XP.   τὸ δ' ἐστὶν οὐ τοιοῦτον, ἀλλ' ἑτέρως ἔχον.
BΛ.   μῶν οὐ κέκλοφας ἀλλ' ἥρπακας;

Here ἀλλ' ἥρπακας (+ + steal) appears *para prosdokian* after οὐ κέκλοφας (– steal), magnifying the effect. As Rogers points out, ἁρπαγή includes violence whereas κλοπή is simple larceny.[178]

Plut. 706. Narrating the treatment of Wealth to Chremylus' wife, Carion mentions that he broke wind in the Asclepieion during the procedure but Asclepius' priest did not react:

ΓΥ.   αὐτὸς δ' ἐκεῖνος;
KA.   οὐ μὰ Δί' οὐδ' ἐφρόντισεν.

---

178 Cf. κλέψαι τε χἁρπάσαι βίᾳ, Soph. *Phil.* 644.

| ΓΥ. | λέγεις ἄγροικον ἄρα σύ γ' εἶναι τὸν θεόν. | 705 |
| ΚΑ. | μὰ Δί' οὐκ ἔγωγ', ἀλλὰ σκατοφάγον. | |

Again, there is a 'magnifying' *para prosdokian* conclusion: Carion utters a worse blasphemy than the one he has just been accused of (Sommerstein). The content is justified 'either because doctors make their living by inspecting the body's excreta and urine or because Hippocrates, the leader of medicine, was said to have tasted human shit in order to assess whether a patient would live or die'.[179] It is noteworthy that such 'magnifying' *para prosdokian* structures are absent in the *Acharnians*. This reasonably leads to the next question (section): are there any norms in Aristophanes' use of the figure, and how do they change over the course of time?

1.5 Tracing the Norms (A Comparative Analysis)

By comparing the standard (according to the criteria set out before) cases of *para prosdokian*, this section seeks to identify some norms in the employment of the figure, and potential differentiations in the course of Aristophanes' career, to the extent permitted by the four plays under examination. Norms and differentiations are traced over three aspects: the typology of the figure, the context it 'thrives' in, and the characters who use it. The data on which the following discussion is based is presented in tables 8–11 of the Appendices.

1.5.1 Typology

'Typology' is used here as an umbrella-term for the morphological and semantic components of the figure which regularly appear. Which grammatical, syntactical, and metrical forms are used, and what kind of vocabulary?

---

[179] Σ *ad loc.* (transl. Kazantzidis 2016). Hippoc. *Prog.* 11–12 speaks of the colour, quantity, and consistency of faeces and urine. There is no reference to tasting them and the only references to smell (that the faeces of a healthy man should be μὴ λίην δυσῶδες and that θανατωδέστερα δὲ τῶν οὔρων τά τε δυσώδεα) implies a routine self-check by people rather than a test by the doctor. Only Hippoc. *Epid.* 7.25 (οὖρα στρυφνά, ὁποειδέα, 'urine astringent, like fig juice') might refer to tasting urine – Kazantzidis 2016, 47 takes it as an unmistakable indication of the practice – but it might refer to its consistency instead. At any rate, the joke does not require that such practices were applied – only that this was the common belief (on which, unfortunately, we do not have other testimonies).

Starting with the width of application, that is, the linguistic structure-levels in which *para prosdokian* is observed, the vast majority of the occurrences of the figure (> 85%) are found in phrases or small sentences. Only a few cases in the material examined occur within single words – and still they are 'marginal', in the sense that the phrasal context contributes significantly to their comprehension. Consider the following cases.

Ach. 336. When Dikaiopolis threatens that he will slay the charcoal-basket, in a hilarious parody of Euripides' *Telephus*, the chorus exclaim: ἀπολεῖς ἄρ' ὁμήλικα τόνδε φιλανθρακέα; As Olson notes, φιλανθρακέα appears *para prosdokian* for φιλάνθρωπον, contributing to the fluctuation of the tragic tone (ὁμήλικα is from a high poetic register),[180] thus making it paratragic. It is noteworthy that the entailed contradiction occurs not only between the words ὁμήλικα (+ human) and φιλανθρακέα (– human), but also within φιλανθρακέα itself, since the first part 'φιλανθρ' phonetically predisposes us to expect an 'ωπον' ending. The same applies to *Pax* 308, where the chorus refers to Peace as τὴν θεῶν πασῶν μεγίστην καὶ φιλαμπελωτάτην, a *para prosdokian* for φιλανθρωποτάτην (Plaey, Platnauer). However, once such parallelisms have been established, one cannot consider them as unexpected when they reoccur thereafter. Thus, in *Pax* 557, when the chorus exclaim προσειπεῖν βούλομαι τὰς ἀμπέλους instead of 'I want to salute Peace', this is not a *para prosdokian* anymore (as it is per Sharpley).

Ach. 751. In answering Dikaiopolis' question about everyday life in Megara, the Megarian replies with bitterness, or sarcasm:

ΔΙΚ.   πῶς ἔχετε;
ΜΕΓ.   διαπεινᾶμες ἀεὶ ποττὸ πῦρ.

The scholia propose that διαπεινᾶμες appears *para prosdokian* for διαπίνομεν. Given that the latter particularly means 'to have a drinking-contest',[181] διαπεινᾶμες is not just 'we are hungry' but 'we have a hunger-contest'; drinking by the fire, a typical sympotic image of felicity, has been replaced by an image of suffering, in tragicomical mode. One could fairly object that we cannot have a *para prosdokian* in the first part of the phrase, as this chapter has repeatedly argued. In this case, however, the *para prosdokian* does not occur between διαπεινᾶμες and ποττὸ πῦρ (indeed, there is no antithesis in +hunger, +fire) but within διαπεινᾶμες itself: its first part (διαπειν-) phonetically predisposes us to

---

180 Hom. *Il.* 9.54; Hes. *Op.* 444; *Theog.* 1063; Eur. *Hipp.* 1098.
181 Hdt. 5.18, 9.16; Pl. *Resp.* 420e; Anaxandr. 57.

expect διαπίνομεν – given that διαπεινᾶμες is a *hapax*, it could not have been expected. As for ποττὸ πῦρ, it only follows to confirm the audience's suspicion of the underlying διαπίνομεν.

In these instances of single-word *para prosdokian*, the unexpected meaning is constructed at the level of morphemes and phonemes. The poet coins words (φιλανθρακέα, φιλαμπελωτάτην, διαπεινᾶμες) which display a *sufficient syllabic/ phonetic overlap* with the 'expected' words (φιλάνθρωπον, φιλανθρωποτάτην, διαπίνομεν). This means that not any word starting with φιλ- or δια- would capture the pun, but more clues (i.e. syllables) are needed. It is the entire φιλανθρ- and διαπειν- that enable the hint at the 'original' φιλάνθρωπον and διαπίνομεν; as for φιλαμπελωτάτην, which does not display the maximum syllabic overlap possible with φιλανθρωποτάτην, the poet has made sure that he coins a word with the same total number of syllables and the same superlative suffix with the word towards which he wants to hint. An explanation drawn from cognitive linguistics would be that a single-word *para prosdokian* is too short for the mind to process – the semantic complexity of the 'acoustic image' being disproportionate to its duration – and requires an alertness which is impossible in terms of performed (oral) speech.[182] This also explains why διαπεινᾶμες ἀεὶ is followed by ποττὸ πῦρ: technically, the *para prosdokian* occurs within the first word itself but it is too obscure to be perceived; thus an explanatory comment follows to give time for the mind to process the acoustic image, and to provide an additional interpretative hint. As for φιλανθρακέα and φιλαμπελωτάτην, it is the preceding ὁμήλικα and τὴν θεῶν πασῶν μεγίστην, respectively, that make the contradictions clear.[183] Since language is not parsed from left to right a word at a time, but as a sequence of sense-blocks which come into focus in turn as syntactic units are completed, placing explanatory hints around such 'microscopic' jokes is a useful, if not a necessary, tactic.

At the other end, there are a couple of *para prosdokian* instances extending over wider sentences and periods. *Ach.* 68–75, though an underappreciated passage, constitutes the most elaborate *para prosdokian* in the play.[184] The corrupt

---

182 Jokes with punchlines elicit brain response ('ERP reflection') in such timings: detection of the incongruity comes 350–500 milliseconds after the acoustic stimulus; resolution of the incongruity comes 500–700 ms after it; humour appreciation (emotional response) comes 800 – 1500 ms after it. Laughter (observable response) may come after the humour appreciation. Chen *et al.* 2017, 286.
183 Thus, I take these cases both as phrasal and single-word *para prosdokian*.
184 Rogers 1910 alone has noticed the *para prosdokian* and only in 73. In his brief discussion, Dover 1987, 288 speaks of 'blending two tones'.

ambassador describes a fictitious mission to Persia and Dikaiopolis replies in an analogous manner:

ΠΡ.   καὶ δῆτ' ἐτρυχόμεσθα διὰ Καϋστρίων
      πεδίων ὁδοιπλανοῦντες ἐσκηνημένοι,
      ἐφ' ἁρμαμαξῶν μαλθακῶς κατακείμενοι,
      ἀπολλύμενοι.
ΔΙΚ.   σφόδρα γὰρ ἐσῳζόμην ἐγὼ
      παρὰ τὴν ἔπαλξιν ἐν φορυτῷ κατακείμενος.
ΠΡ.   ξενιζόμενοι δὲ πρὸς βίαν ἐπίνομεν
      ἐξ ὑαλίνων ἐκπωμάτων καὶ χρυσίδων
      ἄκρατον οἶνον ἡδύν.

The dipole 'we suffered in luxury – I rejoiced in misery' is actually a *para prosdokian* chiasmus; properly, happy feelings should be joined to pleasurable activities, and discomfort with harsh activities. However, the surprise lies not only in the contradiction within each of the statements, but also in their sequence. Imitating the ambassador's attitude, Dikaiopolis responds with an ironic γὰρ ('Right, sure') as if he agreed,[185] and uses the same word as they do to describe his own condition (κατακείμενοι, κατακείμενος), even though he means the exact opposite (they are 'resting' – he is 'standing guard'). The ambassador in turn, as if he does not perceive the irony, continues his narration even more passionately (emphatic δὲ) and provocatively (πρὸς βίαν ἐπίνομεν), prolonging this game of 'who makes fun of whom'. Even though comically effective, it seems that the lengthier a *para prosdokian* is, the harder it is for it to be perceived as such. In this passage, it is the irony between Dikaiopolis and the ambassador that prevails, rather than the *para prosdokian* itself (which explains why it has escaped the notice of most commentators). The other extended *para prosdokian* passage is *Thesm.* 130–3, which is discussed later from another perspective.[186]

In terms of grammar and syntax, the core of the figure, i.e. the unexpected meaning, often (≈ 60%) lies in a noun, which in most instances operates as an object (e.g. ἀπένεγκέ μου τὴν μορμόνα, *Ach.* 582; ποτέχετ' ἐμὶν τὰν γαστέρα, *Ach.* 733) and seldom as a prepositional phrase (ἄνευ σκάνδικος, *Ach.* 480; ποττὰν μᾶδδαν, *Ach.* 732; ἐν πᾶσι βολίτοις, *Ach.* 1026) or a complement (γυναῖκες, *Thesm.* 532; κλεπτίστατον, *Plut.* 27). Subjects are reasonably avoided for *para prosdokian*,

---

185 Cf. *Eccl.* 773–6:
   ΓΕ.   λέγουσι γοῦν ἐν ταῖς ὁδοῖς. ΑΝ. λέξουσι γάρ.
   ΓΕ.   καί φασιν οἴσειν ἀράμενοι. ΑΝ. φήσουσι γάρ.
   ΓΕ.   ἀπολεῖς ἀπιστῶν πάντ'. ΑΝ. ἀπιστήσουσι γάρ.
186 pp. 75–6.

since they usually come at the beginning of sentences and thus have nothing preceding to contradict. Indeed, the rare times when a *para prosdokian* noun is the subject, it is always reserved for the end (e.g. οὐδὲν πονηρόν, ἀλλ' ὅπερ καὶ Κιλλικῶν. *Pax* 363). Occasionally (≈20%), the figure lies in an adjective (e.g. κακόν *Ach*. 909; κακοηθέστεροι *Pax* 823; θηλυδριῶδες καὶ κατεγλωττισμένον καὶ μανδαλωτόν *Thesm*.131–2; σκατοφάγον *Plut*. 706) and equally frequently in a verb, as in the following example.

Plut. 165. An argument used to cajole Wealth is that all professions exist for him, i.e. for profit. The poet here exploits his much-loved accumulation technique, in the form of a word catalogue:

ΧΡ.   ὁ μὲν γὰρ αὐτῶν σκυτοτομεῖ καθήμενος·
      ἕτερος δὲ χαλκεύει τις, ὁ δὲ τεκταίνεται·
      ὁ δὲ χρυσοχοεῖ γε χρυσίον παρὰ σοῦ λαβών –
ΚΑ.   ὁ δὲ λωποδυτεῖ γε νὴ Δί', ὁ δὲ τοιχωρυχεῖ –   165

Carion's verbs appear *para prosdokian*, since being a thief and a burglar – though aiming to profit and sometimes executed very professionally – are not jobs like the preceding examples. The joke is emphasised through rhyming endings (σκυτοτομεῖ – χρυσοχοεῖ – λωποδυτεῖ – τοιχωρυχεῖ).

Only in individual cases are other parts of speech employed for *para prosdokian* jokes (infinitive: βδεῖν, *Ach*. 256; adverb: ἔνδον, *Ach*. 396).

Three quarters of the identified instances are metrically highlighted, appearing either at the end of a line, or within an *antilabē*, or before a strong internal pause:

ΕΥ. ὤνθρωπ' ἀφαιρήσει με τὴν τραγῳδίαν· (*Ach*. 464)

ΘΕ. καὶ χοανεύει. – ΚΗ. καὶ λαικάζει (*Thesm*. 57)

ΧΟ. ὦ μειρακίσκη· πυνθάνει γὰρ ὡρικῶς. (*Plut*. 963)

The common feature in all these methods is pausing, which enables the mind to process the joke. Other metrical devices are alliteration and rhyme, whose function is emphasis:

πεδίων ὁδοιπλανοῦντες ἐσκηνημένοι,
ἐφ' ἁρμαμαξῶν μαλθακῶς κατακείμενοι,
ἀπολλύμενοι. (*Ach*. 69–71)[187]

---

187 For triple rhyme of participles, cf. *Pax* 451–3; *Lys*. 26–8. Data from experimental studies of prosodic features of humour do *not* confirm – they rather challenge – that that participants in a conversation use a set of prosodic phenomena to mark the presence of the humour and to set the

ἀλλ' εἰς ἀπόπατον ᾤχετο στρατιὰν λαβών,
κἄχεζεν ὀκτὼ μῆνας ἐπὶ χρυσῶν ὁρῶν. (*Ach.* 81–2)

παίειν, ὀρύττειν, πὺξ ὁμοῦ καὶ τῷ πέει· (*Pax* 898)

Zimmermann notes that a passage is a metrical *aprosdokēton* when a typically choral/tragic metre such as the dochmiac or the dactylo-epitrete expresses a content that is inappropriate to the lofty genres.[188] *Para prosdokian* in Aristophanes is not a metrical *aprosdokēton*, since it occurs in the usual metres of comedy.

With regard to the vocabulary preferred, a wide range of concepts is employed: animals (γαλᾶς, πιθήκοις), monsters (μορμόνα), political terms (συκοφάντην, ῥήτωρ), coined words (φιλανθρακέα). However, three groups alone represent more than half of the *para prosdokian* instances listed. Unsurprisingly, scatology is one of them. *Ach.* 80–2, discussed earlier from a different perspective,[189] is characteristic of such vocabulary:

ἔτει τετάρτῳ δ' ἐς τὰ βασίλει' ἤλθομεν·
ἀλλ' εἰς ἀπόπατον ᾤχετο στρατιὰν λαβών,
κἄχεζεν ὀκτὼ μῆνας ἐπὶ χρυσῶν ὁρῶν.

The scholia suggest that εἰς ἀπόπατον ᾤχετο appears instead of ἐπὶ πόλεμον ᾤχετο and Triklinios notes that Aristophanes ἔπαιξε δέ, which means that this replacement was a joke. However, ἐπὶ πόλεμον could not have been expected, because στρατιὰν λαβών comes afterwards and because the preceding τὰ βασίλεια is not primarily a military word. What *is* a *para prosdokian*, instead, is the στρατιὰν λαβών, as the second part of the phrase. Given that the supposed Persian king went 'to take a shit', one would expect something like σπογγιάν λαβών (cf. *Ran.* 483), but he instead took his entire army as company.[190] If the principle that the second part overwrites the first part is true, then instead of a 'shitty expedition', the poet rather projects the imagery of an 'epic shitting'. That the scatological element is the core of the image and not a surprising interpolation is confirmed by the next line, where κἄχεζεν appears at the beginning. As for

---

humour aside from the rest of the conversation; Gironzetti 2017, 400–2. These studies, however, concern spontaneous oral conversation (mostly in English).
188 Zimmermann 2011, 706.
189 pp. 41–2.
190 On toilet hygiene in antiquity, see Charlier *et al.* 2012.

χρυσῶν ὁρῶν, it is not a *para prosdokian* since it metaphorically combines a military meaning (golden mountains = Persia)[191] and a scatological one (piles of golden shit).[192]

Plut. 818. Proclaiming the new era, after the rehabilitation of Wealth, Carion is thrilled to announce that:

> ...ἀποψώμεσθα δ' οὐ λίθοις ἔτι,
> ἀλλὰ σκοροδίοις ὑπὸ τρυφῆς ἑκάστοτε.

Garlic was a common, cheap savoury food and the notion here is that in the new era of wealth, people will not deign to use them unless for 'wiping their asses'. In this context, σκορόδιον (diminutive of σκόροδον) must be a pun on σκῶρ ('shit'). Apart from the novelty of the concept (one would rather expect a sponge; the σαβάνοις proposed by the scholiast is a medieval word) there is a *para prosdokian* linking of garlic, the burning effect of which makes it unsuitable for applying on sensitive areas, to τρυφή, which alongside 'luxuriousness' means 'softness', 'delicacy'.

The second distinctive group of *para prosdokian* vocabulary conveys gluttony and wine drinking (σκάνδικος, μᾶδδαν, γαστέρα, διαπεινᾶμες, κρεῶν, βότρυς, ἔσθιε, κριβανωτῶν ὁρμαθῷ, ἔπινες). The respective passages have been discussed earlier and two more examples are given below.

Pax 123. Addressing his daughters, Trygaeus attributes the necessity of his mission to Olympus to their current hunger and he promises them that:

> ἢν δ' ἐγὼ εὖ πράξας ἔλθω πάλιν, ἕξετ' ἐν ὥρᾳ
> κολλύραν μεγάλην καὶ κόνδυλον ὄψον ἐπ' αὐτῇ.

The practice of someone beating his children for punishment was not uncommon. However, a 'slap in the face' is certainly not an expected 'side-dish' or 'sauce' (ὄψον) for one's loaf; κόνδυλον stands *para prosdokian* for κάνδυλον or κάνδαυλον, a luxury Lydian dish (Platnauer). In light of the proverb cited by the scholia,[193] the point is that Trygaeus will punish his daughters as a precautionary measure, so they do not become demanding after enjoying the loaf. If the scholiast is right that κολλύρα means a small loaf, then κολλύραν μεγάλην is another

---

191 *Persarum | montis, qui esse aurei perhibentur* (Plaut. *Stichus* 24–5).
192 For golden faeces, cf. *Pax* 1176–7.
193 Schol.: ἢν δ' οἶνον αἰτῇ, κονδύλους αὐτῷ δίδου ὑπὲρ τοῦ ἐθίζειν τοὺς παῖδας μηδέν τι περιττὸν αἰτεῖν.

para prosdokian – two in the same line – and the meaning is even more disappointing: the girls will actually continue to starve. A fair question would be why Trygaeus makes a discouraging comment just before he launches his ambitious plan. Is he pessimistic and prejudging his failure? Does he intend to keep all the goods for himself? Or does he simply tease his daughters? More likely, what matters here is the pun *per se*.

Thesm. 509. Trying to defend Euripides, by arguing that women actually do worse things than what the tragedian presents in his plays, the disguised in-law narrates an alleged incident of a fake parturition:

| τὸ δ' εἰσέφερε γραῦς ἐν χύτρᾳ, τὸ παιδίον, | 505 |
| [...] τὸ γὰρ ἦτρον τῆς χύτρας ἐλάκτισεν· | 509 |

That the baby came out of the pot cannot be considered as a surprising development, since the χύτρα has been introduced in 505. On a verbal level, however, τῆς χύτρας stands out semantically as it comes after ἦτρον (the lower part of the abdomen) and is thus a *para prosdokian* for τῆς μητρός (Austin/Olson).

Finally, sexual vocabulary could hardly be left off the list. Consider the following examples. *Thesm*. 50:

ΘΕ.   μέλλει γὰρ ὁ καλλιεπὴς Ἀγάθων
         πρόμος ἡμέτερος—
ΚΗ.   μῶν βινεῖσθαι;

Just like with καὶ λαικάζει (57), mentioned earlier,[194] the in-law insults Agathon with a sexual *para prosdokian*. After καλλιεπὴς and πρόμος, the reasonable question would be 'will he perform for us?' rather than 'will he be fucked with us?' Note that βινεῖσθαι here is middle voice, implying that Euripides, Agathon, and the in-law would all have a 'versatile' sexual role in this orgy (cf. *Eq*. 1242).[195]

Thesm. 130–3. When Agathon sings a maidens' song he has composed, as if he were one of the maidens, the in-law expresses his sexual excitement:

ὡς ἡδὺ τὸ μέλος, ὦ πότνιαι Γενετυλλίδες,	130
καὶ θηλυδριῶδες καὶ κατεγλωττισμένον	
καὶ μανδαλωτόν, ὥστ' ἐμοῦ γ' ἀκροωμένου	
ὑπὸ τὴν ἕδραν αὐτὴν ὑπῆλθε γάργαλος.	

---

194 p. 53.
195 Passive voice is used for women (Eup. fr. 385.2, Philetaer. fr. 9.4). For βινεῖν see Collard 1979, Sommerstein 1980a, Baldwin 1981, Jocelyn 1980, Bain 1991.

The in-law is not excited by the song itself (which is a very conventional worshipping of Apollo, Artemis, and Leto) but by Agathon's acting. If the in-law's remarks are taken literally, the mask of Agathon must have had very 'fleshy' and wide-open lips (in connection to λαικάζει, 57). The passage is surprising in multiple ways. First, it comes after a song devoted to Artemis, a virgin goddess, but the girls whom Agathon represents are now called Genetyllides (deities associated with Aphrodite and feminine lust)[196] instead of Nymphs, and are treated as sexual objects. Moreover, ὡς ἡδὺ τὸ μέλος, ὦ πότνιαι anticipates a high-toned vocabulary (μειλίχιος, σεπτός vel sim.), so that all three following adjectives and especially the striking coinage θηλυδριῶδες (on the model of θηριῶδες) appear *para prosdokian*.[197] The final line, too, must be a *para prosdokian* appropriation of Archil. 191 (τοῖος γὰρ φιλότητος ἔρως ὑπὸ καρδίην ἐλυσθεὶς / πολλὴν κατ' ἀχλὺν ὀμμάτων ἔχευεν): ἔρως has become γάργαλος and ὑπὸ καρδίην has become ὑπὸ τὴν ἕδραν.[198]

Thesm. 254. Once the in-law has been shaved and singed, Agathon offers him some of his feminine clothes to wear, and first of all his κροκωτόν.[199] The in-law takes it and comments: νὴ τὴν Ἀφροδίτην, ἡδύ γ' ὄζει ποσθίου, with the latter word standing *para prosdokian* for μύρου vel sim. Even though ἡδύς is occasionally used for sex,[200] its principal meaning is for a sweet smell or taste and, as long as the in-law sniffs the garment, the expected ending would be a kind of perfume. In light of Ar. fr. 613 (ἡδύς γε πίνειν οἶνος, Ἀφροδίτης γάλα), this could be the smell of mellow wine.[201] Instead, Agathon's robe smells 'sweetly of a little-dick', i.e. his own penis – probably an allusion to masturbation (Prato). Here πόσθιον[202] must be an affectionate diminutive of πόσθη ('sweetie penis'), rather than a mocking one ('small penis'), the idea being that by wearing Agathon's clothes, the in-law acquires Agathon's queerness and yearns for male genitals.[203]

---

196 Cf. *Nub.* 52, *Lys.* 2. Misled by Aristophanes, schol. and Hsch. γ 343 associate them with Artemis.
197 For κατεγλωττισμένον cf. *Ach.* 380, *Nub.* 51; for μανδαλωτόν cf. *Ach.* 1201.
198 For the latter, cf. Filippo 2001–2002, 106.
199 It is not clear whether Agathon strips off his own clothes or gives similar ones from his wardrobe; the latter is only certainly the case for the ἔγκυκλον, a kind of himation (261). For κροκωτόν as a feminine garment, cf. *Lys.* 645; *Eccl.* 332, 879; *Ran.* 46.
200 Cf. Xen. *Hier.* 1.30.5: ὁ ἄπειρος ὢν ἔρωτος ἄπειρός ἐστι τῶν ἡδίστων ἀφροδισίων.
201 The fragment also proves that the reference to Aphrodite in 254 does not predispose to a sexual conclusion.
202 Not ποσθίον as in Austin/Olson 2004, 137; cf. Hippoc. *Ulc.* 12.21
203 Cf. Eur. *Bacch.* 925 f. (Pentheus displaying feminine behaviour after wearing feminine clothes).

Plut. 152. Trying to persuade Wealth that people do everything for the sake of money, Chremylus refers to the behaviour of prostitutes:

καὶ τάς γ' ἑταίρας φασὶ τὰς Κορινθίας,
ὅταν μὲν αὐτάς τις πένης πειρῶν τύχῃ,   150
οὐδὲ προσέχειν τὸν νοῦν, ἐὰν δὲ πλούσιος,
τὸν πρωκτὸν αὐτὰς εὐθὺς ὡς τοῦτον τρέπειν.

In principle, a reference to sex in a context that mentions *hetairai* is not surprising. However, whereas in the case of poor men the prostitutes do not give 'their attention', which is a very coy metonymy for their actual services, in the case of rich men they are said to give 'their anus', which stylistically lies at the other extreme and thus constitutes a *para prosdokian*. At the same time, it is a cultural *para prosdokian*: anal penetration between men is well attested in late archaic and early classical vases, but women (even prostitutes) display some kind of opposition or are shown to be forced;[204] yet here it is alleged the Corinthian prostitutes *pursue* anal penetration.[205]

1.5.2 Context

The focus in now turned to the position where *para prosdokian* appears. In which parts and themes of comedy, and near what other figures does it occur?

The figure usually occurs in the prologue and the episodes, occasionally in the parodos (in its spoken portion), and rarely in the parabasis (only twice, with chanted anapaests) or the lyric parts (*Pax* 864; *Thesm.* 529–30). This observation supports Berk's theory that *para prosdokian* is connected to dramatic developments, rather than an irrelevant interpolation. Given that the progression of the plot happens precisely in these parts – the prologue introduces a surprising 'great idea' and the episodes feature surprising arguments between the characters – it seems legitimate to say that *para prosdokian* is coordinated with dramatic surprise, and that they go together emphasising one another. As for the general avoidance of *para prosdokian* in the lyric parts, this can be attributed to the music and the dancing, which would distract the audience from focussing carefully on

---

[204] See Kilmer 1990, 270–2; 1993, 33–43. Cf. *Pax* 896, *Lys.* 231, *Thesm.* 498.
[205] While Corinthian prostitutes were the most expensive – there was a saying οὐ παντὸς ἀνδρὸς ἐς Κόρινθόν ἐσθ' ὁ πλοῦς 'Not for every man the trip to Corinth' (Ar. fr. 928) – there is no evidence that they offered a wider variety of services than Athenian prostitutes. In fact, Lais would even refuse sex in spite of money (Auson. *Epig.* 17).

language. Moreover, with regards to the dispersion/frequency of *para prosdokian* jokes, there is a tendency for them to gather in the first half of the play (prologue and first episode) and progressively reduce towards the end. This tendency can be attributed to the audience's ability more easily to notice details (linguistic, scenic, or others) at the beginning of a play. After some point, mental alertness naturally falls and attention is paid to the plot itself; this is a reason why the exodus is conventionally a formulaic, unrefined carnival – so that little thinking is required. Being a challenging task to decode, *para prosdokian* towards the end of a play would go to waste. This is not to say that Aristophanes read cognitive theories before composing his plays, but that he was poetically perspicacious. Finally, a noticeable feature is the occasional accumulation of the figure, i.e. consecutive *para prosdokian* jokes (*Ach.* 68–75, 119–20, 255–6, 732–3; *Thesm.* 130–3, 935–7) aiming at inducing non-stop laughter.

Turning to the contextual themes, i.e. the themes of the wider passages in which *para prosdokian* jokes are found, one can identify some popular categories (apart from paratragedy, discussed earlier). One of them is political criticism, for example denouncing the appropriation of public money by phantom-bodies or the orators' lurking (*Ach.* 68–75 and *Thesm.* 529–30 respectively, discussed earlier). Other examples are:

Ach. 904. A Boeotian is selling animals to Dikaiopolis and asks to be paid in kind with some Athenian goods. After negotiations, Dikaiopolis suggests:

BOI. ἀλλ' ὅ τι παρ' ἁμῖν μή 'στι, τᾷδε δ' αὖ πολύ.
ΔΙΚ. ἐγᾦδα τοίνυν· συκοφάντην ἔξαγε,
       ὥσπερ κέραμον ἐνδησάμενος.   905

The *para prosdokian* lies in the insertion of a human being after a series of products that were under negotiation, and most importantly, in the characterisation of sycophants as exportable *goods*. Dikaiopolis' intention is simply to get rid of a sycophant, to the benefit of Athens.

Thesm. 937. When the Prytanis comes to punish the in-law, the latter asks him for a last favour:[206]

ὦ πρύτανι, πρὸς τῆς δεξιᾶς, ἥνπερ φιλεῖς
κοίλην προτείνειν, ἀργύριον ἤν τις διδῷ,
χάρισαι βραχύ τί μοι καίπερ ἀποθανουμένῳ.

---

206 For this motif, cf. Hdt. 1.24.2–5; Eur. *Alc.* 299–310; *HF* 327–31; *IT* 597–615.

The in-law lets his acidic comment slip into his petition, as if not caring about the consequences. Of course, such realistic objections are not applicable to the dramatic 'reality' of comedy; the Prytanis acts as if he never heard the comment but the audience/readers are expected to perceive the paradox. The *para prosdokian* lies in the juxtaposition of the respectful opening address ὦ πρύτανι with the entire following line. According to the context, one would expect: 'which hand you like to offer generously, if someone asks for help'.[207] Cf. *Eccl.* 782–3 (ἕστηκεν ἐκτείνοντα τὴν χεῖρ' ὑπτίαν, / οὐχ ὥς τι δώσοντ' ἀλλ' ὅπως τι λήψεται), said about the gods.

Para prosdokian also serves social criticism. In the scenes with the Megarian and the farmer in the *Acharnians*, the figure expresses their self-pity: they complain about hunger (732–3; 751) and robbery (1026) respectively, as a result of war and unfair internal policy. In *Peace*, Trygaeus blames the Athenians for malignancy (821–3). In *Thesmophoriazusae*, the in-law attacks women for marrying for profit (289–90) and pretending pregnancies (509). In *Wealth*, Chremylus illustrates the economic inequality with the example of prostitutes serving only the rich (152). The criticism is sometimes implied, as in the case below.

Pax 425. Hermes is intransigently opposed to the rescuing of Peace, until he is offered a golden libation-bowl as a bribe. Profoundly touched, he exclaims: οἴμ', ὡς ἐλεήμων εἴμ' ἀεὶ τῶν χρυσίδων,[208] with the last word appearing *para prosdokian* for τῶν ἱκετῶν (Platnauer), τῶν ἀνθρώπων (Olson) *vel sim*. Apart from the contrast between moral values and profiteering, the surprise also lies in the disarming sincerity with which Hermes makes this confession – possibly an aside joke. Clearly, Aristophanes' target is not Hermes and the gods in general, but the merchandising of religion.

Personal abuse, more or less coarse, explicit or implicit, is a common function of *para prosdokian*. In *Pax* 756, the chorus describes Cleon as a monster, among the atrocious qualities of which 'a hundred heads of... fawners are licking him all around'. The 'fawners' appear *para prosdokian* for the hundred 'snakes' which lick Typhoeus (Sharpley, Olson), but would not come as a great surprise for those who remembered *Vesp.* 1033. The form of the monster and its semiology are discussed in detail later.[209]

---

207 For the concept of a hand of help, cf. Eur. *IA* 915–6: ἢν δὲ τολμήσῃς σύ μου / χεῖρ' ὑπερτεῖναι, σεσώμεθ'·
208 For οἴμ' as cry of joy, cf. *Nub.* 773.
209 pp. 99–100.

Thesm. 829. The chorus is praising the superiority of women over men.[210] Among many insults, they blame men for:

πολλοῖς δ' ἑτέροις ἀπὸ τῶν ὤμων
ἐν ταῖς στρατιαῖς
ἔρριπται τὸ σκιάδειον.

Here there is no 'personal' abuse in the sense of abuse against a specific individual, but abuse against a group of people (who are not public figures, thus a case of 'political criticism'). The last word, 'umbrella', appears *para prosdokian* and hence is reserved for the end. Within the military context (ἐν ταῖς στρατιαῖς), ἀσπίς would be expected. Σκιάδειον is selected not only as a non-military vocabulary, but as a female vocabulary in particular (echoing 823). It is an implicit way to call the men 'pussy-wussies'.

It becomes clear that *para prosdokian* serves a wide range of functions which are all located on the spectrum of subversion: irony, satire, parody, self-sarcasm. Thus, the linking with the type of *eirōn* becomes inevitable (see discussion in the next section).

A special case of *para prosdokian* in terms of its contextual function is *Ach.* 255–6. Dikaiopolis wishes his daughter a grotesque birth:

ἄγ' ὦ θύγατερ ὅπως τὸ κανοῦν καλὴ καλῶς
οἴσεις βλέπουσα θυμβροφάγον. ὡς μακάριος
ὅστις σ' ὀπύσει κἀκποιήσεται γαλᾶς   255
σοῦ μηδὲν ἥττους βδεῖν, ἐπειδὰν ὄρθρος ᾖ.

Here 'weasels' appears *para prosdokian* for 'children' or 'daughters' (scholia, Rogers, Starkie, Olson), since a human is not expected to give birth to animals. The weasel-metaphor for women traditionally bears unpleasant connotations; Semon. 7.53:

τὴν δ' ἐκ γαλῆς, δύστηνον οἰζυρὸν γένος·   50
κείνηι γὰρ οὔ τι καλὸν οὐδ' ἐπίμερον
πρόσεστιν οὐδὲ τερπνὸν οὐδ' ἐράσμιον.

In Aristophanes' passage, these unpleasant connotations become tangible, or better, 'odourous'. The farting weasel also appears in *Plut.* 693 (ὑπὸ τοῦ δέους βδέουσα δριμύτερον γαλῆς), again as a metaphor for a female character. Henderson suggests that βδεῖν is also a *para prosdokian* for βινεῖν ('to fuck'), which is

---

[210] This is the only Aristophanic parabasis which contains no lyrics; Sommerstein 1994, 204.

doubtful.²¹¹ Aristophanes is fond of the word and concept of βινεῖν, so he would hardly miss the opportunity to use it. The concept of a father anticipating that his daughters will become sex-experts, having their mother as an example, is present in the play, in the episode with the Megarian (781–3):

ΜΕΓ. αὕτα 'στὶ χοῖρος;
ΔΙΚ. Νῦν γε χοῖρος φαίνεται.
 ἀτὰρ ἐκτραφεῖς γε κύσθος ἔσται.
ΜΕΓ. πέντ' ἐτῶν,
 σάφ' ἴσθι, ποττὰν ματέρ' εἰκασθήσεται.

However, whereas in the latter case the comic effect lies in the sexual connotations of χοῖρος ('pig', 'cunt'), the weasel-metaphor had the opposite meaning, i.e. disgust, as the Semonidean passage shows. Therefore, it is true that βδεῖν is a *para prosdokian*, but only as an extension of the weasel-metaphor, i.e. with *no* sexual connotations. Within the larger context, one would expect the positive descriptions καλὴ, καλῶς, and μακάριος (223–4) to be followed by some graceful talent suitable to a young girl, like singing²¹² – not farting. The mockery here does not target an enemy (politicians, society, or Euripides) but rather, Dikaiopolis addresses it to his beloved daughter. It is the festive context that enables, or better imposes, such a surprising, Rabelaisian wish: it is said during the phallic litany organised by Dikaiopolis in order to solemnise their family treaty. As in the case of carnivals, obscenity here is merely a ritual necessity, said with no malice. Evoking sex (ὀπύσει) and scatology (βδεῖν) is a kind of sympathetic magic, pleading the gods to favour the fertilisation of the land and the health of animals. Not surprisingly, *Peace* too features festive *para prosdokian* lines.

1.5.3 Characters

Turning to the characters who use *para prosdokian*, it is appropriate to ask whether this figure can be attributed to a certain type of character. Silk convincingly rejects the neo-Aristotelian trisection *eirōn – alazōn – bōmolochos*,²¹³ highlighting the discontinuities of Aristophanic characters. They are 'inconsistently inconsistent' both *per se* and in the way they express themselves, and *eirōn –*

---

211 Henderson 1991, 196–7.
212 Aesch. *Ag.* 245.
213 This scheme is applied in detail by Cornford 1914, 132–71. See also Whitman 1964, 281–7; McLeish 1980, 53 f.; Baldwin 1997, 120–237; Silk 1990, 163 f.; Rosen 2014.

alazōn – bōmolochos are only *functions* which may be transferred from one character to another. Nevertheless, one has to admit that there are some primary functions for each role, and thus the three terms are hereafter used for convenience.

More than half of the *para prosdokian* jokes are said by the protagonists (Dikaiopolis, Trygaeus, the in-law, and Chremylus). Even though these characters are not equally or exclusively *eirōnes* – in fact, their plans for private treaties, neglecting the orders of Zeus, and invading secret rituals rather signify *alazōneia* – the employment of the figure is clearly ironic. First, in the sense of oneself being ψευδόμενος μὴ ἀγνοῶν.[214] For example, when listening to the corrupt ambassadors' story, Dikaiopolis pretends not to understand that these men are lying, and replies with γὰρ ('indeed'), using *para prosdokian* in his turn (*Ach.* 71–3, discussed earlier).[215] Secondly, *para prosdokian* is used ironically in the sense of 'pretence in the form of understatement'.[216] For instance, in the parodic ὦ θύμ' ἄνευ σκάνδικος ἐμπορευτέα (*Ach.* 480), suffering has been degraded into not having vegetables. Similarly, when Dikaiopolis faces Lamachus, he pretentiously underestimates himself and uses a reductive, childish *para prosdokian*.

Ach. 582. Lamachus' shield bears a prominent *gorgōn*, a typical armour-device, symbol of ferocity and means of intimidating the enemy.[217] Dikaiopolis pretends to have been scared:

HMIX. ἰὼ Λάμαχ', ὦ βλέπων ἀστραπάς,
βοήθησον, ὦ γοργολόφα, φανείς,
...

ΛΑΜ. πόθεν βοῆς ἤκουσα πολεμιστηρίας;
ποῖ χρὴ βοηθεῖν; ποῖ κυδοιμὸν ἐμβαλεῖν;
τίς Γοργόν' ἐξήγειρεν ἐκ τοῦ σάγματος;
...

ΔΙΚ. ὑπὸ τοῦ δέους γὰρ τῶν ὅπλων εἰλιγγιῶ.
ἀλλ', ἀντιβολῶ σ', ἀπένεγκέ μοι τὴν μορμόνα.   566–582 *sel.*

---

[214] Arist. *Eth. Eud.* 3.7.
[215] p. 71. To use Raskin's terms (1985, 100–4), there is a pretend *bona-fide* communication mode.
[216] προσποίησις ἐπὶ τὸ ἔλαττον (Arist. *Eth. Nic.* 2.7, 4.7).
[217] Athena also bears such a shield in Eur. *El.* 1257; *Ion* 210.

Μορμόνα appears *para prosdokian* for γοργόνα (Olson). In contrast to the fierce monster, Mormon was a female-bogey evoked by nurses to frighten the children.[218] Dikaiopolis is equally scared of Lamachus. The joke must had received laughs, since Aristophanes repeats it in *Pax* 473–4:

> ΤΡ.   ὦ Λάμαχ', ἀδικεῖς ἐμποδὼν καθήμενος.
>   οὐδὲν δεόμεθ', ὤνθρωπε, τῆς σῆς μορμόνος.

This time, however, Aristophanes did not have to mention *gorgōn* in order to prepare the pun, because he knew that his audience would recall their initial expectation, from four years ago.

Even though *eirōn* and *bōmolochos* are not easily distinguishable, one can reasonably classify personal assault into the latter function.[219] Some examples are the coarse, 'homophobic' addresses by Dikaiopolis and the in-law to Cleisthenes and Agathon respectively (*Ach.* 119–20; *Thesm.* 50, 57) and when Carion calls Zeus σκατοφάγον (*Plut.* 706).

As for the *alazōn* function, the attribution of *para prosdokian* jokes to such characters could only be argued for the case of *Acharnians* (from the plays under examination). Dikaiopolis repeatedly calls the corrupt ambassadors impostors: ἄχθομαι 'γὼ πρέσβεσιν καὶ τοῖς ταῶσι τοῖς τ' ἀλαζονεύμασιν (62–3), τῶν ἀλαζονευμάτων (87), σὺ μὲν ἀλαζὼν εἶ μέγας (109), ἕτερος ἀλαζὼν οὗτος ἐσκηρύττεται (135). They are indeed impostors, performing προσποίησις ἐπὶ τὸ μεῖζον in the sense that they are only masquerading as ambassadors; and they indeed employ *para prosdokian* (68–71, 73–5, 81–2, discussed earlier).[220] However, it is wrong to say that the figure also belongs to the type/function of *alazōn*, because even when used by such characters, *para prosdokian* is explicitly described as an ironic manner of speaking. Immediately after the outrageous *para prosdokian* by the corrupt ambassadors (about 'suffering in luxuries'), Dikaiopolis exclaims irritatedly:

> ΔΙΚ.   ὦ Κραναὰ πόλις   75
>   ἆρ' αἰσθάνει τὸν κατάγελων τῶν πρέσβεων;

---

218 φοβεῖσθαι τοὺς πελταστάς, ὥσπερ μορμόνας παιδάρια (Xen. *Hell.* 4.4.17); also Erinn. *SH* 401.25; Luc. *Philops.* 2.
219 ἔστι δ' ἡ εἰρωνεία τῆς βωμολοχίας ἐλευθεριώτερον· ὁ μὲν γὰρ αὑτοῦ ἕνεκα ποιεῖ τὸ γελοῖον, ὁ δὲ βωμολόχος ἑτέρου (Arist. *Rhet.* 3.18).
220 p. 71.

Κατάγελων points out that the corrupt ambassadors have been acting as *eirōnes*, in that specific occasion. The only instance of *para prosdokian* that could be somehow likened to an *alazōn* is Euripides' ἀφαιρήσει με τὴν τραγῳδίαν (*Ach.* 464), in the sense that he upgrades rags and pots (the items Dikaiopolis takes from him) into a tragedy. But still, this parodic persona is inherently ironic: he rather degrades his tragedy into rags and pots, in kind of self-sarcastic confession.

To sum up, a typical *para prosdokian* joke occurs within a phrase or short sentence. It is a semantically distinct noun, adjective, or verb, often with gastronomic, sexual, or scatological meaning, and is metrically highlighted. It occurs almost exclusively in the spoken parts of a comedy, it is often said by the protagonist, and serves a wide range of ironic and buffoonish functions: political, social, and literary criticism, parody, self-sarcasm, and personal assault.

1.5.4 Changes Over the Course of Time

So far we have seen the various possibilities of Aristophanic *para prosdokian* on a timeless basis, i.e. as they emerge from an overall comparison of the occurrences of the figure in the four plays under examination. This approach has been useful in drawing a coherent theory for this understudied figure, but it is of no less interest to trace the changes in its employment over the course of the poet's career. Even though the discussion of *para prosdokian* in the previous sections has not followed a temporal arrangement of the material, this perspective is facilitated by the play-by-play structure of tables 8–11 of the Appendices.

The first observation is quantitative: slightly more instances of the figure exist in *Acharnians*, but the plays otherwise display almost the same number of *para prosdokian* jokes – a striking coincidence.[221] Since there is no substantial change in numbers, we shall focus on the qualitative differences. To this end, the comparison between the two ends of Aristophanes' career, *Acharnians* and *Wealth*, is illuminating. In fact, not even a single *para prosdokian* in *Wealth* is of the type that prevails in *Acharnians*. In terms of form, the poet moves from mainly employing noun-based *para prosdokian* (στρατιὰν, πρωκτὸν, πώγωνα, γαλᾶς, σκάνδικος, μορμόνα, μᾶδδαν, γαστέρα, βολίτοις etc.) to mainly employing verb-based *para prosdokian* (λωποδυτεῖ, τοιχωρυχεῖ, ἐμπέσοι, δικάζει, ἥρπακας, πείσῃς, ἐκπιεῖν, ἔπινες etc.). I would argue that noun-based *para prosdokian* are

---

221 Mitchell's assertion that *Knights* have the most *para prosdokian* words (1835, 1) is not confirmed even in his own commentary; he proposes lines 19, 98, 174, 508, 517, and 1238.

more imaginative and 'redemptive' than verb-based *para prosdokian*, in the sense that the former *adorn* the world of comic fantasy by importing into it some familiar *objects* (pots, vegetables, animals), whereas the latter *undermine* the world of comic fantasy by projecting into it familiar *behaviours* (to be corrupt, to steal, to judge). Other factors also suggest a weakening of the figure. The majority of *para prosdokian* jokes in *Acharnians* are (a) metrically highlighted, (b) often accumulated in consecutive lines, (c) placed early in the play in view of the audience's readiness to decode them, (d) serving political, social, or literal criticism, (e) said by the protagonist, thus gaining authority. In *Wealth* on the other hand, (a) emphasis with internal pauses and alliterations is rare, while a fair amount of *para prosdokian* jokes do not even appear at the end of the line, (b) consecutive *para prosdokian* jokes appear only once (*Plut.* 277–8), (c) there is a reasonable dispersion of the jokes across several parts of the play, but this does not facilitate the audience's comprehension, (d) there are no *para prosdokian* jokes serving political criticism, and social criticism is restricted to a single case (ὁ δὲ λωποδυτεῖ γε νὴ Δί', ὁ δὲ τοιχωρυχεῖ, *Plut.* 165); the figure is used almost exclusively for personal abuse, (e) the slave Carion says as many *para prosdokian* jokes as his master, challenging (and rather conquering) his comic primacy. Beyond any technical explanations, a minimal sense of humour is enough to perceive the difference between e.g. *Ach.* 81–2 and *Plut.* 180:

    ἀλλ' εἰς ἀπόπατον ᾤχετο στρατιὰν λαβών,   ΚΑ. ὁ Τιμοθέου δὲ πύργος
    κἄχεζεν ὀκτὼ μῆνας ἐπὶ χρυσῶν ὀρῶν.   ΧΡ. — ἐμπέσοι γέ σοι.

While it might be tempting to say that *Wealth* proves exceptional in this respect, as a case of 'Middle Comedy', we need to remind ourselves that Aristophanes' later period is poorly represented through the extant comedies, and any late developments probably arose gradually; in fact, *Thesmophoriazusae* already attests to some of the changes in the use of the figure. Less political, less emphasised, less imaginative, less dramatically needed, *para prosdokian* seems to become less *para prosdokian* over time. However 'decaying' this might seem when judging the evolution of ancient comedy in retrospect, it should rather be viewed, from a synchronic perspective, as a symptom of Aristophanes' never-ending poetic experimentation.

1.6 And What About Oxymoron?

An oxymoron (ὀξύς + μωρός = 'a sharp foolishness') is an absolute contradiction. In fact, the very word oxymoron is an oxymoron, since ὀξύς also means δριμύς ('smart'), hence oxymoron is 'a witty foolishness'. Hansjörg Büchner's thesis 'Das Oxymoron in der griechischen Dichtung' (1950) is a useful compilation of passages which contain some kind of paradox, but having set no solid theoretical and consistent methodological frames, it fails to identify actual oxymorons, or at least passages with the same kind of paradox.

Generally speaking, oxymoron places side-by-side two opposite semantic values. With few exceptions (e.g. Eur. *Alc.* 141, καὶ ζῶσαν εἰπεῖν καὶ θανοῦσαν ἔστι σοι), oxymorons are constructed either by a word + οὐ + the same word, or by a word + the same word with the privative prefix ἀ(ν). This figure is extensively used by Euripides and a brief selection from his plays suffices to show its difference from *para prosdokian*:[222]

> With οὐ: ἔστιν τε κοὐκέτ' ἔστιν (*Alc.* 521); ὁ δ' οὐ θέλων τε καὶ θέλων (*Hec.* 566); θανῆι γὰρ οὐ θανοῦσα σὺν νεκρῶι (*Tro.* 1223); οὐχ ἑκὼν ἑκών (*IT* 512); ἔστ', ἄθλιός γε, κοὐδαμοῦ καὶ πανταχοῦ (*IT* 568); ὁ κατθανών τε κοὐ θανὼν φαντάζομαι (*Ion* 1444); πέποιθα μέντοι μητρὶ κοὐ πέποιθ' ἅμα (*Phoen.* 272); φρονῶν εὖ κοὐ φρονῶν ἀφικόμην (*Phoen.* 357); τεθνᾶσι κοὐ τεθνᾶσι (*Hel.* 138); τὸ καλὸν οὐ καλόν (*Or.* 119); τὸ σοφὸν δ' οὐ σοφία (*Bacch.* 395).

> With ἀ(ν): νύμφην τ' ἄνυμφον παρθένον τ' ἀπάρθενον (*Hec.* 612); κακῆς γυναικὸς χάριν ἄχαριν ἀπώλετο (*IT* 566); δι' ἔργ' ἄνεργ' ὄλλυσαι (*Hel.* 363); καταστένει γάμον ἄγαμον <ἐμόν> (*Hel.* 690); δεσμὸν δ' ἄδεσμον τόνδ' ἔχουσα φυλλάδος (*Supp.* 32).

Even though oxymorons have a much stricter form than *para prosdokian* as the list above shows, the two figures work in the same way from a cognitive-linguistic perspective (the 'erasure and replacement' mechanism mentioned early in this chapter).

One might expect that comedy is also full of oxymorons. Aristophanic comedy is certainly not.[223] Apart from οὐκ ἔνδον ἔνδον ἐστίν (*Ach.* 396) and οὐ γὰρ πείσεις, οὐδ' ἢν πείσῃς (*Plut.* 600) there are no other oxymorons in the four plays under examination, and even these two instances are used in a paratragic context.[224] In *Frogs*, too, Euripides' oxymorons are both satirised (φασκούσας οὐ ζῆν τὸ ζῆν, *Ran.* 1082) and parodied (τίς οἶδεν εἰ τὸ ζῆν μέν ἐστι κατθανεῖν, [= Eur. fr. 638] τὸ πνεῖν δὲ δειπνεῖν, τὸ δὲ καθεύδειν κῴδιον; *Ran.* 1477). In all these cases, it is not the Aristophanic voice that uses the figure but the para-Euripidean voice.

---

222 For more examples, see Mitchell 1839, 312–13; Synodinou 1978.
223 Other poets of Old Comedy used the figure in one form or another – to what extent we cannot know. E.g. δίκας τ' ἀδίκους (Cratin. fr. 353), πόλιν δούλων (Cratin. fr. 223 with Zelnick-Abramovitz 2012, 124), θήλεια Φιλόξενος (Eup. fr. 249 with Gilula 1983, 362), ἀ]νάνδρους ἄνδρ[ας (Eup. fr. 99.75), τοὺς θανόντας ο{ὐ}κ ἐᾷς τεθνηκέν{αι;} (Eup. fr. 99.102; cf. Eur. fr. 507.1).
224 See p. 59 and p. 62 respectively.

As it seems, it is precisely Euripides' preference for this figure of speech that made Aristophanes avoid it. Since oxymoron was a stylistic signature of Euripides, Aristophanes had to invent, and invest in, a signature of his own. Far from being a 'not particularly fashionable' category invented by the scholiasts, *para prosdokian* is an inherent element of Aristophanes' works and the definition of *his* comedy.

2 Thematic Surprise: Appropriating Myths

Whereas verbal *para prosdokian* is something technical and thus measurable, identifying thematic surprises presents a true methodological challenge, which arises from the non-realism of comedy. If the treatment of a theme is paradoxical in terms of reality and logic (truth > validity > soundness), this does not guarantee a surprise effect; because in the theatrical context – and indeed in the comic context – such terms are abandoned *a priori*, both within the play and on the part of the audience. Especially with comedy, the surprise would be to expect no surprises. Therefore, in order to establish what thematic surprises are with some certainty, we need to look at themes which are not restrained by realism or logic; at themes which are 'surprising' in themselves, so that their appropriation can undoubtedly be taken as a surprise. The theme most fitting with this criterion is myth.[225]

From the surviving titles of Aristophanic comedy and Old Comedy in general, we can assume that a fair proportion of the plays had mythological content – with the reservation that a title does not necessarily describe the exact content, as for example in *Frogs*, in which the chorus of the frogs was possibly invisible.[226] None of Aristophanes' eleven comedies is mythological *per se* but they do use mythical elements, either as explicit references or as underlying structural patterns. From the latter perspective, *Birds* draws from Titanomachy and polis-foundation myths, *Lysistrata* from the Amazons and the Lemnian women,[227] *Peace* from Persephone's rape and other myths about the salvation of maidens and the *anodos* of underworld divinities or fertility goddesses,[228] *Frogs* from Hercules' decent to Hades and from the psychostasia etc. Bowie (1993) offers a brilliant analysis of such patterns, as well as those from rituals (e.g. *Acharnians* as anomalous Rural Dionysia) and rites of passage (e.g. Philocleon in *Wasps* as undergoing a reversed *ephēbeia*). Following Bowie in his play-by-play method of discussion, but focus-

---

225 Except for its introduction and its last section, the present chapter was first published in *Logeion* 7 (2017). I owe special thanks to the anonymous reviewer of the journal and the editor-in-chief Professor Stavros Tsitsiridis for their comments and corrections on that occasion.
226 For a statistical account see Carrière 1997, 413–7. Bowie 2010 for an overall account from Sicilian to New Comedy; esp. p. 145 on Old Comedy. On *Frogs*' chorus of frogs, see schol. on 209; Stanford 1957, 68; Higgins 1977, 60; Allison 1983; and Zimmermann 1984, 164–6 in favour of its invisibility. Sifakis 1971, 94–5; Dover 1972, 177–8; and MacDowell 1972 in favour of its visibility.
227 See Bowie 1984 and 1993, 184–95; Martin 1987.
228 See Bowie 1993, 142–50; Olson 1998, xxxv–xxxviii.

https://doi.org/10.1515/9783110677034-003

sing on explicit references to myths (rather than the structure of the plots), I compile and analyse the myths appropriated in the eleven extant comedies from a typological perspective (what is changed, why it is changed, and how the myth is embodied in the play) and from a poetological one (what the myth implies for comedy as a genre).[229] The comic poet exploits myths in various ways, from mere quotation and adaptation to appropriation or even creation of his own quasi-mythical narratives (e.g. Amphitheus' genealogy in *Ach*. 48–52),[230] but this chapter is only concerned with appropriated myths.

The clarification of a couple of terms is necessary. As the reader will soon observe, *myth* is here used as an umbrella term for material of different kinds: mythical stories, known from the oral tradition, literary treatments of myths in poetic genres – such as tragedy and epic – popular legends, allegorical or wisdom concepts, Aesopic fables and others, without strict differentiation. This is a deliberate choice which, far from aiming to generate confusion or to ignore historical and anthropological approaches to Greek mythology, intends to show that the techniques of appropriation (reversal, replacement, exaggeration, de-contextualisation, vulgarisation etc.) apply to all of these categories. At any rate, *myth* is not used in the Aristotelian sense, i.e. as the plot of a play.

In Reception Theory, *adaptation* and *appropriation* are two terms commonly used to describe the degree of fidelity, or proximity, of a 'recipient' text or artwork to the source it draws on, with *appropriation* being the most divergent version, and hence more likely to be surprising.[231] It is used for cases where the 'recipient' artist is openly inspired by, but freely deviating from the prototype in composing an authentic work. But 'proximity' is often understood in a historical sense. For Julie Sanders, 'adaptation can be a transpositional practice, casting a specific genre into another generic mode, an act of re-vision in itself' whereas 'appropriation frequently affects a more decisive journey away from the informing source

---

229 A typological approach is also offered by Moessner 1907, 82 f., arranged in thematic sections: description of the gods; parody of epic myth; parody of tragic myth; parody of legends; other mythic elements (passing references). Though a very informative survey, it collects a lot of material (mythology in Old Comedy in general) at the expense of detailed analysis.
230 On that passage, see Méautis 1932; Griffith 1974; Kanavou 2011, 388–91.
231 'Proximity', which is a descriptive category, is often preferred to 'fidelity', which implies a qualitative judgement based on the moral nuance of the word. Other taxonomies of the degrees of 'proximity' are: *borrowing, intersection,* and *transformation* (Andrew 1980, 10–12); *analogy, commentary,* and *transposition* (Wagner 1975, 222–31).

into a wholly new cultural product and domain'.[232] For Lorna Hardwick, *adaptation* is 'a version of the source developed for a different purpose' whereas *appropriation* is 'taking an ancient image or text and using it to sanction subsequent ideas or practices'.[233] The editors of the 2014 volume *Shakespeare and the Ethics of Appropriation*, explain that: 'In choosing appropriation over adaptation, the most common alternative, we [...] seek to highlight the active potential of appropriation and the openness of its forms, which encompass cultural deployments in addition to discrete works'.[234] It was with Shakespearean studies, indeed, that *appropriation* became a prominent term, especially after Jean Marsden's oft-quoted definition:

> Associated with abduction, adoption and theft, appropriation's central tenet is the desire for possession. It comprehends both the commandeering of the desired object and the process of making this object one's own, controlling it by possessing it. Appropriation is neither dispassionate nor disinterested; it has connotations of usurpation, of seizure for one's own uses.[235]

The difference, according to Thomas Cartelli, is that *appropriation* serves the interests of the appropriator and works against the interests of the appropriated work or author – the term itself implies a hostile takeover – [236] whereas *adaptation* merely adjusts or accommodates the original work, with which it retains a tributary relationship.[237] It is this conception of *appropriation* as a hostile technique (rather than as a passing to another cultural context) that is employed in this chapter; the antagonistic context (festivals) and content (genres) of Greek drama strongly endorse this conception. Even if one accepts that the difference between *adaptation* and *appropriation* is a 'difference in degree rather than kind',[238] i.e. that there are no prescribed motives behind either phenomenon, the particular implementations (which is our focus here) do serve certain functions. Speaking of Aristophanes as a recipient of myths, two examples of *adaptation* are Dionysus introducing himself as υἱὸς Σταμνίου (*Ran.* 22) instead of 'son of Zeus', and the assertion that Menelaus dropped his sword at the sight of Helen's breasts (*Lys.*

---

232 Sanders 2006, 18, 27. In Hutcheon 2006, 20, on the contrary, *appropriation* and its relation to *adaptation* are not developed.
233 Hardwick 2003, 9.
234 Huang/Rivlin 2014, 2.
235 Marsden 1991, 1.
236 Sanders 2006, 9.
237 Cartelli 1999, 15.
238 Desmet/Iyengar 2015, 16.

155–6) instead of her overall beauty; these are minor comic interpolations in order to make the myths 'relevant'.[239] Here, however, we shall focus on *appropriations*; i.e. on elaborate reworking of myths with a surprising effect.

2.1 *Acharnians*

In the parodos, after having concluded his treaty with the Spartans, Dikaiopolis defends himself before the chorus of the Acharnians who have come to stone him. The scene is a parody of Euripides' *Telephus* (438 BC) from which only fragments survive.[240] Telephus, son of Hercules and Auge, was the king of Mysia, which the Greeks attacked mistaking it for Troy. In the battle, Achilles wounded Telephus who was later advised by the oracle to go to Argos and seek cure from the perpetrator. Telephus went as a suppliant disguised in rags to Agamemnon and received Achilles' cure, in exchange for showing the Greeks the exact way to Troy. In Euripides' version, when Telephus' identity was discovered during the negotiations, he threatened to kill the infant Orestes on the altar, whereas in Aeschylus' version it seems that the hero merely held the baby up to raise sympathy.[241] As for Sophocles' *Telephus*, we cannot tell because only one word survives. Whether the idea of threatening Orestes was Euripides' innovation or not, Aristophanes is clearly parodying his version, directly quoting, or alluding to Euripidean lines and dressing his protagonist with the rags that Euripides (as a *dramatis persona*) had used to costume his own Telephus. As Bowie (1993, 28–9) points out, Telephus is well chosen not only as a device for generating sympathy, given that Dikaiopolis is in an equally weak position, asking to be heard by a hostile audience, but also as a reflection of the comic hero's negative aspects: Dikaiopolis made a private peace with the Spartans abandoning Athens, similarly to Telephus who betrayed Troy (the homeland of his wife and an ally of his own) to the Greeks for his personal salvation.

The surprise in the Aristophanic scene can be found on many levels; most obviously, in the replacement of Orestes with a basket of charcoal, which Dikaiopolis threatens to slay with a sword on the altar. The replacement of a noble figure from mythology with a shabby utensil from rural life makes the passing from tragedy to comedy tangible.[242] At the same time, the retention of the sword

---

239 Sanders 2006, 19.
240 See Handley/Rea 1957; Webster 1967, 43–8; Heath 1987; Collard *et al.* 1995, 17–52; Preiser 2000; Aguilar 2003. On the parody see Rau 1967, 24–41; Foley 1988.
241 Schol. on *Ach.* 332. See Csapo 1990.
242 On replacement as a technique of comic parody, see Tsitsiridis 2010.

further mocks the limits of tragedy as a genre: comedy is capable of including tragic, high-register objects. But would tragedy ever dare to show a basket of charcoal? If this is meant to allude to the staging of Euripides' play as closely as possible, we could assume that in *Telephus* Orestes would have been brought on stage in his cradle. Alternatively, Aristophanes is simply insinuating that the presentation of an infant on the tragic stage (whether it was a real baby or a doll) is a cheap device and the solemnity of tragedy is merely an illusion.[243] Just before Dikaiopolis grabs the basket, the chorus assumes that he is about to seize a baby (μῶν ἔχει του παιδίον / τῶν παρόντων ἔνδον εἴρξας; *'He hasn't got somebody's child, one of ours, locked up in there, has he?'* 329–30), reinforcing and dictating the audience's anticipation that a baby is indeed about to appear, as in *Telephus*. Against this deliberately encouraged expectation, Dikaiopolis enters with the charcoal-basket, shown with emphatic *deixis* (τουτονί, 331). And here comes the second surprise: the chorus neither rejects nor, at least, notices the deception, but they become part of the illusion (of the drama within the drama), as if they deliberately want to collaborate with Dikaiopolis in his deceit. They cry for the basket no less than they would cry for a baby being threatened and they finally succumb to Dikaiopolis' demands. A third surprise is that, whereas Telephus' appeal to Agamemnon was a rhetorical exaggeration (Eur. fr. 706, Ἀγάμεμνον, οὐδ' εἰ πέλεκυν ἐν χεροῖν ἔχων / μέλλοι τις εἰς τράχηλον ἐμβαλεῖν ἐμόν, / σιγήσομαι δίκαιά γ' ἀντειπεῖν ἔχων. *'Agamemnon, not even if someone with an axe in his hands were about to strike it on my neck, shall I keep silent; for I have a just reply to make'*), Dikaiopolis is willingly placing his head on the ἐπίξηνον, the butcher's chopping block (318, 355, 365, 366). Again, we can read this as comedy competing with tragedy: if the tragic hero is brave (only) in words, the comic hero can afford to put himself in 'real' danger, because in the end he never dies. Finally – one more surprise – the outraged chorus is suddenly silenced and Dikaiopolis has plenty of time to visit Euripides in order to borrow the rags he had used for his Telephus (393–489). Only when he returns can the action move on. What we actually have here is a rehearsal on stage, an actor looking for his costume in order to get a feeling for his role.

---

[243] The use of a real infant as Orestes in Euripides' tragedy should not be precluded on grounds of practical inconvenience. In fact, if the infant cried, that would be most suitable for the play. On the other hand, it is highly unlikely that Orestes was presented as a toddler, played by an older child like the children in *Medea*, given that the fourth-century iconography always depicts an infant (*LIMC* vii.2: *Telephos* 55–63).

Dikaiopolis starts his defence by blaming the Athenians for the Peloponnesian War. Some young Athenians, he maintains, got drunk and kidnapped a Megarian prostitute named Simaitha, and in revenge some Megarians kidnapped two Athenian prostitutes belonging to Aspasia (524–9). Then Pericles was outraged and passed the Megarian Decree, leading the Megarians to ask for the involvement of Sparta.[244] The background story with the prostitutes parodies Herodotus' story (attributed by the historian to Persian learned men) that the enmity between Europe and Asia arose from a series of mutual rapes of princesses (Hdt. 1. 1–1.5).[245] The Phoenicians seized Io from Argos; the Greeks seized Europe from Tyre, and then Medea from Colchis; Paris seized Helen, and the Greeks started the Trojan War in response. In the comedy, the Trojan War is replaced with the Peloponnesian War; the dispute between the Greeks and the Phoenicians with the hostility of the Athenians against the Megarians; the three mythical generations with contemporary time. However, some details have been retained or exaggerated. First, the number of the women involved: four (Simaitha, πόρναι δύο, and Aspasia who for the purposes of comedy – at least – was a whore).[246] Secondly, the detail that one of the opposing sides (the Greeks in Hdt./the Megarians in *Ach.*) disproportionately seized two girls in revenge for the abduction of only one girl.[247] Last and more striking, Dikaiopolis' conclusion that the war essentially began ἐκ τριῶν λαικαστριῶν, 'because of three cocksuckers' (529) rather echoes Herodotus' judgement that εἰ μὴ αὐταὶ ἐβούλοντο, οὐκ ἂν ἡρπάζοντο, 'the women would never have been carried away, had not they themselves wished it' (1.4.9). Whereas the surprising appropriation of the myth of Telephus consists of theatrical replacements and exaggerations, this latter case exploits historical de-contextualisation and verbal vulgarisation, displaying how Aristophanes – already from his first extant comedy – experiments with different techniques of parody.[248]

---

244 On Pericles' insistence on the Megarian Decree, Thuc. 2.21.3; 1.140–144. On him having personal motivations for the Decree, cf. *Pax* 605–9.
245 Since we do not know the publication date of the *Histories*, or whether they were read in public, it is uncertain whether the parody draws on this version of the tale or another source. On the issue, see Fornara 1971.
246 Eup. fr. 110.2. In fr. 267 he calls her 'Helen' implying that she led Pericles to start the Samian War.
247 Hdt.'s comment (1.2.1): ταῦτα μὲν δὴ ἴσα πρὸς ἴσα σφι γενέσθαι· μετὰ δὲ ταῦτα Ἕλληνας αἰτίους τῆς δευτέρης ἀδικίης γενέσθαι. 'So far, then, the account between them stood balanced. But after this (say they) it was the Greeks who were guilty of the second wrong'. This detail makes me assume that Ar. draws on Hdt. directly.
248 For the parody of the Trojan War here and in other comic poets, see Wright 2007.

2.2 Knights

The slave Demosthenes reports to the Sausage-Seller an oracle, according to which the latter is meant to succeed Paphlagon as a leader of the Demos (197–201):

> "ἀλλ' ὁπόταν μάρψῃ βυρσαίετος ἀγκυλοχήλης
> γαμφηλῇσι δράκοντα κοάλεμον αἱματοπώτην,
> δὴ τότε Παφλαγόνων μὲν ἀπόλλυται ἡ σκοροδάλμη,
> κοιλιοπώλῃσιν δὲ θεὸς μέγα κῦδος ὀπάζει,
> αἴ κεν μὴ πωλεῖν ἀλλᾶντας μᾶλλον ἕλωνται."

> "Yea, when the crook-taloned rawhide eagle shall snatch in its beak the dimwitted blood-guzzling serpent, even then shall perish the garlic breath of the Paphlagons, while to tripe sellers the god grants great glory, unless they choose rather to sell sausages."

'Dactylic hexameter meter, oracular and dialectal formulae (ἀλλ' ὁπόταν), αἱ for εἰ (cf. *Birds* 978), the replacement of humans with animals, long compound words like "leather eagle" and "blood drinking", as well as the presence of epicisms like κῦδος and ὀπάζει [...] and the heavy, spondaic rhythm of the final line [...], all contribute to the serious tone of a text meant to be received with respect.'[249] The imagery comes from the *Iliad*, where an eagle flies above the Trojans, snatching a snake, which in turn curls and bites the eagle and gets released; Hector alone refused to accept that this was a bad sign (*Il.* 12.200–9). The Sausage-Seller wonders about the meaning, in fact expressing the audience's question. Demosthenes, in his answer, identifies Paphlagon as the eagle and the Sausage-Seller as the snake, with the comic exegesis that a snake is long like a sausage (202–10) – perhaps a satire of the practices of oracle interpreters. It is interesting that the snake is called κοάλεμον, 'stupid',[250] which ought to be counted as one of the many negative qualities of the Sausage-Seller, who is essentially no better than Paphlagon. That he is called πονηρός (181) is not a contradiction, because this is a moral term ('sly', 'rogue', 'malicious'), not a term of pure intelligence. More telling is that, whereas in the Homeric version the snake, after being released by the wounded eagle, eventually dies before the Trojans' eyes (κείμενον ἐν μέσσοισι, *Il.* 12.209), here we do not learn about its fate; we only learn that Paphlagon, the eagle, perishes. One would say that Aristophanes simply keeps the part of the imagery that facilitates his foreground meaning: the Sausage-Seller's victory. One could argue, however, that Aristophanes conceals the information which he

---

249 Platter 2007, 116.
250 Cf. *Eq.* 221; Aeschin. Socr. 16; Plut. *Cim.* 4; Hsch. *ad loc.*

would expect the audience – at least its most learned part – to guess: that neither will the Sausage-Seller last for ever, which goes beyond the end of the play. So the surprise lies in the comic exegesis of the myth, which subverts its initial solemnity, and the concealment of its end, which raises doubts in the minds of the informed audience. Aristophanes reworks this Homeric scene also in *Vesp.* 15–20 (see below).

2.3 Clouds

Along with *Ecclesiazusae*, these two plays are the poorest in terms of mythological material.[251] Of course, the conception of clouds as deceptive entities is well attested in mythology, the most famous cases being Helen's ghost in Troy, referred to as νεφέλη,[252] and the cloud in the shape of Hera, which Zeus made for Ixion to mate with, in order to reveal his lustful intentions for the actual goddess.[253] But explicit references to these or other myths are rare.[254] One notable case in *Clouds* is the surprising, poetological treatment of Electra in the parabasis (534–7):

> νῦν οὖν Ἠλέκτραν κατ' ἐκείνην ἥδ' ἡ κωμῳδία
> ζητοῦσ' ἦλθ', ἤν πού 'πιτύχῃ θεαταῖς οὕτω σοφοῖς·   535
> γνώσεται γάρ, ἤνπερ ἴδῃ, τἀδελφοῦ τὸν βόστρυχον.
> ὡς δὲ σώφρων ἐστὶ φύσει σκέψασθ'·

> So now this new comedy of mine, like the legendary Electra, has come on a quest, hoping somewhere to find similarly intelligent spectators: for she will recognize the lock of her brother's hair if she sees it. Look how naturally decent she is.

In Aeschylus' *Choephoroi*, Electra goes to Agamemnon's tomb bringing offerings, and finds a tuft of hair, left there by Orestes, which she recognises as similar to her own; thus, she knows that her brother is back. Here, Electra is *this* comedy

---

[251] Carrière 1997, 424. The fact that I devote the smallest section to *Knights* does not contradict this principle. Simply, *Knights* contains more non-surprising (i.e. not *appropriated*) mythological references (e.g. 551–63), which as such are not discussed here.
[252] Eur. *Hel.* 45, 705, 707, 750, 1219.
[253] Soph. *Phil.* 676–80; Diod. 4.69; Plut. *Mor.* 777 e; Luc. *DDeor.* 9.4–5.
[254] Passing references are made to Athamas, husband of Nephele and later of Ino (257), and to Iapetos, Cronos' brother (998). See Bowie 1993, 127–30 on Ixion and Athamas; Reckford 1991 on Iapetos.

(and Aristophanes by extension, one could say)²⁵⁵ who is looking for 'wise spectators', to be recognised through a proper sign; the equivalent of the βόστρυχος is presumably a favourable vote or an applause.²⁵⁶ As for the wise spectators sought out, they probably correspond, in mythical terms, to Orestes, given that the βόστρυχος is τἀδελφοῦ. This is a surprising reversal of the tragic original, where Electra does not seek Orestes, who is instead looking for her.²⁵⁷ According to Telò, however, the spectators stand for the father Agamemnon, to whom the poet-Electra is dedicated.²⁵⁸ Be that as it may, there is one more fundamental question to face: why is a tragic figure chosen to personify comedy, especially within this comedy which does not otherwise employ paratragedy? Other mythical figures, associated with comic style (like Thalia or Iambe), would have been more appropriate; but Aristophanes chooses Electra.²⁵⁹ If his purpose was merely to discuss the play's relationship to its spectators, then Iambe could perfectly have been brought in: the spectators/Demeter have been looking for the lost joy/Persephone, and this comedy/Iambe offers them consolation through jokes. Therefore, the decision to employ a figure from the realm of tragedy reveals that there was another intention. Silk suggests that 'Aristophanes now (plausibly) identifies this play as a "new mode" [(καινὰς ἰδέας, 547)] in the particular sense of a textual hybrid, a "serious comedy", a tragicomedy (or comitragedy) even (*hence* the reference to a tragic "Electra" at line 534)'.²⁶⁰ But what the poet says in 547 is that he *always* brings in new ideas (ἀλλ' αἰεὶ καινὰς ἰδέας εἰσφέρων σοφίζομαι), not only on the occasion of *Clouds*. As for the 'severity' of the comedy (σώφρων, 537), it is not the first time Aristophanes makes such a claim (cf. *Ach.* 500). A plausible suggestion could be that the selection of a tragic figure to personify comedy is a surprising, poetological comment on the genre as a whole: the poet confesses that comedy is not actually self-defined but mimics the ways of tragedy (Ἠλέκτραν κατ' ἐκείνην, 534). But ironically, this heteronomy is given in the parabasis, i.e. the most self-referential part of the play, which is something

---

255 'Of course, the comparison of our comedy and Electra is facilitated by the fact that the *komodia*, like Electra, is feminine', O'Regan 1992, 203 n. 22.
256 Hackforth 1938; refuted by Newiger 1961, 425–6.
257 Dover 1968 *ad loc*. Cf. Starkie 1911 *ad loc*.; Sommerstein 1982 *ad loc*.
258 Telò 2016, 127–35. His interpretation, however, relies heavily on the spectators' assumed remembrance of the *Wasps*.
259 Our first explicit references to Thalia as the muse of comedy are Hellenistic, but she is associated with some kind of κῶμος as early as in Pind. *Ol.* 14.15–16. Iambe was a servant who cheered the mournful Demeter with her jokes; *Hom. Hymn Dem.* 202.
260 Silk 2013, 38.

not observed in tragedy. Through this 'meta-surprise', comedy manifests its uniqueness.

The second appropriated mythological figure in the play is Peleus (1061–70), whom the Better Argument mentions as an example of a man who was rewarded for his virtue. According to the story, Peleus was once Acastus' guest in Iolcus. When the latter's wife Hippolyte (or Astydamia) tried to seduce him, he resisted, and in revenge she falsely accused him of trying to rape her. Acastus abandoned Peleus in a forest with wild animals, taking away his sword as punishment, but the gods bestowed him a knife to defend himself.[261] '*A knife? What a civilised reward the poor sucker got! Now Hyperbolus, the man from the lamp market, has made a vast amount of money by being a rascal, but never a knife, no indeed!*' replies the Worse Argument.[262] He is essentially reckoning the knife in its monetary value, which is low indeed, and disregards its vital (for Peleus) practical value. In real life, as opposed to mythology, profit is the only benefit, the Worse Argument implies, and thus mentions a counter-example from contemporary Athens, that of the politician Hyperbolus.[263] The juxtaposition of a mythical and a real person here works in two directions: not only is Peleus degraded (ἀστεῖόν γε κέρδος ἔλαβεν ὁ κακοδαίμων, 1064), but Hyperbolus is elevated to the level of a 'legendary' rascal. The Better Argument now tries a second mythical *exemplum*, given that the point with the knife did not work:

KP.   καὶ τὴν Θέτιν γ' ἔγημε διὰ τὸ σωφρονεῖν ὁ Πηλεύς.   1067

B.AR.   And Peleus got to marry Thetis by being decent.

That Thetis was given to Peleus as a reward for his virtue is an arbitrary assertion. In Homer, Thetis married the hero by the command of Zeus, against her will (πολλὰ μάλ' οὐκ ἐθέλουσα).[264] According to Philodemus, both the *Cypria* and Hesiod presented Zeus as outraged and swearing that he would make Thetis marry a mortal after she rejected him.[265] Herodotus reports that Peleus carried her off.[266] According to Pindar, Zeus and Poseidon were rivals for Thetis' hand, but they

---

261 Pind. *Nem.* 4.57–61; Pl. *Resp.* 3.319 c; Apollod. *Bibl.* 3.13.3.
262 μάχαιραν; ἀστεῖόν γε κέρδος ἔλαβεν ὁ κακοδαίμων.| Ὑπέρβολος δ' οὐκ τῶν λύχνων πλεῖν ἢ τάλαντα πολλὰ | εἴληφε διὰ πονηρίαν, ἀλλ' οὐ μὰ Δί' οὐ μάχαιραν.
263 For his lamp-making business cf. *Pax* 690, *Eq.* 739, 1316. The accusation concerning Hyperbolus' illegal enrichment is a comic commonplace rather than a reference to an actual scandal.
264 *Il.*18.430–3.
265 *Cypria* fr. 2 West; Hes. fr. 210 Merkelbach–West.
266 Hdt. 7.191.2

became afraid when they learnt that she was destined to give birth to a son mightier than his father, so they married her off to Peleus.[267] The real surprise, however, lies in the Worse Argument's following reply:

> HT. κᾆτ' ἀπολιποῦσά γ' αὐτὸν ᾤχετ'· οὐ γὰρ ἦν ὑβριστὴς
> οὐδ' ἡδὺς ἐν τοῖς στρώμασιν τὴν νύκτα παννυχίζειν·
> γυνὴ δὲ σιναμωρουμένη χαίρει·   1070

> W.AR. And then she up and deserted him because he wasn't a
> roughneck, and no fun to spend the night with between the
> sheets. A woman enjoys being lewdly used.

Actually, Thetis left Peleus because she felt offended by his disrespectful reprimanding, when he saw her holding their son Achilles over the fire.[268] Here, Thetis is said to have abandoned Peleus because (in bed) he treated her with *too much* respect![269] This can be read as a comic parallel to Peleus' aforementioned troubles with Hippolyte: Peleus is always punished by women whom he fails to satisfy.

2.4 *Wasps*

In the beginning of the play, the slave Xanthias shares with his fellow slave Sosias and with the audience a peculiar dream he has had (15–9):

> ΞΑ. ἐδόκουν αἰετὸν
> καταπτάμενον εἰς τὴν ἀγορὰν μέγαν πάνυ
> ἀναρπάσαντα τοῖς ὄνυξιν ἀσπίδα
> φέρειν ἐπίχαλκον ἀνεκὰς εἰς τὸν οὐρανόν,
> κἄπειτα ταύτην ἀποβαλεῖν Κλεώνυμον.

> XA. I saw a great big eagle swoop down into the market and snatch up
> a bronzed shield in its talons and take it right up to the sky, and then
> it became Cleonymus and lost its shield!

Aristophanes reworks, in a very different way, the Homeric passage discussed above in connection to *Knights*. Whereas in *Knights* the appropriated myth was associated with the core theme of the play (the snake/Sausage-Seller overthrowing the eagle/Paphlagon), here it only serves the 'abuse of a single individual,

---

267 Pind. *Isthm.* 8.27–41.
268 Ap. Rhod. 3.13.6. Soph. fr. 151.
269 Sommerstein 1982 *ad loc.*

with no substantial larger implications for the plot of the play'.[270] The humour here lies in ἀσπίς meaning both 'asp' (Hdt. 4.191) and 'shield', with the following ἐπίχαλκον confirming that the latter meaning is the one which applies here.[271] The eagle here symbolises Cleonymus, a democratic politician who is repeatedly charged with ῥιψασπία in Aristophanes,[272] and the snake is a shield, a bitter foe for its holder! The description of the eagle as μέγαν is also an alteration of the Homeric model, in which the snake, not the eagle, is large, the enormous eagle suiting Cleonymus' corpulence.[273] Sosias replies that Cleonymus is apt to become a riddle at the symposia (21–3):

> ΣΩ. προερεῖ τις τοῖσι συμπόταις, λέγων
> ὅτι "ταὐτὸν ἐν γῇ τ' ἀπέβαλεν κἀν οὐρανῷ
> κἀν τῇ θαλάττῃ θηρίον τὴν ἀσπίδα."

> SO. A man could challenge his fellow drinkers by asking,
> "what beast sheds its shield on land, in the air, and at sea?"

According to Athenaeus, the original riddle was τί ταὐτὸν ἐν οὐρανῷ καὶ ἐπὶ γῆς καὶ ἐν θαλάττῃ; and the possible answers were ἄρκτος, ὄφις, and αἰετός, with each being the name of a constellation, an animal, and a sea creature.[274] But here, the right answer will be 'Cleonymus', the man who drops his shield on the land (as a soldier), on the sky (as an eagle), and in the sea (during naval battles, presumably). Or better, not 'the man', but the θηρίον. The word was a widely-used abusive term (*LSJ* III), but in this case it might be a further allusion to Cleonymus' size and is indeed a very ironic term for someone who is afraid to fight. As is the case with Hyperbolus in *Clouds*, the myth and the riddle are here appropriated in order to picture Cleonymus as a 'legendary' coward.

The most striking case of a beast employed as a means of personal abuse is the hybrid monster Cleon, against whom Aristophanes is fighting like another

---

270 Biles/Olson 2015 *ad loc.*
271 Cf. MacDowell 1971 *ad loc.* On the contrary, Biles/Olson 2015 *ad loc.* state that ἐπίχαλκον is firstly understood as describing τὸν οὐρανόν (cf. the Homeric 'brazen sky', *Il.* 17.425) and only after Κλεώνυμον is heard in the end, do we understand the proper syntax (ἐπίχαλκον describing ἀσπίδα) and meaning (ἀσπίδα as shield).
272 Cf. 592, 822–3, *Nub.* 353–4; *Pax* 444–6, 673–8, 1295–1301; *Av.* 290, 1473–81.
273 Biles/Olson 2015 *ad loc.*
274 Ath. 10.453b.

Hercules (1030–5, repeated with few variations in *Pax* 752–8).[275] A Frankensteinian patchwork of Cerberus,[276] Hydra or Typhoeus (with a hundred licking fawners instead of snake-heads),[277] and Chimaera (with Lamia's testicles,[278] a camel's arse, and a seal's odour),[279] this creature is more repugnant than terrifying. Not only is the monster itself surprising, but also the progression of the description, which reverses the traditional course of Hercules' labours. Starting from the hauling of Cerberus, which traditionally is the final labour, the passage essentially ends with the most atypical labour, the cleaning of the stables (to which the version in *Peace* alludes much more clearly).[280] The labour of the Augean stables is first attested in Pind. *O.* 10.27 f. and a contemporary metope from the temple of Zeus at Olympia (the right end of the east porch). Interestingly, adjacent to this is another metope depicting the fetching of Cerberus. Furthermore, the Olympian metopes are the only source in which the labour of cleaning the stables appears after Cerberus (Fig. 2).[281] Aristophanes may have been inspired for the merging of these two images by the sequence on the temple, or he may have found inspiration in an earlier narrative of the labours which also served as the source of the stonemasons in Olympia.

---

[275] See Mastromarco 1989; Lauriola 2004; Peigney 2009; Sommerstein 2009, 168–9.
[276] For Cleon as Cerberus, cf. *Eq.* 1007, 1030, discussed by Lind 1990; *Pax* 313.
[277] Typhoeus appears in Hes. *Theog.* 824–30. For Cleon as T. cf. *Eq.* 511. Cerberus was his offspring.
[278] The explanation given by Biles/Olson 2015 *ad loc.* is that Lamia (a children's bogie) could transform herself into any form, and by MacDowell (1971) *ad loc.* that she was hermaphroditic. I prefer Sommerstein 1983 *ad loc.* 'Since Lamia is elsewhere always female, the "balls of a Lamia" may mean "no balls at all".' For Cleon as a passive homosexual, cf. *Ach.* 664.
[279] For the animal's repulsive smell cf. *Od.* 4.406, 435–43. MacDowell 1971 *ad loc.* noticed the structural similarity of 1035 (φώκης δ' ὀσμήν, Λαμίας δ' ὄρχεις ἀπλύτους, πρωκτὸν δὲ καμήλου) with Chimaera's description in *Il.* 6.181 (πρόσθε λέων, ὄπιθεν δὲ δράκων, μέσση δὲ χίμαιρα).
[280] Cf. schol. and Platnauer 1964 on *Pax* 753. *Peace* was produced the year after *Wasps*, when Cleon was dead (*Pax* 269); for the problem of mocking a dead person in the present tense, cf. *Pax* 47; Platnauer *ad loc.* and xvi.
[281] For the course of Hercules' labours, cf. Apollod. *Bibl.* 2.5.1–12; Diod. Sic. 4.11–13; Hyg. *Fab.* 30. The labour of the stables is absent in Eur. *HF* 359 f. but again the Cerberus labour is the last one.

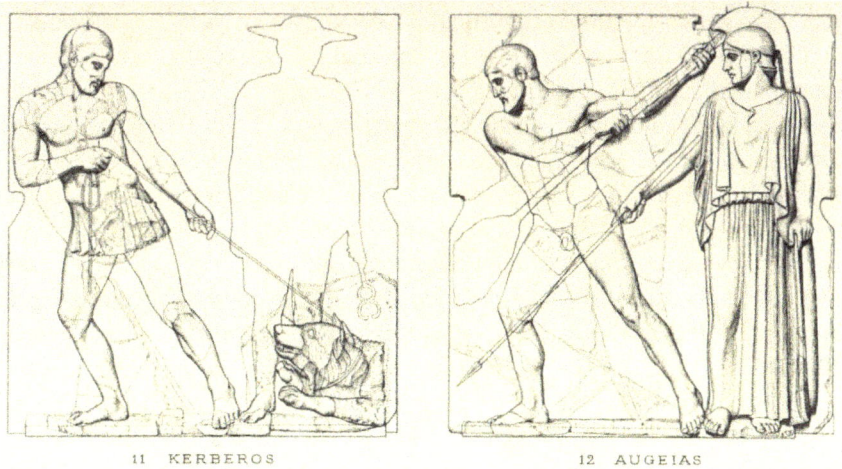

Fig. 2: Sketch of the fifth and the sixth metope of the pronaos, Temple of Zeus at Olympia. Drawing by Max Kühnert, in E. Curtius/F. Adler (eds.), *Olympia: Die Ergebnisse der von dem Deutschen Reich veranstalteten Ausgrabung*, vol. 3, Berlin 1894, pl. xlv.

Early on in the play, after many unsuccessful attempts made by Philocleon in order to escape his house (climbing the chimney, 144–8; breaking the door open, 152–5; ripping the mesh off the windows, 164–5), where his son Bdelycleon has restricted him in order to prevent him from going to the courts, the old man slips out suspended beneath a donkey, as another Odysseus escaping Polyphemus' cave (169–91; cf. *Od.* 9).[282] Given that there are no close verbal similarities to the Homeric version,[283] that the latter was adapted for the stage many times,[284] and that this version is scenically elaborate (with the donkey braying and with Philocleon clinging to it backwards, i.e. facing its tits, penis, or arse),[285] it is clearly suggested that here we probably have a parody of a previous production, rather than one of the *Odyssey* itself. The donkey was probably not a real one, given that it needs to walk, stand, and bray at specific moments, but a pair of actors.[286] This

---

[282] For a detailed discussion, see Moessner 1907, 94–7.
[283] MacDowell 1971, 156.
[284] Cf. *Plut.* 290–301; Cratinus' *Odysseis*; Euripides, Aristias, Callias, Epicharmus and Antiphanes, all had a *Cyclops*. For Cyclops and Odysseus in Old Comedy and satyr play in general, see Mastromarco 1998; Casolari 2003, 179–57 and 209–11.
[285] Biles/Olson 2015, 146–7.
[286] Arnott 1959, 177–8.

humorously corresponds to the Homeric version, where each fellow was suspended beneath three sheep (9.430–2). The mighty Odysseus has now become a dotard, the sheep flock (woolly and usually white animals) have been turned into a single donkey (an animal with dark, short, and rough hair), the mass-escape becomes a one-man show, and the successful plan becomes a resounding failure. Bdelycleon detects him – with Sosias' help and with some delay for better comic effect – and sends him back to the house. Also, the original sequence of events has been reversed or compressed: Philocleon's self-introduction as Οὖτις comes after the escape attempt – unlike the *Odyssey* – and his re-introduction with his (supposedly) true name comes immediately afterwards, again unlike the *Odyssey* (184–5, cf. *Od.* 9.505). Philocleon claims to be the 'son of Escapehorse from Ithaca' (Ἰθακος Ἀποδρασιππίδου), which is a very ironic patronymic for someone who did not manage to escape and did not have a horse but a donkey. That Philocleon conceals his real identity even after he has been detected is a sign of his petty chicanery, but can also be read as a metatheatrical comment: the concept of 'recognition', a central element both for tragedy and comedy, is nothing but an illusion. It never actually happens, because there is always a layer that is not revealed: the actor behind the mask.

2.5 *Peace*

While in *Wasps* Aristophanes transforms a successful mythical plan (the escape from the Cyclops' cave) into a failure, in *Peace* he does exactly the opposite from as early as its opening scene, appropriating Euripides' *Bellerophon*. Having been falsely accused of rape, having been sent to face Chimaera, having lost his children, having been sent into exile and suffering from melancholia, it is obvious that this tragic hero was especially hated by the gods. So he rides Pegasus towards Olympus, in order to complain to them, but halfway there he is thrown off Pegasus, back to earth.[287] Given our otherwise limited information about this tragedy, we cannot estimate the extent to which Aristophanes appropriates this play, apart from the replacement of Pegasus by a giant dung-beetle and the allusion to, or quotation of, a few lines.[288] And although it seems convenient to assume that

---

[287] See Dixon 2014; Collard *et al.* 1995, 98–120; Luppe 1990; Gregorio 1983; Webster 1967, 109–11. For gods' hatred of him, cf. *Il.* 6.200. For his fall from Pegasus, cf. Pind. *Isthm.* 7.43–8. For his injury after the fall, cf. *Ach.* 427–9. For the parody in *Pax*, see Ruffell 2011, 314–60; Telò 2010; Dobrov 2001, 89–104; Bowie 1993, 134–8; Rau 1967, 89–97.

[288] 76 ≈ Eur. fr. 306; 154–5 ≈ Eur. fr. 307; 722 ≈ Eur. fr. 312. There are also lines from *Stheneboia* (126 ≈ Eur. fr. 669.4) and *Aiolos* (119 ≈ Eur. fr.18).

the parody was rather more concentrated on the scenic effects than on the text,[289] this cannot be proven on the basis of the few surviving fragments. Even for the stagecraft, we can only make speculations about the original, such as that 'the tragic hero must have been carried off by Pegasos behind the *scaenae frons*, after which his disastrous fall was described to the audience in a messenger speech, rather than being allowed to land again on stage'.[290]

What is of particular importance in this case is that Trygaeus succeeds in his journey in opposition to the tragic hero – claiming thus the superiority of comedy. Driven by a collective motive (ὑπὲρ Ἑλλήνων πάντων πέτομαι, 97), and not by a personal one like Bellerophon, he reaches Olympus riding his giant dung-beetle, in order to complain to Zeus about destroying ('sweeping', 55) the Greeks with war. The specific substitute for Pegasus, the giant dung-beetle, is chosen as a symbol of 'the corruption and unnaturalness of wartime Athens', and of the 'shit-eater' Cleon in particular.[291] However, the explanation that Trygaeus gives for its use is that the dung-beetle alone has ever managed to reach Olympus, according to Aesop (127–34). Here, in order to justify the surprising use of a (tragic) *mythos*, Aristophanes employs another type of wide-spread popular narrative, which was also commonly designated as a *mythos* by the ancient Greeks – viz., a fable. According to the fable referred to by Trygaeus, an eagle once offended a beetle, and the beetle in response broke the eagle's eggs; then the eagle nested in Zeus' lap to lay its eggs safely, but the beetle followed it and pestered Zeus, so that the god leaped up and smashed the eagle's eggs.[292] Thus, strictly speaking, it was the eagle that went to Olympus first, not the beetle; this is why Trygaeus does not get to tell the whole fable, because it does not actually serve him (no less than because the fable would be well known). Of course, given that Trygaeus goes to Olympus to defend a rightful claim, the wicked eagle would not fit.

Here there is a surprise that scholarship has failed to address hitherto: even though the dung-beetle represents in most distasteful terms the abnormality of war, at the same time it becomes the vehicle (literally) of elevation, pacification, and purification.[293] Therefore, it is more plausible that the primary function of the beetle lies with its scenic and parodic effect, rather than with some political allegory, despite the fact that the text offers explicit support of such considerations

---

289 E.g. Ruffell 2011, 320.
290 Olson 1998, xxxiv.
291 Henderson 1991, 63. On the significance of scatology *vs* fragrance in the two halves of the play, as well as of homosexual *vs* heterosexual sex, see *ibid.* 62–6; Whitman 1964, 109–10.
292 fab. 3 Perry; *Vit. Aesp.* 135–9 Perry; schol. 129–30 (with some variations). Also used at *Vesp.* 1446–8 and *Lys.* 695. For Aesop in Aristophanes, see Schirru 2009; Hall 2013.
293 Hubbard 1991, 141.

(47–8). In this respect, instead of reversing the audience's expectation outright – that the rider will fall and not reach his destination – Aristophanes chooses to create suspense: the beetle does not take off determinedly, as Pegasus must have, but wavers as it smells 'scrumptious shit', endangering its rider (150–2). And then, when they eventually reach Olympus and Trygaeus hears the news from Hermes (196–7), 'what more striking substitution could there be for Bellerophontes' tragic punishment at the hands of Zeus than the glaring absence of the gods, an abandoned Olympos?'[294] This wavering between mythic expectation and its reversal is exemplified in the dung-beetle itself, and in the names given to it by Trygaeus throughout the scene: first κάνθων (82), then Πήγασε (154),[295] but eventually a ἱπποκάνθαρος (181). So, in fact, it is not the Aesopic beetle that surprisingly replaces the Euripidean Pegasus, but the Aristophanic horse-size dung-beetle that replaces both of them by combining the two. If comedy manifests its differentiation from tragedy, it does so without identifying with other genres either.

2.6 Birds

With a plot resembling Gigantomachy, Titanomachy, and myths of city-foundation;[296] with Tereus, Procne, Prometheus, Iris, Poseidon and Hercules as *dramatis personae*; with an invented avian theogony and cosmogony (465–521, 693–702); with two Aesopic fables (771–5, 651–3) and with a ξουθὸς ἱππαλεκτρυών (800),[297] *Birds* is the comedy most permeated by myth among the extant comedies (along with *Frogs*) – so much so that there is an entire monograph on the topic.[298]

Tereus' presence is explicitly a parody of the Sophoclean version of the relevant myth in the lost tragedy *Tereus* (100–1): τοιαῦτα μέντοι Σοφοκλέης λυμαίνεται / ἐν ταῖς τραγῳδίαισιν ἐμὲ τὸν Τηρέα, '*That's how shabbily Sophocles treats me–Tereus!– in his tragedies.*' The legend was as follows: the Thracian king Tereus raped his sister-in-law Philomela and cut off her tongue in order for her not to reveal the deed to her sister and his wife, Procne. However, Philomela depicted her rape through a woven tapestry and Procne, in revenge, chopped and served to Tereus their son Itys. On realising what he had just eaten, Tereus pursued the sisters with a spear, until the gods intervened and transformed all three

---

294 Dobrov 2001, 100.
295 The verb βουκολήσεται (153) does apply to horses; cf. *Il.* 20.221.
296 For these structural patterns, see Bowie 1993, 151–77; Dunbar 1995, 7–9.
297 Taken from Aesch. fr. 134.
298 Hofmann 1976.

of them into birds: a hawk (Tereus), a nightingale (Procne), and a swallow (Philomela).[299] It was Sophocles who invented (and established) Tereus' transformation into a crested hoopoe, instead of a hawk.[300] The three metamorphoses were reported in the final *rhēsis* of the play (fr. 581) and, conceivably, the actors appeared motionless on the *ekkyklēma* with some kind of avian accoutrement, like crests or feathers.[301] So Aristophanes had to compete with an already unusual and scenically elaborate imagery and, as if he ostentatiously wanted to prove that comedy is unrivalled in surprise, he stretched or reversed every aspect of the performed myth. First of all, he made the 'snapshot' of the metamorphosis a permanent condition: stuck in the conventions of tragedy, which is too serious to dress the characters as proper animals, Tereus remained a miserable hybrid, neither a man nor a hoopoe. He has a triple crest (94), a beak (99), plucked plumage (94, 103–4), and he lives among the birds. At the same time, he speaks (Attic, even though a Thracian), has taught the birds to speak (199–200; rather an irony for someone who cut off someone else's tongue), he has a servant, and uses a bowl and a spoon to eat (78).[302] Procne is also a hybrid: she is referred as τοὐρνίθιον (667) and ὦ φίλτατον ὀρνέων πάντων...ἀηδοῖ (677–9), bearing a ῥύγχος (672), but at the same time she is summoned as Πρόκνη (665), is treated in erotic terms appropriate for humans (ἐγὼ διαμηρίζοιμ' ἂν αὐτήν, 669; κἂν φιλῆσαί μοι δοκῶ, 671), and plays the flute (683); ὅσον δ' ἔχει τὸν χρυσόν (670) either refers to her wearing jewellery or is a pun for the female genitals, both cases referring to a human characteristic.[303] In contrast to Tereus and to the Sophoclean intertext where Procne was the protagonist, here she is a mute character and lives with Tereus in love (τὴν ἐμὴν ἀηδόνα, 203; ἄγε σύννομέ μοι, 203). Her crime, as well as Tereus' crime, is passed over in silence: the lamentation of Itys *is* mentioned (212) but not explained; no word of Philomela. From a cruel tyrant, Tereus becomes a nice and helpful friend; from a ruthless revenger, Procne becomes a

---

299 Cf. *Lys.* 564; Aesch. *Supp.* 58–67. 'The later Roman mythographers [Ovid's *Metamorphoses*] somewhat absurdly inverted the transformation of the two sisters, making Procne the swallow and the tongueless Philomela the songstress nightingale', Frazer 1921, 100. Also, later sources speak of an axe instead of a spear (Apollod. *Bibl.* 3.14.8).
300 Cf. Aesch. *Supp.* 62; Hyg. *Fab.* 45; Pearson 1917, 223–4. For some explanations of this replacement, see Dunbar 1995, 140–1.
301 Dobrov 2001, 115. However, a painted tableau could also have been used. Entirely on Sophocles' play, see Hourmouziades 1986; Stähler 2000; Fitzpatrick 2001; Hofmann 2006; Luppe 2007; Coo 2013; Finglass 2016.
302 Dobrov 2001, 115. On Tereus, see also Koenen 1959; Hoffman 1976, 71–9; Griffith 1987; Holmes 2011.
303 Dunbar 1995 *ad loc.* On the physical appearance of the nightingale-piper, see Romer 1983.

charming entertainer; from a means of divine punishment, the transformation into birds becomes something to covet for Peisetairos and Euelpides; all in all, a total reversal of the myth. As for the invention of Tereus' bird-servant, whose appearance causes terror to the two Athenians (61, 65, 68), and his introduction as a prelude to the entrance of Tereus on stage, the most appropriate analysis was given by Gelzer:

> By this duplication Aristophanes is able, without adding anything new and by the mere parallelism of the process, to use expectations, aroused by the fact that apparently exactly the same is going to happen again, to delude and surprise his spectators, making them anticipate by analogy what is in fact *not* going to happen: in the repetition of the pattern the king appears *un*summoned and his appearance is the *opposite* of frightful... and yet the same items are used: the door, the bird's costume, the beak... It is precisely through all this repetition that the audience's expectations are deluded and surprised.[304]

In order to persuade the birds about their ancient origin and reign, supposedly dating before the Olympians, and the Titans, and the earth (468–9), Peisetairos employs a series of τεκμήρια (482), all of which are in fact comic inventions. The claims that the rooster was the first king of Persia, the hawk of Greece, and the cuckoo of Egypt and Phoenicia are supported via wordplay, proverbs, the appearance of these birds, or people's reactions to them (e.g. people waking up with the cry of the rooster denotes their obedience to his rule). Moreover, the fact that several kings and gods have a bird siting on their sceptre or crown indicates, according to Peisetairos, the birds' royal status, but fails to explain their antecedence. As for the fable attributed here to Aesop, that the first bird in the world, the Lark, buried its father within its head, since the earth did not yet exist (471–5), we cannot appreciate the extent to which Aristophanes adapted or appropriated this fable. It is, however, certain that he did not invent it.[305] Conceivably, a fable could speak of a Lark burying its father in its head for some reason (cf. Zeus devouring Metis), but such a pragmatic justification, as there being no burial land, must be a comic addition. In any case, the fact that the first bird ever is said to have had a father is surprising in its own right. Apart from serving the advancing of

---

304 Gelzer 1996, 200.
305 Aelian (*Nat. Anim.* 16.5) cites a similar Indian aetiological fable about the hoopoe and its crest. There are also parallel fables in Rabbinic Jewish literature. Indian mythographers and Jewish rabbis may well have taken material from the Greek fabulistic tradition, but they are unlikely to have read Aristophanes. It must be assumed that there was originally a Greek aetiological fable about the lark, which spread towards Israel and India and which was comically adapted by Aristophanes in *Birds*. See Schirru 2009, 103–8; Dijk 1997, 197–200; Adrados 1990, 223.

the comic plot, i.e. to take the birds into partnership, this ornithological genealogy works as a parody of well-known techniques of oratory – blandishing the audience about their nobility and invoking glaringly unfounded arguments as τεκμήρια.³⁰⁶

Not surprisingly, the birds are persuaded, change their prior attitude, and agree to follow Peisetairos' plans (and so do the gullible Athenians in reality, the poet seems to comment). But surprisingly, even though they had no knowledge of their glorious past until a few lines ago (470), now they 'put on airs' and narrate with great authority (688–90: προσέχετε τὸν νοῦν... ἵν' ἀκούσαντες πάντα παρ' ἡμῶν ὀρθῶς..., '*pay attention to us... once you hear from us an accurate account*') an avian cosmogony which Peisetairos never actually taught them! One would say that since we are in the parabasis, the chorus is omniscient. But this explanation ignores the inherently surprising context: this is the first (as far as we can tell) non-parabatic parabasis in Aristophanes. The birds do step forward – which is what parabasis technically means – addressing the audience, but they are not speaking on behalf of the poet on matters relating to the contest, or to current politics.³⁰⁷ They are not supposed to be omniscient here. Their cosmology is a parodic concoction of Orphic cosmogonies,³⁰⁸ pre-Socratic philosophy (Empedocles and perhaps Epimenides), and mainly of Hesiod's *Theogony* (116 ff.).³⁰⁹

---

306 From a different perspective, Kanavou 2011, 392–400 reads it as a satire of myths themselves (of traditional genealogies, city-foundation stories, and eponymous heroes).
307 Moulton 1996, 220–1. An implicitly 'parabatic' moment in the play is 1274–5 (στεφάνῳ σε χρυσῷ τῷδε σοφίας οὕνεκα| στεφανοῦσι καὶ τιμῶσιν οἱ πάντες λεῴ, '*With this crown of gold all the people recognize and reward you for your wisdom*'), said by the herald to Peisetairos, which is also appropriate for the poet who is about to win the first prize.
308 There are solid indications that the egg concept goes back to fifth-century Orphic Theogony and was known to the author of the Derveni papyrus. See West 1984, 70–1, 86–7, 101–6, 111–2, 178–83, 198–203, 230; Kouremenos *et al.* 2006, 20–31. However, for a fourth-century author, the concept of a cosmic egg was not necessarily connected to Orphism; Betegh 2004, 148–9.
309 For a detailed analysis, see Dunbar 1995, 437 ff. For a full diagram of Hesiod's *Theogony*, see Lattimore 1959, 222–6.

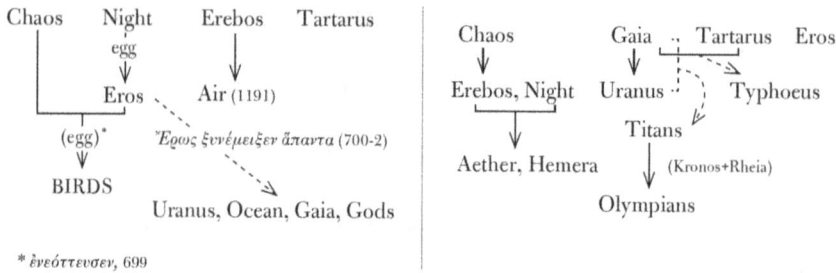

Fig. 3: A schematic comparison of Aristophanes' cosmogony (left frame) and Hesiod's *Theogony* (right frame).

Even though the concept of a cosmic egg was probably not unknown, its introduction into the otherwise Hesiodic model (where there is no egg), its duplication (both Night and Eros appear to lay eggs), and the attribution of wings to Chaos (Χάει πτερόεντι, 698) are certainly Aristophanes' innovations. Eros, who remains inactive in Hesiod's narrative, here becomes the father of the birds, and Night becomes their 'grandmother'. Both entities are traditionally winged (Νὺξ ἡ μελανόπτερος, 695; στίλβων νῶτον πτερύγοιν χρυσαῖν, 697),[310] thus being appropriate as the birds' ancestors. In this context, Ἔρως ὁ ποθεινός (696) seems a most intentional phonologic pun for Ἔρως ὁ πετεινός.[311] At the same time, in addition to his winged nature, Eros is a central concept for the play. He is the force that led Peisetairos and Euelpides towards the birds (ἔρως βίου διαίτης τε καί... ξυνοικεῖν τέ... καὶ ξυνεῖναι, 412–5). And again, after Nephelokokkygia is established, the birds brag that κατέχουσι δ' ἔρωτες ἐμᾶς πόλεως [sc. ἀνθρώπους] ('*Passion for my city grips the world*' 1316). In the exodus, ὁ δ' ἀμφιθαλὴς Ἔρως is invoked during the marriage of Peisetairos with Basileia (1737–41). Even here, as part of the cosmogony, the deified Eros is referenced just after Procne's dance, which has sparked the sexual and romantic interest of the viewers (667–84). Therefore, apart from an appropriate (in so far as he is winged) ancestor of the birds, Eros exemplifies that 'love is in the air' throughout the play.[312]

---

310 Cf. 574 (Νίκη πέτεται πτερύγοιν χρυσαῖν καὶ νὴ Δί' Ἔρως γε); 1737–8 (Ἔρως χρυσόπτερος). See Christopoulos 2010.
311 Note the alliteration of τ throughout the period.
312 On the role of *erōs* in *Birds*, see Arrowsmith 1973.

2.7 Lysistrata

In this comedy, *erōs* is exclusively a sexual term, and in what is a fundamental surprise, *erōs* is omnipresent (as an instinct) through its total absence (as an act).³¹³ Appropriated mythology is once again employed, with Lysistrata praying (551–4):

> ΛΥΣ. ἀλλ' ἥνπερ ὅ <τε> γλυκύθυμος Ἔρως χἠ Κυπρογένει' Ἀφροδίτη
> ἵμερον ἡμῖν κατὰ τῶν κόλπων καὶ τῶν μηρῶν καταπνεύσῃ,
> κᾆτ' ἐντέξῃ τέτανον τερπνὸν τοῖς ἀνδράσι καὶ ῥοπαλισμούς,
> οἶμαί ποτε Λυσιμάχας ἡμᾶς ἐν τοῖς Ἕλλησι καλεῖσθαι.
>
> LYS. If Eros of the sweet soul and Cyprian Aphrodite imbue our thighs and breasts with desire, and infect the men with sensuous rigidity and bouts of truncheonitis, then I believe all Greece will one day call us Disbanders of Battles.

Traditionally, Eros – appearing in various forms – either paralyses or shakes people's entire body or strikes their hearts or minds (καρδίαν, θυμὸν, φρένας).³¹⁴ Here Lysistrata becomes more explicit and realistic: *erōs* strikes with the spasms of erection (τέτανον τερπνὸν makes an oxymoron),³¹⁵ and with 'bludgeon-dicks' (a *hendiadys* – so unrestrained is the drive). Even though the physiology of sex is not something unknown, the grotesque obscenity within a prayer of otherwise pious language (Κυπρογένει', καταπνεύσῃ) is a surprise. One of the most popular mythical examples of this kind of pathology is Menelaus' love at first sight of Helen (155–6):

> ΛΑΜΠ. ὁ γῶν Μενέλαος τᾶς Ἑλένας τὰ μᾶλά πα
> γυμνᾶς παραϝιδὼν ἐξέβαλ', οἰῶ, τὸ ξίφος
>
> LAMP. Like Menelaus! As soon as he peeked at bare Helen's melons,
> he threw his sword away, I reckon.

---

313 The fact that men could have sex with their hetairai, pornai, or male lovers is ignored, as is also masturbation and the women's option to use slaves and dildos (107–10), in order for the sex strike to have a point. See Dover 1972, 160 and 1993, 40; Henderson 1980, 177.
314 οὐ γάρ πώ ποτέ μ' ὧδέ γ' ἔρως φρένας ἀμφεκάλυψεν (*Il.* 3.442; cf.14.294). Cf. Archil. 191 (as fog), Sappho 47 (as wind), Sappho 130 (as snake); note the sensational oxymoron λυσιμέλης δόνει, 'Eros the limb-paralyser is shaking me'), Ibyc. 286 (as lightning), Eur. *Tro.* 255 and *IA* 547–51 (as archer). Eros' association with honey is later (Theocr. *Idyll* 19; cf. Anacreont. 28 West). See Calame 1999.
315 Henderson 1987 *ad loc.*

Even though the scholia *ad loc.* maintain that *Little Ilias* (fr. 28 West) had the same version, the claim that Helen's breasts caused Menelaus to drop his sword is attested for the first time in Eur. *Andr.* 628–30: οὐκ ἔκτανες γυναῖκα χειρίαν λαβών, / ἀλλ', ὡς ἐσεῖδες μαστόν, ἐκβαλὼν ξίφος / φίλημ' ἐδέξω.[316] It is highly possible that *Andromache* was first performed outside Athens (*ca* 425 BC),[317] but it could still have become familiar to the Athenians in the late 410s BC, conceivably through a re-performance. In any case, whether originating from epic, melic, or tragic poetry, or from vase-painting, the detail of the breasts was already known and

Fig. 4: The Persephone Painter (Greek, Attic), *Bell Krater; Front: Helen fleeing from Menelaos*, 440–430 BC, earthware. H: 32.5 cm; Diam (lip): 37.5 cm; Diam (foot): 18 cm. The Toledo Museum of Art. Purchased with funds from the Libbey Endowment, Gift of Edward Drunmond Libbey, 1967.154. Even though the motif of Menelaus' dropping his sword was very popular, here alone it is combined with Helen's (semi)nudity.

---

[316] '*You did not kill your wife when you had her in your power, but when you saw her breasts, you threw away your sword and kissed the traitorous bitch*'. For Menelaus' dropping his sword at the sight of Helen's beauty, in general, cf. Eur. *Or.* 1287; Ibyc. 296; Stesichorus 201. For Helen's breasts, see Maguire 2009, 52–5.

[317] Schol. on *Andr.* 445. See Allan 2000, 149–60.

would certainly have been more surprising to hear in high-register poetry rather than here, in comedy. Instead of surprising appropriation, Aristophanes here aims at the dramaturgical adaptation of the myth: Helen's example is cited by the Spartan Lampito – herself a woman with impressive breasts (ὡς δὴ καλὸν τὸ χρῆμα τιτθίων ἔχεις, 83) – by way of bragging about the 'legendary boobs' of her native land.

A second mythical exemplum, that of Tereus, is employed to allude to another aspect of the pathology of sex drive: to sexual abuse.[318] Lysistrata complains to the Proboulos that soldiers come to the market dressed in full armour – a ridiculous outfit for this place – and misbehave (ἀγοράζοντας καὶ μαινομένους, 556). Most of the examples she provides are indeed funny (557–62) but the last one, about a Thracian mercenary, is ambivalent (563–4):

> ἕτερος δ' <αὖ> Θρᾷξ πέλτην σείων κἀκόντιον ὥσπερ ὁ Τηρεύς,
> ἐδεδίττετο τὴν ἰσχαδόπωλιν καὶ τὰς δρυπεπεῖς κατέπινεν.
>
> Another one, a Thracian, was shaking his shield and spear like Tereus;
> he scared the fig lady out of her wits and gulped down all the ripe ones!

Tereus was not only a Thracian and an armed persecutor, which is the superficial reason why the mercenary is compared to him, but was also a rapist. As for πέλτην σείων κἀκόντιον, it can well be understood as a *double entendre* for the man waving his erected genitalia (cf. the ῥοπαλισμούς mentioned just a few lines above (553) and a δόρυ in place of an erected penis in 985). Secondly, even though the usual metaphor for the female genitalia was σῦκον/συκῆ (*Pax* 1350, Archil. 331), ἰσχάς, the dried fig, was used by Hipponax (124) to indicate the 'cunt' and could also mean the 'anus'.[319] Thus a ἰσχαδόπωλις, 'fig seller', can be understood as implying a mature prostitute or a bawd; and δρυπεπεῖς was definitely understood in this way.[320] Therefore, through the funny incident of a swashbuckler stealing and devouring figs in the market, the appropriated myth and the ambiguous vocabulary allude to stories of coarse exploitation of women. 'Although prostitution was state regulated, prostitutes and hetairai were still abused by

---

318 Aeschin. *In Tim.* 191 attributes a series of crimes, from robbery to *coups d'état*, to unrestrained physical pleasures.
319 Henderson 1991 §122 with n.137.
320 Cf. Ar. fr. 148: ὦ πρεσβῦτα, πότερα φιλεῖς τὰς δρυπεπεῖς ἑταίρας | ἢ <σὺ> τὰς ὑποπαρθένους, ἁλμάδας ὡς ἐλάας, | στιφράς; '*Old man, do you fancy the girlfriends* [Henderson's rendering] *who are ripe, or the fresh ones, firm as salted olives?*'

male clients. Paintings on cups showed men abusing and beating them with sandals and sticks. Vase paintings depicted men kicking prostitutes and pulling them by the hair'.[321]

But far from denouncing such behaviour, *Lysistrata* duplicates it, presenting us with mutual abuse between the two sexes. If Tereus exemplifies male violence, an Aesopic fable is used to exemplify female violence, with the old women's semichorus threatening the old men's semichorus as follows (691–5):

ὡς εἰ καὶ μόνον κακῶς <μ'> ἐρεῖς, ὑπερχολῶ γάρ,
αἰετὸν τίκτοντα κάνθαρός σε μαιεύσομαι.

If you so much as curse at me, I'll boil over with such rage,
I'll be the beetle midwife to your eagle's eggs.

The allusion is to the fable discussed above in connection to *Peace*, about the beetle's revenge on the eagle by making Zeus to break its eggs. With this intertext, "I'll midwife you" is a euphemism for "I'll smash your eggs". However, I find it hard to agree with Sommerstein's and Henderson's certainty that "I'll smash your eggs" points to the men's testicles,[322] firstly because there is no parallel for this metaphor, however evident it might seem (as the former admits); secondly because the usual threat was to tear off one's testicles, not to smash them;[323] last but not least, because "I'll smash your eggs" is in itself something implied, so that "I'll smash your testicles" would be a second-level implication – probably hard to be decoded in the course of oral speech.[324] In any case, the fable is well chosen, since the beetle that overpowers the eagle suits the women's ostensible inferiority to – and eventual victory over – men. The suitability of this fable is also explained in connection with, and as continuation of, the previous exemplum of Tereus: it fictionalises the afterlife of Tereus and Procne as winged animals (even though not a hoopoe and a nightingale, but an eagle and a beetle) and redresses the balance between them. If the eagle's initial offending of the beetle corresponds to Philomela's rape, and the beetle's first breaking of the eagle's eggs corresponds to the murder of Itys, then the second 'smashing of eggs' conceptualises that Procne is not just crying for her Itys passively in her afterlife,[325] but she takes revenge on Tereus eternally – not only for the rape, but for also attempting to kill her.

---

[321] Tetlow 2005, 80–1. For such iconography see Keuls 1993, 174–86.
[322] Sommerstein 1990 *ad loc.*; Henderson 1991 §83 and 1987 *ad loc.*
[323] Cf. 363; *Eq.* 772; *Plut.* 312; 955–6.
[324] μαιεύομαι usually applies to the birth of mammals and ideas (the Socratic method).
[325] Cf. Aesch. *Ag.* 1140–5.

This technique, which is here called by the term of 'responsive' or 'antiphonal' myths, is clearly used, for the first time in Aristopanes, in the second stasimon:

| ΧΟΓΕΡ. μῦθον βούλομαι λέξαι τιν' ὑμῖν... | 782 |
| ΧΟΓΥΝ. κἀγὼ βούλομαι μῦθόν τιν' ὑμῖν ἀντιλέξαι... | 805 |

MEN I want to tell you all a tale that once I heard...
WOM. I too want to tell you all a tale in reply...

The old men's semichorus invokes, as an example to imitate, Melanion, a man who hated women so much that he decided to live in the wilderness as a huntsman forever (785–95). In response, the old women's semichorus reports the story of Timon, who hated the evil men (only the evil ones) but loved women (805–20). However, both tales are appropriated according to the interests of each side: 'Melanion was famously the lover and conqueror of Atalanta; he did indeed stay in the countryside, but with Atalanta. Timon is not known to have had time for anyone, male or female.'[326] Conceivably, by citing legends like these, Aristophanes wanted to test his audience's readiness to perceive the paradox. If the paradox is not perceived (because, for instance, Melanion's story was not well-known), the debate between the two semichoruses seems valid; if it was perceived on the other hand, the audience would laugh. In both cases, this would be a good result for the poet. Viewing the passage under this light, we can say that Aristophanes' insistence on characterising these tales as real μῦθοι (782, 805; and indeed, in the first occasion, μῦθον... ὅν ποτ' ἤκουσ' αὐτὸς ἔτι παῖς ὤν, 'which I heard when I was a child') is a misleading *deixis*, a playful puzzle for his well-versed spectators. The surprise lies not only in the appropriation of the myths, but also in the very labelling of the generated stories as 'myths'. As for the antiphonal arrangement, a first attempt at this pattern can be traced in the first stasimon of *Knights*, where the chorus evokes Poseidon in the strophe (551–63) and Athena in the antistrophe (581–4). In evoking the contrast of the two gods for the patronship of Athens, one could reasonably link Paphlagon to the former and the Sausage-Seller to the latter god, in a way that the myth becomes a prelude of the comic *agōn*.[327] Be that as it may, in *Knights* there are no antiphonal semichoruses (but rather a single united chorus), no incorporation of the myth in the characters' arguments, and no surprising appropriation.

---

[326] Bowie 2007, 198. For Melanion and Atalanta, cf. Xen. *Cyn.* 1.7; Apollod. *Bibl.* 3.9.2. For Timon as a legendary misanthrope (whether a historical or a proverbial figure), cf. *Av.* 1549; Phryn. Com. 19. For Timon in *Lys.* see Hawkins 2001. Antiphanes had written both a *Timon* and a *Melanion*.
[327] Bowie 1993, 69–71.

2.8 *Thesmophoriazusae*

Appropriation of tragic myth is the *raison d'être* of this play, with its second half being a collage of parodies of Euripides' *Telephus* (687 f.), *Palamedes* (770 f.), *Helen* (850 f.), *Andromeda* (1011 f.) and perhaps *Cyclops* (1200 f).[328] Aristophanes' mastery is especially shown in the first one of these parodies, in the way in which he differentiates it from – and makes it more surprising than – the Telephus parody in *Acharnians*. It is not simply that he replaces the basket of charcoal with a sack of wine. In *Acharnians*, Dikaiopolis tried to deceive the chorus by telling them that he would slay their 'beloved ones' (τοὺς φιλτάτους 326) and they reasonably took this to mean a παιδίον (329) instead of a basket of charcoal. Here, it is the protagonist who gets deceived by the chorus. The in-law truly believes that he is holding an actual baby and he is surprised when he unwraps it (733–4): τουτὶ τί ἐστιν; ἀσκὸς ἐγένεθ' ἡ κόρη | οἴνου πλέως, *'What is this? The baby girl's become a skin full of wine'*. As for the reaction of the choruses, in both plays they participate in the illusion (since they lament for an object as if it were a human being) but in opposite ways. The Acharnians, as already noted, recognise the basket as such. In *Thesmophoriazusae*, Mika (the mother) and the women's chorus insist on calling the wine-sack a baby (690, 706), even after the in-law has discovered its true nature (744, 754), and even after it is 'slain' (761). Moreover, the wine-sack replaces not any kind of baby, but specifically a daughter (κόρη 733, τὴν παῖδα 761) instead of a boy like Orestes – another misleading *deixis*. In this case the poet's intention was not to test his audience's knowledge of the myth – which was widely known from many sources – but to repeat the comic aphorism that women are drunkards; if wine runs in the arteries of this baby instead of blood (694), it is certainly a girl. Yet the most unexpected element is that, contrary to the myth, to the tragedies, and to *Acharnians*, here the petitioner does slay the hostage, spilling its 'blood' on the altar.[329] Comedy is once more claiming its dramaturgical superiority over tragedy (it 'dares' to show on stage events that tragedy only reports through messengers) and its proximity to realism (on the comic stage, miraculous rescues are not an option).[330]

This latter point is especially emphasised by the parody of *Palamedes*. Accused by Odysseus for conspiracy against Agamemnon, Palamedes was executed

---

[328] For the last one, see p. 62.
[329] For the famous depiction of the scene on the Apulian bell-krater by the Schiller Painter, *ca* 370 BC (Würzburg, Martin von Wagner Museum H 5697), see Kossatz-Deissmann 1980; Csapo 1986; Taplin 1987, 102–5; Austin/Olson 2004, lxxv–lxxvii.
[330] On the parody of *Telephus*, see also Miller 1948; Rau 1967, 42–50; Farmer 2017, 167–72.

while in Troy, and his brother Oiax reported the news to their father Nauplios in Euboea by inscribing them on oars which he threw in the sea, so that their father would prepare their revenge.[331] The in-law attempts to imitate Oiax,[332] but as he soon realises that such stage-properties are not simply lying around in normal life,[333] he grabs some wooden tablets (dedications) from the altar beside him. His difficulty with carving ρ, while trying to write 'Euripides' (according to the scholia), increases the bathos. This is necessary, because the original mythical model is so surprisingly successful (an oar floating from Troy to Euboea and reaching its addressee), that only a total failure (not even having the proper supplies for the plan to begin with) could compete with it. The replacement of oars with small tablets could very well be a metatheatrical allusion. The judges of the dramatic competitions cast their votes by inscribing the name of their favourite competitor on a tablet (ἔγραψε μὲν ταῦτα εἰς τὸ γραμματεῖον, Lys. 4.3.3).[334] Even though we have no information on whether the γραμματεῖα were wooden, clay, or stone, and even though the tablets here, the dedications, are initially called ἀγάλματα (773), the overall wording is tempting: ῥίψω γράφων (771), γράφων διαρρίπτοιμι (774), and especially πινάκων ξεστῶν δέλτοι (778). Thus, it is possible that the in-law is dispersing the ballots for (and towards) the judges to find, not for Euripides. In that case, the ρ would not come from 'Euripides' but from the prospective winner's name, i.e. 'Aristophanes'.

Both in the parody of *Telephus* and that of *Palamedes*, the in-law performs a one-man show, appropriating a single scene from the tragedies (the hostage, the oars), and the chorus and Mika participate in the illusion. In the following parodies of *Helen* and *Andromeda*,[335] both produced the year before *Thesm.*, exactly the opposite happens. 'Euripides' becomes a deuteragonist, playing Teucrus and Menelaus in the first case, and Echo and Perseus in the second; the parodies are

---

331 *Cypria* arg. and fr. 27 West; schol. on *Thesm.* 770. Aeschylus, Sophocles, and Astydamas II also had a *Palamedes* of their own. For Euripides' play, see Webster 1967, 174–6; Scodel 1980, 43–63; Kovacs 1997; Mariscal/Presentación 2007. For the parody here, Rau 1967, 51–3; Farmer 2017, 172–4.
332 ὡς ἐκεῖνος (770) does not refer to Palamedes, even though it comes immediately after his name, but to his brother ('the man I'm thinking of', cf. *Ach.* 428; Austin/Olson 2004 *ad loc.*)
333 Bowie 1993, 222.
334 On the judging system, see Pickard-Cambridge 1988, 95–9; Pope 1986; Csapo/Slater 1995, 157–65; Wilson 2000, 98–102 and 346–7 nn. 222–37; Marshall/Van Willigenburg 2004; Todd 2007, 368–70.
335 On the parody of *Helen*, see Rau 1967, 56–65; Farmer 2017, 177–81. On the parody of *Andromeda*, see Rau 1967, 65–89; Mastromarco 2008; Major 2013; Farmer 2017, 182–8. For the original *Andromeda*, see Webster 1967, 192–9; Bubel 1991; Wright 2005; Bañuls Oller/Morenilla Talens 2008.

not 'photographic' but combine several (appropriated) scenes, restaging *Helen* and an *Andromeda* in fast-forward, and in contrast to Mika, Critylla and the Scythian archer are not deceived by the in-law (862–3; 1111–2). Reversing the Euripidean original, Aristophanes' 'Helen' is not a dynamic woman, 'Menelaus' is not a dolt, and 'Theonoe' (supposed to be played by Critylla; 897–8) is not an ally.[336] The couple's *anagnorisis* is perfunctory, and most importantly their escape plan fails, as happens also with the parody of *Andromeda*. For this latter case we cannot assess the characterological and structural surprises since we miss the original,[337] but things are better on the level of form and stagecraft. In the first part of the parody, while anticipating the arrival of Euripides, the in-law (impersonating Andromeda) reaches such a degree of desperation that he confuses his identities, mixing male and female adjectives and pronouns; in 1022–38 alone: τὸν πολυστονώτατον βροτῶν... κώλοον ἄφιλον... / ἕστηκ' ἔχουσ'[α]... ἐμπεπλεγμένη / ος, ὦ τάλας ἐγώ, τάλας. The second part is a slanging match with 'Echo' – not a witty device indeed, but this is precisely what Aristophanes blames Euripides (the real one) for, concerning his decision to employ Echo as a *dramatis persona*. The last part is a homoerotic play between 'Perseus' and 'Andromeda' as a transvestite (1114–24). Whether Euripides/Perseus entered on the *mēchanē* as in the original is controversial, but Sommerstein offers a compelling case for him doing so.[338] However, this is not on the basis of παρέπτετο (1014) or διὰ μέσου γὰρ αἰθέρος / τέμνων κέλευθον πόδα τίθημ' ὑπόπτερον ('*through the empyrean cutting a swath I aim my winged foot*' 1099–10), which can be mere exaggerations by the pretend-Euripides, but on the basis of dramatic technique. All previous parodies use a prop as a point of reference: the wine-sack/baby for *Telephus*, the wooden tablets/oars for *Palamedes*, the altar/tomb for *Helen* (888). Likewise, the *mēchanē* would remind the audience of what they had seen a year earlier, on the same stage.

Even though the second part of the comedy exclusively deals with tragic myth, there is also a cosmogonic myth at the very beginning of the play: the separation of the senses of sight and hearing during the creation of the animals (13–8). Any attempt to identify the Euripidean version, and the influence of specific

---

336 Austin/Olson 2004, lxi.
337 At least with regard to the Scythian archer, who is sleeping by the captive in-law until 'Echo' wakes him up with 'her' fuss (1007–81), I would suggest that he stands for the sea monster rather than for Andromeda's father Kepheus (as Austin/Olson 2004, lxiii).
338 Cf. Sommerstein 1994, 229 and Prato 2001, 315. The use of the *mēchanē* in the original is attested by Pollux 4.128.7.

philosophers in it, is abortive due to limited fragments from either side.[339] A parallel between this myth of separation of the senses that Aristophanes attributes to Euripides, and the myth of separation of the sexes that Plato (who was between 12 and 18 years old the year of *Thesm.*) ascribed to Aristophanes,[340] would tempt one to argue that the theory of the senses is more Aristophanic than truly Euripidean. But likewise, is the theory of the sexes truly Aristophanic or rather Platonic? In any case, we cannot appreciate the paradoxes in the myth itself (if any),[341] but we can see the surprising manner in which it is incorporated into the play. The play begins with the in-law asking Euripides where they are going and Euripides replying '*you don't need to hear what you shall see soon*' (4–6) instead of 'we are going to Agathon', which is not revealed until 29. And then Euripides digresses into his para-philosophy. So his initial call for taciturnity and simplicity in fact leads to abundant chatter, perpetrated indeed by the admonisher himself.

2.9 Frogs

With Dionysus' and Hercules' descent to the underworld as background stories,[342] with the figures of these two gods plus Charon, Aeacus, and Pluto as *dramatis personae*, with the chorus of Iacchus' initiates,[343] with the weighing of the tragic verses that resembles a *psychostasia* (*Il.* 22.208–13; Aesch. fr. 279–280a), with references to Theseus (142), to Empousa (288–96), to Oedipus (1188–94) and other mythic/tragic figures, this play is fundamentally linked to mythology, no less

---

339 For Αἰθήρ as an originator in Euripides, cf. Eur. fr. 839; for generation as a process of separation, cf. Eur. fr. 484; for Euripides' 'obsession' with Αἰθήρ, cf. *Thesm.* 51, 272, 1099; *Ran.* 892.
340 *Symp.* 189c–193e. See *i.a.* Dover 1966; Eisner 1979; Saxonhouse 1985; Carnes 1998, 104–21; Dobson 2013.
341 The images of the sun as an eye and of ears as funnels were commonplace. E.g. ἀκτὶς ἀελίου... ὦ χρυσέας ἁμέρας βλέφαρον (Soph. *Ant.* 100–4); διὰ τῶν ὤτων ὥσπερ διὰ χώνης (Pl. *Resp.* 411a.6).
342 For the myth of Dionysus' descent to save Semele, known in Aristophanes' time, see Whitman 1964, 233–4. Both Dover 1993, 40 and Sommerstein 1996, 9 n. 44 note that an allusion to that myth would spoil the plot, i.e. Dionysus' supposed ignorance of the underworld. For Dionysus and Hercules in comedy and satyr play, in general, see Casolari 2003, 112–26 and 249–92 respectively.
343 Scholars have noticed, but have poorly explained why, Dionysus does not recognise himself as Iacchus, despite the fact that the two divinities were identified with each other in Aristophanes' time (Soph. *Ant.* 1120–54; Eur. *Bacch.* 725) and the fact that Dionysus here accepts the chorus' invitation, addressed to Iacchus, to join them (404–19). Dover 1993, 40; Sommerstein 1996, 184; Whitman 1964; 234. A very simple explanation is that Dionysus still tries to pass for Hercules, hence does not confirm that *he* is Iacchus.

than *Birds*. In *Birds*, however, appropriated mythology performs a more dynamic function, given that the hoopoe's past as Tereus justifies his role as a mediator, and the avian cosmogony becomes the catalyst for the realisation of Peisetairos' plan. Here mythology, though omnipresent, is dramaturgically in the background; it offers a setting, but not the plot. There is no doubt that the first half of the play is entirely a Dionysian drama, but this is a common comic theme (cf. Cratinus' *Dionysalexandros* and Eupolis' *Taxiarchoi*), not an interplay with mythology *per se*. Nor can we perceive the merging of opposite identities into Dionysus' persona (male-female, beast-human-god, Herculean-Dionysian, primitive-civilised, cheerful-painful etc.) as a comic surprise, because this is precisely what Dionysus was in religion, vase painting, and tragic theatre as well: 'a personified *Oxymoron*'.[344] What comedy does is merely to stretch these known qualities. In Riu's most suitable words:

> Dionysus favours the change of social roles, inversion, reversal: in comedy he walks and the slave rides. [...] Is he not the god of laughter, who can male his foe up as a woman to expose him to the laughter of the people? Now he is a buffoon accoutred in such an outlandish way that Heracles cannot stop laughing. [...] And if he has an effeminate look, comedy connects him in a series of equivocations with Clesthenes (48–9, 57). [...] Dionysus' comic figure is, then, based on his serious figure, where what we might call the "comic reasoning" is applied.[345]

Even the scene of the alternate thrashing of Dionysus and Xanthias, conducted so that the real god is revealed (635 f.), can been seen as a comic σπαραγμός.[346] In the same way, the assumption that Hercules during his own descent to fetch Cerberus (467) had encountered '*harbours, bakeries, brothels, rest areas, turnings, springs, streets, cities, restaurants, hostels with the fewest bedbugs*' (112–5) and had mistreated two innkeepers, eating all their stock without paying the bill

---

344 Stanford 1958, xxix. See Lada-Richards 1999, 17–44, esp. 33, 43.
345 Riu 1999, 116–8.
346 A more obvious occasion is Aeacus' threats (470–477: διασπαράξει, διασπάσονται) but this remains on a verbal level. See Lada-Richards 1999, 94–7. Σπαραγμός was inflicted not only on animals and Dionysus' opponents (Lycurgus, Actaeon) and initiates (Pentheus), but also on Dionysus himself according to Orphism (e.g. Kern 34, 35, 210, 211, 214).

(549–67), are perfectly in line with the stereotypical gluttony of Hercules,[347] his libido,[348] and his intimidating behaviour.[349]

The limited surprise in the usage of myth in the first half of the play is also seen in some passing references. Hercules informs Dionysus that he will have to pay a two-obol fee to get into Charon's boat, which alludes either to the θεωρικόν (the charge for admission to the theatre) or the διωβελία (a state subsidy for the poor).[350] Amazed at how 'money makes the (under)world go round', Dionysus asks him how money had reached there, and Hercules replies Θησεὺς ἤγαγεν (140–2). As the mythical king of Athens, Theseus is the most legitimate authority for 'exporting' Athenian policies into the underworld. As for the question of why two-obols instead of one, which was the standard amount to put into corpses' mouths,[351] Dover (*ad loc.*) is right that 'to imagine that Herakles takes account of Xanthias as well as Dionysos, or of a return fare payable in advance, is to spoil the point of the joke', which is precisely to satirise the expensive living costs: even to die, one needs a subsidy. What is more important for our discussion here is that we have an adaptation rather than appropriation of the myth. Theseus had descended to the underworld with his best friend Peirithous in order to abduct Persephone, whom Peirithous wanted as a wife. Dionysus is also about to descend accompanied by an ally, Xanthias, in order to bring back someone he feels πόθος about (53, 66). Therefore, even though the myth is *prima facie* evoked in order to explain the two-obol fee in a surprising way, its occurrence is contextually something fairly expected.

This is not to argue that *Frogs* is not surprising – see the final chapter. But as far as myth is concerned, the exploitation of surprise seems to be limited to the second half of the play, where *tragic* myth enters the debate (literally). The most

---

347 Cf. *Ra* 63; *Vesp.* 60; *Pax* 741; *Av.* 1583 f. For discussion and examples from more comic poets, see Ath. 9.80–10.2; Wilkins 2000, 90–7; Hill 2011, 82–90.
348 'He was twice married, and for three years played the gigolo to Queen Omphale of Lydia. He consorted with Echidna [...] and sired the warlike Scythians. [...] Hercules was the guest of King Thesipus [who granted him] the right to sleep with all fifty of his daughters, a different daughter every night for fifty nights [Diod. Sic. 4.29.2–3; Ath. 13.4; Apollod. *Bibl.* 2.4.10] or, in one version [Paus. 9.27.7], all fifty in one night.' Austin 1990, 114.
349 See, for instance, Hercules' ghost gripping his bow and horrifying the dead around (*Od.* 11.604–8); shooting his arrows against Helios (Pherec. fr. 18a *FGrH* 3; Apollod. *Bibl.* 2.5.10); holding the Erymanthian boar over King Eurystheus' head and making him hide into a *pithos* (in sculpture and vase painting since 6th century; Diod. 4.12.2; Mitchell 2009, 121–3).
350 See Roselli 2009, 24–6. The only attested association of Theseus with money is his donation of a sum to the locals in Cyprus, in order to sacrifice and set two statues in honour of the dead Ariadne (Plut. *Thes.* 20.4).
351 *AP* 7.67.6; 11.168.6; Luc. *Luct.* 10; *Dial. Mort.* 2.1. See Stevens 1991.

striking example is Aeschylus' lament over a lost rooster (1331–64), which he credits to, or better blames on, Euripides. We cannot tell whether this is an *ad hoc* invention of a paratragic myth, an appropriation of a Euripidean scene from a lost play,³⁵² or a direct borrowing from a comedy. We can only appreciate the use of tragic language and emotional exaggeration for οἰκεῖα πράγματα (959). Cf. ὦ θύμ' ἄνευ σκάνδικος ἐμπορευτέα, also in a para-Euripidean context (*Ach*. 480). More importantly, we can appreciate that a supposedly 'tragic myth' is here used meta-theatrically, i.e. for a quality of comic theatre. We do not listen to Euripides singing his own supposed monody, but we watch Aeschylus who appropriates Euripides' supposed monody, or better, it is Aristophanes who appropriates Aeschylus' persona who appropriates Euripides' supposed monody. Is this not the surprise of meta-paratragedy?

2.10 *Ecclesiazusae*

Only one mythical reference occurs in this play, which is a surprise in itself from a poetological perspective. What could have led Aristophanes to such a decision – should it be a conscious decision at all – is something we can hardly speculate about, since we do not know the year and festival of performance,³⁵³ hence we do not know the rival plays and the previous year's titles which would help to argue that Aristophanes either followed a trend or differentiated himself from a trend followed by others. We also do not know the result of the contest but '*Ecclesiazusae*, it is certain, has won very little favour since. It is seldom referred to in antiquity, and only three manuscripts transmit the text in full. Scholars and critics are, with few exceptions, hostile'.³⁵⁴ This negative reception can be attributed to the general alteration of Aristophanes' previous well attested, and much praised poetic idiolect. The absence of mythology here (but not in *Wealth* and definitely not in fourth century comedy altogether)³⁵⁵ can be seen as an aspect of this 'deterioration' which nonetheless proves that the old Aristophanes was poetically young enough to experiment. A justification of this attitude can be found in the text (578–80):

---

352 The closest parallel in extant Euripides is *Orestes* 1368–502, as Sommerstein 1996 *ad loc*. points out, but he is wrong in that the parody contains no verbal reminiscences of it. Aristophanes parodies the obtrusive doubling words in the Phrygian's monody; Dover 1993, 358; Stanford 1958, 185. *Hec*. 68–72 is also parodied in the first lines.
353 For an account of the proposals, ranging from 393 to 389 BC, see Sommerstein 1998, 1, 7.
354 Ussher 1973, xiii.
355 On the flourishing mythological burlesques, see Konstantakos 2014; Nesselrath 1995.

δεῖται †γάρ τοί γε† σοφοῦ τινος ἐξευρήματος ἡ πόλις ἡμῶν.
ἀλλὰ πέραινε μόνον
μήτε δεδραμένα μήτ' εἰρημένα πω πρότερον·
μισοῦσι γὰρ ἢν τὰ παλαιὰ πολλάκις θεῶνται.

Yes, our city needs some kind of sage scheme; describe it in full, making sure only that none of it's ever been said or done before: they hate to watch the same old stuff over and over again!

Apart from the contextual meaning (the demand to overcome inequality, patriarchy, and corruption), it would be tempting from a poetological perspective to read τὰ παλαιά as 'the old stories', i.e. mythology, which would have no place in modern comedy. However, we should not attach much weight to this, because claiming to be innovative and unconventional is just a comic commonplace and not a trustworthy programmatic statement of what a dramatist will actually introduce or omit.[356]

In the single mythic reference, a young woman describes the consequences of Praxagora's sexual communism as: ὥστ' εἰ καταστήσεσθε τοῦτον τὸν νόμον, | τὴν γῆν ἅπασαν Οἰδιπόδων ἐμπλήσετε ('*If you people start enforcing a law like this, you'll fill the whole country with Oedipuses*' 1041–2). Of course, Praxagora has only suggested that children will not know who their father is and vice versa (635–9) whereas nothing alike is said for mothers (which is the case in Plato *Resp.* 460b–d). But this can be fairly assumed through analogy or the mythical exemplum can be taken as a metaphor for gerontophilia rather than for incest. Not to mention that the reverse case, i.e. young women having to copulate with older men (which falls within the declaration of 628–9), could lead them to copulate with their fathers. What is poetologically interesting, and a surprise, is that the comic dystopia is described in terms of tragic myth: if the communistic scenario (i.e. the comic idea) happens, then comedy would become tragedy. In fact, it would become 'more of a tragedy' than a tragedy itself, since Oedipus is an exceptional case in tragedy but here everyone will be an Oedipus – note the pleonasm ἅπασαν, ἐμπλήσετε.[357] However, this scenario, even though it has been

---

356 Cf. *Nub.* 546–8; *Vesp.* 1044, 1053, 1536; Pherecr. fr. 84; Metag. fr. 15; Eup. fr. 60. See Wright 2012, 77–8; Moulton 1996, 217–8.
357 The only other attested comic use of Oedipus' myth is Euboulos' *Oedipus* (fr. 72), in which 'Oedipus would have been portrayed as a comic parasite, going about in search of free meals and invitations from generous hosts—a humorous distortion of the mythical hero who wandered destitute in exile after his fall and expulsion from Thebes', Konstantakos 2014, 172. Plato Com. *Laius* (frr. 65–8) must also have had references to Oedipus.

voted for and is about to be put into effect, is not realised within the play; it is only kept for after the exodus. Comedy remains comedy.

2.11 *Wealth*

Through appropriated myths, however, comedy competes not only with tragedy but with all genres that interlope in its territory, as we have noticed with regard to the Aesopic fables in *Peace*. Here the case is dithyramb, which provides a highly significant instance of competition with comedy, since the two genres often shared the same stage.[358] The inclusion of a para-dithyramb in *Wealth* cannot itself shed light on whether the comedy was produced in the Dionysia or the Lenaea, because Aristophanes' point could either be to mock the genre staged in the same festival (thus Dionysia) or to offer the audience a comic substitute for the absent genre (thus Lenaea). As the scholia let us know, the dithyramb concerned is the famous *Cyclops* or *Galatea*,[359] by the contemporary poet Philoxenus, which Carion parodies in collaboration with the chorus, despite the two parties being hostile to each other in the course of the parody. The former pretends to be the Cyclops, assigning to the chorus the role of his docile sheep, and the chorus responds that they will play the role of Odysseus' fellows instead, and will blind him (290–301). It is certain that Philoxenus' dithyramb itself included comic elements,[360] and in all probability it also had a satirical intention, against the Sicilian tyrant Dionysius I (represented as Polyphemus) who had condemned Philoxenus (as Odysseus) for having seduced his mistress (as Galatea).[361] Thus 'Aristophanes has singled the *Cyclops* out of parody in part because Philoxenus was beginning to blur the boundary between dithyramb and drama'.[362] Even though one need be cautious with the scholia that attribute some lines to the original *Cyclops*, at least two comic interventions can be named: θρεττανελὸ (290; cf. *Ran* 1285–6) which

---

358 Dithyramb contests in Athens, with ten men's choruses and ten boys' choruses of fifty members each, date from Pindar and Bacchylides' time to AD 200; Pickard-Cambridge 1988, 74–5. In City Dionysia, the dithyrambs were performed either all together on a separate date (Csapo/Slater 1995, 106–108) or on two out of the five days when comedies were performed (Pickard-Cambridge 1988, 66). For the absence of dithyramb from the Lenaea see Haigh 1907, 25 n. 4.
359 *PMG* 814–24. See Holzinger 1940, 109–11; Sutton 1983a; Hordern 1999; Sommerstein 2001, 156; Casolari 2003, 127–34; Rosen 2007, 55–9; Farmer 2017, 213–9.
360 Arist. *Poet.* 1448a mentions that it depicted characters worse than actual people, which he accounts a characteristic of comedy.
361 Ath. 1.6e–7a (a tale credited to Phaenias of Eresus) = 816 *PMG*.
362 Farmer 2017, 215.

seems to parody the sound of the *kithara* that Philoxenus had invented for Polyphemus, and the circumcised chorus (ἀπεψωλημένοι, 295) which comes in sharp contrast to the dithyrambic choruses' solemn clothing.[363]

Aristophanes, however, does not only compete with the comic effect of the rival genres (through parody) but also with the very *process* of constructing surprise: if Philoxenus appropriated mythology in order to mock Dionysius about his mistress, Aristophanes – accepting the challenge, one would say – also appropriates mythology, from the very same epic, to mock another contemporary for his mistress. Now (302–15) Carion becomes Circe the sorceress, calling the chorus to follow 'her' as swine, in the same way that Polyphemus had earlier manipulated his flock. But instead of Circe from Aeaea manipulating Odysseus' fellows, we read Circe from Corinth manipulating Philonides' friends. The mockery targets Philonides, a nasty but wealthy man who could afford the services of the (in)famous Corinthian courtesan Nais.[364] So, if the dithyramb was suggestive in its satire, comedy is straightforward. And if the dithyramb innovated in exploiting comic elements, here comedy 'raises the bar', flaunting its very own theme, scatophagy (305, 313).[365] Finally, at the peak of the surprise, the chorus once again denies their role as swine; they become Odysseus' fellows (in their human version) and threat to hang Circe/Nais from 'her'…. balls, thus bringing the illusion to an end.

Now we can better appreciate the much underestimated coherence of the two sketches, which goes beyond their metrical and structural similarity (Carion distributing roles and the chorus redistributing them).[366] From a poetological perspective, the parody of *Cyclops* as the first sketch, comes to deride the rival genre

---

363 Demosthenes, as a dithyrambic choregos in 358, dressed his chorus in golden-embroidered robes and golden crowns (Dem. 21.14–8). Cf. ἱμάτια χρυσᾶ παρασχὼν τῷ χορῷ, Antiph. fr. 202.6. For the Greeks' negative attitude on exposure of the glans, see Hodges 2001, esp. 392–4.
364 οἱ ἀμφὶ Φιλωνίδη is merely a periphrasis for Philonides himself; Rogers 1907 *ad loc*. For his affair with Nais, cf. schol. *ad loc.*; 179; Lys. fr. 82 Carrey. The scholia name the mistress Lais, the other famous Corinthian hetaira, but given the similarity of the two names, we can assume an early corruption of the text; Sommerstein 2001, 148.
365 Of course, the theme is as old as *Il.* 23.777 (Ajax falling into a pile of dung face forward) but that brings disgust, whereas in comedy it is often a voluntary act of pleasure (cf. 706; *Pax* 48), sometimes of sexual pleasure (*Pax* 11; *Lys.* 1174; and *ad hoc*). See Henderson 1991, 192–4.
366 Another symbolic interpretation is Bowie 1993, 287–8, that both Cyclops and Circe symbolise the lifestyle which Penia suggests and which the chorus denounces. A more prosaic explanation would be that both these Homeric episodes were treated in Philoxenus' dithyramb, and therefore pass into Aristophanes' parody of it. The superficial explanation by the scholia that in *Odyssey* Circe's episode comes after the Cyclops, ignores the intervening episodes of Aeolus' windbag and the Laestrygonians.

of dithyramb; the second part, Circe's allegory, comes to give the superior – in terms of more surprising – version of comedy. Therefore, we can include this pair in the group of 'antiphonal' myths. Last but not least, if it is right that dithyrambic choruses did not wear masks,[367] then Aristophanes through these passages also declares that comedy, compared to dithyramb, knows no restrictions due to its use of masks. In fact, it is comedy and not dithyramb that allows multilevel role changes (actor/Carion/Polyphemus/Circe; and dancers/chorus/flock/Odysseus' fellows/swine/Odysseus' fellows again), despite the masks.

The central allegory of the play, the blindness of Wealth, his mistreatment of righteous people, and the enriching of the wicked, occurs already in Hipponax.[368] On the other hand, the attribution of the god's blindness to Zeus' envy (87–92) and his eventual healing (635) must have been Aristophanes' innovations.[369] It is hard, however, to call them surprising; the former innovation merely offers a formulaic and rather perfunctory premise for the plot and has no comic content (in contrast to 234–44 for example); the latter innovation has been progressively planned since 94 and was probably disclosed already in the *proagōn*. It thus appears that mythical innovation is not a necessary (let alone a sufficient) condition for surprise.

2.12 The Intra-Dramatic Functions of Appropriated Myths

The chapter has so far offered a close reading of the surprising appropriation of each myth in each of the eleven extant comedies, with special emphasis on its poetological intention, which is to claim the superiority of comedy over other genres. Either suggestively or openly, all of the appropriated myths point to such a reading. In this section, considering together all the passages discussed above, their intra-dramatic function is examined, i.e. how they operate within the plot.[370] We have already mentioned some adapted (and not appropriated) myths, whose functions range from offering the background of the plot (e.g. Dionysus' ambivalence in *Frogs* or Wealth's blindness in *Wealth*), to supporting an argument (e.g.

---

367 Pickard-Cambridge 1962, 34.
368 Hippon. 36. Cf. Eur. fr. 776; Timocr. 731; Pl. *Leg.* 631c; Antiph. 259; Men. fr. 74; Theocr. *Id.* 10.19.
369 Sommerstein 2001, 8. The most famous punitive blindings, Phineus' and Teiresias', were a result of their affronting the gods (Ap. Rhod. 2.178; Callim. *Hymn* 5.75–82). Here, Zeus envies human beings *a priori*, and indeed only the virtuous ones.
370 For other conclusions, Moessner 1907 should be consulted (154–5 for myth in general and 111 for tragic myth specifically).

Helen's breasts for the power of sex, in *Lysistrata*) or a joke (e.g. Theseus and Peirithous' descent for the two-obol fee, in *Frogs*). Naturally, there are some myths that are neither appropriated nor adapted, but merely mentioned with no creative intention at all (e.g. *Av.* 651–3 ~ Aesop. 1 Perry).

Appropriated myths, which are our subject, can be grouped into five categories according to their intra-dramatic function. (1) 'Persuasive myths' are those used by a character in order to make an argument. (2) 'Aetiological myths' are those used in order to explain a statement. (3) 'Responsive' or 'antiphonal' myths are those juxtaposing two ideas. (4) 'Abusive myths' are those used to mock someone. Finally, (5) 'structural myths' are those used to form the plot. Functions might overlap; e.g. Hyperbolus' mythicisation (*Nub.* 1065–6) is 'antiphonal' towards the virtuous exemplum of Peleus that precedes it, but is also an 'abusive' myth in itself. Of more interest is to clarify the distinction between 'persuasive' and 'aetiological' myths, since they seem similar to each other. *Birds* offers the most suitable examples for this distinction; both the avian genealogy (466–521) and the cosmogony (688–702) explain more or less the same thing, the birds' seniority. But the former is used as an argument by Peisetairos in order to persuade the birds to follow his plans, whereas the latter only affirms/extends what has already been established. 'Persuasive' myths promote the plot, or aspire to promote the plot without success (e.g. *Eccl.* 1041–2), whereas 'aetiological' ones are static. The only surprising myth that does not fit in this proposed schema, and which retains only a poetological function, is 'comedy as Electra' (*Nub.* 534–44), but it definitely belongs to the revised version of the play, which was never performed.[371]

From the allocation of all the appropriated myths into these five groups (see table 12 of the Appendices), it is evident that Aristophanes did not have a preferred method; the balance among the five functions is striking. As for the sources of the appropriated myths (literary treatments in other genres or the broader oral tradition), one can only assume a preference for tragedy and satyr drama with regard to 'structural' myths.

2.13 A Comparison with Tragedy

The preceding analysis may have left the reader with the misleading impression that appropriating myths towards a surprising outcome is a privilege of comedy.

---

[371] See hypothesis VI [=I Dover]; Dover 1968, lxxx–xcviii; Tarrant 1991.

In the closure of this chapter, it should be underlined that tragedy, the competitive sibling, has first and foremost employed this trope, and that comedy only differs in the methods of appropriating myths.

For tragedy, using myths is not an optional or an ornamental element as it is for comedy, but a constitutional one. Since tragedy drew on mythology for its plots, the very word μῦθος was used to name them. Given, however, that mythology was a common material and that the tragedians aspired to win the competition, they had to differentiate themselves from their colleagues in the treatment of myths, no less than in other dramatic aspects. For instance, all the three major tragedians had an *Iphigenia* (Euripides had two), an *Ixion*, an *Oedipus* (Sophocles had two), a *Palamedes*, a *Philoctetes*, and a *Telephus*. In fact, the more popular a myth was (and the more success it had in the festivals), the more productions we are likely to find.[372] For *Oedipus*, apart from the versions by the three major tragedians, there are also versions by Achaeus, Philocles the Elder, Xenocles, Nicomachus of Athens, Meletus the Younger (*Oedipodeia*), Carcinus the Younger, Diogenes of Sinope, Theodectes, Timocles, Lycophron (two versions), and Nicomachus of Alexandria.

This particular case sheds light on a joke by Aristophanes. In *Ecclesiazusae*, if Praxagora's sexual legislation comes into effect, then there is a fear that γῆν ἅπασαν Οἰδιπόδων ἐμπλήσετε (1042). This joke has been always interpreted within its intra-dramatic context: if young men have to sleep with old women, and if children do not know who their parents are, as Praxagora suggests, then there is a chance of incest between boys and their mothers. For the fourth-century Athenian audience, however, the joke would also have a metatheatrical semiology: how many *Oedipus* productions can this stage afford? On a broader scope, we can fairly imagine the Athenians in the theatre or in the agora comparing the various versions of the same myth they would have watched over the years, or indeed during the same festival, and sometimes arguing about their preferences. The surprise effect in the treatment of a myth must have been an important factor in judging the tragedies, either positively or negatively, and therefore an important consideration on the dramatists' part.

Even though there is only scanty evidence for the treatment of the myth of Agamemnon between Homer and Aeschylus, it appears that *Agamemnon* invests significantly in surprise, especially on the level of characterisation. The focus on

---

[372] Aeschylus' *Oedipus* already won the first prize in 467 BC City Dionysia, in a tetralogy comprising *Laius, Oedipus, Seven against Thebes*, and the satyr play *Sphinx*. The rule might not always hold: for example no post-Sophoclean *Electra* is known – but we do have post-Euripidean *Oresteses* (by Euripides II and the comedians Alexis and Sopater) which probably featured Electras.

Clytemnestra, her presentation as a capable ruler and a hurt wife and mother, the emphasis on Agamemnon's wrongs, and the downplayed role of Aegisthus must represent a surprising departure from tradition.[373] In the prologue of Sophocles' *Ajax*, Odysseus appears to know part of the traditional version of the myth, that Ajax has killed the animals and herdsmen and he is mystified. The explanation given by Athena, however, is not what the audience would traditionally expect, i.e. that Ajax had gone mad due to his defeat in the adjudication, but that he was plotting against the Greek Leaders.[374] Odysseus is clearly surprised by this revelation (44) and so must have been the audience. In Euripides' *Phoenissae*, contrary to the audience's expectations – created from previous treatments of the myth – Polynices is not an unjust, blood-thirsty, terrifying warrior, but a positively described character who makes a wary entrance.[375] In the lost *Oedipus* by Euripides, Oedipus is overpowered and forcibly blinded by the servants of Laius, instead of blinding himself (fr. 541).

Identifying appropriations requires that we know the preceding treatments of the myths.[376] The invention of Helen's ghost and Iphigenia's rescuing the sacrifice would have been credited to Euripides, if we did not have earlier testimonies by Stesichorus and *Cypria*, respectively. But with most other cases we are not so lucky.

> Was Euripides the first to have Medea deliberately kill her children? Had the motif of the wresting of a soul from death been attached to the story of Admetus and Alcestis before Euripides presented Heracles bumbling into the mourning king's palace? How much had Hennione and Andromache had to do with each other before the murderous plottings of the *Andromache*?[377]

Irrespectively of the novelty of one or another case, it becomes evident that appropriating myths is a field of competition among tragedies, no less than a means of comedy to antagonise tragedy as a whole.

The consequent question is how comedy differs from tragedy in appropriating myths. Such an investigation exceeds the scope of this book, which is not comparative – but some initial thoughts might be useful. The first and most obvious difference is the range of the 'incoming' material. Tragedy deals exclusively

---

373 Bednarowski 2015, 181–4.
374 Heath/Okell 2007, 366.
375 Lamari 2010, 49–50.
376 For more examples, see Sommerstein 2005 and Anderson 2005, 130–4.
377 McDermott 1991, 123. Her proposal is that when Euripides was consciously making innovations to received myth, he also had his characters signal those innovations through double meaning.

with mythology in the narrow sense (the deeds of gods and heroes found in the epics), whereas comedy is equally, or more dependent upon non-heroic folktales, fables, and legends. As for the techniques employed, a seminal observation deriving from our extended analysis on Aristophanes and the few, aforementioned examples from tragedy, is that in tragedy the attempted surprise effect is centred on the plot and the characters, whereas in comedy it is centred on language (vulgarisation, parody) and the visual outcome (beetles instead of horses, wine sacks instead of babies, ballots instead of oars, and so on). Last but not least is an observation by Aristotle, regarding the degree of appropriation; criticising the tragedians who exceed the limits, he says (*Poet.* 1453a35):

> It is suitable to comedy, not to tragedy, if the worst enemies in the story, like Orestes and Aegisthus, should become friends and go off without anybody being killed by anybody.

No matter how innovative and surprising a tragic myth may be, its structure and its ethos remain unquestionable; and if they are questioned, then the entire tragedy is no longer treated as such and bears the 'stigma' of a tragicomedy. Comedy on the other hand knows no such limitations: the more impossible, i.e. the less κατὰ τὸ εἰκὸς ἢ τὸ ἀναγκαῖον, the better. In that sense, poetologically speaking, tragedy promotes reform whereas comedy promotes revolution.[378]

---

[378] These political terms have passed into literary theory. For Eco 1976, 19–21, 'reformative' literature – with romance novel being the most characteristic genre – denounces the atrocious contradictions of society (think of *Notre-Dame de Paris* or *Les Misérables*) but at the same time offers consolatory solutions, whereas 'revolutionary' literature (Balzac, Proust, Joyce) entails everlasting problematisation and the solution rests upon the free will of each reader. Under this definition, Eco is right to classify Greek tragedy to the latter category. Here, however, I use the terms 'reform' and 'revolution' very differently: to denote the relation of a play with literary tradition, rather than with social reality.

3 Theatrical Surprise

In what follows, the term 'theatrical' is used to refer to all of the non-textual aspects of a performance. Clearly, this definition is used only for convenience, since comic and tragic texts are theatrical *ipso facto*: they are scripts. In other words, the non-textual aspects are sometimes – and to varying degrees – incorporated into the texts. That said, here I consider as 'theatrical' the following aspects of any given play: (a) the theatrical space, setting, and machines; (b) the costumes, masks, and props; (c) the actors' entrances, exits, kinesiology and gestures; and (d) music, singing, and dancing.

Examples of surprising incidents in Aristophanes, which scholars have pointed out in the respective areas, are: (a) *Birds* 264 ff: Euelpides looks upwards for the birds to arrive, but the chorus fills the orchestra, below the actors' level;[379] *Clouds* 218 ff: we expected Socrates to roll out on the *ekkyklēma*, instead of swinging from the crane, along the lines of 'Euripides' in *Acharnians*;[380] (b) *Knights* 1321–34: the rejuvenation of Demos is wholly unexpected and paradoxical, employing a change of mask and costume which depicts a young man, but signifying a nostalgic shift to the glorious past of Marathon.[381] (c) *Peace* 1315: Trygaeus invites the chorus to attend the wedding feast and they – according to Sommerstein – do in fact eat some of the offerings – a *hapax* practice in Greek theatre;[382] (d) *Frogs* 1370–77: the stanza builds up and then breaks away from the expected pattern of alternation between resolved and unresolved metra, and culminates in an 'ithyphallic' clausula, which is unusual for trochees;[383] *Wasps* 1518–37: in the context of a discussion of dancing in tragedy, unexpectedly, Philocleon and the three sons of Carcinus dance the comic *kordax*, instead of the stately *emmeleia*.[384]

Defining what can be considered to be a theatrical surprise entails three essential problems. The first is that the audience (any audience) displays various responses to a single performance. Even when the entire cavea laughs at the same moment, not everyone laughs for the same reasons. What is surprising for one can be trite for another, and yet both may still laugh. Certainly, the same subjectivity applies to the reading of the texts. But whereas the texts are fixed and

---

379 Slater 2002, 137.
380 Brown 2008, 358.
381 Revermann 2006, 120–1.
382 Sommerstein 1984, 148, 152 n. 36; Slater 2002, 130.
383 Parker 1997, 26–7. 'Generally, surprise effects produced by the disruption of common rhythms belong to sophisticated, not to popular poetry', *ibid*. 295.
384 Dale 1968, 209; MacCary 1979, 142.

https://doi.org/10.1515/9783110677034-004

known to us – hence some consensus between our readings is possible – the (ancient) performances are not recorded, and this is the second problem.

Our knowledge of theatrical practice is fragmentary, based on textual evidence (scripts, treatises, inscriptions, scholia) and archaeological evidence (theatrical venues, vase paintings, terracotta miniatures, masks, reliefs). The gaps, however, are incomparably greater than our knowledge; even some very essential questions about performances remain unanswered. In which theatre were the dramas of the Lenaea performed? Did women play some mute roles or even attend the theatre? Did all comic male roles bear a phallus? What did the *proagōn* include? The list could expand over multiple pages and, as a matter of fact, 'moderate speculation' is often the best solution in order to address such questions. This is not to say that a survey of the theatrical aspect is trivial. On the contrary, emphasis is to be put on the fallacy of such biases. Texts are fragmentary too; even with extant plays, like the eleven Aristophanic comedies, our textual readings are often informed by speculation – speculation over what Old Comedy was in general; over what Aristophanes' rivals might have written on the basis of fragments; of what a 'typical' Aristophanic comedy was, etc. The texts themselves are based on some speculation, such as the attribution of lines to characters, deletions, and *variae lectiones*. Consequently, if one is allowed to make textual speculation, he ought not be apologetic about dealing with stagecraft as well. In both cases, it is methodology that makes speculation tenable. Revermann sets out three criteria, or better three stages, for assessing theatrical speculation: any proposal is to be discarded if it can be disproved by the scripts we have. The proposals that have not been discarded at first need to be examined within the theatrical codes (to the extent to which we can reconstruct them); if a character is said to weep, for example, a realistic rendering of weeping is precluded by the use of masks. Finally, one needs to outline all available options and explain their preference.[385] As a matter of fact, the latter is precisely what a textual critic does as well.

The third problem is the concept of surprise itself, with reference to the comic stage. If, for the textual and thematic surprise, we had to resort to logic and intertexts in order to identify their subversion, what should we employ to speak of theatrical surprise? What is the point of reference for the audience's horizon of scenic expectations? Our first guide is obviously the text: what we are told to expect versus what we eventually get. Words and actions, says Revermann, can be identical to each other, complementary, or contradictory. But, whereas Revermann brings examples from Aristophanes for the first two categories, he claims that in Greek drama there is no obvious instance where a character is doing the

---

385 Revermann 2006, 63–4.

opposite of what is being said.[386] A few pages later, however, he repeats a well noted counterexample from tragedy: Orestes in *Choephoroi* says that he will speak like a Phocian (564) but he never does.[387] Undoubtedly, such occasions are not plentiful. This is not necessarily because what is written in the script *must* have happened on stage (an assumption which is often taken as an axiom)[388] but also because the poet may simply be *unconcerned* about referring verbally to what the spectators can see,[389] or *intentionally* avoids preoccupying the audience with what is going to happen on stage. Surprise is not only reversing what has been heralded, but also presenting something totally 'out of the blue'.

A secondary enquiry in search of theatrical surprise is whether, when (in what contexts), and how Aristophanes deviates from the theatrical conventions. Here we find ourselves between Scylla and Charybdis. On the one hand, it seems arbitrary to judge the theatrical practices of comedy on the basis of the theatrical conventions of tragedy. The most characteristic example is the parabasis, the 'breaking of the theatrical illusion': its absence in tragedy does not make its presence in comedy a surprise.[390] On the other hand, we have almost no evidence for the theatrical practices of contemporary comic poets, and therefore we may slip into circular arguments, forming judgements through comparing Aristophanes to himself. For instance, if it was Aristophanes who introduced the fourth and/or fifth actor,[391] then it would certainly have been a surprise for the audience to watch, for the first time ever, the stage getting more and more crowded, like a small orchestra. However, we cannot tell who the pioneer was. Despite both forms of comparison – with tragedy and with Aristophanes himself – being misleading, the former is less so. The regulations and the programme of the festivals marked a clear-cut distinction, and even the festivals themselves had an almost specialist reputation: the Dionysia for tragic contests and the Lenaea for comic ones. Nonetheless, the common aspects of the two genres – at least on a superficial level – are more essential than the differences: the context was the same (the venues, the occasions), the technical means (the crane, the platform) and limitations (the daylight, the use of masks) were common. We should also consider that

---

386 Revermann 2006, 47–8.
387 For Dover 1987, 240 this occasion is not surprising, because in tragedy, by convention, heroes coming from all over the Greece and from abroad, as well as the gods, speak Attic. Surprising or not, it is still a contradiction to what has been heralded.
388 Taplin 1977, 28–39; he acknowledges, however, that in comedy the rule is less rigid (31 n. 1).
389 Poe 2000, 259.
390 Sifakis' claim (1971, 7–14) that there was no 'illusion' at all in Old Comedy has been rejected.
391 Only *Knights* and *Wealth* can be performed without a fourth actor, while *Clouds* and *Acharnians* appear to require five; Csapo/Slater 1995, 222. See the table in Dearden 1976, 96–100.

the Athenians were more exposed to tragedy; during the Peloponnesian War, they attended three times more tragedies (9) than comedies (3) in the Dionysia, and one tragedy more (4) than comedies (3) in Lenaea.[392] Therefore, it is not arbitrary to assume that *some* expectations about the tragic stage were transferred onto the comic stage – after all, it was the same stage.

The third method is to resort to recorded modern performances of Aristophanic plays, and to trace moments of theatrical surprise on the basis of the audience's responses or our own responses. That the conditions of modern performances and the expectations of modern audiences are fundamentally different from those of the ancient performances and audiences is unquestionable. But still, modern performances provide us with *a gauge of the surprising dynamics* of specific scenes, or tropes. If modern directors have been tempted to invest a certain scene with visual or aural surprises, this is because the Aristophanic script provides this possibility in the first place. Naturally, as in the case with literature in general, we do not aim to prove what the poet intended, but what interpretations the text itself promotes, permits, or eliminates.

Let us take a characteristic example: the first version of Koun's historic performance of *Birds*, which generated a negative kind of surprise. Apart from many technical problems, the priest of the play (863–94) was presented as an Orthodox priest, both in terms of clothing (black robe) and of praying style (nasal accent). The audience disapproved and the government banned the performance on grounds of blasphemy.[393] A year later, the performance was reproduced with the controversial scene modified. With this incident in mind, it is easier to appreciate that Aristophanes could also have been considered 'blasphemous' by his audience in this scene – the criteria of blasphemy differing of course from those in the very conservative Greece of the 50s – had he used certain non-textual signs (e.g. profaning the Mysteries).[394] Or it is easier to imagine that a (badly received) scenic

---

[392] Defending the *communis opinio*, Storey 2002 refutes Luppe's 1972 arguments for assuming no reduction of plays during the war.

[393] 29 August 1959 at the Odeon of Herodes Atticus. See Van Steen 2000, 124–189.

[394] Cf. the reported story that Aeschylus was prosecuted for *revealing* (i.e. not even parodying?) the secrets of the Eleusinian mysteries in one or more of his plays; Arist. *Nik. Eth.* 1111a and the schol. *ad loc.*; Ael. *Var. Hist.* 5.19; Clem. *Strom.* 2.14; Murray 1940, 151. Sutton 1983 suggests that the tragedian 'represented onstage the kind of pig-sacrifice associated with the Thesmophoria and the Eleusinian mysteries, perhaps in a highly comical way'.

surprise had contributed to the failure of the first version of *Clouds*, and was abolished in the second version that we have.[395] Consulting modern performances thus becomes a means of revisiting the texts and exploring their theatrical potential in constructing a surprise effect, even when the texts *per se* are uninformative. For this method to obtain as much validity as possible, some conditions are recommended: (a) that we consult a good number of performances of the same play; (b) that we consult performances whose scripts are translations or 'moderate' adaptations of the original text; (c) that we prefer recordings of live performances with audience. In trying to decode their responses, we can assume that, even though laughter does not necessarily express surprise, a bursting-out, uncontrolled laughter (in contrast to a mild or a crescendo-ing laughter) is a very likely indicator.

The following sections correspond to the three aforementioned methods of approaching theatrical surprise. In contrast to the previous chapters, in which an exhaustive identification of the unexpected cases was attempted, here the focus is on selected scenes.

3.1 Actions Contradictory to Words

Revermann is right that there are no obvious cases in which scenic actions contradict the words of the characters, where a character says 'I will do X' and proceeds to do Z (or even – X, if a sharp contradiction is intended). But this is far from saying that *there were no* such cases at all. This would be methodologically wrong, because we cannot rely (merely) on textual evidence in order to appreciate the reversal of the text. The characters, even though they wore masks and could not make facial expressions, could nevertheless react with gestures to what happened on stage, without need to make any comment. In fact, they did not even have to react at all, and it could be left for the audience to notice the paradox themselves. This is precisely what happens with 'aside jokes'. These are short ironic comments which a character interpolates when another character speaks, supposedly said *sotto voce* in order for the latter not to listen; they remain nonetheless perfectly audible to the audience. The interrupted speaker does not react

---

[395] It appears, for example, that the Right and Wrong arguments were presented as fighting cocks in the first version (schol. on 889c; Dover 1968, xc–xci). This cannot have been provocative of course; the modification was rather for reasons of clarity.

to them, as if he does not even understand that he is being interrupted. But the audience does perceive these jokes.[396]

In analogy to 'aside jokes' we can reasonably accept 'aside actions'. We can define them as actions which contradict a character's words without provoking any (verbal) reactions among the other characters, but are noticed by the audience. As long as there are no textual markers for such scenic tricks however, one can only speculate. But though this be madness, yet there is method in't.[397] Maintaining that we are not talking about modern Surrealism, one cannot 'deconstruct' the text saying that every single word can be contradicted on a scenic level. The chorus of Birds was a chorus of birds, as the text emphasises in every occasion, and not a chorus of elephants (which in the case of Surrealism could very well happen, precisely because the text emphasises the opposite). Secondly, since the contradiction among words and actions was not an end in itself, it would only be employed in moments where a 'minor' comic effect would emerge, i.e. as a momentary embellishment which does not ruin the cohesion of the play. In the same way that excessive aside jokes create an impression of tackiness,[398] excessive aside actions would be viewed as equally distasteful.

The concept of 'actions contradictory to words' does not essentially refute Taplin's principle that 'we should allow *significance* only to those actions which are sanctioned by the words'.[399] Indeed, significant actions are in line with the text, but in a comedy not everything is a significant action. Taplin himself produces an example from *Wealth*: someone knocks on Chremylus' door but when Carion comes to open no one is there; then Hermes appears and Carion asks him if he was the one who knocked, but the god denies it and says that he was just *about to* knock (1097–101). Despite what Hermes (the text) says, there is no one else who could have knocked on the door. The only possible explanation is that Hermes had entered from the beginning, knocked on the door, hid, and then reappeared to have the above exchange with Carion.[400] This is indeed an insignificant incident, yet a funny one.

---

[396] See Bain 1977.
[397] This is an example of an 'aside' remark, said by Polonius for Hamlet's speaking nonsense (*Ham*. 2.2.207).
[398] See, for example, Artotrogus in *Miles Gloriosus* (Act I) and 'the inartistic asides in which he explains directly to the audience his motive – parasitic greed – and his true opinion of the soldier'; Wilner 1931, 267.
[399] Taplin 1977, 31. Italicisation is my own.
[400] Holzinger 1940 *ad loc.*; Taplin *ibid.*; Brown 2008, 370–1. The latter scholar also points out the reversal of our expectations in the fact that Hermes, the door-keeper of Olympus, is now knocking on a door himself. The reasons for Hermes' hiding and for his denial are not explicit.

A second example comes from *Birds*. The Triballian is among the representatives of the gods who have come to negotiate with Peisetairos. He does not speak Greek, but his words are intelligible to some degree: such a degree that allows Aristophanes to play with ambiguity. When asked whether he consents to give Basileia as a wife to Peisetairos, the Triballian responds: καλάνι κόραυνα καὶ μεγάλα βασιλιναῦ / ὄρνιτο παραδίδωμι (1678–9). Grammatically speaking, it is not clear whether this answer is affirmative or negative,[401] and indeed Hercules understands it as παραδοῦναι λέγει whereas Poseidon as οὐχ οὗτός γε παραδοῦναι λέγει. It is possible that the Triballian did not accompany his words with any gesture to clarify his intention (e.g. a nod to say 'yes' or jerk his head backwards to say 'no'), a scenario which would make both interpretations tenable.[402] But taking into account the characters (Poseidon being severe and Hercules a glutton) and the order they speak (Poseidon speaks second, correcting Hercules) the most likely interpretation is that the Triballian had jerked his head negatively, and Hercules deliberately misinterpreted it as an affirmative answer in order to go to the roasts faster, which is his only true concern from the beginning (1583, 1585–6, 1590). Hercules talks over the Triballian (in *antilabē*), since he knows in advance what he needs to say for his own benefit, and we can imagine Hercules nodding his head at the same moment that the Triballian is jerking his own backwards.

We have already seen two occasions for which we know from the text that a heralded action is immediately cancelled: when the in-law plans to inscribe his name on some oars, but he cannot find any (*Thesm.* 769–74); and when a celebratory sacrifice is about to happen on stage, but is reserved for backstage (*Pax* 1017–22). Another example from the latter play is when Trygaeus repeatedly asks the peasants who have come to rescue Peace to stop dancing and shouting, so as not to get caught by Polemos. They do not stop, regardless of this, for at least thirty lines (309–37), even though at some point they claim to have already stopped (327):

XO.   ἢν ἰδοὺ καὶ δὴ πέπαυμαι.
TP.   φῄς γε, παύει δ' οὐδέπω.

Presumably, he is hiding because he feels ashamed of going to a mortal to beg, and then he denies knocking on the door because Carion has just threatened to slam that noisy door (1099), which Hermes perceives as a threat to himself.
401 Dunbar 1995, 735–6.
402 In the parallel scene of Pseudartabas' responses in *Ach.* 113–4, someone felt it necessary to add the nods (ἀνανεύει/ἐπινεύει) as stage directions in the MSS text.

CHO. Here, look, I've just stopped!
TR. You say so but you don't stop at all!

If music accompanied the dancing chorus in this scene, the spectacle would resemble the children's game known as 'musical statues' or 'freeze dance'. The chorus dances around as long as the music is playing, and when Trygaeus interrupts, the music pauses and the chorus stands still, until the music starts again. One can even imagine the members of the chorus quitting the dance one by one, as in these games the players are eliminated in similar manner, until the winner is left dancing (note the singular in the last dancing act of 334–5, in contrast to the plurals before).

In *Acharnians*, when Amphitheus returns from Sparta bringing the drafts for the treaty, Dikaiopolis is greeting him before he has actually arrived (175–7):

ΔΙΚ.   ἀλλ' ἐκ Λακεδαίμονος γὰρ Ἀμφίθεος ὁδί.
        χαῖρ' Ἀμφίθεε.
ΑΜΦ.   μήπω γε πρίν γ' ἂν στῶ τρέχων·
        δεῖ γάρ με φεύγοντ' ἐκφυγεῖν Ἀχαρνέας.

DIK. Amphitheus from Sparta is now here. Welcome, Amphitheus!
AMP. Not till I've stopped running! I have to outrun the Acharnians!

Dikaiopolis utters his greeting as soon as Amphitheus enters from the *parodos*; although he is rushing, it will take him some time to become visible to the audience and reach the *skēnē*,[403] hence he calls Dikaiopolis to not greet him yet. This withholding of expectations can be read as a meta-theatrical, self-sarcastic comment. Even though comedy denies realistic spatio-temporal rules (Amphitheus leaves for Sparta, and returns from it, within only 4 lines; 133–74) and even though Amphitheus is 'a god on both sides' (47–8), he implicitly complains that it is impossible to annihilate time, and protests against the physical strains placed upon comic actors.[404]

In *Clouds*, when Strepsiades wants to ask about the progress of his son, he knocks at the door of the Thinkery and shouts παῖ, ἠμί, παῖ, παῖ (1145). In analogy to his first visit to the Thinkery, when he had knocked at the door shouting παῖ, παιδίον (132) and a student of Socrates had appeared, we now expect a student to

---
[403] It is not clear whether the Acharnians who are chasing him are imaginary (who supposedly follow him and do not appear on stage) or real members of the chorus (who confront him in his way towards the *skēnē*). In the latter case (a parody of obstacle racing), it would take Amphitheus more time to reach Dikaiopolis.
[404] Indeed, the reason for hurrying is pragmatic, since the specific actor had to change roles multiple times; see Marshall 1997, 79.

answer the door again. Now, however, Socrates himself answers the door. Dover is right that it would be dramaturgically inconvenient and time-wasting to have a similar scene here,[405] since nothing has changed in Socrates' appearance that would require suspension. But then, why does Strepsiades not simply call Socrates by his name, as he has actually done in a previous occasion (866–7: Δεῦρο δεῦρ' ὦ Σώκρατες, ἔξελθ·)? More than just an 'accelerated and compressed doorkeeper scene',[406] this scene can be viewed as an intentional contradiction of what is heralded: we expect to see a young boy and we see Socrates. And even though Socrates was not old at the time (forty-five years old in 423 BC, when *Clouds I was staged), his ugliness would not have been rendered very differently from portrayals of the elderly.

Conceivably, there were similar occasions of 'withholding the expectations' which are nevertheless not marked as such in the text itself. In the quasi-parabasis of *Lysistrata*, the semichorus of old men strips off, and so does the semichorus of old women in response, as indication of their hostility to each other (perhaps in the model of wrestlers). Only when they are reconciled do they dress themselves again.[407] The text offers us no information about the visual rendering of that nudity, but it is unlikely that Aristophanes missed this opportunity to ridicule the bodies of the elderly. First, the men say that they should throw their clothes off in order to show the women that they 'have balls' (661; a timeless metaphor for bravery), and having awareness of their age, they conclude (669–70):

νῦν δεῖ νῦν ἀνηβῆσαι πάλιν κἀναπτερῶσαι
πᾶν τὸ σῶμα κἀποσείσασθαι τὸ γῆρας τόδε.

Now we must rejuvenate and give wing to
our whole bodies and slough off this skin.

A very funny but not very plausible scenic rendering is to accept the 'rejuvenating' process, taking κἀναπτερῶσαι very literally: instead of the expected leather phalluses, the actors would wear winged phalluses, which at the time were a popular theme in pottery, reliefs, and miniatures – but there are no parallels for winged phalluses on actual bodies.[408] The most possible staging, therefore, is

---

405 Dover 1968 *ad loc.*
406 Revermann 2006, 184.
407 The old women offer a coat to the old men in 1021, but we are never told when the women put on the clothes – perhaps during 889–951; Sommerstein 1990, 192.
408 The earliest phallus-bird is found on a late seventh century lekanis from Delos (inv. B 6149). In Roman religion and magic it is treated as a deity, known as Fascinus.

that the spectacle is far from threatening or impressive: once the men drop their clothes off, a body (i.e. leotard) full of wrinkles and a loose penis appear. And maybe the preceding warning that they 'have balls' is now proven to be ironically literal: with a shrunk phallus, the only thing to display are the testicles.[409]

3.2 Breaching Theatrical Conventions

Gazing at the constellations (Aesch. *Ag.* 4), the watchman is patrolling overnight on the roof of the palace, waiting for the beacon to signal the fall of Troy and Agamemnon's imminent return. Before dawn, when the stars are still shining (*Eccl.* 20, 83), Praxagora is conspiring with the other women at Pnyx, and so is Lysistrata, at the propylaea (*Lys.* 60, 72). Also before dawn (*Nub.* 2–4), Strepsiades complains about his debts and his son's indolence. And yet, all these and all other night scenes were staged under the daylight; to us, modern spectators accustomed to indoor theatres and evening performances with light effects, this incongruity would be (if we could somehow time-travel to the cavea of the Theatre of Dionysus in antiquity) surprising, ambiguous, problematic, or even disturbing; in any case, something particularly noticeable. But for the audience of the time it was nothing but a convention. A real surprise for them would be to be called to attend the theatre in the evening. This is the case for the males acting female roles as well; for all actors wearing masks; for extravagant gestures; or for the stage effects being non-illusory – not only the ropes of the crane, but the entire construction was visible. Even if *we* find something inherently paradoxical in such practices, for the ancients they were the norm, to which they paid little or no attention.[410]

So what kind of 'conventions' are we talking about, and what kind of breaching of them? It is necessary to distinguish between conventions in the sense of basic elements of theatrical grammar (e.g. the above-mentioned examples) from the looser use of the term to denote traditional but optional elements of scenic business. It is mostly the latter group of conventions that allow for innovation, and therefore open a window for surprise; such practices are the appropriation of

---

[409] Similarly, Peisetairos' bragging θαυμάζειν ὅπως / οὕτω γέρων ὢν στύομαι τριέμβολον ('*It is amazing how, though I am old, I've a hard-on for three rammings!*', *Av.* 1255–6) is not necessarily reflected in his costume.

[410] And yet, Aristophanes sometimes manages to create a surprise effect out of such 'unescapable' conventions, without breaching them. In *Eq.* 498–9, for example, the chorus complains '*See how he [=Cleon] keeps up his boundless brazenness without even changing his usual colour!*', as if the mask could ever change colour. Cleon is *technically* incapable of feeling ashamed.

the theatrical machinery and of the standardised repertoire of body language, which are discussed in the following sections. In the introduction to this chapter it has been argued that a comparison with the theatrical practices of tragedy enables a plausible survey, or at least something more plausible than comparing Aristophanes with the lost plays by other comic poets, or to himself. Besides, if we were to adopt the latter method, the spare evidence would rather advocate against Aristophanes' originality. In the (reworked) parabasis of the *Clouds*, the poet claims that his comedy is superior to that of others, because it does not deign to follow some of the scenic conventions (538–43):

> οὐδὲν ἦλθε ῥαψαμένη σκύτινον καθειμένον,
> ἐρυθρὸν ἐξ ἄκρου, παχύ, τοῖς παιδίοις ἵν' ᾖ γέλως·
> οὐδ' ἔσκωψεν τοὺς φαλακρούς, οὐδὲ κόρδαχ' εἵλκυσεν,
> οὐδὲ πρεσβύτης ὁ λέγων τἄπη τῇ βακτηρίᾳ
> τύπτει τὸν παρόντ', ἀφανίζων πονηρὰ σκώμματα,
> οὐδ' εἰσῇξε δᾆδας ἔχουσ' οὐδ' "ἰοὺ ἰού" βοᾷ,

> She didn't come with a red, thick, dangling leather stitched to her to make the children laugh; nor did she mock the bald, nor dance a *kordax*; nor does an old man beats his interlocutor with his stick in order to distract attention from his bad jokes; nor did she dash across the stage brandishing torches and yelling "ow ow".

But as a matter of fact, Aristophanes exploits all these kinds of slapstick in his comedies. In *Ach.* 158, for instance, the Odomantians (Thracian soldiers) appear with hanging circumcised phalluses.[411] In *Vesp.* 1518–37, Philocleon and Carcinus' sons dance the *kordax*.[412] In *Lys.* 356–7, the chorus of old men threaten to hit the women with their crooks and, in *Nub.* 1297–1300, Strepsiades bludgeons the creditor Ameinias. In *Lys.* 382, the old men attack the women with lit torches and do exclaim οἴμοι once they are drenched. Finally, in the end of *Clouds*, the arson of the Thinkery, and the students and Socrates' cries (1493, 1497, 1504) prove Aristophanes' claims to be notoriously untrue.[413] As for his claim that he is not making fun of the bald, Sommerstein maintains that this is hardly surprising, since Aristophanes was bald himself (*Eq.* 550; *Pax* 771–4). But in fact, when not referring to *his own* baldness, Aristophanes is not so sympathetic with the bald in general. Carion, for example, introduces Wealth as ῥυπῶντα, κυφόν, ἄθλιον, ῥυσόν,

---

411 See Dover 1987, 293–4.
412 See p. 129 n. 384.
413 Dover 1968 *ad loc.*, Sommerstein 1982 *ad loc.*, Zimmermann 2014, 156. This is the only non-celebratory ending of a comedy and was part of the revision of *Clouds*. See Revermann 2006, 226–8.

μαδῶντα, νωδόν ('*grubby, hunched, miserable, shrivelled, losing hair, toothless*') and we can see a hanging circumcised phallus again (*Plut.* 266–7). Therefore, if there is something surprising here, it is not the breach of 'trite' conventions of comedy, but the false claim that such a breach is taking place.

As a consequence, comparison with tragedy appears to be a more promising approach in investigating the poetics of surprise. Joe Park Poe has discussed the characters' entries and the use of props from this standpoint. In tragedy, the departures and arrivals of actors are moments of high expectation, at least in the sense that the spectators acknowledge an intention behind them. Aristophanes violates this dramatic norm, inserting into his plays plenty of occasions where entries and exits do not serve the overall plot. For example, he presents mutes who enter and leave the stage without any motive, or characters who exit and return within the same scene repeatedly.[414] Whereas in tragedy exiting actors depart at a slow pace accompanied by lyric parts, Aristophanes often eliminates this time. For example, in *Av.* 1336–410 three episodes succeed one another in haste, with each of the characters (Parricide, Cinesias, Sycophant) entering before the preceding character has properly left. The audience is thus surprised by a new entry before their expectation for an exit is fulfilled.[415]

As for props, the main difference between comedy and tragedy is not the nature of the objects. A clear-cut attribution of homely, everyday objects to comedy and of heroic, extraordinary objects to tragedy is obviously invalid. For example, the cloth which Clytemnestra orders to be laid for her beloved husband has been identified with various textiles (a carpet, a blanket, a garment, a tapestry), but in any case it is a textile that comes from the domestic sphere, regardless of how luxurious it may be.[416] If the difference does not lie in the nature of the props themselves, it should be sought in the expectations raised by their use. Tragic props have dramatic importance and bear symbolism: the red carpet leading to the interior of the palace renders Agamemnon's path to a bloody death, for instance. But comedy very often employs objects which are of no use, even if they briefly become the centre of dramatic activity. The spectators, Poe suggests, recognise this technique and therefore harbour no expectation that the incoming object will advance the plot.[417] This last assertion is doubtful, because comedy

---

[414] Poe 2000, 277–82.
[415] Poe 1999, 200–1.
[416] A bridal cloth would have been versatile enough to serve all these functions; McNeil 2005, with further bibliography on each interpretation (n. 2).
[417] Poe 2000, 286. For props in both genres, see English 1999; 2000; 2007; Raeburn 2000; Taplin 2003, 56–74; Revermann 2013; 2006, 203–5, 244–6; Diamantakou 2007, 245–53; Chaston 2010; Konstan 2013; Tordoff 2013; Mueller 2016.

also features props that promote the plot (such as the setting up of the court in *Wasps*), hence the audience can hardly avoid having their expectations raised at any point.

3.2.1 Scenic Effects

Another illuminating yet overlooked aspect of comparison is the main theatrical machinery, the *ekkyklēma* (platform) and the *mēchanē* (crane). (I am not concerned here with the various technical questions, such as where exactly the devices were placed, how they operated, what their capacity was, or where they emerged from, because these conditions were common in both tragedy and comedy). One first needs to consider the certain and the possible uses of these devices in Aristophanes. The distinction between 'certain' and 'possible' hinges on whether there is clear *deixis* in the text (i.e. technical terminology) or some less clear evidence which nevertheless makes the use of the devices a tenable scenario (there are various degrees of plausibility). The instances when the crane was certainly used are Trygaeus' riding the dung-beetle (ὦ μηχανοποιὲ, *Pax* 173), Socrates' appearance in a hanging basket (οὑπὶ τῆς κρεμάθρας, *Nub.* 218; cf. Plato, *Ap.* 19c3), and two cases in fragments.

Daedalus fr. 192: ὁ μηχανοποιὸς ὁπότε βούλει τὸν τροχὸν
ἐᾶν †κἀνεκάς† λέγε, χαῖρε φέγγος ἡλίου

Crane operator, when you decide to pull the gear
and lift me up, say 'O blessed the light of the sun!'

Gerytades fr. 160: περιάγειν ἐχρῆν | τὸν μηχανοποιὸν ὡς τάχιστα τὴν κράδην

The operator should have deployed the crane faster.

The instances when the crane might have been used are Iris' invasion of Cloudcuckooland (ποῖ ποῖ πέτει; *Av.* 1198) and Euripides' masquerade as Perseus (διὰ μέσου γὰρ αἰθέρος, *Thesm.* 1099). The platform was certainly used to show the interior of Euripides' house (ἐκκυκλήσομαι, *Ach.* 408) as well Agathon's house (οὗτος οὑκκυκλούμενος, *Thesm.* 96), as well as to carry Paphlagon inside after being defeated by the Sausage-Seller (κυλίνδετ' εἴσω τόνδε τὸν δυσδαίμονα, *Eq.* 1249).[418] It was possibly used to bear Strepsiades' and Pheidippides' beds in the

---

[418] It is not clear, however, at which point the platform comes out. See Sommerstein 1980, 53–4.

opening scene of *Clouds*,[419] to show the interior of the 'Thinkery' (ἄνοιγ' ἄνοιγ' ἀνύσας τὸ φροντιστήριον, *Nub.* 181; cf. Σ184), to present the statue of the rescued Peace (*Pax* 517),[420] and to host the entire *agōn* between Aeschylus and Euripides (*Ran.* 830 ff.)[421] In *Thesm.* 276, the Ravenna manuscript preserves the stage direction τὸ ἱερὸν ὠθεῖται, according to which the sanctuary of Thesmophoria is rolled out on the platform, to mark that the action has now moved from Agathon's house to the venue of the festival. The proposal that Charon's boat (*Ran.* 182) could have been conveyed with the *ekkyklēma* is the least plausible.[422] The most popular and scenically elaborate solution is the boat being dragged across the orchestra with ropes or pulled by the chorus of frogs, assuming that they were visible.[423]

Wasps, *Lysistrata*, *Ecclesiazusae* and *Wealth* seem to not feature either device. One might have reservations about *Wasps*, despite the commentators' consensus, because the scene in which Philocleon tries to escape from the window fastened with a rope (379, 397) might have exploited the crane, instead of a mere rope, given that the machine could provide vertical motion in addition to horizontal.[424] To return to the *communis opinio* however, one can account for the lack of the theatrical machinery in those plays not for 'practical' reasons, like the unfounded assumption that there was no crane available at the Lenaeon theatre,[425] but dramatic ones. In *Wasps*, the lack of crane and platform accords with the general concept of Philocleon's entrapment: he has no means of escape. In *Lysistrata*, their absence is in line with the enclosure in the Parthenon: women are not allowed to break the strike – despite the efforts of some of them (719 ff). Another dramatic explanation is that these two plays are the most extravagant in terms of filling the stage with props (setting up the court in *Wasps*, and preparing Myrrhine's bed in *Lysistrata*). Therefore, these plays do not need the crane or the platform to create spectacle. As for *Ecclesiazusae* and *Wealth*, the last extant 'old'

---

419 Revermann 2006, 182, with further bibliography in the footnotes.
420 Webster 1956, 19; Dale 1957, 210–11; Newiger 1965, 236–7; Dearden 1976, 62–4.
421 Both the throne of Pluton and the contestable throne of tragedy would feature on the platform (*Ran.* 765). Schmid 1920; Dearden 1976, 69–70; Sommerstein 1996 *ad loc.* Dover 1993 *ad loc.* argues against it.
422 Dearden 1976, 69. Even though he assumes that the boat would have been presented broadside on rather than *en face*, which is a fair hypothesis according to the depictions of boats in pottery, he does not address the most obvious objection: that the *ekkyklēma* moves forward, not sideward.
423 For the debate, see p. 88 n. 226.
424 Chondros 2004, 92.
425 Russo 1994, 3. Be that as it may, Aristophanes' plays were produced at a time when Lenaea also took place at Dionysus' theatre.

comedies, we may assume that 'the trend' of using the devices had by now – the early fourth century BC – faded. Indeed, the fragmentary evidence from middle comedy supports this assumption, at least as far as the crane is concerned: Antiphanes makes fun of the tragedians for abusing the crane (fr. 189.13–16), which suggests that contemporary comedians had abandoned that technique.

Turning to tragedy, we cannot speak of 'certain' uses of the machinery in the sense of the text embodying technical vocabulary, since tragedy avoids metatheatrical references. We only have possible uses, for some of which the consensus of scholars (and sometimes evidence from vase paintings) has led us to believe in their certainty. Nonetheless, even the chariot of the Sun in *Medea*, a widely accepted case for the use of the crane,[426] is in fact questionable: Aristotle's testimony comes a century after the initial performance,[427] and vase iconography only suggests that the chariot appeared on a higher level – presumably placed on the roof of the *skēnē*, and not hung from the crane. The entrances of Oceanus in *Prometheus*,[428] of Iris and Lysa in *Heracles*,[429] of Thetis in *Andromache*,[430] of Perseus in *Andromeda*,[431] of Dioscuri in *Helen*,[432] of Bellerophon in the homonymous tragedy,[433] of the Muse in *Rhesus*,[434] and many other entrances of deities and heroes may have well employed the crane.[435] It is certain that the chorus in *Prometheus* could not have appeared on [or have been suspended from?] the crane as the scholia maintain,[436] because of the enormous load-durability that would be required. As for the most plausible employments of the platform, in *Choephori* ἀνοίγεται ἡ σκηνὴ καὶ ἐπὶ ἐκκυκλήματος ὁρᾶται τὰ σώματα, Orestes standing beside the corpses of Clytemnestra and Aegisthos.[437] Whether that was also the case

---

426 Eur. *Med.* 1317. See Cunningham 1954; Mastronarde 1990, 264–6.
427 Arist. *Poet.* 1454b.
428 τί χρῆμα λεύσσω; (Aesch. *PV* 298–9) verbalises Prometheus' surprise, since he could not have expressed it with gestures, being chained to the rock. See Taplin 1977, 262–5.
429 Eur. *HF* 817. See Lee 1982.
430 Eur. *Andr.* 1226–30. See Stevens 1971, 241–2.
431 Eur. fr. 124; Pollux iv 128. See Hourmouziades 1965, 154.
432 Eur. *Hel.* 1665. See Burian 2007, 290–1.
433 Eur. fr. 308; Pollux iv 128.
434 *Rhes.* 886–8. See Fries 2014, 440.
435 For a detailed list, see Mastronarde 1990, 280–9.
436 Schol. 128a: ταῦτα δέ φασιν διὰ μηχανῆς ἀεροδονούμεναι.
437 Schol. 973. Garvie 1986, lii–liii.

in *Agamemnon* 1372, with Clytemnestra standing on the *ekkyklēma* over Agamemnon's and Cassandra's corpses, is less clear.[438] Amongst more clear cases, Ajax is presented sitting alongside the slaughtered sheep;[439] Phaedra's corpse is revealed;[440] Hercules is tied to a pillar, surrounded by the corpses of his wife and children;[441] Amphion and Zethus ambush Lykos supposedly inside a cave.[442]

Before focussing on how surprise is constructed in the use of these devices, a preliminary disclaimer is necessary: I do not intend to argue that all occurrences of the crane and the platform by Aristophanes are unexpected. For instance, the rescuing of Peace on the *ekkyklēma* does follow the conventions: the platform represents an interior space (a cave, like in *Antiope*), and the event presented on it is both crucial to the plot, and imposing as a spectacle.[443] Conversely, I do not aim to argue that the employment of the machinery by the tragedians was never surprising, or less surprising than it is in Aristophanes. To take some aforementioned examples, the scholiast in *Ajax* (*ad* 346a) evaluates that:

ἐνταῦθα ἐκκύκλημά τι γίνεται, ἵνα φανῇ ἐν μέσοις ὁ Αἴας τοῖς ποιμνίοις.
εἰς ἔκπληξιν γὰρ φέρει καὶ ταῦτα τὸν θεατήν, τὰ ἐν τῇ ὄψει περιπαθέστερα.

At this point the ekkyklēma is used, showing Ajax in the midst of the flock.
And this is a surprise for the spectator, a most pathetic spectacle.

The scholiast does not make clear why exactly he considers this spectacle surprising. It cannot be the slaughter itself or the bloody sword that the killer holds, because this is precisely what the platform normally revealed (cf. *Choephori*). The

---

438 No clue is given in the scholia; Fraenkel 1950, 644 avoids taking a position; Taplin 1977, 325–7 hesitantly denies the platform; Raeburn/Thomas 2011, xlvi, 213 are certain about its employment. Also, in *Eumenides* 64, the scholia speak of στραφέντα μηχανήματα which reveal Orestes holding his bloody sword and Erinyes guarding him in a circle. Some revolving panels must be implied here, rather the *ekkyklēma* – contrary to Sommerstein 1989, 33, 93. See Taplin 1977, 369–74.
439 Soph. *Aj.* 344–53, with schol. on 346.
440 Eur. *Hipp.* 808–10, with Barrett 1964 *ad* 811.
441 Eur. *HF* 1029–38, with Bond 1981 *ad* 1028 ff.
442 Eur. *Antiope* fr. 223. 47–63, with Csapo/Slater 1995, 61.
443 If it is true that Aristophanes τὸ τῆς εἰρήνης κολοσσικὸν ἐξῆρεν ἄγαλμα and that he was ridiculed for this by his colleagues (schol. on Pl. *Ap.* 19c), then we may assume that there was something surprising – even though the meaning of κολοσσικὸν is not clear. At any rate, the surprise would lie with the statue and not the use of the *ekkyklēma*. See Taplin 2014, 66–8.

extraordinary element here is that the victims are animals and not humans: a theatrical disorder coordinated with the mental disorder of Ajax.[444] In the exodus of *Medea*, when Jason listens to what Medea has done to their children (1306–11) and urged by the chorus (1313), he asks for the doors of the palace to be opened to see the corpses (1314–6). Both the eyes of Jason and the audience are focused on the doors – note the accumulation of 'door vocabulary': πύλας ἀνοίξας, χαλᾶτε κλῇδας, ἐκλύεθ' ἁρμούς, κινεῖς κἀναμοχλεύεις πύλας – and everything suggests that we will have the *ekkyklēma* coming out. To everyone's surprise, Medea appears on the crane. From the status of a murderer (if she were to appear on the platform), she has been elevated – quite literally – to the status of a goddess, which also has a surprising semiology: are we to suppose that Medea is justified?

The preceding overview allows us to imagine what was considered conventional (i.e. expected) in tragedy, with respect to the crane and the platform. Furthermore, as I have advocated earlier, such expectations were transferred to the audience's responses to comedies as well. Regardless of how sceptical one might be about any single case, we can still deduce the essential patterns: (a) the crane carries gods or heroes; (b) the platform reveals what is supposed to happen indoors; (c) both devices are used in moments of dramatic tension, usually at its peak. These principles have always been acknowledged by scholars, but are often 'pigeonholed' to readings of individual cases. If we keep them in mind as a point of reference, it is easier to appreciate their paradoxical reverse in Aristophanes – or indeed, in the tragedians.[445]

Take the *ekkyklēma* in *Knights* for example, one of the 'certain' cases. As we said, Paphlagon collapses on it and retreats into the *skēnē* (1249). But when does the platform first come out? According to Dearden, the platform appears already in 751 and represents the Pnyx, where the debate between Paphlagon and the Sausage-Seller supposedly takes place, or according to Sommerstein's opinion the platform only appears *ad hoc*, to receive the collapsing Paphlagon after he has lost the debate; in both cases we have a surprising reversal of conventions. In the former scenario, the platform represents an outdoors and public space, whereas the convention is that it represents an interior and private space, while in the second scenario, the platform does not represent *any* space, but merely

---

[444] Whether the tableau featured actual dead animals or representations of them, either facsimiles or paintings, is unclear. See Ley 1988, 90.

[445] For an overview on the machinery in both genres, see Taplin 1977, 442–7; Newiger 1989. His most interesting remark, relevant to our discussion, is that we should not preclude the use of the crane at any time this is not announced, because the epiphany of a god via the *mēchanē* is supposed to be a surprise for the *dramatis personae* (rather than for the audience); 179–80. Dioscuri in *Helen* is such a case.

becomes a 'coffin' for Paphlagon. His symbolic, 'political' death on the *ekkyklēma* could be paralleled with the exposure of the corpses of Agamemnon and Cassandra, of Clytemnestra and Aegisthos, of Hercules' children, and many others, on the platform. Even bearing that in mind, the 'intention' of the platform/coffin is the opposite in either case: in tragedy it brings us face to face with horror, where in comedy it relieves us from the parasite.

As for the *ekkyklēma* in *Acharnians*, Mastromarco (1983) makes a weak case that the entrance of Euripides on it entails a surprise, in the sense that the spectators would have expected the tragedian to appear 'upstairs' (on a balcony mounted on the platform?) but instead he appears on the lower level, sitting 'upside down' on a sofa. This case is based on the supposed ambiguity of ἀναβάδην (to mean 'upstairs' in 399, but 'with the feet upwards' in 410), which is allegedly the source of the ancient scholiast's confusion. Judging, however, from the only other instance of ἀναβάδην, the word just meant 'with the feet upwards'.[446] Therefore, that Euripides lies on the sofa with his feet pointing up – no matter how unusual it may be – is not surprising, precisely because it has been announced. Moreover, it seems unlikely that Euripides' position has any sexual connotations.[447] The text itself explains that Euripides' position is responsible for him composing lame characters (οὐκ ἐτὸς χωλοὺς ποιεῖς, 411), not open-legged women.

Leaving aside Euripides' position and focussing on the use of the *ekkyklēma* itself, we can appreciate how this scene, as well as the relevant scene with Agathon in *Thesmophoriazusae*, breaches the conventional use of the platform. By 'conventional' I mean its use in the tragic theatre, and to forestall any objections which may maintain that Aristophanes may simply follow the comic conventions instead of breaching the tragic ones, one should remember that these two specific scenes are paratragic, i.e. that tragedy is the *deliberate* measure of comparison. The audience is invited not only to compare the *dramatis personae* Euripides and Agathon to the real Euripides and Agathon, but also to compare the parodied theatrical practices of the former group against the actual theatrical practices of the latter group. From this perspective, what *is* in line with the conventions of tragedy is the spatial semiology of the platform, i.e. the fact that it is used to reveal an interior space. In fact, I believe that the role of this alignment is precisely to make

---

446 νυνὶ δὲ πεινῶν ἀναβάδην ἀναπαύομαι, *Plut.* 1123. Reversing the mostly clear meaning of this line, Mastromarco borrows van Leeuwen's impossible interpretation that ἀναβάδην is heaven.
447 Ruck 1975, 21: '*anabaden* means «with an erection» or at least in some sexual position'. Such (over)interpretations are rather a symptom of confusing Euripides' persona with that of Agathon in *Thesmophoriazusae* (151–2), and with Aeschylus' accusations against Euripides in *Frogs* (1045–7).

us recall our expectations from tragic theatre, so that any later misalignment becomes more evident. There is, however, a slight disparity in the spatial semiology: we could say that in tragedy, *we* are virtually transferred to the interior of the *skēnē* to witness personal deeds and sufferings, whereas in comedy the *skēnē* is transferred in front of us. With the *ekkyklēma* in tragedy, the public sphere invades the domestic life; with the *ekkyklēma* in comedy, domestic life invades the public sphere. Even with Paphlagon's appearance on the platform – to which someone might object that it holds nothing individualistic/domestic, but instead is purely political/public – we should not forget that both Paphlagon and the Sausage-Seller are domestic slaves in the household of Demos.

However, the true breaching of conventions does not lie in the spatial semiology but in the dramatic function of the platform. Instead of presenting great deeds and sufferings, it brings us face-to-face with the most trivial things (rags, pots, radishes, arse-searing). Instead of serving a dramatic climax, it rather serves an anticlimax. This is not, however, to say that the audience of a comedy would have expected to watch corpses on the *ekkyklēma* even within a paratragic scene, but rather it is to suggest that they were not even seeing something 'important' in terms of the comic plot. In *Acharnians*, the scene with the platform comes after Dikaiopolis has threatened to kill the charcoal basket and put his own head to the chopping block, and before he delivers his controversial speech to the Assembly. Between two moments of high tension, the *ekkyklēma* only appears to offer a break. In fact, if we were to use realism as a criterion, the entire scene is useless for the progress of the plot, since Dikaiopolis is not concealing his identity with Euripides' rags; he is merely trying to raise sympathy, and even there he is unsuccessful judging from the semichorus' reaction (557–9). In *Thesmophoriazusae* on the other hand, the scene with Agathon is necessary due to the in-law concealing his identity, a prerequisite for the progress of the plot. Once more, this is not a moment of dramatic tension; it may be a moment of tension for the poor in-law who suffers the searing, but not a moment of climax at any rate. The same with the opening scene in *Clouds*, in which the platform may have been employed to present Strepsiades and Pheidippides' bedroom. Strepsiades' emotional tension in this scene is the catalyst for the plot, but the *ekkyklēma* itself (if it was used) has totally lost its conventional dramatic value. Not only does it not appear at a peak moment but, even worse, it is already rolled-out before the play begins. Should it also have been used to reveal the Thinkery, the spectators would not have expected to watch something grandiose and solemn, but nor would they have expected to see Socrates' students studying astronomy with their rear-ends (191–4).[448]

---

448 Dover 1968 *ad* 191: γάρ perhaps verbalises a start of surprise.

Let us turn to the *mēchanē*. We have seen how our expectations for the employment of the *ekkyklēma* in *Medea* are subverted and the crane appears instead. The same trick (more or less) occurs in *Clouds*. We watch the Thinkery on the platform, and its students, and their equipment. It is therefore natural to expect Socrates, the headmaster of the Thinkery, to step onto the platform as well. Not only a natural expectation, but this is also what the text prepares us for. When Strepsiades had asked for 'the doors to be opened' (i.e. for the *ekkyklēma* to be rolled out), he explicitly expected to see Socrates: ἄνοιγ' ἄνοιγ' ἀνύσας τὸ φροντιστήριον | καὶ δεῖξον ὡς τάχιστά μοι τὸν Σωκράτη ('*Go open the Thinkery and show me Socrates as soon as possible*' 181–2). But some thirty lines later, when the platform has been established in our visual consciousness as the main dramatic space, Socrates suddenly appears with the crane. Russo claims that Socrates' aerial entrance was intended as an *unheralded* surprise.[449] In fact, it is not unheralded, but *heralded* to happen from the platform, leading to a double surprise.

The surprise effect of Trygaeus' riding the dung-beetle has already been discussed from a mythical perspective. Focussing on the function of the crane itself, we can also spot some unexpected elements, apart from the metatheatrical reference to the crane operator. The crane seems to have been traditionally used for transporting actors on a horizontal axis and with a steady movement, as one can assume from the common expression used for the characters appearing with it, 'to cross the air'. On the contrary, the crane is here moving on the vertical axis (the beetle lowers itself as it smells shit, 157–8) and is unbalanced. In *Bellerophon*, which is the explicit intertext of this scene, even though we know that the tragic hero eventually fell, there is actually nothing in the surviving fragments (frr. 306–9) to suggest that Pegasus' flight involved undulations. Since according to myth the cause of Bellerophon's fall occurred suddenly,[450] it is almost certain that Pegasus' taking off was steady. It is also quite certain that the fall was not presented, because according to myth, only Bellerophon fell and Pegasus completed the flight to Olympus; the actor, however, could not have jumped from the crane.[451] Therefore, Trygaeus' wavy journey was a rare spectacle, if not a *hapax*. This naturally is also owed to the dung-beetle itself as a prop attached to the crane.[452] How large or small,

---

[449] Russo 1994, 117–8. Italicisation is my own.
[450] Either from fear or from giddiness, or being thrown off by Pegasus, who was rendered furious by a gad-fly which Zeus had sent. Pind. *I.* 7.44; *O.* 13. 92; schol. on Pind. *O.* 13.130; Hygin. *Poet. Astr.* 2.18.
[451] Moreover, Ar. *Ach.* 427 maintains that Bellerophon appeared crippled, which means that the actor would have needed some time backstage to arrange his outfit.
[452] The wobbly journey envisaged here only requires a rotating crane, not one with high load-capacity; even a large dung-beetle prop can be a very light construction.

how realistic or artificial, how lovable or monstrous could its appearance have been? Was it fixed, or did it have moving parts, such as its wings or jaws? Any option and combination of those (and other) qualities is possible and all of them have the potential for surprise. Since the text is not informative on such aspects, modern performances can always help us appreciate this potential for surprise.

Fig. 5: Christoforos Nezer as Trygaeus on the dung-beetle in *Peace* directed by Alexis Solomos for the Greek National Theatre, 1964. Photograph by Dimitris Harissiadis, Benaki Museum. The anonymous critic of *Ακρόπολις* newspaper (23/07/1964) spoke of 'acrobatics with helicopter-beetles' and 'barbarous surprises in the costumes and the setting'.

3.2.2 Body Language

In *Knights* 169–75, the servant Demosthenes invites the Sausage-Seller to look far and wide, at islands, harbours, and boats; and then asks him to direct his right-eye sight towards Caria, and his left-eye sight towards Carthage. The Sausage-Seller complains διαστραφήσομαι, which either means that he will twist his neck, or turn cross-eyed. Given the actual orientation of the Theatre of Dionysus, if the actor is facing the audience when saying these lines, he is looking north. Therefore, Caria is on his right side and Carthage on his left, precisely as he is directed to turn each of his eyes. But if the actor has turned his back to the audience, looking south, then he is expected to look left with his right eye (at Caria) and look right with his left eye (at Carthage). Both options have their theatrical advantages, and hence are equally plausible. In the former option, the audience is invited to stare at the actor, trying to see through the holes of his mask. In the latter option, the actor can render his 'visual chiasmus' by crossing his hands above his head.[453] In *Birds* 174–7, the Hoopoe also exclaims διαστραφήσομαι, when Peisetairos asks him to inspect the place where the birds shall build a new city, looking down, then upwards, and then sideways; the Hoopoe can only see clouds and the sky.[454]

In their commentaries, scholars have always cited these passages as similia, and Dunbar also points out their interpretative similarity: in both cases, the characters look at far-off areas which, it is alleged, are about to become their empire.[455] What has been overlooked, however, is the paratragic tone of this head movement. In the parodos of *Oedipus at Colonus*, the chorus enters in search of the person who has entered the sanctuary of Eumenides (117–22):

> ὅρα. τίς ἄρ' ἦν; ποῦ ναίει;
> ποῦ κυρεῖ ἐκτόπιος συθεὶς ὁ πάντων,
> ὁ πάντων ἀκορέστατος;
> προσδέρκου, προσφθέγγου,
> προσπεύθου πανταχᾷ.

---

[453] Sommerstein 1981 *ad loc.* takes for granted that the actor faced the audience, on the assumption that the right eye must be looking right, and the left eye must be looking left.
[454] The Hoopoe sees the clouds and the sky when he looks *upward*, because the dramatic space is still the ground level. It is not clear when the transition to the clouds happens, but this is certainly after 264 (κέχηνά γ' ἐς τὸν οὐρανὸν βλέπων) and before 817–8 (ἐντευθενὶ | ἐκ τῶν νεφελῶν καὶ τῶν μετεώρων χωρίων). On the fluidity of dramatic space in Ar. see Lowe 2006.
[455] Dunbar 2005 *ad loc.*

> Look! Who was he, then? Where is he? Where has he rushed to out of the way, the man most impudent of all, of all? Look, speak out, enquire everywhere!

The staccato singing, the alliteration of π, the anadiplosis ὁ πάντων / ὁ πάντων, and the accumulation of προσ-compounds provide the necessary signals for the actors to know when to turn their heads in a synchronised manner. The multiple rhythmical breaks indicate that the chorus is indeed looking everywhere around, for it would be ridiculous to watch them turning their heads only towards their left or right repetitively.

In the prologue of *Iphigenia in Tauris*, Orestes and his friend Pylades are entering the stage in search of a statue of Artemis, which they have to take back to Athens, as Apollo has ordered. Since the mission must remain secret (83), Orestes warns Pylades (68–9):

> ΟΡ. ὅρα, φυλάσσου μή τις ἐν στίβῳ βροτῶν.
> ΠΥΛ. ὁρῶ, σκοποῦμαι δ' ὄμμα πανταχῇ στρέφων.
>
> OR. Look carefully to see whether there is anyone on the path.
> PYL. I'm looking, casting my glance in all directions.

What they see in the temple of Artemis are walls dyed with the blood of the Greeks (72–3), along with their skulls, which are hanging from the entablature (74–5). Thus, Pylades is speaking literally when he says ὄμμα πανταχῇ στρέφων, since the two men are turning their heads both on the horizontal axis (noticing the walls) and on the vertical axis (noticing the entablature). Despite the atrocious spectacle, they must continue looking around, Pylades repeats: ἀλλ' ἐγκυκλοῦντ' ὀφθαλμὸν εὖ σκοπεῖν χρεών (76).

In the first episode of *Phoinissai*, Polynices is hesitantly entering the stage (representing Thebes) in fear of an ambush. Thus, he says to himself (265–6):

> ὧν οὕνεκ' ὄμμα πανταχῇ διοιστέον
> κἀκεῖσε καὶ τὸ δεῦρο, μὴ δόλος τις ᾖ.
>
> For this reason I must turn my eyes this way and that for fear of trickery.

Κἀκεῖσε καὶ τὸ δεῦρο suggests that he is looking only on a horizontal axis, but he might have also looked above, because of suspicion that they might try to trap him with a net (263) which could be thrown from the roof of the *skēnē*.

In the third stasimon of *Orestes*, Electra is keeping watch in front of the palace while Orestes and Pylades are plotting to kill Helen inside. Electra divides the chorus into two parts – setting them in front of each of the parodoi (1258–60) – and instructs them to keep watching with her (1261–7):

HΛ. Δόχμιά νυν κόρας διάφερ' ὀμμάτων.
XO. Ἐκεῖθεν ἐνθάδ' εἶτα πάλιν σκοπιὰν
ἔχομεν, ὡς θροεῖς.
HΛ. Ἑλίσσετέ νυν βλέφαρον,
κόρας διάδοτε πάνται διὰ βοστρύχων.

EL. Sideways turn the glance of your eyes.
CH. From that side to this and then back again
we turn our watchful gaze, as you command.
EL. Wheel your eyes about, turn your glance
in all directions through the locks of your hair.

Both semichoruses are looking both left and right, and not just towards their respective parodos. *'Turn and look everywhere, through your hair'* simply means 'even at the edges of your field of vision'.[456] Here, for instance, their gazing is only on the horizontal axis.

We can now appreciate better the head movements in Aristophanes' passages, as a deviation from the conventional pattern. First, it must be clarified that all the aforementioned tragic passages come from plays subsequent to *Knights* and *Birds*, hence Aristophanes cannot be parodying them. However, the similarities among them (for example πανταχᾷ/πανταχῇ/πανταχῇ/πάνται in the four passages respectively) suggest that there was a pattern established already, of which Aristophanes was aware. With this precaution in mind, we can deduce that in tragedy, looking around is a means of discovering someone who is hiding (*OC*) or a means of remaining hidden from others (*IT, Phoen., Or.*). The point of reference is intra-dramatic (looking for other *dramatis personae*) where the emphasis is put on *what* is (wished to be) seen or not seen, and the purpose is to create suspense. In *Knights* and *Birds* looking around is a means of fantasising the future. The point of reference is extra-dramatic (looking up to the sky or far towards the sea from the cavea of the theatre) where the emphasis is put on the person who looks around and his complaints; there the purpose is to create visual humour. The dramatic tension of looking around in tragedy is degraded into muscle tension in comedy, and the metatheatrical implications seem inevitable: is it truly the Sausage-Seller/Hoopoe that complains to Demosthenes/Peisetairos about the physical strain, or could it be the actor speaking to the *didaskalos*?

---

456 West 1987 *ad loc.*

3.3 Consulting Modern Performances

The purpose and methodology of this survey have been outlined in the introduction to the chapter. The plays under examination in this section are *Wasps, Lysistrata*, and *Ecclesiazusae* and the performances selected are:

Tab. 2: A selection of modern productions of Aristophanic plays

Year	Director	Translator	Production
Wasps			
2006	S. Evangelatos	P. Matesis	S. Evangelatos' Amphi-Theatre
1991	E. Gabrielides	L. Zenakos	Cyprus Theatre Organisation
1977	N. Giannopoulos	T. Stavrou	Nat. Theatre of Northern Greece
Lysistrata			
2004	K. Tsianos	K. Tsianos	Greek National Theatre
1997	D. Chronopoulos	G. Varveris	Greek National Theatre
1972	A. Solomos	T. Stavrou	Greek National Theatre
Ecclesiazusae			
2015	G. Mbezos	M. Volanakis	Greek National Theatre
1996	A. Voutsinas	P. Dimitrakopoulos	Greek National Theatre
1998	S. Evangelatos	S. Evangelatos	S. Evangelatos' Amphi-Theatre

This selection has been made on the basis of the availability of recorded performances, either online or in private collections. The fact that they are all modern Greek productions, and indeed acclaimed productions, was not deliberate nor does the selection entail any bias; it is simply that these performances are more frequently archived.[457] At the same time, modern Greek productions of ancient drama are themselves part of a system of 'rivalry', of expectation, and of high self-consciousness vis-à-vis comic and cultural traditions, and it is also very common for the annual summer Athens and Epidaurus Festival to feature more than one production of the same play. This renders modern Greek productions extremely

---

457 Professor Kaiti Diamantakou kindly offered me access to the recordings of the first two performances of the list. Other acclaimed productions, which unfortunately are not recorded, are Alexis Solomos' *Wasps* (1963), Karolos Koun's *Lysistrata* (1969), and Peter Hall's *Lysistrata* (1993).

appropriate for understanding the central place of surprise and innovation within an antagonistic context.

3.3.1 Stagecraft as Meaning

To highlight the importance of stage action in the construction of surprise, I would like to begin with an example in which stage action is *complementary* to the text, and not contradictory (to follow Revermann's terminology). In such cases, performance comes to specify the meaning of the text; in other words, here a certain interpretation which is not prescribed in the text is proffered. For example, the oath to abstain from sex that Calonice takes on behalf of all women, under Lysistrata's pressure, is textually 'uncoloured'. Except for a παπαῖ ὑπολύεταί μου τὰ γόνατ' ὦ Λυσιστράτη (*'Oh god, my knees are buckling, Lysistrata!'* 215–6), Calonice is repeating Lysistrata's words of the oath verbatim. As a reader, one may find it a boring passage (very much like Echo in *Thesmophoriazusae*), because it is just the same text twice. But for a spectator, this passage is one of the most comic in the entire play. In all three performances of *Lysistrata* under examination, Calonice maintains and exaggerates her παπαῖ attitude throughout the otherwise (textually) unmarked passage.[458] She exclaims '*may I never surrender*' and '*may I never bend over*' (232) in lament, instead of determination. By contrast, she utters '*may my husband suffer from a burning erection*' (222) and '*if my husband tries to rape me against my will*' (226) in pure excitement, instead of abhorrence. Effectively, she yearns for the opposite of what she is swearing to do. But this meaning is only constructed on a theatrical level; facial expressions are essential in depicting this hilarious incongruity (Fig. 6a–b). However, even in an ancient theatre where masks were used, the intonation and the gestures could perfectly display the contrast between Calonice's moods.

---

458 Tsianos 2004 at min. 25:15; Chronopoulos 1997 at 31:30; Solomos 1972 at 13:10.

Fig. 6a–b: Mary Aroni as Lysistrata and Anna Kyriakou as Calonice in *Lysistrata* directed by A. Solomos, 1972. Screenshots from the video-recording of the performance. In the left frame Calonice says 'if he rapes me' with a big smile, while in the right frame her jaw drops when she is asked to say 'never shall I open my legs'.

Chronopoulos, owing to the witty translation of the passage, provides the funniest version of the scene. One of the tricks he uses is that Lysistrata (Katia Dandoulaki) dictates the oath, and Calonice (Eleni Gerasimidou) repeats the sentences verbatim but with an intonation which changes the meaning:

| ΛΥΣ. | Με κέφι να του κάτσω αποκλείεται. | ≈ 223 |
| ΚΑΛ. | Με κέφι να του κάτσω! Αποκλείεται; | ≈ 224 |

LYS. To put out willingly? Never!
CAL. To put out willingly! Never?

The same technique could have been applied to the original text too, and one must not forget that punctuation in the transmitted texts is only an invention by Hellenistic scholars.

Despite the incongruity between words and feelings, stage action here is complementary and not contradictory in relation to the text, as explained earlier. Indeed, the text never implies that women enjoy abstaining from sex; it is rather explicit that they really miss their husbands (99–104, 763). Therefore, this example illustrates that contradiction between the text and the action is not a necessary precondition for scenic surprise. Complementary action ('colouring' the text or 'filling in its gaps') can be an equally successful method, and it certainly is more frequent.

In *Wasps*, we know from the very beginning that Philocleon wants to escape from the house and will try all means possible (69–70, 112–3, 125–32). But *how* this plan is scenically realised is what generates surprise. In Giannopoulos' performance, the setting representing Philocleon's house is a particularly complex wooden construction, rather dissimilar to actual Athenian houses which were very simple. A one-metre-high platform rises from the orchestra, on the centre of which a two-level tower stands; there is a balcony on the left side of the tower, and a mezzanine on the right side, beneath which a storage room is formed; a staircase leads from the platform level to the mezzanine, and from there to the upper floor of the tower; three frontal doors and two lateral are available, as well as multiple ladders. Facing this labyrinth, the spectators know that the jury-addict will attempt many exits, but they do not know where to look each time. Aiming to maximise the surprise effect, the director has the actor emerging from the two furthest ends: the roof and the door on the orchestra level. Moreover, he adds some tricks that are not prescribed in the text, but they are not precluded either. According to the text, Philocleon first attempts to sneak out from the chimney *like* smoke (143–4); in the performance, there is a real explosion and smoke before the old man appears, which generate some exclamatory remarks from the cavea. A few lines later, Philocleon invokes as his excuse that he needs to go to the market to sell his donkey (169–73); in the performance, he is disguised as an old woman during this short exchange. Later on, just before he delivers his speech on the benefits of being a juror (548 f.), he breaks wind twice, and the audience breaks into laughter.

One could claim that such tricks do not necessarily entail surprise, but instead that they are simply funny. Indeed, there is nothing inherently surprising in someone breaking wind or crossdressing on the comic stage, but it is the context and the timing that attach such an effect. For example, Philocleon farts not at any random moment, but at the very moment he is least supposed to do so. From 521 onward, we see hints that a weighty debate begins: the men of the chorus will be the witnesses (521); Philocleon promises to commit suicide if he loses (523–5); Bdelycleon will keep the minutes (536–7); the chorus heaps all of *their* expectations on Philocleon (540–7). The peak of this crescendo, however, is nothing but passing wind. We may assume that the director's purpose is to imply that Philocleon's following arguments are merely 'bullshit'.

3.3.2 Mutes, Babies, Animals

Mute characters are another suitable means for conveying theatrical surprise. It is precisely their muteness that endows them with a surprising potential. More precisely, it is their muteness *in the text*, i.e. the lack of textually prescribed expectations, that enables (and challenges) the director to improvise and make them 'scenically speaking' roles. They impersonate slaves, girls, children, or animals (however, not all slaves, girls, children, or animals are mutes). There is a great deal of debate and speculation over who played these roles. For example, were mute female characters played by male actors in leotards or by real women (hetairai)?[459] Were animals played by actors as pantomime; were they represented by facsimiles; or were real animals brought on stage?[460] In such questions scholars tend to advocate one or another side, seeking what the 'rule' was, but it is equally plausible that the dramatists had all options available. They might have been able to use real women to play mutes, and still have preferred male actors in certain cases. This is established at least in the case of animals.

In the trial episode of *Wasps*, the plaintiff dog (Cydathēnaion) is obviously played by an actor, given that he has a speaking part (907–30). But what is the defendant dog Labes? For MacDowell, an actor dressed as dog comes out, whereas for Biles/Olson, Labes is represented by a real dog or a reasonable facsimile.[461] Both sides are equally dogmatic – not even mentioning the alternatives – whereas, in fact, all three options are equally possible. The commentators are also dogmatic when (in agreement with each other this time) they pronounce that the donkey beneath which Philocleon attempts to escape must be a 'pantomime' one, played by an inventively costumed mute extra, or pair of extras.[462] But it could also be – and *it is* in Giannopoulos' and Evangelatos' performances – a trolley in the shape of a donkey. As for the usual scepticism over the use of real animals on grounds of practical inconvenience, this reflects our contemporary concerns about animals in public (and indeed urban) space rather than the ancients' experiences. In the opening scene of *Frogs*, for instance, iconographic evidence suggests that a real donkey was used.[463] Especially in the case of dogs, training them when and where to enter and exit, when to sit down, or when to bark for the purposes of a performance, was anything but impractical.[464] In fact, there is iconographic evidence suggesting that real dogs were used in the ancient comic performances (e.g. vases 1402 and 36955, Museo Jatta).

---

459 See Stone 1981, 148–9; Zweig 1992; Marshall 2000; Hughes 2012, 211–4.
460 See Arnott 1959.
461 MacDowell 1971, 251; Biles/Olson 2015, 351, 362.
462 MacDowell 1971, 155; Biles/Olson 2015, 143.
463 Taplin 1993, 45–7.
464 Different kinds of dogs received much more complex training: from guarding houses and supervising the sheep (*Vesp.* 955–7; *Lys.* 1213–5; *Thesm.* 414–7), to hunting (Xen. *Cyn.*) and joining wars (Forster 1941; Cook 1952; Phillips 2001). We have no reference to guide dogs for the blind

Taking as a principle the idea that all options were available, and that none of them are inherently unexpected, one only need examine how the surprise effect is constructed in the exploitation of these options within specific contexts. In the trial scene from *Wasps*, a cup, a pestle, a cheese-grater, a brazier, a pot, and other utensils are brought in as witnesses (936–9). Of them, the cheese-grater alone is summoned to testify (963–6), and even though it has no speaking part according to the text, both Bdelycleon and Philocleon are reacting to its 'testimony', with credence (φησὶ κατακνῆσαι) or disbelief (νὴ Δί' ἀλλὰ ψεύδεται) respectively. For MacDowell, 'the most effective way of handling this passage in performance would *clearly* be to have them *all* played by mute actors. [...] The alternative is to suppose that the various objects are carried into the court by slaves, but that would make the performance, especially of 963–6, more awkward and *less effective*'.[465] Biles/Olson on the other hand, prefer the alternative case objecting that *too little is made* of the utensils' appearance to make MacDowell's suggestion likely.[466] MacDowell is probably wrong that *all* of the utensils were played by mute actors, firstly due to the cheese-grater alone having a prominent role, and secondly because the number of the utensils is large enough (καὶ τἄλλα τὰ σκεύη, 939), so that to employ a respective number of costumed actors would be a considerable expense. MacDowell is also mistaken that the use of actual utensils would be less effective.

A look at the cover illustration of Biles/Olson's commentary is the best answer: a man judging real dogs and interrogating a real cheese-grater, as if he could ever receive an answer from them, is indeed a hilarious surprise (Fig. 7). This is the case precisely because we would expect actors to play these roles. At the same time, it is untrue that *too little* is made of the utensils' appearance to have them played by mutes. Textually speaking, there is indeed nothing on their part; but their theatrical potential is far from limited. In Giannopoulos' performance, the cheese-grater *is* an actor. When it is summoned to testify, it only shouts 'ggrrr grrr ggrrr' (the actress scratches her costume) and Bdelycleon assumes the role of the interpreter (Fig. 8). The audience laughs at the incongruity of Bdelycleon understanding everything while Philocleon understands nothing, as if the latter stands outside the theatrical illusion. Finally, it is noteworthy that in Giannopoulos' performance the dogs are also played by actors, in contrast to the illustration in which the dogs depicted are actual dogs. It seems that in both

---

in ancient Greece; the first testimony for this practice is a 1st century AD mural from the House of Julia Felix, Pompeii (MANN 9059).
465 MacDowell 1971, 255. Italicisation is my own.
466 Biles/Olson 2015, 360. Italicisation is my own.

cases the artists wanted to be consistent: if the litigants are actors, then the witness should also be an actor; but should the litigants not be actors, the witness should not be either.

Fig. 7: Cover illustration by John Taylor, Biles/Olson 2015, Oxford Publishing Limited. Reproduced with permission of the Licensor through PLSclear.

Fig. 8: Gianna Kourou as the cheese-grater in *Wasps* directed by N. Giannopoulos, 1977. Screenshot from the video-recording of the performance.

Let us turn to a human figure this time: Myrrhine's baby in *Lysistrata*. The text preserves a cry μαμμία, μαμμία, μαμμία (879), but Henderson maintains that the infant was probably represented by a doll and its cries were made by Cinesias.[467] More confidently, Sommerstein pronounces that *no doubt* the 'child' was *in fact for theatrical convenience* a dummy, its voice being that of Cinesias. First, it is unclear what is 'theatrically inconvenient' about the use of a real baby. If a real baby was used and cried or even wet itself on stage, that would be most convenient for the context of the play, according to which the infant suffers neglect by its mother. Secondly, why should it be a doll and not an actor? In fact, in all three performances of *Lysistrata* examined the baby is played by an adult, leading to fairly surprising outcomes. Solomos' and Tsianos' versions are similar at this point: a mute brings on stage a wheeled cradle, which is initially covered; the covers are suddenly removed and an oversized 'baby' emerges and cries in bass voice and makes grotesque facial expressions. In Solomos' performance, the 'baby' stands up in the cradle, so that everyone can see how much taller than his father Cinesias he is (Fig. 9). In Tsianos' performance, when Myrrhine comes to breastfeed the 'baby', the latter's facial expressions, exclamations, and vigorous sucking of the breast have clear sexual connotations. The impression formed is of an actor having sex with an actress, rather of a mother feeding her son (Fig. 10). Therefore, we see that both directors invest in stretching the 'adultness' of the actor for intensifying the surprise, and indeed, the audience breaks out in laughter in both cases.

The same is true of Chronopoulos' version, which features a toddler instead of an infant – also played by an adult actor. Consequently, Myrrhine comes to feed him with a bottle, instead of her breast; the bottle is oversized, matching the toddler's physique, but also acts as a counterweight to the oversized phallus of Cinesias. Myrrhine holds the bottle upside down for the baby to drink milk, but she does not pay any attention because she is quarrelling with Cinesias. She is nervously waving her hands (and the bottle) here and there, and the toddler is desperately trying to follow her moves, with his mouth wide open in an attempt to get any drop of milk (Fig. 11). On a theatrical level, the paradox lies in the contrast between Myrrhine's expressed compassion for her child (882, 884) and her incompetence at feeding him. On a metatheatrical level, the surprise lies in the actress treating her colleague with remarkable indifference, like a mere prop.

All three cases suggest that the surprising dynamics entailed in employing an adult actor to play a baby should make us rethink (at least) the commentator's certainty that a doll was used.

---

[467] Henderson 1987 *ad loc.*; Sommerstein 1990 *ad loc.* Italicisation is my own.

Consulting Modern Performances — 161

Fig. 9: Cinesias, the baby, and a nurse in *Lysistrata* directed by A. Solomos, 1972. Photograph from the Archive of the Greek National Theatre.

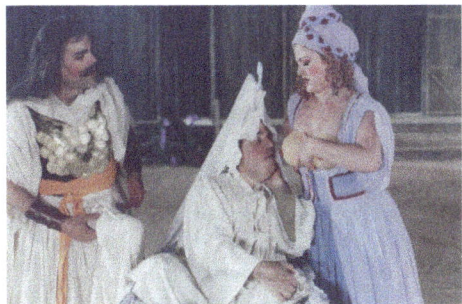

Fig. 10: Cinesias, the baby, and Myrrhine in *Lysistrata* directed by K. Tsianos, 2004. Photograph from the Archive of the Greek National Theatre.

Fig. 11: A sleeping nurse, the toddler, and Myrrhine in *Lysistrata* directed by D. Chronopoulos, 1997. Screenshot from the video-recording of the performance.

3.3.3 Accidents

A distinct category of theatrical surprise is the accidents that happen during a performance: actors falling or forgetting their lines, spectators disturbing the process, sets collapsing, costumes being torn, special effects failing to operate, even people dying. In his speech *On the Crown* 262, Demosthenes makes fun of Aeschines for (allegedly) collecting the fruit and vegetables that the audience violently threw at him while he was acting.[468] These are surprising moments not only for the audience but for the actors too, and their readiness to deal with such incidents is considered an indication of their talent. Even though such accidents are unintentional – rather undesirable – and therefore do not (normally) reflect the dynamics of the script,[469] they are still an important factor in the construction of comic effect (leaving the macabre incidents aside). Especially in the context of ancient theatre, in which technological means were poor, where the theatre of Dionysus could accommodate 14,000 to 17,000 spectators, where weather conditions, external noises, or even animals could spoil the accumulative efforts of a year, accidents would have been routine during festivals. In this respect, comedy has an important advantage in comparison to tragedy: in the former, accidents normally enhance hilarity, whereas in the latter, accidents may ruin solemnity. Chickens invading the orchestra would be a 'gift from the gods' for Aristophanes but, probably, a curse for Sophocles. Apart from any inherent hilarity in chickens, the reason is that accidents are moments of metatheatre, and metatheatre is a concept alien to tragedy.[470]

In Solomos' performance, when Lampito introduces the girl from Boeotia (86) and Lysistrata goes to take her by the hand, the protagonist trips over her dress and falls. Even though the recording is poor, we can still hear an exclamation of *oh!* from the audience. The experienced actress stands up supporting herself on her colleagues, and instead of pretending that her fall never happened, she decides to build on it. 'I told you that the orchestra is a mess and we'll crash

---

[468] The other interpretation of the passage is that Aeschines performed at the Rural Dionysia, and thus had the opportunity to steal fruit from the fields around.

[469] I say 'normally' because an actor's heart or panic attack on stage may be a result of his tension while performing a character who suffers a heart or panic attack. The most prominent example is Molière's death from a coughing fit and haemorrhage while performing *The Imaginary Invalid*.

[470] Here, I do not use 'metatheatre' in the sense of a play within a play (indeed, tragedy has such instances, like Pentheus' transvestism) but with its 'primitive' definition of referring to the extra-theatrical context: addressing the audience and the technicians, referring to the festival and the contemporary socio-political environment. See Taplin 1986.

down' she complains, and extends her leg out of her dress – in an otherwise very conservative staging with no nudity. The confident actress does on stage what the confident Lysistrata does in the play: she 'tells it like it is', and self-directs her body as a sign of protest. As for her complaint, it invites us to revisit a much-discussed passage from *Peace* in which Trygaeus warns the crane operator to be careful not to throw him down (169–76). It is possible that such an accident had actually happened to some other colleague at an earlier date (perhaps on the occasion of *Gerytades* fr. 160).

In Chronopoulos' performance, when Cinesias enters in full erection in search of his wife Myrrhine, a hilarious 'sexident' happens.[471] The erection of the husband is conveyed by the actor carrying and waving a phallus prop. At one point, however, and indeed when Cinesias boastfully says to Lysistrata '*take it if you fancy it*' (861–2), the prop falls with the 'glans' facing the floor (Fig. 12a–c). This is a total reversal of expectations, as if theatrical reality – in contrast to the 'overambitious' text – comes to remind Cinesias that in practice everyone has 'his ups and downs'. The audience bursts out laughing, the actor tries to rectify his phallus with his leg, but the prop does not balance well and falls again! Apparently, it is not Cinesias' lucky day, and Myrrhine's rejection will complete his humiliation. As with the previous example, we see that the actor insists on drawing attention to the accident, rather than discreetly skipping over it.

Fig. 12 a–c: Nikos Mbousdoukos as Cinesias, dealing with a phallus prop collapsing, in *Lysistrata* directed by D. Chronopoulos, 1997. Screenshot from the video-recording of the performance.

---

[471] Nikos Mpousdoukos as Cinesias was received as one of the most successful Cinesiases of the last decades. See Spyros Pagiatakis' review, *Η Καθημερινή*, 10 August 1997.

Given the extensive use of phalluses in Greek comedy, is seems statistically certain that similar accidents had happened, especially with elaborate uses. When for example, Reconciliation drags the Athenian and the Spartan representatives by their phalluses up to the stage (1119, 1121), or when the in-law repeatedly brings his phallus forwards and backwards from between his legs, so that it remains hidden from Cleisthenes and Mika (*Thesm.* 643–8), a detachment of the accessory would have been plausible.

In the same performance, accidents become a theme; in other words, the performance entails *pretend* accidents. When a girl faints on hearing Lysistrata's proposal to quit sex (127), someone from within the audience, an actor himself, jumps in and tries to resuscitate her; some actors pull him away saying 'she is acting!'. Later on, when Lysistrata exclaims 'If peace won't come, then dick won't come!' (≈152–4), an orthodox priest – an actor again – invades the orchestra and shouts 'Shame on you!'. In both cases the audience reacts by laughing; in the second case by clapping as well, approving in this manner Chronopoulos' clear parody of the puritanical reaction to Koun's *Birds* in 1959.[472] Chronopoulos' message is that comedy does not cede its scenic expression to censorship.

Returning to the ancient texts, an obvious case of pretend accidents (which are therefore incorporated into the text) is *Thesm.* 770–2, where the in-law tries to communicate with Euripides:

ἐκ τοῦ Παλαμήδους. ὡς ἐκεῖνος, τὰς πλάτας
ῥίψω γράφων. ἀλλ' οὐ πάρεισιν αἱ πλάται.
πόθεν οὖν γένοιντ' ἄν μοι πλάται; πόθεν;

Like Palamedes I will inscribe on oars – fuck, I have no oars!
Where could I find some oars? Where? Where?

The norm in Aristophanes is that when a character asks for a prop, this is made immediately available, usually brought in by mutes. Think for example of Myrrhine, who effortlessly finds a mattress, a mat, a pillow, a blanket, and perfume – one immediately after the other (*Lys.* 915–40). Or Philocleon, who is brought a chamber pot, a brazier with a pot on top, a rooster, a miniature of a shrine, some barriers, and a pair of vessels as ballot boxes, before he commences the trial of the dogs (*Vesp.* 805–55). But here, the in-law is desperately looking around the stage;

---

472 The scenes concerned are at 24:00 and 26:45, respectively. Chronopoulos was Koun's student and later (2004–2014) director of *Theatro Technis*. The reference to Koun's performance becomes apparent by the fact that the parodos adapts Manos Hadjidakis' renowned music for the parodos of *Birds* (19:15).

presumably, the three instances of πόθεν in 772 correspond to the in-law inspecting the orchestra and the two *paraskēnia* (where props were stored) respectively. But eventually he never finds the oars, and compromises with some tablets. It comes as a surprise for the audience who were used to an abundance of props overwhelming the stage that no props are now available as if a technical problem had prevented the bringing of the oars.[473] As with the pretend accidents in Chronopoulos' *Lysistrata*, here metatheatre and parody play a prominent part as well. In the former, metatheatre is expressed on an extra-dramatic level (a priest interrupting the performance) and the parody is political (against puritanism). Here, metatheatre is expressed on an inter-dramatic level (a prop interrupting the performance of the in-law) and the parody is literary (against Euripides). Aristophanes' message is that comedy does not cede its scenic functionality to tragedy.

3.3.4 Public Figures

Aristophanes' theatre is heavily dependent on public figures. On the one hand, there are cases in which such people explicitly become *dramatis personae*, like Lamachus in *Acharnians*, Socrates in *Clouds*, Euripides in *Acharnians*, *Thesmophoriazusae*, and *Frogs*, Agathon in *Thesmophoriazusae*, and Aeschylus in *Frogs*. On the other hand, there are cases in which a public figure provides the inspiration for a role, which is nevertheless not named after the real person, such as Paphlagon in *Knights* who caricatures Cleon.[474] The latter choice may be dictated by practical needs: if the testimony that Cleon had sued Aristophanes for his satire in *Babylonians* is true, then Aristophanes had to avoid ὀνομαστί κωμῳδεῖν.[475] In both cases, however, we are not able to fully appreciate the hilarity, simply because Cleon, Lamachus, Euripides and the rest, are not figures familiar to us on an experiential level. Again, it is modern performances that come to shed light on the dynamics of this technique.

In the 2015 production of *Ecclesiazusae* by the Greek National Theatre, the director and protagonist Giannis Mbezos conceived and embodied Praxagora as the contemporary president of the Hellenic Parliament, Zoe Konstantopoulou.

---

473 The comic logic of the episode, too, enhances that surprise: the in-law does have the appropriate means to impersonate Telephus (a knife, 692–4) and Helen (a dress, 851), so by analogy one would also expect that the oars here would be available; the expectation that the plan will eventually fail *in its execution* is another story.
474 On portrait-masks, see Dover 1967; Marshall 1999, 194–5; Olson 1999; Varakis 2010, 28–9.
475 Schol. on *Ach*. 378. In *Knights* there is only one clear mention of Cleon (976).

This became evident in Praxagora's costume which imitated the outfit of Konstantopoulou on the day Tsipras' government was sworn into office (Figs. 13–14). The latter ceremony was broadcast live on all television channels and the gossip over Konstantopoulou's stylistic choices – both in the yellow press and in acclaimed media – was disproportionate; she had definitely stolen the show (as was the case on a political level until Tsipras dismissed her a few months later). In his interview for the play, Mbezos said that he was inspired by the figure of Zoe Konstantopoulou primarily on a visual level, sarcastically commenting that his body structure is similar to hers.[476] Artistic reasons aside, we cannot deny that Konstantopoulou's publicity (and the publicity that this specific outfit of hers received) was a convenient means for Mbezos to advertise his own show. Leaving the director's intentions aside, the choice itself is theatrically justified, because Konstantopoulou is a feminist and a radical leftist like Praxagora – to the degree that such terms can be used anachronistically. There is no reason to speculate about whether Aristophanes had also portrayed his Praxagora as a contemporary female public figure. Had that been the case, however, he would undoubtedly have chosen wisely, very much like Mbezos, and not many women would have been more suitable for this than the intelligent and influential Aspasia.[477]

---

[476] G. Mbezos, interview on MegaTV channel, 25/07/2015: www.youtube.com/watch?v=L6xHWS78u60 [Accessed on 1 November 2019].

[477] Scholars have noticed the analogies between Aristophanes' heroine and Aspasia, but Vickers alone seems to accept an equation, i.e. a deliberate allusion. A good reason to be skeptical is that Aspasia was likely dead when *Ecclesiazusae* was staged, and that she was last mentioned in *Acharnians* over thirty years previously. But, on the other hand, her memory was certainly alive in fourth century comedy (in the same way that a caricature of Thatcher, for example, would work in a comedy today). Ussher 1973, 108; Rothwell 1990, 92–5; Henderson 2000, 140; Vickers 2004.

Figs. 13–14: Zoe Konstantopoulou on 27 January 2015. Photograph from *thetoc.gr* (left frame). Giannis Mbezos as Praxagora in *Ecclesiazusae* directed by himself, 2015. Photograph by Marilena Stafylidou (right frame).

The example of Mbezos' *Ecclesiazusae* underlines two important elements with regards to the comic appropriation of public figures. Firstly, that it is not only the multiple historical persons that may be caricatured, but also some very specific public appearances of them on particular occasions. It is a *communis opinio*, for instance, that the portrayal of Socrates in *Clouds* is the archetype of the arrogant empty-talking philosopher; or that Lamachus' triply-plumed and crested helmet and his gorgon-decorated shield in *Acharnians* exemplify the stock character of the boastful soldier. But we should not preclude the possibility that the real Socrates had indeed been seen philosophising on a swing, or that the real Lamachus wore a memorably ostentatious costume on a certain occasion. Mbezos appropriated the specific outfit of Zoe Konstantopoulou, not because he had no other way to portray her – in fact she is usually dressed in dark clothing – but because he already had an impressive image (in the sense that it had been impressed on the memory of his audience) which he could build upon.

Mbezos' performance also makes us appreciate that the claim that Aristophanes' comedies drew the audience's attention to public figures is a half-truth. To an equal (or a greater) extent it was the publicity that these persons already enjoyed that drew the citizens' attention to Aristophanes' plays. This is true even in *Frogs*: Aeschylus was dead long ago, but his plays were known in Aristophanes' time through re-productions.[478] And if *Frogs* has been so popular to this day, this is not only for its merits as a comedy, but also for being a pretext for studying Euripides and Aeschylus. This kind of 'promotion' is not always beneficial, whether for the persons parodied, or for the play itself. If Plato is correct that Aristophanes' *Clouds* played such an important role in the accusations against Socrates,[479] it is no less true that Socrates (the *dramatis persona*) harmed Aristophanes' *Clouds* and contributed to its failure. That might have been simply because the audience never really had such a one-sided impression about Socrates.

A last remark prompted by Mbezos' performance is on the role of the *proagōn*. Held in the Odeion from 444 BC onwards, the *proagōn* preceded the festival and was the occasion for the poet to announce his play and to introduce the actors and the chorus to the public. We do not know how much information about the plot was given out, but it clearly generated some expectations about the play. Conceivably, apart from giving the ὑπόθεσις, the dramatist would also give some hints on individual scenes or characters, in order to generate interest, but he would certainly avoid any 'spoilers' (as is the case with posters, flyers, television spots, and posts on Facebook, which are the modern equivalent of *proagōn*). Even if the audience knew in advance that they would see Socrates, Euripides, Lamachus, or an Aspasia-like Praxagora on stage, they would still experience the suspense of waiting to see how the poet portrayed these figures, both in terms of their physique and their personality. The (potential) spectators knew that Mbezos would portray his Praxagora as Zoe Konstantopoulou as seen in the media, but still they had the curiosity to see it for themselves; in fact, this is precisely why they went to watch the performance. The surprise does not lie in *whether* a public figure will appear on stage – we all expect comedy to have contemporary references – but in *how* that figure will be appropriated.

---

[478] They were enabled by a decree that was passed soon after Aeschylus' death; *Vita Aesch.* 12; schol. on *Ach.* 10.
[479] Plat. *Apol.* 19c.

3.3.5 Men as Women?

In ancient Greek theatre both male and female roles were played by male actors.[480] Often in the plays, male characters cross-dressed as women; the most prominent examples are the in-law in *Thesmophoriazusae* and Pentheus in *Bacchae* (the latter possibly imitating the former).[481] The reverse practice, however, is rare. In fact, *Ecclesiazusae* is the only play in which we have male actors (the protagonist and the members of the chorus) playing female roles (Praxagora and the other Athenian women) who are in turn disguised as men (shoemakers in particular; 385, 432).[482] Even if this was not *the first* occasion of 'female' cross-dressing in the Athenian theatre, it was certainly a hardly-paralleled spectacle and thus an unexpected one. This is why Aristophanes puts so much emphasis not only on the cross-dressing procedure (60–7, 74–5, 268–79) – which is also the case in the male characters' cross-dressing scenes – but also in the 'restoration' procedure (493–513). All disguises of characters pose a metatheatrical effect, in the sense that they present on stage what in real theatrical practice happens backstage. The cross-dressing in *Ecclesiazusae* has an extra metatheatrical intention: to surpass the gender restrictions regarding the casting; within the dramatic world, the actors are women.

On an extra-dramatic level, however, Aristophanes obeys the convention, since Praxagora and the other women are played by male actors. But even within this expected framework there is plenty of room for surprise, as Voutsinas' performance demonstrates. His Praxagora, played by Giorgos Michalakopoulos, uses an ostentatiously deep voice and restrained movements, not allowing us to concede to the illusion that he is a woman in the first place. We know that actors in antiquity trained their voice very well – with respect to its volume, pitch, and rhythm – and female roles were probably given to actors with a true tenor-range voice (rather than sung in falsetto).[483] But Aristophanes – just like Voutsinas – may have deliberately chosen a bass-voiced actor to play Praxagora, contrary to the audience's expectations, in order to sarcastically acknowledge that the Greek stage is an exclusively male world. Voice aside, the costume, the mask, and the

---

480 For a possible exception in this rule, see p. 157 n. 459.
481 See Kanellakis 2017–2018, 71–4.
482 Crates' fr. 24 from *Lamia* (ἀνδριστὶ μιμεῖσθαι φωνήν) does not necessarily require cross-dressing.
483 E.g. the actor playing Electra in Euripides' *Orestes* sung ὀξείᾳ φωνῇ (schol. *Or.* 176). See Hall 2002, 10, 23–4; Slater 1997, 101.

gestures can also contribute to such a surprisingly ambiguous effect. When Praxagora tries to excuse herself for the fact that she had borrowed her husband's coat, she claims that it was cold outside and that she is weak and thin, and so needed a heavy cloth (539). However, Michalakopoulos' body-structure (enhanced with paddings) is anything but weak and thin; and yet, the actor fondles his large waist when he utters these lines. The audience bursts into laughter with the incongruity and the 'offended' Praxagora looks askance at them. Taaffe maintains that 'in the first half of the play, gender definitions and representations are built up only to be taken apart', in the sense that 'the female characters in *Ecclesiazusae* never really become men'.[484] Voutsinas' performance, however, suggests that gender definitions and representations are *not even built up* in the first place; in his staging, Praxagora does not even pass as a woman.

That the same technique was used by Aristophanes himself is evident from Lampito's entrance in *Lysistrata*. The protagonist addresses the Spartan woman:

> ὦ φιλτάτη Λάκαινα χαῖρε Λαμπιτοῖ.
> οἷον τὸ κάλλος γλυκυτάτη σου φαίνεται.
> ὡς δ' εὐχροεῖς, ὡς δὲ σφριγᾷ τὸ σῶμά σου.   80

> Greetings, Lampito, my very dear Spartan friend! My darling, how vivid your beauty! What rosy cheeks, what firmness of physique!

And concludes:

> κἂν ταῦρον ἄγχοις.

> You could throttle a bull!

If we did not have this last line, we would not know that Lampito was presented not as feminine as γλυκυτάτη suggests. One should not assume that the characterisations in the text are a necessary condition for the actual appearance of the actors, i.e. that Lampito would not have been presented as masculine if that was not noted in the text. Theatrical practice refutes such text-centred axioms: Praxagora can be as masculine and bulky as Lampito, even without the text's 'permission'.

---

[484] Taaffe 1991, 92, 105. A Greek translation of this article, by Elena Patrikiou, was included in the brochure of Voutsinas' performance.

3.3.6 New Old Songs

Music was an extensive element in Greek drama and offered another inviting area for conveying surprise. The dramatists could (and can) appropriate popular songs, investing their music with invented lyrics that are relevant to the play; or even adapt them without changing the lyrics, should the original ones fit the context of the play. In the first case, the surprise lies in the incongruity between a familiar part (music) and an unfamiliar part (lyrics), which indeed are synchronised – contrary to *para prosdokian* jokes in which the unexpected comes as the end.[485] In the second case, when the original lyrics are maintained, the surprise lies in the audience discovering a new, comic meaning to them. The most comically successful option is possibly the 'middle ground': to change only a few words of the given lyrics, usually the concluding words of each verse. In all cases, it is important for the 'source' song to be well known, in order for the surprise to be perceived. And given that audiences include people of different ages and education, selecting a song known to everyone can be a challenging task for the dramatist.

In Evangelatos' *Ecclesiazusae*, the appropriation of a popular song plays a significant role in the moral of the performance. In the parodos of the play, the women are departing for the assembly disguised as men while singing. The song in Evangelatos' performance borrows its melody from *Περνάει ο στρατός της Ελλάδος φρουρός* – a popular march during the Greco-Italian War (1940) and well-known to the contemporary audience as well. The (new) lyrics talk about the coming of a new era where everything is communal – including sex and children – where there are no property and no bosses, and where the state provides food to everyone. Praxagora and the rest of the women are dressed in red clothes. Indeed, Praxagora as the leader of an 'army' raises a red banner which reads 'Everything public'. The same music returns in the exodus, now presenting a feast in celebration of the new era. The lyrics, the spectacle, and the ideology, however, are different. The participants, including a man who did not give his property but demands to take share in the communal goods (853–76), are sitting around a big table, plunging into the food and fighting about who will have the lion's share. They exclaim 'everything public, except for what is mine' and praise property,

---

485 Synchronisation does not mean that there is no expectation, but that the expectation (the familiar) is being summoned at the same time with its subversion (the unfamiliar), like when we encounter a stranger in the street who eerily resembles a familiar person, yet has his own individual characteristics; the combination is a surprising spectacle to us, even though we had no *previous* expectation of meeting our known person.

capitalism, investments, and money. Praxagora stands away – speechless and repulsed by the situation[486] – while a green light in the shape of a rising sun – a clear hint at PASOK – is shed upon this table of corruption.[487] Praxagora's utopian plan has been turned into a dystopia, in the same way that the political system of the Metapolitefsi (the period after the fall of the military junta of 1967–74) failed to establish a fair democratic state in Greece. That this disappointment is conveyed by a march of the Greek Resistance is a bitter surprise.

Could it be that Aristophanes too – staging this play in *ca* 392 BC – wanted to speak of failed expectations during the years following the overthrow of the 404/3 BC oligarchy? As the text stands, the only clear sign of a forthcoming dystopia in *Ecclesiazusae* is the scene with the old women forcing themselves on the young lover. Evangelatos' performance, however, comes to suggest that the finale of the play (a well-intentioned celebration *prima facie*) is also a dystopic symptom. Indeed, the abundance of food and the excessiveness entailed in the very compound word of 1169–75 (the longest attested in Greek) are a visualisation of greed, profiteering, and individualism.[488] Therefore, the end of the play marks a return to the status quo ante, preceding Praxagora's reform. That is, effectively, the real political situation in Athens about which the protagonist was complaining (206–8):

τὰ δημόσια γὰρ μισθοφοροῦντες χρήματα
ἰδίᾳ σκοπεῖσθ' ἕκαστος ὅ τι τις κερδανεῖ,
τὸ δὲ κοινὸν ὥσπερ Αἴσιμος κυλίνδεται.

---

486 In the text, Praxagora is absent in the later scenes of the play. In the finale she might have been present but mute; cf. Henderson 1987, 214–5 for Lysistrata. For Zeitlin 1999a, 82 Praxagora's absence 'is certainly not a fatal flaw. On the contrary, once she has dictated the terms of the new regime, she is no longer needed on stage'. For Fletcher 2012, her absence is justified by the fact that she had abolished law courts (657, 676), so that now there is no official agency left in the city to enforce the decree or deal with any violation. For Rothwell 1990, 61, 73–4 there is an intended semiology: that Praxagora's positive *peithō* has been replaced by the hags' brute force and self-interest. On the other end, Rothfield 1999, 223–4 suggests that Aristophanes might have just removed some scenes which initially included Praxgora, feeling that the scene with the hags was enough to ridicule communism. I follow Rothwell regarding the dystopian semiology, but I extend it until the very end of the play.
487 PASOK is the Greek 'socialist' party which dominated from the Metapolitefsi until the burst of the current financial crisis, and has been accused of populism, abuse of public money, and corrupt public administration. The emblem of the party is a green rising sun. The parallel with the festive table is a successful choice, given that PASOK's days are commonly characterised as 'το μεγάλο φαγοπότι'.
488 The linking of overeating with corruption is a commonplace in Aristophanes. Cf. the Sausage-Seller asking Paphlagon: φέρε, τί σοι δῶ καταφαγεῖν; ἐπὶ τῷ φάγοις ἥδιστ' ἄν; ἐπὶ βαλλαντίῳ; (*Eq.* 606–7).

For while drawing your civic pay from public funds, each of you angles for a personal profit.
Meanwhile the public interest flounders like Aesimus.

Evangelatos' *Wasps* entails a merry example of appropriating popular songs. To gain Philocleon's sympathy during the domestic trial, Labes the defendant dog is whimpering, while Bdelycleon is delivering a defence on his behalf (949). Labes is accused of having eaten a truckle of cheese on his own; Bdelycleon tries to excuse this and raise pity for Labes, saying: 'the poor soul is uneducated, he hasn't studied at a conservatoire' (≈ κιθαρίζειν γὰρ οὐκ ἐπίσταται, 955). Labes – who is otherwise only barking – is now uttering his only human words singing Ἀλλοθι, δεν ἔχω ἀλλοθι (*I have no alibi*). This is a variation of the popular song by Vasilis Karras Ἀλλοθι, δεν ἔχεις ἀλλοθι (*You have no alibi*) slightly altered to fit the plot. This song belongs to a certain genre of popular modern Greek music, derogatorily called *skyladika* ('dog songs'). These are cheap songs with clichéd lyrics for the amusement of the masses in night clubs, and they are called *skyladika* on the presumption that the performers are 'barking', rather than singing. In the dog-face of Labes, Evangelatos found the most appropriate way to parody this kind of music, and to offer unrestrained laughter to his audience. And it is possible that many members of the audience will still recall and laugh at this 'new interpretation' of the popular song when they listen to it, as if Karras had sung it not referring to an unfaithful girlfriend, but to a greedy dog.

It is clear that Aristophanes himself appropriated popular songs, either in order to parody the songs themselves (like Evangelatos in *Wasps*) or to satirise a person or a situation (like Evangelatos in *Ecclesiazusae*). A good example of both of these modes is found in the exodus of *Peace*, which in effect presents an 'antiphonal' use of songs. Lamachus' son sings some verses from the epic *Epigonoi* (1270–87) and then Cleonymus' son sings Archil. 5 (ἀσπίδι μὲν Σαΐων τις ἀγάλλεται, 1298–301). The former poem has a martial content, totally inappropriate for the festive occasion, whereas the latter promotes an anti-war message.

Naturally, Trygaeus welcomes neither Lamachus' son (ἀμαθές γ' εἶ καὶ κατάρατον, 1272), nor his song. He subverts the song in three stages, which work in a climactic order; first by interrupting the son's dactylic hexametres with iambic trimetres in which he is asking him to revise the content of his song (1284–5); second by completing with *antilabē* the son's ongoing hexametre (1286) offering an ironic conclusion to his verse (based on the ambiguity of θωρήσσοντο = *they armoured themselves/they got drunk*); and finally by singing entire hexametres of his own making (1288–9, 1292–3) in which he curses the child. In other words, when Trygaeus sees that he cannot change the son's mind with trimetres, he decides to play by the son's rules to defeat him, i.e. using epic form, but with iambic content.⁴⁸⁹ This strategy of Trygaeus is probably a reflection of Aristophanes' own strategy: he begins with exhortations when he is still mild, then moves to joyful parody when things become annoying, but he ends up brutally offensive when his tolerance and limits are exhausted.

As for the other child who sings Archilochus' elegy, one might expect that Trygaeus would be well-disposed towards his anti-militaristic spirit. In fact, we are told to expect a pleasant song from this child, as he is the son a wise father (1297). But we are also told, just a couple of lines above, that Cleonymus is the father of this child. Anyone in the audience who had watched an Aristophanic comedy before knew that σώφρονος πατρός was a very suspicious compliment for Cleonymus. Indeed, by listening to the first two verses of Archilochus' poem, Trygaeus suspects that the ῥίψασπις concerned is Cleonymus (1300);⁴⁹⁰ by listening to half of the following verse, he lashes out against the child (κατῄσχυνας δὲ τοκῆας, in *antilabē*), as if he was the ῥίψασπις. Whether the father is the ῥίψασπις or the son, the very fact that a two-century-old song is employed to attack a contemporary family is inherently surprising; it is a comment on what historic cowards they are. But it is still worth asking *why* there is such an attack in *Peace*, a play in which any anti-war voice should be welcome. One possible answer is to deny any special semiology; to say simply that Aristophanes would never miss an opportunity to mock Cleonymus. The other possible answer is to say that Aristophanes admits some restrictions to his plan: peace is certainly desirable, however not under any conditions, not with ῥίψασπία, i.e. not by surrendering to the Spartans.

What all these cases show is that while modern performances cannot tell us what happened on stage in the ancient performance, they offer a pointer for discarding the monolithic scenic interpretations found in traditional scholarship, a pool to draw new possible interpretations from, and a crucial tool for making a more reasoned speculation about alternative options (i.e. which option is more surprising form a technical point of view – without assuming that Aristophanes aimed for surprise in every single occasion). Not only do modern performances call for an expansion of Revermann's three-stage assessment of theatrical speculation, but also challenge its very premise that scenic action cannot contradict the script. Combining philological analysis with performance analysis help us move from axiomatic pessimism, i.e. that textual-scenic contradiction cannot be proven, to experiential optimism, i.e. that the text itself does not preclude its contradiction.

---

489 The best example for cursing in dactylic hexametre is Hippon. 128.
490 cf. *Vesp.* 15–9; pp. 98–9.

4 Brekekekex, Surprise! Surprise!

This final chapter offers a close reading of *Frogs* from the perspective of surprise. Reference will also be made to the following modern performances:

Tab. 3: Two modern productions of *Frogs*

Year	Director	Translator	Production
1998	K. Tsianos	K. Tsianos	Greek National Theatre
2013	H. Eastman	H. Eastman[491]	Cambridge Arts Theatre

The purpose is threefold: to demonstrate that verbal, thematic, and theatrical surprises cooperate in practice; to argue that failed expectations contribute to the overall 'logic' of the specific comedy, which generates a sense of futility; and to fill the gap noted by Ian Storey in his review of Mark Griffith's *Aristophanes' Frogs*: 'we need more about the physical and visual aspect of the comedy'.[492] I am not interested here in attempting a systematic connection with, or integration of, the particular applications analysed earlier (*para prosdokian* jokes, appropriation of myths, and scenic action contradictory to the script), but in highlighting the role of accumulation as a catalyst for surprise. For that purpose, the discussion takes the form of a running commentary, i.e. follows the spectators' progressive understanding and appreciation of the play. We may have approached the verbal, thematic, and theatrical aspects separately so far, but in experiencing a theatrical event it is their intersection that allows an overall (as opposed to a sporadic) effect. When combined, they can mark a play as thoroughly paradoxical. *Frogs* is such a play; it is indeed so cumulatively surprising that it can be considered a piece of primitive surrealism.

One should start with what makes *Frogs* surprising on a macroscopic level. Structurally speaking, the play is in effect two plays, with the prologue extending over the half of the comedy and with the thematic cohesion of the two parts being debatable. There have been some compelling arguments in favour of the unity of

---

[491] The triennial Cambridge Greek Play (since 1882) is performed in ancient Greek with English surtitles. The 2013 production paired abridged versions of *Prometheus* and *Frogs*. According to the director, this combination helped those who had not read Aeschylus before to gain a first impression of his poetic style in *Prometheus*, so that they could understand the parody of it in *Frogs*.
[492] Griffith 2013; Storey 2013.

https://doi.org/10.1515/9783110677034-005

the play, concentrating on the role of Dionysus. If he is presented as a buffoon in the first part and a solemn critic in the second part, these qualities simply correspond to the historical development of the cult of the god, from an alien to a much-institutionalised deity. They also portray his personal and artistic development, in the sense that he initially likes Euripides out of naivety, but once he reaches maturity, he prefers Aeschylus.[493] Dionysus' swapping of roles throughout the play could be indeed what provides unity: he plays a god (Hercules), a slave (Xanthias), a member of two choruses, a spectator, a judge, and patron of drama.[494] It could also be his contest with the frogs: Dionysus is farting more 'artistically' than the frogs are coaxing, as Aeschylus is proven to be better than Euripides later on.[495] All of these interpretations, however, speak of unity on a level of symbols rather than dramatic coherence – even a comically distorted one.

On the level of themes, scholars have noticed the surprising silence about comedy throughout the play.[496] In terms of casting, *Frogs* alone has two independent choruses (not to be confused with semi-choruses, as in *Acharnians*, *Wasps*, or *Lysistrata*), whether both were visible or not.[497] As for characterisation, it is striking how Dionysus' role is eliminated in the second part, both in terms of frequency of speaking and of comic primacy, which is now assumed by Aeschylus and Euripides. If we also examine the deities of the underworld featured in the play, we notice that Charon is a cynical but friendly ferryman (181 ff.); then Aeacus is a terrifying doorkeeper (464 ff.) and a cruel torturer (605 ff.), but also a rascal servant (743 ff.); hence one would expect Pluto – as the King of the underworld – to be the peak of this climax, an absolutely macabre figure, but in fact he is a totally colourless character.

Finally, the premise of the plot is undermined by the absence of Sophocles, which is extra-theatrically justified (since the tragedian had died so soon before the performance that a thorough revision would be impossible), but is nevertheless poorly excused within the play. As a matter of fact, the dramatists had to

---

[493] Segal 1961.
[494] Habash 2002.
[495] Wills 1969. Less convincingly, Vaio 1985 and Padilla 1992 suggest that the scene with Hercules prefigures the final choice of Aeschylus as the winner. For a review of all these theories, see Riu 1999, 129–34.
[496] Heiden 1991.
[497] In tragedy, 'subsidiary choruses' were probably used in Aeschylus' *Eumenides* (Athena's temple-staff, finale 1032–47) and *Suppliants* (Egyptians 825–65 and Argive soldiers 1034–62) and Euripides' *Hippolytus* (huntsmen 58–72) and *Suppliants* (young boys 1113). See Pickard-Cambridge 1988, 236–7; Carrière 1977; Sommerstein 2010, 24, 108–10. This may be the very reason why *Frogs*, a tragedy-themed comedy, features two choruses.

apply well in advance (χορὸν αἰτεῖν) to receive the approval of the government, and that would include the submission of a detailed summary, if not of the entire script.[498] However, it is unlikely that the audience would be aware of the procedural barriers. Sophocles' recent death was a big public affair, and it is thus inherently surprising how lightly it passes in *Frogs*, especially when at the same festival (Lenaea of 405 BC) Phrynichus' *Muses* devoted an entire encomium to the dearly departed tragedian.[499]

4.1 Prologue

The prologue of *Frogs* works as a programmatic statement about the surprising nature of the play. It opens with Dionysus entering on foot, and his slave Xanthias riding on a donkey and carrying a heavy load on his shoulder. The pressure which Xanthias feels in his stomach from this load offers an excuse for scatological jokes; but Dionysus forbids him to utter any, because such jokes are most cliché and distasteful. The impression that this comedy will not imitate that kind of humour collapses immediately, as the two collocutors give a list of scatological jokes which are not supposed to be told. The entire construction ('say neither this, nor that, nor that…') is in effect a *priamel* which remains without conclusion (20: τὸ δὲ γέλοιον οὐκ ἐρεῖ, 'won't tell the joke'). Xanthias is not allowed to say πιέζομαι ('*I am pressed tight*'), θλίβομαι ('*I am compressed*'), χεζητιῶ ('*I need to take a shit*') or ἀποπαρδήσομαι ('*I will fart it all out*'). Within this order, the latter seems anticlimactic to Sommerstein, who proposes the alternative meaning: 'a rapid and copious defaecation (here involuntary) accompanied by noisy wind'.[500] There is, however, good evidence – the obvious etymology aside – that what is meant here is just passing gas: ἀποπαρδήσομαι seems a very intentional choice (instead of *περδήσομαι or βδέσω), with the alliteration of π making the word an onomatopoeia for the action that is being described. In Tsianos' performance, the play begins with Xanthias (Petros Philippidis) asking Dionysus (Giannis Mbezos)

---

498 A passage from *Laws* suggests that the poets had to read out extracts from their plays; Pickard-Cambridge 1988, 84. The selection of plays lay with the *Eponymous archon* for the Dionysia, and with the *Basileus archon* for the Lenaea (Arist. *Ath. Pol.* 56.3; 57.1). We do not know how early the applications were made, but presumably that was at the beginning of the Athenian new year when the magistrates changed, i.e. in July (Lenaea took place in late January and Dionysia in late March).
499 fr. 32. It won the second prize after *Frogs*.
500 Sommerstein 1996 *ad loc.*

'Να ρίξω κανά χοντρό;' which can both imply a joke and a shit (cf. the English 'crack a joke/a fart').

A now lost Apulian vase probably depicted this opening scene, with reference to a reproduction of the comedy in South Italy (Fig. 15).[501] That the painter on this occasion portrayed Xanthias riding a real donkey does not preclude the possibility that a facsimile was used. I would like to argue in favour of a facsimile – not however on grounds of 'impracticality' of having a real donkey (a statement which would not do justice to the patient nature of these creatures). Xanthias complains about the load he is carrying, and Dionysus reminds him that he has offered him the donkey for his convenience, even though he, as a god, should be the one enjoying convenient transportation (21–4). Dionysus goes further in denying that Xanthias is carrying any load, arguing that since the donkey bears the rider who bears the load, then the accumulative weight burdens the donkey only and that the rider feels no pain himself. This theory sounds outrageous to Xanthias who is really suffering from pain in his shoulders (25–30), and it is a clear parody of the sophists, who were thought to blend wordplays with bad physics in order to reverse the truth. In the peak of his *non sequitur*, Dionysus asks Xanthias: '*Since you don't admit that the donkey is to your benefit, then why don't you carry the donkey?*' (30–2). Prima facie, this is just an ironic, rhetorical question; but in light of the theatrical conventions it can receive a very realistic sense: if a facsimile is used as a donkey, then Xanthias is literally asked to lift the donkey and carry it. Therefore, he is not only not unburdened by his load (which Dionysus was quibbling about), but burdened by an additional one. Such a rendering is scenically elaborate and involves multiple layers of surprise that gain in comicality. First we are surprised by the fact that the master has granted the donkey to his servant; then we are surprised by Dionysus' absurd theory; and finally we are surprised by the scenic realisation of the exact opposite of that theory. In retrospect, we are triggered to question Dionysus' expressed intentions: did he honestly provide the donkey out of charity for Xanthias, or simply because he knew that someone would have to undertake the chore of carrying the facsimile off stage?

Tsianos' performance invests heavily in the artificiality of the donkey, achieving a fairly comic result (Fig. 16). The facsimile, representing the head and body of the animal, is placed around the waist of the actor and is held with suspenders from his shoulders; the legs of the actor peep out under the facsimile and represent the legs of the donkey (two in number!). The actor 'gallops' around the orchestra, while his upper part is playing the role of Xanthias. When he and Dionysus reach the

---

501 Discussed in Taplin 1993, 45–7 and Csapo 2010, 58–61.

house of Hercules, Xanthias dismounts from the donkey (or more precisely he unfastens the suspenders and leaves the facsimile down) and addresses it with the aside apostrophe 'do not leave', as if it could, which makes the audience laugh.

Fig. 15: Apulian red-figured bell krater 375–350 BC (formerly Berlin F3046). M. Bieber, *Die Denkmaler zum Theaterwesen im Altertum*, Berlin/Leipzig 1920, pl. 80).

Fig. 16: Giannis Mbezos as Dionysus and Petros Philippidis as Xanthias in *Frogs* directed by K. Tsianos, 1998. Photograph from the Archive of the Greek National Theatre.

Dionysus is knocking on Hercules' door shouting παιδίον, παῖ, ἠμί, παῖ (37), but instead of a servant answering the door first, here Hercules emerges at once. This is not only different from what Dionysus expects but also different from what the audience knew from other plays (knocking at Euripides' house in *Acharnians*, the Thinkery in *Clouds*, Hoopoe's nest in *Birds*, Agathon's house in *Thesmophoriazusae*). What is also different is that here it is not the visitors who are surprised by the appearance of the character who comes out, but the reverse. Hercules bursts into laughter as he sees his half-brother dressed like him, in a quasi-drag-queen way. Dionysus explains the motivation behind his plan: it is the excitement (ἐξαίφνης πόθος) he felt when he read Euripides' *Andromeda* (52–5):[502]

HP.   πόθος; πόσος τις;
ΔΙΟΝ.   σμικρός, ἡλίκος Μόλων.

HER.   An excitement? How big?
DION.   Tiny, like Schwarzenegger.[503]

The *para prosdokian* comment about the size has been discussed earlier. As for the double entendre of πόθος, it resembles that of τὸ πρᾶγμα in *Lys*. 23:

ΚΑΛ.   τί τὸ πρᾶγμα; πηλίκον τι;
ΛΥΣ.   μέγα.
ΚΑΛ.   μῶν καὶ παχύ;
ΛΥΣ.   νὴ τὸν Δία καὶ παχύ.

CAL.   What is the matter? How big?
LYS.   Huge!
CAL.   Oh god, and thick?
LYS.   Thick indeed!

In Tsianos' performance, this is nicely conveyed with Dionysus saying 'Μου σηκώθηκε... πόθος μεγάλος στην καρδιά' ('What an arousal... of emotions in my soul' ≈ 53–4). The occasion on which Dionysus read *Andromeda* was when he 'boarded for Cleisthenes', i.e. when he served in the navy under his command. Hercules, however, takes this as a (homo)sexual metaphor (48–50).

Dionysus is asking what the fastest way (ὁδός: 117, 135) to death is, and Hercules suggests a series of suicide methods: hanging, poisoning, and falling. Due to his cowardice, Dionysus rejects all of them with the excuse of them being 'inconvenient' (suffocating, blood-freezing, and brain-smashing, respectively). In

---

502 See Sfyroeras 2008.
503 Molon, in the Greek text, was an actor of big size; see p. 50.

fact, these are the very qualities that make the abovementioned methods lethal; hence we understand that Dionysus does not really intend to die. In the modern performance, Hercules (Christos Mbiros) proposes an additional method, this time a literal ὀδός: 'Σα βγεις στον πηγαιμό για τη Λαμία' ('As you set out for Lamia'), an appropriation of the first line of Cavafy's *Ithaka*, with Lamia appearing *para prosdokian* for Ithaka, making the audience laugh. Dionysus replies 'Σε μια νταλίκα θες να γίνω εγώ θυσία;' ('Do you want me to become an offering to a truck?'), given that Athens-to-Lamia is one of the biggest motorways in Greece, with a notably high record of accidents. Instead of these very realistic and painful methods, Dionysus prefers a metaphorical death, by visiting the underworld through the Acherusia Lake, in the example of Hercules.

Before embarking on Charon's boat, Dionysus tries to persuade a corpse passing by to carry Xanthias' load in his coffin. The best deal that Dionysus can offer for this service is nine obols, which the corpse declines by saying ἀναβιῴην νυν πάλιν (177), a comic reversal of the formula 'better I die', in order to fit the context. The financial motivation behind this reaction seems to bear a paratragic hint:

> τί δῆτ' ἐμοὶ ζῆν κέρδος... ;
> ...κρεῖσσον γὰρ εἰσάπαξ θανεῖν
> ἢ τὰς ἀπάσας ἡμέρας πάσχειν κακῶς.
>
> What good does life do me? ...It is better to die once and for all
> than to suffer terribly all the days of my life. (Aesch. *PV* 747–51)
>
> ὅστις γὰρ ἐν πολλοῖσιν ὡς ἐγὼ κακοῖς
> ζῇ, πῶς ὅδ' οὐχὶ κατθανὼν κέρδος φέρει;
>
> For does not whoever lives among many troubles,
> as I do, gain by death? (Soph. *Ant.* 463–4)
>
> τί δέ μοι ζῆν ἔτι κέρδος;
> φεῦ φεῦ· θανάτῳ καταλυσαίμαν
> βιοτὰν στυγερὰν προλιποῦσα.
>
> What profit any longer for me in life? Ah, ah! may I find
> my rest in death and leave behind my hateful life! (Eur. *Med.* 145–7)

In such passages from tragedy, κέρδος means the emotional or moral benefits which the hero is being deprived of as long as (s)he remains alive, and therefore (s)he prefers to die. Conversely, the corpse here is more concerned with a tangible benefit – which he is being deprived of as long as he remains dead – and therefore he prefers to be resurrected. This is clearly far from praising life *per se*, like the dead Achilles does when he proclaims '*better be a worker on earth than a king in the underworld*'.[504] The dead in our case would be very content to be 'a king' (rich) in Hades, and since this is not possible, returning to earth is only a necessary evil. When discussing mythology in a previous chapter, we saw how Aristophanes differentiates himself from one tradition not by resorting to another tradition, but by creating a new one. The same applies here: the pessimistic attitude about life is not replaced by a humanistic one, but by a mercenary one. In the end, as the negotiations fail, Xanthias has to carry the load himself and meet his master at the end of the lake; he is probably waiting behind the *skēnē*, rather than walking around the orchestra, because the latter would distract the audience during the rowing episode.

Dionysus is embarking on the boat, 'misguidedly' sitting on the oar – like on a dildo – rather than by the oar (199). Charon fixes his position and informs him that their journey will be accompanied by beautiful songs, βατράχων κύκνων θαυμαστά (207). Apart from being told that what follows will be extraordinary, the very equation between frogs and swans is unexpected. The rather disturbing noise and funny (if not ugly) appearance of the former species seem irreconcilable with the elegance and alleged charming singing of the swan. Far from being stereotypes imposed through modern fairytales (like Brothers Grimm's *Frog Prince* and Hans Christian Andersen's *Ugly Duckling*), these characteristics were already acknowledged in Greek antiquity.[505] What Aristophanes attempts with this surprising parallel is possibly a hint at the swans of *Birds* (769–84), as the similarities of two passages suggest. The frogs cry βρεκεκεκὲξ κοὰξ κοάξ (*lēkythion* metre); the cry of the swans presents multiple textual problems (as for the number of the constituent syllables) but there was at least one *lēkythion* metre (τιο τιο τιοτίγξ : Coulon 772, 774, 783; Dunbar 773; Wilson 784). The frogs are singing in the lake (211, 217, 234); the swans in the river (774). The frogs are praising (ἰαχήσαμεν) Dionysus (216–7); the swans are praising (ἴαχον) Apollo (772), who also features in the song of the frogs (231–3). Both songs are musically elaborate (ξύναυλον, *Ran.* 212; συμμιγῆ, *Av.* 771) and most pleasant to the Muses (*Ran.* 229; *Av.* 783). Olympus thunders all around in response to the swans (780) and so does Dionysus, breaking wind, in response to the frogs. Of course, *Frogs* was staged nine years after *Birds*, but some modern parallels (most notably, Hadjidakis' music for Koun's *Birds*) suggest that some compositions endure in the collective theatrical memory for decades and are always open to 'musical dialogue'.

---

504 Hom. *Od.* 11. 489–91. Cf. 'Better live badly than die nicely', Eur. *IA* 1252.
505 Cf. *Eq.* 523 on the frog; Hom. *Hymn Apoll.* 1, Alcm. 1.101, Eur. *IT* 1104 on the swan.

A second possible intertext in this episode is the choral genre of *paeans*. Among other purposes, the *paean* was used in order to provide a marching pace for the army and a rowing tempo for the navy. Doric in origin and devoted to Apollo, it was sung by men accompanied by the aulos (rarely the kithara), with antiphonal elements and sometimes a single-phrase refrain (like *ie Paean!*). There is no prescribed metric form, but 'paeons' were a prominent feature, synecdochically named after the genre.[506] In this episode of *Frogs* there are indeed a chorus and an *exarchos* singing antiphonally; an aulos (212); a reference to Apollo (772); a naval and antagonistic context; and the refrain βρεκεκεκὲξ κοὰξ κοάξ. The latter is composed in 'lecythion' metre, which in fact begins with (i.e. predisposes the audience to) a 'paeon':

‿ ‿ ‿ –	‿ – ‿ –	
βρεκεκεκὲξ	+ κοὰξ κοάξ	= lecythion
fourth paeon	2 iambs	

That these intertexts come as a surprise is better understood in the modern performance, where the lyricism of the swans' song and the pomposity of the paean have been replaced with some analogous motifs. When Charon asks Dionysus to extend his hands (201), the latter does so, imitating (as he admits) Leonardo DiCaprio in the *Titanic*. The blockbuster was released only a few months before Tsianos' performance (1998) and the Greek director could not have missed the opportunity to allude to it. The joke does not go far but it was enough to make the audience laugh, not only for the reference to a contemporary work but also for the dramatic semiology of this reference. A trip to Hades is certainly not a romantic boat ride, but at the same time this is such an ironically accurate parallel, when one considers the end of the Titanic (and of the fictional character Jack). In a similar way, in the original play the song of the swans – beautiful but at the same time foretelling their death – is a surprisingly fitting intertext, since Dionysus is virtually dying by visiting the underworld. The second intertext in our modern performance, equivalent to the *paean*, is the horn of a ferry. Dionysus' intense rowing and the prolix singing of the frogs fill him with irritation (a very physical one; 236–7), until he bursts into farting. Thanks to a mechanism underneath his costume, the actor emits fumes which dim the atmosphere and repulse the frogs.

---

506 Rutherford 2001, 42–5, 58–83.

The latter are coaxing in an operatic way, singing three high fermatas, and Dionysus responds by expelling three farts, respectively, sounding like the horn of a ferry. The audience cannot stop laughing with this antiphony.[507]

What happens on a scenic level in the original play (whether the chorus is visible or just audible; whether the boat is pulled/dragged/rolled across the orchestra, or rolled out with the *ekkyklēma*;[508] whether Dionysus is actually passing gas or competes with the frogs only by accelerating his rowing pace) has generated a great deal of scholarly debate. However, the vast majority of modern performances stand in favour of the first solution in each of these questions. If modern directors would not miss the opportunity to exploit the maximum scenic potential of the script, it is unlikely that its very writer would have done otherwise.

Dionysus has now reached his destination, disembarked from the boat, and met again with Xanthias. Once more (cf. 41), the god is bragging about his bravery and wishes for a monster to appear, so that he can prove his strength (279–84). When somebody wants something, all the universe conspires in helping them to achieve it (at least in Greek comedy),[509] and so a monster does appear on the spot – or at least Xanthias says so. The common scholarly interpretation is that Xanthias is either trying to terrify his master with an imaginary monster,[510] or that he is indeed facing the Empousa but the audience cannot see her (because her successive metamorphoses would be impossible to produce).[511] More recently, Andrisano rebutted the latter reasoning and suggested that both Xanthias and the audience could see the bogie. Empousa, she argues, was played by a mute dancer who changed dancing (pantomime) styles every time that the monster transformed.[512]

The 2013 production of *Frogs* directed by Helen Eastman offers a brilliant example, close to Andrisano's idea that there must be some visual humour. In this performance, every time that the Empousa transforms, we see (through change

---

[507] According to the international navigation signals, three short blasts mean 'I am operating astern propulsion', which is indeed the case here, since the chorus of the frogs is standing behind Dionysus receiving his fumes – although this might have been a mere coincidence.
[508] See p. 142.
[509] Even episodes that seem to be a failure *prima facie*, such as Philocleon's unsuccessful attempts to escape the house or the in-law's search of oars to inscribe, are eventually surpassed with comic alternatives.
[510] Stanford 1963 *ad loc.*; Borthwick 1968, 201–2.
[511] Brown 1991, 41 n. 2; Dover 1993 *ad loc.*; Sommerstein 1996 *ad loc.*
[512] Andrisano 2007.

of lights) a different portrait mask. First, when Xanthias says that he sees a 'horrible beast' (288), a portrait of David Cameron emerges. That beast is 'a shape shifter' (289), says Xanthias, and Nick Clegg's portrait appears next to the previous one, in what is clearly a comment on their coalition (Fig. 17). Then the monster becomes 'an ox' represented by Ed Miliband; then an 'ass' represented by Nigel Farage; then 'a beautiful woman' represented by Kate Middleton and finally 'a horrible hag' represented by Camilla Parker – not a 'bitch' however, as in the original Greek text (κύων 292). The audience's laughter is unrestrained; more than just laughing with the interpolation of contemporary figures into the plot, they are laughing with the specific characterisations attributed to each one of them. In Tsianos' version on the other hand, the audience is laughing modestly in this scene and solely due to verbal signs, since Empousa remains invisible. This comparison suggests that either as a dancer or group of dancers, or as a sketch with portrait masks, or as moving tableau (περίακτοι), or as a film projection in the case of a modern production, the more present that Empousa is, the more humour it enables.

Fig. 17: Portrait masks of David Cameron and Nick Clegg as the Empousa in *Frogs* directed by H. Eastman, 2013. Screenshot from the video-recording of the performance.

4.2 First Episode

As we saw, the opening scene of the play introduces an exchange of roles between the master and the slave, on the basis of who rides the donkey. Such an exchange now becomes the main theme, already from the first lines. The master asks his slave for advice on how to knock on Aeacus' door, and the slave commands him with a bossy manner (οὐ μὴ διατρίψεις, '*don't waste time*' 462). Dionysus introduces himself as Hercules to Aeacus, who addresses him...

> ὦ βδελυρὲ κἀναίσχυντε καὶ τολμηρὲ σὺ
> καὶ μιαρὲ καὶ παμμίαρε καὶ μιαρώτατε,
>
> You disgusting, shameless, insolent scum!
> You filthy filth, the filthiest of all!

...the reason being that (the true) Hercules had seized Cerberus (465–7). This is exactly how Hermes also addressed Trygaeus, when the latter had knocked on the door of Olympus (*Pax* 182–3). Of course, sixteen entire years separate the two comedies, so it is unlikely that an allusion was intended; more likely, Aristophanes just dug out an old (successful) joke from his desk drawer. Be that as it may, for those in the audience who would remember the first instance, it would be surprisingly funny to imagine Aeacus as Hermes and, by extension, Dionysus as Trygaeus. For Hermes had insulted Trygaeus as '*a total filth*', not in any moral sense, but due to the smell associated with the dung-beetle. By analogy, it can be inferred that Aeacus now abuses Dionysus not so much for the incident with Cerberus, but because Dionysus reeks of shit. This is a very realistic possibility given his soaking in 308. The parodos has emphasised the sense of smell, which is first stimulated by the incense from the initiates' torches (314) and then by roast pork (338). Therefore, Dionysus' subsequent stink can be fairly seen (or smelled) as a natural conclusion: lighting a fire > cooking food > digesting food.

For those in the audience who would miss this intertextual scatological hint, Aristophanes immediately compensates them by presenting an onstage defecation, with Dionysus again soiling himself when faced with Aeacus' threats. In the prologue, Dionysus violated the expectation (which he had raised) that the comedy would not feature scatological jokes; now he goes even further and makes the content of such 'forbidden' jokes a reality. Admitting his action, he utters: ἐγκέχοδα· κάλει θεόν ('*I just shit myself; pray to the god*' 479). The phrase appears *para prosdokian* for ἐκκέχυται, κάλει θεόν ('it has been poured out; pray to the god'), which according to the scholia was uttered after the pouring of a libation in various ceremonies, including the Lenaea. At the same time, it is a surprise that Dionysus – a god himself – invokes another god as a witness to his 'libation'.

A moment later, he asks Xanthias to pass him a wet sponge, to apply it on his chest because he is fainting; but instead he wipes his bottom with it. '*So there you have your heart?*' Xanthias teases him. '*Well, it got scared and it sank under my belly*' Dionysus replies, appropriating the Homeric metaphor παραὶ ποσὶ κάππεσε θυμός (*Il.* 15.280). The god who was not embarrassed to admit that he soiled himself is now embarrassed to admit that he used the sponge for his arse, rather than for his heart. But eventually he admits it, when Xanthias accuses him of cowardice; the god replies that the fact that he stood upon his feet and wiped himself is a sign of bravery. This comic explanation reads as an appropriation of the traditional theme of standing upon one's feet in the battlefield.[513] The wider motif of someone defending his cowardice with silly excuses, when he has clearly made a fool of himself, is a common feature of comedy, linked to the *braggart soldier* character.[514] This motif is not attested in earlier comedy or iambic poetry, so it is likely that Aristophanes himself invented it.[515] The most elaborate instance is that of *Av.* 86–91, where Peisetairos and Euelpides vie in trying to excuse themselves for the fact that the birds which they were holding in their hands flew away. First, Peisetairos calls Euelpides a coward for *letting* his jackdaw leave. Euelpides responds '*so did you*' and Peisetairos objects that, in his case, the crown flew away *on its own*. The implied (comic) reasoning is that Peisetairos faced resistance from his bird, whereas Euelpides did not even try to secure his own. Reversing this reasoning, Euelpides accuses Peisetairos of cowardice, precisely because the latter did not *let* his bird go, i.e. he did not take any initiative at all! Both here and in the scene in *Frogs*, we observe the technique of cumulative surprise: in both cases, an absurd argument (the heart sinking under the belly – the bravery of having a bird escape) is followed by a second absurd argument (the bravery of wiping – letting a bird escape).

---

[513] Cf. ἀσφαλέως βεβηκὼς ποσσί (Archil. 114) and μηδὲ νικηθεὶς ἐν οἴκωι καταπεσὼν ὀδύρεο (Archil. 128). For the parallelism between taking a shit and fighting at war, see pp. 73–4.
[514] In Terence's *Eunuch* (770 f.), when the parasite Gnatho mocks Thraso for avoiding the vanguard and standing in the sidelines giving orders to the others, Thraso says that Pyrrhus, the great general, was applying the same method. In Shakespeare's *Henry IV, Part 1* (2.5) when Harry and Poins expose Falstaff for having run away when he encountered two robbers, Falstaff immediately finds a comic excuse for his cowardice: he claims that he had understood that Harry was one of the disguised robbers and thus did not stay to fight, because it would be inappropriate to kill the heir of the throne. In Corneille's *L' Illusion comique*, when Matamore's servant asks his master why he is hiding from his rival instead of attacking him, Matamore responds that if he made himself visible, he would have killed both the rival *and* his darling girl with his death stare.
[515] For the *braggart soldier* in the comic tradition before Aristophanes and the way that Aristophanes reworks this model in *Acharnians*, see Konstantakos 2015 and 2016 respectively.

In fear of Aeacus' threats, Dionysus forces his slave to exchange their garments, so that Xanthias may pass himself off as Hercules and thus receive all the beating. Contrary to Dionysus' expectation, a welcoming lady comes and offers food and entertainment to 'Hercules'. The god cannot allow Xanthias to appropriate these goods, so he forces him to exchange outfits again despite all of his complaints. Dionysus' argument is: *'How could you, a mortal and a slave, ever become the son of Alcmene?'* (531). To Dionysus' discomfiture, however, the motif is now reversed: an outraged hotelier and a restaurateur come to lynch 'Hercules' for not having paid his bill during his last stay. When these ladies leave the stage to fetch support, Dionysus begs Xanthias to exchange clothes one last time, but Xanthias resentfully responds: *'How could I, a mortal and a slave, ever become the son of Alcmene?'* (582–3). Dionysus manages to persuade him, by swearing *'May I perish if I ever again take these clothes from you! And may my wife, and my children, and Archedemus the bleary-eyed perish too!'* (586–8). This swearing encompasses a series of paradoxes: first, that Dionysus cannot die in any case, as he is an immortal; second, that he had no wife or children; third, the *para prosdokian* attachment of 'Archedemus the bleary-eyed' to an otherwise formulaic oath.[516] Therefore, from the four potential targets of Dionysus' curse (himself, his wife, his children, and Archedemus), only the last one is a realistic candidate for death – perhaps a desirable one.

Aeacus returns to the stage ready to punish Xanthias, who is currently dressed as Hercules, but the cunning slave is now determined to take revenge on his master. He does not deny that he is Hercules, but denies the fact that he ever seized Cerberus and urges Aeacus to torture 'his slave', that is Dionysus, as a means of interrogation (612–7).[517] Dionysus cannot stand this rebellion and reveals his true identity, but Xanthias insists that Dionysus is only a slave and that he himself is the god. The solution for Aeacus is to torture both of them, and whoever cries out of pain first shall be the slave, on the assumption that a true god would not suffer pain (637–9). Thus, the two rivals get undressed and receive Aeacus' thrashings alternately, and even though both of them suffer, they attribute their tears to irrelevant reasons. This is, once again, the motif of the *braggart soldier* excusing his failures, embodied by both Dionysus and Xanthias. Not being

---

[516] Cf. Ant. 5.11; Andoc. 1.98; Lys. 12.10; Dem. 47.70; Aeschin. 3.111. Ten years later, Lysias reports the rumour that Alcibiades, when he was a young boy, was the *erastēs* of 'Archedemus the bleary-eyed' (14.25); hence Aristophanes' description of the politician – who held a financial office in 406/5 – must have received a good laugh and been long remembered.

[517] Interrogating slaves under torture about the accusations against their owners was a real practice; Ant. 1.10; Isocr. 17.15; Dem. 37.40 and 59.124.

able to reach a conclusion, Aeacus takes both of them off stage, so that Pluto and Persephone reveal the true god (670–1). Structurally speaking, the very conception of this scene as a continuation of the previous one is inherently surprising, because the former scene was all about exchanging roles in order *not* to get beaten. Now, however, the proposed solution is to get beaten in order to stop exchanging roles.

The scene must also have presented a number of visual surprises, despite the fact that the text is (as so often) totally uninformative about this aspect. Most strikingly, there is no clue about what happens when the characters strip at Aeacus' command (641). However, it seems likely that Aristophanes would have exploited the occasion for some 'aside' stage action. Equally, we do not know from the text how exactly the alternating beatings are given; with what instrument, pace, or viewpoint for the audience. Once again, modern performances illuminate this aspect and suggest methods that Aristophanes might have utilised himself. In Tsianos' production, much emphasis is placed upon the nudity of the characters, with Dionysus and Xanthias revealing their phalluses: a tiny one and a huge one respectively. The audience is expected to laugh at the contrast of sizes, as well as the very procedure of stripping. Not having much to exhibit, Dionysus removes his pants with one blow, whereas Xanthias unfolds his 'rope' out of his pants inch by inch, until the exposed organ reaches the ground of the orchestra. This depiction is in line with the ancient Greek stereotypes (according to which a small uncircumcised penis was the ideal of male beauty and a large circumcised penis was a barbarian attribute); hence Aristophanes might have applied a similar staging. In Eastman's production, humour is based on an accumulation of props: Aeacus employs a series of imaginative instruments to torture the contestants, such as a leek, a hobby-horse, a guitar, a surfboard, a baguette, and a trident. The text seems to support the idea that the beatings are increasingly painful, since they cause a crescendo of reactions from the contestants: from not reacting at all (645, 647), they proceed to crying out (ἀτταταῖ, 649; ἰοὺ ἰού, 653; οἴμοι, 657) and finally to invoking gods (Ἄπολλον, 659; Πόσειδον, 664). Given that the masks did not allow Dionysus and Xanthias to express their pain through facial expressions, the use of successively larger instruments by Aeacus would have been a good alternative to mark the increasing force of the beatings.

4.3 Second Episode

This short episode is, in effect, a prologue to the second half of the play. Now we are finished with Dionysus' adventures and the focus shifts to the antagonism between Aeschylus and Euripides. As happens in other prologues (*Knights*,

Wasps, *Peace*), here we have two slaves explaining the premise of the plot (757 f.). In other words, this episode not only works as a prologue but it also mimics a prologue in its form, in a self-conscious way. This was probably intended as a surprise for the audience, who would start wondering what was going on: is Aristophanes starting a new play? As far as content is concerned, Aeacus announces that the poetic art of the two tragedians will be measured on the weighing-scales, leaving Xanthias astonished at this announcement (τί δέ; 797–8).[518] For Stanford, the audience is meant to be surprised too, whereas for Sommerstein the audience assumes that Aeacus is speaking metaphorically, with the surprise coming only in the fourth episode, when the weighing is enacted.[519]

4.4 Third Episode

This is the beginning of the *agōn* between the two tragedians, and judging from the text, Aristophanes seems to focus on exposing their personalities rather than on scenic humour. Indeed, the scene is abundant in rhetorical *topoi*, aiming at showing the *ēthos* and the *pathos* of the contestants: these comprise readiness to speak (860), disadvantage in speaking (866–9), praying to the gods for the success of the speech (885–94), outlining the structure of the speech (907–8), generalisations (1008–10), rhetorical questions (1010–2), and the use of *paradeigmata* (1030–6). The appearance of the contestants, however, gives the first and potentially the strongest impression. The degree of similarity between the masks of the actors and the faces of the deceased tragedians, as well as the similarity of their voices, was probably the main attraction in this episode. Aeschylus had been dead for fifty years, but the audience may have been familiar with public portraits of him.[520] In the same way that Aristophanes *stretches* the stereotypical views about the poetry of the two tragedians (presenting Aeschylus as the poet of war and bombast, and Euripides as the poet of whores and colloquial speech), he would also have exaggerated their physical and vocal features. Given, for instance, the anecdote that Euripides had a long beard and moles on his face,[521] a portrait-mask might have exaggerated these features. Such anecdotes usually draw on comedy rather than vice versa (cf. *Thesm.* 190); but we can appreciate

---

518 Stanford 1963 *ad loc.*
519 Sommerstein 1997 *ad loc.*
520 For example, Pausanias (1.22.1–2) implies that Aeschylus featured in the fifth-century painting 'Battle of Marathon' in the *Stoa Poikilē*. See Harrison 1972, 370, 375, 377–8.
521 *Vita Eur.* IA.7.

that whatever the real features of a historical person were, comedy was in a position to laugh at them.[522] In modern performances of *Frogs* these elements can be overlooked since we are not familiar with the images of the historical Aeschylus and Euripides. Some productions, however, have resorted to contemporary figures, such as the 1892 production by the Oxford University Dramatic Society, in which Euripides was clearly modelled on Oscar Wilde,[523] or the 1987 adaptation by George Pavrianos for the shadow theatre, in which Aeschylus and Euripides were presented as the composers Mikis Theodorakis and Manos Hadjidakis.[524] Both of these cases exemplify the principle of imitation through exaggeration.

In addition to visual humour there is verbal humour. When Euripides describes how he managed to heal tragic poetry, which had been suffering from oedema due to Aeschylus' bombast, Dionysus interjects (944):

> ΕΥΡ.   εἶτ' ἀνέτρεφον μονῳδίαις –
> ΔΙΟΝ.   Κηφισοφῶντα μιγνύς.

Here I follow Hall and Geldart's edition, as opposed to other editions where there is no *antilabē* and the entire phrase is attributed to Euripides.[525] Firstly because it makes no sense that Euripides himself would reveal the 'scandal', and second, because the wider passage (up to 958) is full of *antilabai*. According to Stanford, this interjection is only a 'cheap gibe', pointing at the rumours (created by Aristophanes himself) that Cephisophon was involved with Euripides' work, as well as with his wife. Μείγνυμι has indeed sexual connotations, but not exclusively. It is also a verb which describes the preparation of ointments for the cure of patients (cf. *Plut.* 719). Therefore, far from being a 'cheap gibe', this interjection is an aside *para prosdokian* which wittily builds upon the medical terminology of the wider passage, extending it to another semiotic sphere, that of obscenity. In English, this double entendre could be translated as:

> EUR.   Then I started treating the monodies...
> DION.   ...by applying Cephisophon's cream.

Euripides proceeds to pride himself for having made the characters of his tragedies explain their origin (τὸ γένος) from the very beginning (πρώτιστα), for the

---

522 Other famous anecdotes are Demosthenes' stuttering (Plut. *Dem.* 11; Cic. *Orat.* 1.61.260–1), Pericles' oversized skull (Plut. *Per.* 3; 13), and Plato's breadth of eloquence or breadth of forehead (Diog. Laert. 3.4).
523 See Wrigley 2007.
524 See Kanellakis 2018, 165–6.
525 Wilson, Henderson, Dover, Coulon–Daele. The *antilabē* was proposed by von Velsen 1881.

clarity of the plot. A well-disposed interlocutor might respond: 'Well, that was better than to explain it *later*'. Instead, Aeschylus or Dionysus – the attribution is again problematic – responds: '*Well, that was better than to explain* your *origin*' (947).[526]

The peak of mockery against Euripides comes in the *pnigos* (971–91). The tragedian claims that with his dramas he taught the audience how to be insightful, and to always investigate how, and why, things happen. Dionysus replies ironically: '*Indeed now the Athenians go home and interrogate their servants "Where is the pot? Who ate the herring? Where is the garlic from yesterday? Who nibbled my olive?"*' The content of the mockery (i.e. that Euripides' tragedy is a mishmash of trivial everyday matters) is not something new. For that reason, Aristophanes reserves it for the *pnigos*, in order to ensure that it will still have a comic effect. The accumulation of alliteration (e.g. πῶς τοῦτ' ἔχει; | ποῦ μοι τοδί; τίς τόδ' ἔλαβεν; 978–9) and successive long words (e.g. ἀβελτερώτατοι | κεχηνότες Μαμμάκυθοι, 989–90) in a *pnigos* creates a tongue-twister, the tackling of which (even deliberately on the actor's part) is laughable in its own right.

4.5 Fourth Episode

Disproportionately to its small size, the flask has generated enormous scholarship with regard to the ληκύθιον ἀπώλεσεν interjection which Aeschylus ironically attaches to Euripides' prologues (1198–247).[527] Is it a phrase of unimportant content which becomes humorous only through its constant repetition (cf. λαβὲ τὸ βιβλίον in *Av.* 974–89), or is it a meaningful comment expressing poetic criticism? And if so, what is the criticism implied: that Euripides' prologues are all the same, or that they are cheap? Is ληκύθιον a metaphor for a phallus as it has been often argued, or not? Does the joke remain on a verbal level, or is there something happening on stage? There is no reason to repeat here all the possibilities and the arguments (they are nicely summarised in Sommerstein's and Dover's commentaries); we shall content ourselves with only proposing an additional possibility: that *frog-shaped* flasks were brought and broken on stage, every time that Aeschylus uttered ληκύθιον ἀπώλεσεν.

---

526 τὸ σαυτοῦ appears *para prosdokian* for ὕστερον *vel sim*. For Euripides' mother (allegedly) being a greengrocer, cf. 840; *Ach.* 478; *Thesm.* 387, 456.
527 Navarre 1933; Ambrose 1968; Whitman 1969; Griffith 1970; Henderson 1972; Penella 1973; Snell 1979; Anderson 1981; Guido/Filippo 1981; Beck 1982; Robertson 1982; Bain 1985; Sider 1992; Gerö/Johnsson 2002.

Even though there is no evidence for such pottery in mainland Greece, there survive three such flasks from Apulia, fourth century BC (Figs. 18–20). During the sixth and fifth centuries south Italy imported most of its decorated pottery from Greece, mainly from Attica. In late fifth and fourth century local workshops appeared but it seems that they were established by immigrants from Athens; the style, technique, and shape of the vases remained 'Athenian' to a large extent.[528] It is therefore increasingly likely that the Athenians of 405 BC were familiar with (i.e. they were exporting) frog-shaped flasks. Given the diffusion of Greek drama in Magna Graecia and the depiction of tragic and comic scenes in local pottery,[529] it would be reasonable to imagine that the Athenians exported this kind of flask on the very occasion of the re-production of *Frogs* in Apulia (which is also supported by the vase in Fig. 15). The form is probably drawing inspiration from Egyptian art, where frog-shaped pots (though not oil-flasks) had a very long tradition.[530]

Fig. 18–20: Apulian frog gutti, 4th century BC. Left: Cleveland Museum of Art 1985.176, Ohio. Middle: Museo Jatta 1458, Ruvo. Right: Leo Mildenberg Collection II 76, Zurich. Drawings by D. Kanellakis.

If such pottery was indeed known in late classical Athens, it is then only appropriate to ask *how* and *why* Aristophanes would have used it in his play. As stated earlier, it is debatable whether a real flask or any other prop was used *at all*, but 1223 (νυνὶ γὰρ αὐτοῦ τοῦτό γ' ἐκκεκόψεται, '*This time, this [flask] will be knocked right out of his hand*') and 1224 (ἴθι δὴ λέγ' ἕτερον κἀπέχου τῆς ληκύθου, '*go on, say another one and dodge the flask*') give strong evidence to support such a case. Be that as it may, why would it be a frog-shaped flask in particular? First and most

---

528 Carpenter *et al.* 2014, 1, 6.
529 See Taplin 1993, 89–99; Taplin 2007; Dearden 1999; Robinson 2004; Biles/Thorn 2014; Carpenter 2014.
530 See Patch 2011, 30–1.

obviously, that would provide a link between the two halves of the play, both in terms of iconography and in dramatic function. If in the parodos of the frogs the amphibians lose the battle against Dionysus, here too the frog-flasks are smashed by Aeschylus in an antagonistic context. In fact, the very verb κόπτω (1223) is often used to describe the killing of animals (*LSJ* 3). Thus, by breaking the frog-flasks, Aeschylus is in effect *murdering* the prologues of his opponent, which is precisely what he had promised in 1200 (διαφθερῶ). Secondly, such pots would be appropriate for this scene on a symbolic level. In many cultures, frogs are considered symbols of immortality, because various species lie in hibernation during winter and reappear with the first rainfalls of spring; hence an ointment vessel in this shape must have been a funerary gift.[531] Therefore, if Aeschylus is here breaking (what is supposed to be) Euripides' frog-flasks, then he is symbolically ruining his hopes of coming back to life.

Returning to the wider question (whether a prop was used at all), modern performances – even when not employing props – strongly indicate that ληκύθιον ἀπώλεσεν is not sufficient in its own right. In Eastman's production there is no scenic rendering of ληκύθιον ἀπώλεσεν, apart from Aeschylus holding a lotion dispenser which he never uses. This choice undermines the comic dynamics, as might be inferred from the silence of the audience (in the one particular performance that has been recorded). In Tsianos' production there is also no scenic rendering of ληκύθιον ἀπώλεσεν, but the director (and translator) has adequately adapted the phrase to make it stand as a joke on a verbal-only level. Specifically, he has made Aeschylus' interjection *rhyme* with Euripides' lyrics:

ΕΥΡ.   Ο Αίγυπτος πάτησε μια π**λάκα**... (≈ 1206)
       Ο Διόνυσος πλησίασε τη θ**ράκα**... (≈ 1211)
       Ο Πέλοπας ζεύγει το άρμα του τ**άκα-τάκα**... (≈ 1232)
       Ο Οινέας, φορώντας μία β**ράκα**... (≈ 1240)
ΑΙΣΧ. ...κι έσπασε την τσαν**άκα** (x4)

The audience laughs at the sound rather than the content of the interjection.[532] This suggests that Aristophanes too would have felt the need to invest in this scene *more* than what appears in the text. Even if ληκύθιον ἀπώλεσεν was a popular formulaic joke for the ancient Athenians, it would not come as a surprise after its second, third, or fourth repetition. To sustain its humour, there must have been something additional going on – and rhyme was not a standard option in

---

531 On the symbolic meanings of the frog, see Lullies 1960.
532 The same technique is applied by George Pavrianos in his 1978 adaptation of *Frogs* for the shadow theatre; Kanellakis 2018, 165–6.

ancient Greek. This addition could well have been the surprising return of the frogs on stage (in another form), after a 'hibernation' period between the first parodos and this moment. 'Coaxing' (cracking) for a last time, they are now 'killed' for good by Aeschylus.

Surprise escalates in the following scene with the weighing of lyrics (1365–410). It is not the judge Dionysus who initiates this trial, but Aeschylus himself, who as the poet of *Psychostasia*, is reasonably credited with the idea. Indeed, the chorus asks the rhetorical question '*who else could have thought of such an unexpected idea?*' (1371–3):

τόδε γὰρ ἕτερον αὖ τέρας
νεοχμόν, ἀτοπίας πλέων,
ὃ τίς ἂν ἐπενόησεν ἄλλος;

The implementation rather than the notion itself is what is unprecedented, since the notion exists already in *Il.* 22.209–12, where Zeus weighs Achilles' and Hector's destinies. Where literature is specifically concerned, the concept of 'measuring' its quality is already found in stylistic terms such as ὄγκος or ὕψος. How exactly the spectacle looked like in *Frogs* is not clear. We are told that the contestants are standing beside the scales (παρίστασθον παρά, 1377), holding it somehow (λαβομένω, 1379; ἐχόμεθα, 1381; λάβεσθε, 1390), and reciting verses from their plays. But we do not know whether the verses were just uttered (in which case the scales were prearranged to lean towards Aeschylus' side and were brought back into balance by a hidden peg), or whether they were represented by props placed upon the scale-pans (in which case no trick was necessary). In 1407–9 Aeschylus provokes Euripides to stand on the scales himself, loading his wife and Cephisophon and his books too, which suggests that the scales must have been very large. In Eastman's production there is a see-saw replacing the scales, on which the tragedians are competing. This is certainly precluded for the case of Aristophanes' own production (as the text stands) but it is possible that a see-saw was used in re-productions of *Frogs* in South Italy – local pottery attests that the device was indeed used in comic performances.[533]

While we cannot know how much of a surprise effect to attribute to stagecraft, the *logos* (comic reasoning) seems to be the highlight of this scene. If the idea of weighing the 'gravity' of the verses with physical instruments prompts an initial surprise, then the implementation of the idea prompts an even bigger one:

---

533 See Green 2014, fig. 1 and 12.

that eventually it is indeed the *literal* gravity of the verses that is measured. Aeschylus wins all three rounds. The surrealistic explanations given by Dionysus (1386–8, 1394, 1405–6) have parallels in all plays by Aristophanes and often imply a parody of sophistic ideas. In *Nub.* 227–34 for example, Socrates is *physically* swinging high above, in order to *mentally* reach the sky. Similarly, in this scene of *Frogs* there seems to be a parody of Euripides, who indeed is often associated with Socrates in comedy (1491–9);[534] the moral is that sophistry backfires on the sophist-poet. The intersection of verbal, thematic, and scenic surprise, and the pendulum between literality and metaphor, introduces here – maybe for the first time in Greek drama – what one may truly call *surrealism*. Even though comic reasoning was a well-established pattern, this scene in *Frogs* is the first case where such reasoning regulates stage action rather than vice versa.[535] To find a dotard philosopher swinging in a basket for whatever ridiculous purpose is a potentially realistic scenario; but to find scales leaning towards either side by placing on them non-existent loads is impossible.

At the end of the contest, despite the triple victory of Aeschylus, Dionysus still cannot reach a decision, disregards the competition so far, and suddenly changes to asking the contestants for their political advice. A couple of minutes before the finale, the conclusion of the story still remains uncertain. For some in the audience, this would generate suspense, while for others the conclusion would not matter anymore. I believe this is the intention of the playwright in so far as we can infer it from the plot structure. The scene with the scales is a grandiose affirmation of what the play looked like from the very beginning: a total failure of expectations and promises. The play was named *Frogs* in vain;[536] scatology was renounced in vain; Dionysus offered his donkey to Xanthias in vain; he masqueraded as Hercules in vain; he exchanged roles with Xanthias in vain; they both underwent a beating by Aeacus in vain; the poetic contest was staged in vain. Ironically, the Greek text becomes very problematic when it comes to the political advice of the tragedians (1427 f.), in a way that the lines cannot be distributed with certainty, prolonging the feeling of futility (for us modern readers). This is not to say that the play ends by proposing the vanity of comedy, or trag-

---

534 See Worman 2017; Allan 1999.
535 In the example from *Clouds*, it is the action (Socrates' swinging in the basket) that enables a comic reasoning in retrospect – which, after all, is not necessary.
536 In the sense that the audience, who knew the title already from the *proagōn*, would anticipate a traditional animal-chorus, not a secondary and perhaps invisible one; Zimmermann 2011: 707.

edy, or art in general; 'the final scenes of the play do not in fact seem at all despondent or pessimistic, either in political or in poetical terms.'[537] Rather, it is a call to enjoy the play *per re*, as a spectacular gay musical, rather than for the political message – after all, Aeschylus and Euripides do not differ radically in their recommendations (whatever line distribution we make).[538] While existing scholarship on what is surprising in this play has centred on the outcome of the contest,[539] this chapter has shown that through the accumulation of surprises, the criterion of predictability has essentially been waived at this point, and the audience has surrendered to surrealism. With his perfectly messy poetic programme, Aristophanes won the first prize; not in vain, and not surprisingly.

---

[537] Griffith 2013, 215.
[538] Griffith 2013, 207. For him, the ending of the play conveys the message of inclusiveness – with the final procession containing divinities and humans, men and women, free citizens and (probably) slaves (208) – rather than the mere reaffirmation of the values of 'old-style' politics and art (200).
[539] I agree with Dover 1993, 11 that 'Having been told so plainly and emphatically that bad people like Euripides and good people like Aeschylus [771–83], members of the audience are not likely to think that Euripides will win the throne of poetry.' The fusion of Dionysus' original mission (to retrieve Euripides) with the initially separate competition for the throne of tragedy, too, is often considered a surprise; but to say 'we had no idea that Aeschylus was going to figure in the play at all' (Sommerstein 1996, 14) is an overstatement, not least because of the *proagōn*.

Afterword

The observations of this book about the poetological intention of surprise can be thus summarised: comedy manifests its uniqueness through the 'meta-surprise' of being heteronomously defined (i.e. in opposition to tragedy) but through purely comedic means, and without *copying* from genres such as Aesopic myths, iambic poetry, or satyr drama. Aristophanes invents, and invest in, his own stylistic signatures in the struggle for surprise, and over time he tries to surpass himself (e.g. his first parody of Telephus, or his tendency for noun-based *para prosdokian*). Even more, comedy claims its superiority over rival genres, by showing off its unrivalled flexibility and revolutionary vision, even when it has to compete with already elaborate prototypes (e.g. Sophocles' *Tereus* and Philoxenus' *Cyclops*). The theatrical codes are essential in this process: by employing the crane and the platform for anti-climactic purposes, by turning dramatic tension into muscle tension, by assigning active dramatic roles to animals and babies, by creating accidents on stage, and by parodying contemporary figures and popular songs, Aristophanes is not just declaring what comedy can do, but what tragedy cannot. The issue that naturally emerges as a question for further research is what tragedy's own poetological trademark is; if comedy employs surprise, which emotion does tragedy concern itself with? The obvious research hypothesis is fear, not on the basis of the Aristotelian definitions (which have been extensively studied), but because the neuropsychological affinity between fear and surprise would nicely illustrate the affinity between tragedy and comedy. The apparent challenge in such an argument is the paradox of sibling-genres evoking sibling-emotions to promote their uniqueness.

The aim of this book has been to read Aristophanes from the perspective of surprise, rather than to use Aristophanes as a case study for theorising this category. Yet, the typologies sketched and the methods followed throughout provide the keys for the development of a Grammar of Surprise. Grammars, of course, have prescribed temporal, geographical, dialectical, sociolectal and other restrictions, despite bearing general titles. In going to buy a Grammar of Ancient Greek, for example, one will probably end up having a grammar of the Attic dialect as attested in prose of the fifth and fourth century BC. Secondly, grammars have a certain epistemological format: they are normative/prescriptive, descriptive, explanatory, or functional/communicative, but not all-in-one; they include morphology only, or syntax as well; each format, or even each book, uses different labels to name its categories (consider the mess in English terminology for the Greek conditionals). In other words, grammars are neither exhaustive in their scope, nor obligatory in their system. Similarly, this book has only focussed on humorous surprises (as opposed to unpleasant surprises) which mainly arise from the violation of expectations (rather than from suddenness). Moreover, it has not claimed a tripartite typology of verbal, thematic, and theatrical surprise as a holistic mapping of the phenomenon – on the contrary, it has suggested that such a project should consider plot construction, characterisation, and ideology as well – and has only dealt with specific versions of it within each of the three dramaturgical areas under examination. However, the examination of both the morphology (grammar, syntax, metre, vocabulary) and the pragmatics (context, speakers) is not confined to *para prosdokian* jokes but extendable to all verbal surprises. The consideration of both intra-dramatic functions (persuasive, aetiological, responsive, abusive, and structural) and meta-dramatic functions (poetological) is not limited to appropriations of myths but applicable to all thematic surprises. The study of both intra-dramatic relations (contradiction between words and stage action) and inter-dramatic relations (breaching theatrical conventions) is suitable for all theatrical surprises, not just the scenes discussed here. But still, this intersection of aspects and levels of analysis is only indicative. Drawing together the threads in a cohesive overall model, it emerges that a general Grammar of Surprise should examine all possible intersections of dramaturgical aspects (verbal, thematic, theatrical, characterological, narrative, and ideological) with dramaturgical levels (extra-, inter-, intra-, and meta-dramatic). In terms of methods, plurality is again the key element, with textual readings and empirical research (whether this is the examination of specific performances or the conduct scientific experiments) informing one another. Even though a comprehensive typology of surprise is a realistic goal under all these provisions, it is also true that typologies are not an end in themselves, in the same way that a grammar book can never fully depict and explain the dynamics and the beauty of language. The ultimate utility of grammars, quite surprisingly, is to invite us to think outside the box.

Appendices

Tab. 4: Proposed *Para Prosdokian* - *Acharnians* (Abbreviations explained on p. 207)

Line	Proposed by	Given	Expected
18	Σ(b), O	ἐδήχθην ὑπὸ **κονίας τὰς ὀφρῦς**	ὑπ' ὀδύνης τὴν καρδίαν
68–75	+, R	Πρ: **καὶ δῆτ' ἐτρυχόμεσθα διὰ Καϋστρίων πεδίων ὁδοιπλανοῦντες ἐσκηνημένοι,** ἐφ' ἁρμαμαξῶν μαλθακῶς κατακείμενοι, **ἀπολλύμενοι.** Δικ: σφόδρα γὰρ ἐσῳζόμην ἐγὼ **παρὰ τὴν ἔπαλξιν ἐν φορυτῷ κατακείμενος.** Πρ: ξενιζόμενοι δὲ **πρὸς βίαν** ἐπίνομεν ἐξ ὑαλίνων ἐκπωμάτων καὶ χρυσίδων ἄκρατον οἶνον ἡδύν.	Elements in bold should be together (sufferings); non-bold elements should be together (pleasures) R: 'we were kept to hard labour'
81–2	Σ(b), +	ἀλλ' εἰς **ἀπόπατον** ᾤχετο **στρατιὰν** λαβών, κἄχεζεν ὀκτὼ μῆνας ἐπὶ χρυσῶν ὀρῶν.	Σ(b): ἐπὶ πόλεμον ᾤχετο +: σπογγιάν λαβών (cf. *Ran*.483)
83	Σ(b)	πόσου δὲ τὸν **πρωκτὸν** χρόνου ξυνήγαγεν;	τὸν στρατὸν
88	S	ὄρνιν τριπλάσιον **Κλεωνύμου**	[no proposal given]
118	S	Κλεισθένης ὁ Σιβυρτίου	[no proposal given]
10119	Σ(a), S	ὦ θερμόβουλον **πρωκτὸν** ἐξυρημένε,	ὦ θερμόβουλον σπλάγχνον (Eur. fr. 858)
120	+	τοιόνδε γ' ᾧ πίθηκε τὸν **πώγων'** ἔχων	τὴν πυγὴν (Archil. 187 / Aesop. 81 Perry)
121	Re	**εὐνοῦχος** ἡμῖν ἦλθες ἐσκευασμένος;	'a deed of insolent hardihood'
255	Σ(a), S, R, O	κἀκποιήσεται **γαλᾶς**	παῖδας / θυγατέρας
256	H, +	σοῦ μηδὲν ἥττους **βδεῖν**	H: βινεῖν +: anything graceful
336	O	ὁμήλικα τόνδε **φιλανθρακέα**	φιλάνθρωπον
396	+	οὐκ ἔνδον ἔνδον ἐστίν [oxymoron]	οὐκ ἔνδον ἐστίν **or** ἔνδον ἐστίν
464	+	ἀφαιρήσει με τὴν **τραγῳδίαν**	τὴν οὐσίαν
480	+	ὦ θύμ' **ἄνευ σκάνδικος** ἐμπορευτέα	κακοῖσιν ὅμως ἄτλητα πεπονθὼς (Thgn.1029)
500	O	τὸ γὰρ δίκαιον οἶδε καὶ **τρυγῳδία**	πένης ἀνήρ (Eur. *Supp*. 863)

Line	Proposed by	Given	Expected
582	O	ἀπένεγκέ μου τὴν **μορμόνα**	γοργόνα (cf. *Pax* 474)
615	Σ(a)	ὑπ' ἐράνων τε καὶ **χρεῶν**	[no proposal given]
684	Σ(a)	ὁρῶντες... τῆς **δίκης** τὴν **ἠλύγην**	ἀνθρώπων τὴν ἠλύγην / δίκης φάος
732	O	ἄμβατε ποττὰν **μάδδαν**	θύραν
733	Σ(a), S, O	ἀκούετε δή, ποτέχετ' ἐμὶν **τὰν γαστέρα**	τὸν νοῦν (cf. *Eq.* 1014; *Nub.* 575; *Pax* 174)
751	Σ(a)	**διαπεινᾶμες** ἀεὶ ποττὸ πῦρ	διαπίνομεν
756	Σ(b),S,Re,O	ὅπως τάχιστα καὶ **κάκιστ' ἀπολοίμεθα**	τάχιστα καὶ ἄριστα σωθείημεν / σωθῶμεν
889	O	σκέψασθε παῖδες τὴν ἀρίστην **ἔγχελυν**	παρθένον
904	+	**συκοφάντην** ἔξαγε	any commercial product (response to 902)
909	O	Βοι.: μικκός γα μᾶκος οὗτος. Δικ.: ἀλλ' ἄπαν **κακόν**.	καλόν (cf. Eur. *El.* 1003)
950	R, O	πρὸς πάντα **συκοφάντην**	χρήσιμον
967	S, R	ἐπὶ ταρίχει τοὺς λόφους **κραδαινέτω**	φαγέτω
974	Σ(a)	τὰ δ' αὖ πρέπει **χλιαρὰ** κατεσθίειν	ἀνθηρὰ [not explicitly said]
985	S, O	ἐξέχει θ' ἡμῶν βίᾳ τὸν οἶνον ἐκ τῶν **ἀμπέλων**	ἀμφορέων /κρατήτων / κυλίκων / πίθων
1002	O	ἀσκὸν **Κτησιφῶντος** λήψεται	a name of some good regional wine
1021	O	μέτρησον εἰρήνης τί μοι, κἂν πέντ' ἔτη	κοτύλας
1026	Re, O, +	ἐν πᾶσι **βολίτοις**	ἀγαθοῖς (Pherecr. fr. 113.2) +: (response to 1024)

Tab. 5: Proposed *Para Prosdokian* - *Peace*

Line	Proposed by	Given	Expected
6–7	+	μὰ τὸν Δί', **ἀλλ'** ἐξαρπάσας ὅλην **ἐνέκαψε** περικυλίσας τοῖν ποδοῖν.	ἀπέρριψε
34	Pa, Sh	ὥσπερ παλαιστής, παραβαλὼν τοὺς **γομφίους**	Pa: βραχίονας / Sh: τοὺς ὀφθαλμούς
95	Σ(a)	**τί πέτει;** τί μάτην οὐχ ὑγιαίνεις;	τί κάμνεις;
123	Pa, Sh, Pl, +	κολλύραν <u>μεγάλην</u> καὶ **κόνδυλον** ὄψον ἐπ' αὐτῇ.	Sh, Pl: κάνδυλον, κάνδαυλον. +: <u>κολλύραν alone</u>
153	Sh	κατωκάρα ῥίψας με **βουκολήσεται**	[no proposal given]
199	Sh	ὑπ' αὐτὸν ἀτεχνῶς τοὐρανοῦ τὸν **κύτταρον**.	μυχόν, ἀψῖδα
235	Σ(b), Pl	**θυείας** φθέγμα πολεμιστηρίας.	σάλπιγγος
249	Σ(b), Pa, Sh	βαβαὶ βαβαιάξ, ὡς μεγάλα καὶ δριμέα τοῖσιν Μεγαρεῦσιν ἐνέβαλεν τὰ **κλαύματα**.	κρόμμυα
279	Sh, O	ἀποστραφῆναι **τοῦ μετιόντος τὼ πόδε**.	τὸν κίνδυνον ἡμῖν
300	Sh	ἡμῖν αὖ σπάσαι πάρεστιν **ἀγαθοῦ δαίμονος**	+: τοὺς λίθους, τὴν Εἰρήνην *vel sim*
308	Pa, Pl	τὴν θεῶν πασῶν μεγίστην καὶ φιλα**μπελωτάτην**.	φιλανθρωποτάτην
363	Σ(a)	οὐδὲν πονηρόν, ἀλλ' ὅπερ καὶ **Κιλλικῶν**.	+: some benefactor of the city/ πᾶν ἀγαθὸν
378	Σ(b)	ναί, πρὸς τῶν **κρεῶν**	θεῶν
425	Σ(b),Pa,Pl, O	οἴμ', ὡς ἐλεήμων εἴμ' ἀεὶ **τῶν χρυσίδων**.	ἀνθρώπων, ἱκετῶν, πόλεως, Ἑλλάδος
474	O	οὐδὲν δεόμεθ', ὤνθρωπε, τῆς σῆς **μορμόνος**.	γοργόνος
505	Σ(a), R, Pl, O	οὐδὲν γὰρ ἄλλο δρᾶτε πλὴν **δικάζετε**.	φωνεῖται, ἐμποδίζετε, κωλύετε
554	LSJ	μεστὰ τἀνθάδ' εἰρήνης **σαπρᾶς**.	[no proposal given]
557	Sh	προσειπεῖν βούλομαι **τὰς ἀμπέλους**,	[Peace]
627	O	τὰς κράδας **κατήσθιον**.	κατέκοπτον
669	Sh	ὁ νοῦς γὰρ ἡμῶν ἦν τότ' ἐν τοῖς **σκύτεσιν**.	τῷ πολέμῳ, ταῖς ναυσίν

Line	Proposed by	Given	Expected
708	Pa, Sh, O	ταύτῃ ξυνοικῶν ἐκποιοῦ σαυτῷ **βότρυς**	παῖδας, τέκνα
711	Pl, O	τῆς Ὀπώρας κατελάσας;	ἐμπλήμενος, καταφαγών
728	Sh	ποθοῦντες ὑμᾶς ἀναμένουσ' **ἑστυκότες.**	ἑστηκότες
756-7	Sh, O	ἑκατὸν δὲ κύκλῳ κεφαλαὶ **κολάκων** οἰμωξομένων ἐλιχμῶντο	ὀφέων
795	Pl	τὸ δρᾶμα γαλῆν τῆς ἑσπέρας **ἀπάγξαι.**	κλέψαι
821–3	Pa, Sh, Pl, Rb	ἀπὸ τοὐρανοῦ 'φαίνεσθε κακοήθεις πάνυ, ἐντευθενὶ δὲ πολύ τι **κακοηθέστεροι.**	Pa: φαῦλοι / Sh, Pl, Rb: μικροί Rb: **bigger** +: καλοήθεις
864	Pa, R, Pl, So, Rb	εὐδαιμονέστερος φανεῖ τῶν **Καρκίνου στροβίλων**	R, Pl, Rb: Καρκίνου παίδων So: all other men
868	Sh, O	ἡ παῖς λέλουται καὶ τὰ τῆς **πυγῆς** καλά·	τύχης
874	Pl, O, So,	**ἐπαίομεν** Βραυρωνάδ' ὑποπεπωκότες	ἐπέμπομεν, ἐποιοῦμεν, ἐποιούμεθα *vel sim*
898	Σ(a), Pl	παίειν, ὀρύττειν, πὺξ ὁμοῦ καὶ τῷ **πέει·**	σκέλει
1022	S, R	χοὔτω τὸ πρόβατον **τῷ χορηγῷ σῴζεται.**	[no proposal given]
1065	LSJ, Pl	συνθήκας πεποίησθ' ἄνδρες χαροποῖσι **πιθήκοις**	λέουσι
1067	Pl	καὶ **κέπφοι** τρήρωνες ἀλωπεκιδεῦσι πέπεισθε	πέλειαι
1116	S, +	τὴν Σίβυλλαν **ἔσθιε**	+: αἰτοῦ
1186	Σ(b), Pa, R, Pl, So, O	οἱ θεοῖσιν οὗτοι κἀνδράσι **ῥιψάσπιδες**	ἐχθροί

Tab. 6: Proposed *Para Prosdokian* - *Thesmophoriazusae*

Line	Proposed by	Given	Expected
24	R	πῶς ἂν οὖν... ἔτι προσμάθοιμι **χωλὸς εἶναι τὼ σκέλει;**	[no proposal given]
50	+	Θε. πρόμος ἡμέτερος – Κη. μῶν **βι-νεῖσθαι;**	'to sing'
53	AO	κάμπτει δὲ νέας ἀψῖδας **ἐπῶν**	τροχῶν
57	+	Θε. καὶ χοανεύει. – Κη. καὶ **λαικάζει**	any craft-term
130–3	+	ὡς ἡδὺ τὸ μέλος, ὦ πότνιαι **Γενετυλλί-δες**, καὶ **θηλυδριῶδες** καὶ **κατεγλωττισμένον** καὶ **μανδαλωτόν**, ὥστ' ἐμοῦ γ' ἀκροωμέ-νου ὑπὸ τὴν **ἕδραν** αὐτὴν ὑπῆλθε **γάργαλος**.	Nymphs; any complimentary terms appropriate for deities (μειλίχιον, σεπτόν *vel sim.*) καρδίην - ἔρως (Archil. 191)
158	R, O	ἵνα συμποιῶ σοὔπισθεν **ἑστυκὼς** ἐγώ	ἑστηκώς
242	Pr, AO	πρὶν ἀντιλαβέσθαι **πρωκτὸν** ἕτερον τῆς φλογός	οἰκίαν
254	R, Pr, AO, Σ(b),+	νὴ τὴν Ἀφροδίτην, ἡδύ γ' ὄζει **ποσθίου**.	μύρου *vel sim.* +: οἴνου
288	AO	θύειν ἔχουσαν, εἰ δὲ μή, ἀλλὰ νῦν **λαθεῖν**	θύειν
290	[AO]	καὶ τὴν θυγατέρα Χοιρίον ἀνδρός μοι τυχεῖν **πλουτοῦντος**, ἄλλως δ' **ἠλιθίου κἀβελ-τέρου**	πενιχρὸν μέν, ἄλλως δ' εὐπρό-σωπον καὶ καλὸν καὶ χρηστόν (*Plut.* 976–7)
334–7	AO	εἴ τις ἐπιβουλεύει τι τῷ δήμῳ κακὸν τῷ τῶν **γυναικῶν**, ἢ 'πικηρυκεύεται **Εὐριπίδῃ** Μήδοις τ' ἐπὶ βλάβῃ τινὶ	Ἀθηναίων [no proposal given]
346	AO	ἢ καὶ δέχεται προδιδοῦσ' ἑταίρα **τὸν φί-λον**,	τὴν πόλιν
509	AO, Σ(b)	τὸ γὰρ ἦτρον **τῆς χύτρας** ἐλάκτισεν	τῆς μητρός / τῆς μήτρας
515–6	AO	τά τ' ἄλλ' ἀπαξάπαντα καὶ τὸ **πόσθιον** τῷ σῷ προσόμοιον,	ῥινίον *vel sim.*
529–30	Pr, AO	ὑπὸ λίθῳ γὰρ παντί που χρὴ μὴ δάκῃ **ῥήτωρ** ἀθρεῖν.	σκορπίος
531–2	R, Pr, AO	ἀλλ' οὐ γάρ ἐστι τῶν ἀναισχύντων φύσει γυναικῶν οὐδὲν κάκιον εἰς ἅπαντα—πλὴν ἄρ' εἰ **γυναῖκες**.	[any other creature]

Line	Proposed by	Given	Expected
804	Pr	Ναυσιμάχης μέν <γ'> ἥττων ἐστὶν Χαρμίνος· δῆλα δὲ τἆργα.	τὰ ὀνόματα
829	Pr, AO	ἔρριπται τὸ σκιάδειον.	ἡ ἀσπίς
857	Rb, +	λευκῆς νοτίζει μελανοσυρμαῖον λεών.	Rb: μελανόχρως + : τακείσης χιόνος ὑγραίνει γύας.
935	AO	ὀλίγου μ' ἀφείλετ' αὐτὸν ἱστιορράφος.	μηχανορράφος
937	+	ὦ πρύτανι, πρὸς τῆς δεξιᾶς, ἥνπερ φιλεῖς κοίλην προτείνειν, ἀργύριον ἤν τις διδῷ,	generous... help... asks
1024-5	AO, Σ(b)	μόλις δὲ γραῖαν ἀποφυγὼν σαπρὰν ἀπωλόμην ὅμως.	ἐσώθην
1050-1	Pr	εἴθε με πυρφόρος αἰθέρος ἀστήρ— τὸν βάρβαρον ἐξολέσειεν.	[με]
1201	+	μεμνῇσι τοίνυν τοὔνομ'· Ἀρταμουξία.	Ἀρτεμισία
1226	Pr	τρέχε νυν κατ' αὐτοὺς <ἐς> κόρακας ἐπουρίσας	ἐς αὐτόν [=Euripides]

Tab. 7: Proposed *Para Prosdokian* - *Wealth*

Line	Proposed by	Given	Expected
27	Σ(b), R	πιστότατον ἡγοῦμαί σε καὶ κλεπτίστατον.	εὐνούστατον
152	+	οὐδὲ προσέχειν τὸν νοῦν, ἐὰν δὲ πλούσιος, τὸν πρωκτὸν αὑτὰς εὐθὺς ὡς τοῦτον τρέπειν.	τὸν νοῦν
165	+	Χρ. [...] ὁ δὲ χρυσοχοεῖ γε χρυσίον παρὰ σοῦ λαβών- Κα. ὁ δὲ λωποδυτεῖ γε νὴ Δί', ὁ δὲ τοιχωρυχεῖ-	any proper professions
180	Σ(b), (So)	Κα. ὁ Τιμοθέου δὲ πύργος — Χρ. ἐμπέσοι γέ σοι.	οὐχὶ διὰ τοῦτον ἐγένετο; *vel sim.*
219	R	ὅσοις δικαίοις οὖσιν οὐκ ἦν ἄλφιτα	'a grain of fear'
277-8	Σ(b), +	ἐν τῇ σορῷ νυνὶ λαχὸν τὸ γράμμα σου δικάζει, σὺ δ' οὐ βαδίζεις, ὁ δὲ Χάρων τὸ ξύμβολον δίδωσιν.	Σ(b): ἐν τῷ δικαστηρίῳ... ἄρχων +: ὁ Χάρων σε καλεῖ... ῥοΐδιον

Appendices — **207**

Line	Proposed by	Given	Expected
372	+	μῶν οὐ κέκλοφας ἀλλ' **ἥρπακας**;	εὕρηκας *vel sim.*
600	(So)	οὐ γὰρ πείσεις, οὐδ' ἢν **πείσῃς** [oxymoron]	θέλῃ *vel sim.*
706	+	μὰ Δί' οὐκ ἔγωγ', ἀλλὰ **σκατοφάγον**	any religious adjective
737	Σ(b)	καὶ πρίν σε **κοτύλας ἐκπιεῖν οἴνου δέκα**	εἰπεῖν λόγον ἕνα / πτύσαι
765	Σ(b)	νὴ τὴν Ἑκάτην, κἀγὼ δ' ἀναδῆσαι βούλομαι εὐαγγέλιά σε **κριβανωτῶν ὁρμαθῷ**	στεφάνῳ
818	Σ(b)	...ἀποψώμεσθα δ' οὐ λίθοις ἔτι, ἀλλὰ **σκοροδίοις** ὑπὸ τρυφῆς ἑκάστοτε	Σ(b): σαβάνοις +: σπογγίοις
963	+	**ὦ μειρακίσκη**· πυνθάνει γὰρ ὡρικῶς.	ὦ γραῖα (cf. Eur. *Hel.* 441)
972	Σ(b)	ἀλλ' οὐ λαχοῦσ' **ἔπινες** ἐν τῷ γράμματι;	ἐδίκαζες

Abbreviations

Grey   Non-standard (rejected) proposals and interpretations.
+   New proposals and reinterpretations.
Σ(a)   Scholia, using the term παρὰ προσδοκίαν.
Σ(b)   Scholia, misusing other terms (παρ' ὑπόνοιαν, ἀντὶ δὲ τοῦ εἰπεῖν, δέον εἰπεῖν)
AO   Austin/Olson 2004 *ad loc.*
H   Henderson 1991, 196.
O   Olson (in the respective commentary) *ad loc.*
Pa   Paley 1873 *ad loc.*
Pl   Platnauer 1964 *ad loc.*
Pr   Prato 2001 *ad loc.*
R   Rogers (in the respective commentary) *ad loc.*
Re   Rennie 1909 *ad loc.*
Rb   Robson 2006, 51, 140, 170–1.
S   Starkie 1909, lxvii – lxviii and *ad loc.*
Sh   Sharpley 1905 *ad loc.*
So   Sommerstein (in the respective commentary) *ad loc.*

Tab. 8: Norms in *Para Prosdokian* - *Acharnians* (Abbreviations explained on p. 215)

Line	Text	TYPOLOGY					CONTEXT		CHARACTER
		Width	Gram	Syntax	Metre	Vocab	Part	Theme	
68–75	Πρ.: καὶ δῆτ' ἐτρυχόμεσθα διὰ Καϋστρίων πεδίων ὁδοιπλανοῦντες ἐσκηνημένοι, ἐφ' ἁρμαμαξῶν **μαλθακῶς** κατακείμενοι, ἀπολλύμενοι. Δικ.: σφόδρα γὰρ **ἐσῳζόμην** ἐγὼ παρὰ τὴν ἔπαλξιν ἐν φορυτῷ κατακείμενος. Πρ.: ξενιζόμενοι δὲ **πρὸς βίαν** ἐπίνομεν ἐξ ὑαλίνων ἐκπωμάτων καὶ χρυσίδων ἄκρατον οἶνον ἡδύν.	S	Av V N		R A	O	Prologue	Politics	Dikaiopolis & ambassador
81–2	ἀλλ' εἰς ἀπόπατον ᾤχετο **στρατιὰν** λαβών, κἄχεζεν ὀκτὼ μῆνας ἐπὶ χρυσῶν ὀρῶν.	P	N	O	R	S	Prologue	Politics	ambassador
119	ὦ θερμόβουλον **πρωκτὸν** ἐξυρημένε,	P	N	Exclam.		S	Prologue	Politics/Personal abuse	Dikaiopolis
120	τοιόνδε γ' ὦ πίθηκε τὸν **πώγον'** ἔχων	P	N	O			Prologue		Dikaiopolis
255	κἀκποιήσεται **γαλᾶς**	P	N	O	E	O	1st episode	Festive	Dikaiopolis
256	σοῦ μηδὲν ἥττους **βδεῖν**	P	I	O	P	S			Dikaiopolis

Line	Text	TYPOLOGY						CONTEXT		CHARACTER
		Width	Gram	Syntax	Metre	Vocab	Part	Theme		
336	ὁμήλικα τόνδε **φιλανθρακέα**	W/P	Aj	O	E	O	1st episode	Paratragic	chorus
396	οὐκ ἔνδον **ἔνδον** ἐστίν [oxymoron]	P	Av	C		O	1st episode	Paratragic	Eur.' servant
464	ἀφαιρήσει με τὴν **τραγῳδίαν**	P	N	O	E	O	1st episode	Paratragic	Euripides
480	ὦ θύμ᾽ ἄνευ **σκάνδικος** ἐμπορευτέα	P	N	Pp		G	1st episode	Paratragic	Dikaiopolis
582	ἀπένεγκέ μου τὴν **μορμόνα**	P	N	O	E	O	1st episode	Personal abuse	Dikaiopolis
732	ἄμβατε ποττὰν **μᾶδδαν**	P	N	Pp	P	G	2nd episode	Social criticism	Megarian
733	ἀκούετε δή, ποτέχετ᾽ ἐμὶν τὰν **γαστέρα**	P	N	O	E	G	2nd episode	Social criticism	Megarian
751	**διαπεινᾶμες** ἀεὶ ποττὸ πῦρ	W/P	V	V	A	G	2nd episode	Social criticism	Megarian
904	ἐγῴδα τοίνυν· **συκοφάντην** ἔξαγε	P	N	O	P	O	3rd episode	Politics	Dikaiopolis
909	Βοι.: μικκός γα μᾶκος οὗτος. Δικ.: ἀλλ᾽ ἅπαν **κακόν**.	P	Aj	C	E, A	O	3rd episode	Politics/Personal abuse	Dikaiopolis
1026	ἐν πᾶσι **βολίτοις**	P	N	Pp	A, P	S	4th episode	Social criticism	farmer

Tab. 9: Norms in *Para Prosdokian* - *Peace*

Line	Text	TYPOLOGY					CONTEXT		Theme	CHARACTER
		Width	Gram	Syntax	Metre	Vocab	Part			
6–7	μὰ τὸν Δί', **ἀλλ'** ἐξαρπάσας ὅλην **ἐνέκαψε** περικυλίσας τοῖν ποδοῖν.	P	V	V		G/S	Prologue		Personal abuse	servant
123	κολλύραν **μεγάλην** καὶ **κόνδυλον** ὄψον ἐπ' αὐτῇ.	P	Aj, N	O		O	Prologue		Social criticism	Trygaeus
300	νῦν γὰρ ἡμῖν αὖ σπάσαι πάρεστιν **ἀγαθοῦ δαίμονος**	P	Aj, N	O	E	G	Prologue		Festive	Trygaeus
308	τὴν θεῶν πασῶν μεγίστην καὶ **φιλαμπελωτάτην**.	W/P	Aj	O	E	G	Parodos Spoken unit		Festive	chorus
363	οὐδὲν πονηρόν, ἀλλ' ὅπερ καὶ **Κιλλικῶν**.	P	N	S	E	O	»		Personal abuse	Trygaeus
378	ναί, πρὸς τῶν **κρεῶν**	P	N	Exclam.	E	G	»		Personal abuse	Trygaeus
425	οἴμ', ὡς ἐλεήμων εἴμ' ἀεὶ **τῶν χρυσίδων**.	P	N	Gen. Obj.	E	O	»		Personal abuse	Hermes
474	οὐδὲν δεόμεθ', ὤνθρωπε, τῆς σῆς **μορμόνος**.	P	N	O	E	O	»		Personal abuse	Trygaeus
708	ταύτῃ ξυνοικῶν ἐκποιοῦ σαυτῷ **βότρυς**	P	N	O	E	G	1st episode		Festive	Hermes
756–7	ἑκατὸν δὲ κύκλῳ κεφαλαὶ **κολάκων** οἰμωξομένων ἐλιχμῶντο	P	N	Gen. Epexig.	P	O	Parabasis chanted anap.		Politics/ Personal abuse	chorus
822–3	ἀπὸ τοὐρανοῦ 'φαίνεσθε κακοήθεις πάνυ, ἐντευθενὶ δὲ πολύ τι **κακοηθέστεροι**.	P	Aj	C	E	O	2nd episode		Social criticism	Trygaeus
864	εὐδαιμονέστερος φανεῖ **τῶν Καρκίνου στροβίλων**	P	N, N	Gen. Compar.	E	O	Ode Sung		Paratragic/ Personal abuse	Trygaeus

Appendices — 211

Line	Text	TYPOLOGY					CONTEXT		CHARACTER
		Width	Gram	Syntax	Metre	Vocab	Part	Theme	
898	παίειν, ὀρύττειν, πὺξ ὁμοῦ καὶ τῷ **πέει**·	P	N	Dat.Instr.	E	Sex	2nd episode	Festive	Trygaeus
1022	χοὔτω τὸ πρόβατον **τῷ χορηγῷ σῴζεται**.	P	N, V	Dat.Adv. V	E	O	Mesode Spoken unit	Social criticism/ Personal abuse	Trygaeus
1065	συνθήκας πεποίησθ' ἄνδρες χαροποῖσι **πιθήκοις**	P	N	O	E	O	3rd episode	Politics	Hierokles
1116	τὴν Σίβυλλαν **ἔσθιε**	P	V	V	E	G	3rd episode	Personal abuse	Trygaeus

Tab. 10: Norms in *Para Prosdokian* - *Thesmophoriazusae*

Line	Text	TYPOLOGY					CONTEXT		CHARACTER
		Width	Gram	Syntax	Metre	Vocab	Part	Theme	
50	Θε. πρόμος ἡμέτερος – Κη. μῶν βινεῖσθαι;	P	V	V	E	Sex	Prologue	Personal abuse	in-law
57	Θε. καὶ χοανεύει. – Κη. καὶ λαικάζει	P	V	V	E	Sex	Prologue	Personal abuse	in-law
130-3	ὡς ἡδὺ τὸ μέλος, ὦ πότνιαι Γενετυλλίδες, καὶ θηλυδριῶδες καὶ κατεγλωττισμένον καὶ μανδαλωτόν, ὥστ' ἐμοῦ γ' ἀκροωμένου ὑπὸ τὴν ἕδραν αὐτὴν ὑπῆλθε γάργαλος.	S	N Aj, Aj Aj N, N	Exclam. C, C C Pp, S	E –, E P –, E	Sex	Prologue	Personal abuse	in-law
254	νὴ τὴν Ἀφροδίτην, ἡδύ γ' ὄζει ποσθίου.	P	N	O	E	Sex	Prologue	Personal abuse	in-law
289-90	καὶ τὴν θυγατέρα Χοιρίον ἀνδρός μοι τυχεῖν πλουτοῦντος, ἄλλως δ' ἠλιθίου κἀβελτέρου	S	Aj	C x 3	P, E	0	Prologue	Social criticism	in-law
509	τὸ γὰρ ἦτρον τῆς χύτρας ἐλάκτισεν	P	N	Gen.Part		G	1st episode	Social criticism	in-law
529-30	ὑπὸ λίθῳ γὰρ παντί που χρὴ μὴ δάκῃ ῥήτωρ ἀθρεῖν.	P	N	S		0	Antode Sung	Politics	chorus
531-2	ἀλλ' οὐ γάρ ἐστι τῶν ἀναισχύντων φύσει γυναικῶν οὐδὲν κάκιον εἰς ἅπαντα–πλὴν ἄρ' εἰ γυναῖκες.	P	N	C	E	0	1st episode	Social criticism	chorus
829	ἔρριπται τὸ σκιάδειον.	P	N	S	E	0	Parabasis chanted anap.	'Personal abuse'	chorus
857	λευκῆς νοτίζει μελανοσυρμαῖον λεών.	P	Aj	O		0	2nd episode	Paratragic	
935	ὀλίγου μ' ἀφείλετ' αὐτὸν ἱστιορράφος.	P	Aj	S	E	0	2nd episode	Personal abuse	Critylla

Appendices — 213

Line	Text	TYPOLOGY					CONTEXT			CHAR-ACTER
		Width	Gram	Syntax	Metre	Vocab	Part	Theme		
937	ὦ πρύτανι, πρὸς τῆς δεξιᾶς, ἥνπερ φιλεῖς κοίλην προτείνειν, ἀργύριον ἤν τις **διδῷ**,	P	Aj, N, V	O, V	P, –, E	O	2nd episode	Personal abuse		in-law
1201	μεμνῆσι τοίνυν τοὔνομ'· **Ἀρταμουξία**.	W/P	N	O	E	O	Exodus Spoken unit	Para–Satyric		Scythian

Tab. 11: Norms in *Para Prosodokian* - *Wealth*

Line	Text	TYPOLOGY					CONTEXT		Theme	CHAR-ACTER
		Width	Gram	Syntax	Metre	Vocab	Part			
27	πιστότατον ἡγοῦμαί σε καὶ **κλεπτίστατον**.	P	Aj	C	E	O	Prologue		Personal abuse	Chremylus
152	οὐδὲ προσέχειν τὸν νοῦν, ἐὰν δὲ πλούσιος, **τὸν πρωκτὸν** αὐτὰς εὐθὺς ὡς τοῦτον τρέπειν.	P	N	O		S	Prologue		Social criticism	Chremylus
165	Χρ. [...] ὁ δὲ χρυσοχοεῖ γε χρυσίον παρὰ σοῦ λαβών— Κα. ὁ δὲ **λωποδυτεῖ** γε νὴ Δί', ὁ δὲ **τοιχωρυχεῖ**—	P	V, V	V	R	O	Prologue		Social criticism	Carion
180	Κα. ὁ Τιμοθέου δὲ πύργος — Χρ. **ἐμπέσοι γέ σοι**.	P	V	V	E, A	O	Prologue		Personal abuse	Chremylus
277–8	ἐν τῇ σορῷ νυνὶ λαχὸν τὸ **γράμμα** σου **δικάζει**, σὺ δ' οὐ βαδίζεις, ὁ δὲ Χάρων τὸ **ξύμβολον** δίδωσιν.	P	N, V N	O	E	O	Parodos chanted 4ia cat.		Personal abuse	Carion
372	μῶν οὐ κέκλοφας ἀλλ' **ἥρπακας**;	P	V	V	E	O	1st episode		Personal abuse	Blepsidem.
600	οὐ γὰρ πείσεις, οὐδ' ἢν **πείσῃς** [oxymoron]	P	V	V	E	O	1st episode		Paratragic	Chremylus
706	μὰ Δί' οὐκ ἔγωγ', ἀλλὰ **σκατοφάγον**	P	Aj	C	E	S	2nd episode		Personal abuse	Carion
737	καὶ πρίν σε **κοτύλας ἐκπιεῖν οἴνου δέκα**	P	N, V	O, V	E	G	2nd episode		Social criticism	Carion
765	νὴ τὴν Ἑκάτην, κἀγὼ δ' ἀναδῆσαι βούλομαι εὐαγγέλιά σε **κριβανωτῶν ὁρμαθῷ**	P	N	O	E	G	2nd episode		Festive	wife
818	...ἀποψώμεσθα δ' οὐ λίθοις ἔτι, ἀλλὰ **σκοροδίοις** ὑπὸ τρυφῆς ἑκάστοτε	P	N	Instrum. Dative		O	3rd episode		Festive	Carion

Line	Text	TYPOLOGY						CONTEXT			CHAR-ACTER
		Width	Gram	Syntax	Metre	Vocab	Part		Theme	
963	ὦ μειρακίσκη· πυνθάνει γὰρ ὡρικῶς.	P	Aj	Exclam	P	O	4th episode	Personal abuse	chorus
972	ἀλλ' οὐ λαχοῦσ' ἔπινες ἐν τῷ γράμματι;	P	V	V		G	4th episode	Personal abuse	Chremylus

Abbreviations

Width of application: **W** within a single word / **P** phrase (expanding over a line) / **S** sentence (expanding over a wider passage)
Grammar: **N** noun / **I** infinitive / **V** verb / **Aj** adjective / **Av** adverb
Syntax: **S** subject / **O** object / **C** complement / **Pp** prepositional phrase
Metre: **R** rhyme / **A** antilabe / **E** end of line / **P** internal pause
Vocabulary: **Sex** sexual / **S** scatological / **G** gastronomic / **O** other

Tab. 12: The Intra-Dramatic Functions of Appropriated Myths

Play	Persuasive Myths (to argue for...)	Aetiological Myths (to explain why...)	Antiphonal Myths (to juxtapose...)	Abusive Myths (to mock...)	Structural Myths (to provide the...)
Ach.		524–9: 'Vendetta' for whores (the Peloponnesian War began)			325–51: *Telephus* (Assembly's attention to Dikaiopolis)
Eq.	197–201: Omen of the eagle and the snake (the forthcoming overthrowing of Paphlagon)				
Nub.			1061–70: Peleus' knife and marriage with Thetis (virtue is rewarded) vs Thetis' abandoning him and Hyperbolus (virtue is for losers)	1065–6: Peleus' knife (Hyperbolus as profiteer)	
Vesp.				15–9: Omen of the eagle and the snake (Cleonymus as ῥίψασπις); 1030-5: Cerberus (Cleon as a filth)	169–91: Odysseus beneath the donkey (Philocleon's escape; unsuccessful)
Pax		128–34: The fable of the beetle and the eagle (Trygaeus has chosen a beetle to go to Zeus)		752–8 ≈ *Vesp.*1030–5	71 ff: *Bellerophon* (journey to Olympus to complain)

Appendices — 217

Av.	466–521: Avian genealogy (birds' ancient origin and reign)	688–702: Avian cosmogony (birds appeared before the gods)	Tereus (mediator between humans & birds)
Lys.	551–4: Eros & Aphrodite's power (the potential of the sex strike)		
Thesm.		13–18: Separation of senses of sight and hearing (the in-law should not ask to hear what he is about to see)	563–4, 691–5: Tereus (men's violence) vs beetle (women's violence); 785–820: Melanion (hating women) vs Timon (hating men)
			687 ff: *Telephus, Palamedes, Helen, Andromeda* (in-law's escape; unsuccessful); 1200 ff: *Cyclops* (successful escape)
Ran.	1331–64: Lament over a lost cock (Euripides' ridiculous monodies)		
Eccl.	1041–2: Many Oedipuses (the dangers of the sexual communism)		
Plut.		290–315: Cyclops & Cirke (Penia's lifestyle) vs the resisting chorus (Wealth's lifestyle).	302–5: Cirke (Philonides as Nais' swine)

Bibliography

Adrados, F.R. (1990), 'Documentación suplementaria de la fábula greco-latina', *Euphrosyne* 18, 213–26.
Aguilar, R.M. (2003), 'La figura de Télefo en la literatura y en el arte griegos', *CFC(G)* 13, 181–93.
Alden, D./Mukherjee, A./Hoyer, W. (2000), 'The Effects of Incongruity, Surprise and Positive Moderators on Perceived Humor in Television Advertising', *Journal of Advertising* 29, 1–15.
Allan, W. (1999–2000), 'Euripides and the Sophists: Society and the Theatre of War', *ICS* 24/25, 145–56.
Allan, W. (2000), *The Andromache and Euripidean Tragedy*, Oxford.
Allen, W.S. (1968), 'Varia onomatopoetica', *Lingua* 21, 1–12.
Allison, R.H. (1983), 'Amphibian Ambiguities: Aristophanes and his *Frogs*', *G&R* 30, 8–20.
Amado, C./Kovács, G. (2016), 'Does Surprise Enhancement or Repetition Suppression Explain Visual Mismatch Negativity?', *European Journal of Neuroscience* 43, 1590–600.
Ambrose, Z.P. (1968), 'The Lekythion and the Anagram of *Frogs* 1203', *AJPh* 89, 342–6.
Anderson, G. (1981), 'Ληκύθιον and αὐτολήκυθος', *JHS* 101, 130–2.
Anderson, M.J. (2005), 'Myth', in: J. Gregory (ed.), *A Companion to Greek Tragedy*, Oxford, 121–35.
Andreassi, M. (2004), *Le Facezie del Philogelos: Barzellette antiche e umorismo moderno*, Lecce.
Andrew, D. (1980), 'The Well-Worn Muse: Adaptation in Film and Theory', in: M. Conger/ J. Welsch (eds.), *Narrative Strategies: Original Essays in Film and Prose Fiction*, Macomb, IL, 9–17.
Andrisano, A. (2007), 'Empusa, nome parlante di un mostro infernale (Aristoph. *Ran*. 288ss.)', in: A. Andrisano (ed.), *Animali, animali fantastici, ibridi, mostri*, Ferrara, 21–44.
Anstey, F. [as anonymous] (1891), 'Voces Populi', *Punch* 101, 69.
Arnott, P.D. (1959), 'Animals in the Greek Theatre', *G&R* 6, 177–9.
Arnott, W.G. (1973), 'Euripides and the Unexpected', *G&R* 20, 49–63.
Arrowsmith, W. (1973), 'Aristophanes' *Birds*: The Fantasy Politics of Eros', *Arion* 1, 119–67.
Attardo, S. (ed.) (2017), *The Routledge Handbook of Language and Humor*, New York.
Austin, C./Olson, D.S. (2004), *Aristophanes: Thesmophoriazusae*, Oxford.
Austin, N. (1990), *Meaning and Being in Myth*, University Park/London.
Bain, D. (1977), *Actors and Audience: A Study of Asides and Related Conventions in Greek Drama*, Oxford.
Bain, D. (1985), 'Ληκύθιον ἀπώλεσεν. Some Reservations', *CQ* 35, 31–7.
Bain, D. (1991), 'Six Greek Verbs of Sexual Congress (βινῶ, κινῶ, πυγίζω, ληκῶ, οἴφω, λαικάζω)', *CQ* 41, 51–77.
Baldwin, B. (1981), 'The Use of βινεῖν κινεῖν', *AJPh* 102, 79–80.
Baldwin, R. (1997), 'An Aristotelian Critique of Homeric Comic Technique in the *Iliad*', Ph.D. thesis, Florida State University.
Bañuls Oller, J.V./Morenilla Talens, C. (2008), '*Andrómeda* en el conjunto de las tragedias de Eurípides', *CFC(G)* 18, 89–110.
Barrett, W.S. (1964), *Euripides: Hippolytos*, Oxford.
Beard, M. (2014), *Laughter in Ancient Rome: On Joking, Tickling, and Cracking Up*, Berkeley, LA.
Beck, W. (1982), 'Ληκύθιον ἀπώλεσεν (and Theocritus II, 156)', *JHS* 102, 234.

Bednarowski, K.P. (2015), 'Surprise and Suspense in Aeschylus' *Agamemnon*', *AJPh* 136, 179–205.
Berk, L. (1964), *Epicharmus*, Groningen.
Betegh, G. (2004), *The Derveni Papyrus: Cosmology, Theology and Interpretation*, Cambridge.
Bilbao Ruiz, J. (2005), 'Procedimiento de humor ἐκ τῶν παρα προσδοκίαν en los scholia de *Acarnienses*', in: J.F. González Castro/A. Alvar Ezquerra/A. Bernabé/P. Cañizares Herriz/ G. Hinojo Andrés/C. Rueda González (eds.), *Actas del XI Congreso Español de Estudios Clásicos*, vol. 2, Madrid, 245–52.
Biles, Z.P. (2011), *Aristophanes and the Poetics of Competition*, Cambridge/New York.
Biles, Z.P./Olson, D.S. (2015), *Aristophanes: Wasps*, Oxford.
Biles, Z.P./Thorn, J. (2014), 'Rethinking Choregic Iconography in Apulia', in: E. Csapo/ H.R. Goette/J.R. Green (eds.), *Greek Theatre in the Fourth Century BC*, Berlin, 295–318.
Bond, G.W. (1981), *Euripides: Heracles*, Oxford.
Borthwick, E.K. (1968), 'Seeing Weasels. The Superstitious Background of the Empusa Scene in the *Frogs*', *CQ* 18, 200–6.
Bowie, A.M. (1984), '*Lysistrata* and the Lemnian Women', *Omnibus* 7, 17–9.
Bowie, A.M. (1993), *Aristophanes: Myth, Ritual, and Comedy*, Cambridge.
Bowie, A.M. (2007), 'Myth in Aristophanes', in: R. D. Woodard (ed.), *The Cambridge Companion to Greek Mythology*, Cambridge, 190–209.
Bowie, A.M. (2010), 'Myth and Ritual in Comedy', in: G.W. Dobrov (ed.), *Brill's Companion to the Study of Greek Comedy*, Leiden, 143–76.
Bowie, E.L. (1988), 'Who Is Dicaeopolis?', *JHS* 108, 183–5.
Brock, R J. (1986), 'The Double Plot of Aristophanes' *Knights*', *GRBS* 27, 15–27.
Brown, C.G. (1991), 'Empousa, Dionysus and the Mysteries: Aristophanes, *Frogs* 285 ff', *CQ* 41, 41–50.
Brown, P. (2008), 'Scenes at the Door in Aristophanic Comedy', in: M. Revermann/P. Wilson (eds.), *Performance, Iconography, Reception: Studies in Honour of Oliver Taplin*, Oxford, 349–73.
Bubel, F. (1991), *Euripides: Andromeda*, Stuttgart.
Büchner, H. (1950), 'Das Oxymoron in der griechischen Dichtung', Ph.D. thesis, University of Tübingen.
Burgers, C./Van Mulken, M. (2017), 'Humor Markers', in: Attardo 2017, 385–99.
Burgoon, J.K./Jones, S.B. (1976), 'Toward a Theory of Personal Space Expectations and their Violations', *Human Communication Research* 2, 131–46.
Burian, P. (2007), *Euripides: Helen*, Oxford.
Calame, C. (1999), *The Poetics of Eros in Ancient Greece*, Princeton.
Campbell, D.W./Wallace, M.G./Modirrousta, M./Polimeni, J./McKeen, N.A./Reiss, J.P. (2015), 'The Neural Basis of Humour Comprehension and Humour Appreciation: The Roles of the Temporoparietal Junction and Superior Frontal Gyrus', *Neuropsychologia* 79, 10–20.
Carnes, J.S. (1998), 'This Myth Which Is Not One: Construction of Discourse in Plato's *Symposium*', in: D. Larmour/P.A. Miller/C. Platter (eds.), *Rethinking Sexuality: Foucault and Classical Antiquity*, Princeton, 104–21.
Carpenter, T.H. (2014), 'A Case for Greek Tragedy in Italic Settlements in the Fourth Century BCE', in: Carpenter et al. 2014, 265–80.
Carpenter, T.H./Lynch, K.M./Robinson, E.G.D. (eds.) (2014), *The Italic People of Ancient Apulia: New Evidence from Pottery for Workshops, Markets, and Customs*, Cambridge/New York.

Carrière, J. (1977), *Le chœur secondaire dans le drame grec (Sur une ressource méconnue de la scène antique)*, Paris.
Carrière, J. (1997), 'Les métamorphoses des mythes et la crise de la cité dans la Comédie Ancienne', in: P. Thiercy/M. Menu (eds.), *Aristophane: la langue, la scène, la cité*, Bari, 413–42.
Cartelli, T. (1999), *Repositioning Shakespeare: National Formations, Postcolonial Appropriations*, London/New York.
Casolari, F. (2003), *Die Mythentravestie in der griechischen Komödie*, Muenster.
Chamberland, J./Roy-Charland, A/Perron, M./Dickinson, J. (2017), 'Distinction between Fear and Surprise: An Interpretation-Independent Test of the Perceptual-Attentional Limitation Hypothesis', *Social Neuroscience* 12, 751–68.
Charlier, P./Brun, L./Prêtre, C./Huynh-Charlier, I. (2012), 'Toilet Hygiene in the Classical Era', *British Medical Journal* 345, e8287.
Chaston, C. (2010), *Tragic Props and Cognitive Function: Aspects of the Function of Images in Thinking*, Leiden.
Chen, H.C./Chan, Y.C./Dai, R.H./Liao, Y.J./Tu, C.H. (2017), 'Neurolinguistics of Humor', in: Attard 2017, 282–94.
Ching, M. (1980), 'A Literary and Linguistic Analysis of Compact Verbal Paradox', in: M. Ching/M. Haley/R. Lunsford (eds.), *Linguistic Perspectives on Literature*, London, 175–81.
Chondros, T.G. (2004), 'Deus-ex-machina Reconstruction and Dynamics', in: M. Ceccarelli (ed.), *International Symposium on History of Machines and Mechanisms*, Dordrecht, 87–104.
Christopoulos, M. (2010), 'Dark-Winged Nyx and the Bright-Winged Eros in Aristophanes' "Orphic" cosmogony', in: M. Christopoulos/E. Karakantza/O. Levaniouk (eds.), *Light and Darkness in Ancient Greek Myth and Religion*, Lanham, 207–20.
Collard, C. (1979), 'Βινεῖν and Aristophanes, *Lysistrata* 934', *LCM* 4, 213–4.
Collard, C./Cropp, M.J./Lee, K.H. (eds.) (1995), *Euripides: Selected Fragmentary Plays*, vol. 1, Warminster.
Coo, L. (2013), 'A Tale of Two Sisters: Studies in Sophocles' *Tereus*', *TAPhA* 143, 349–84.
Cook, R.M. (1952), 'Dogs in Battle', in: T. Dohrn (ed.), *Festschrift Andreas Rumpf*, Cologne, 38–42.
Cornford, F. (1914), *The Origin of Attic Comedy*, London.
Courchesne, E./Hillyard, S.A/Galambos, R. (1975), 'Stimulus Novelty, Task Relevance and the Visual Evoked Potential in Man', *Electroencephalography and Clinical Neurophysiology* 39, 131–43.
Crane, G. (1990), '*Ajax*, the Unexpected, and the Deception Speech', *CPh* 85, 89–101.
Csapo, E. (1986), 'A Note on the Würzburg Bell-Crater H5697 (Telephus Travestitus)', *Phoenix* 40, 379–92.
Csapo, E. (1990), 'Hikesia in the *Telephus* of Aeschylus', *QUCC* 63, 41–52.
Csapo, E. (2010), *Actors and Icons of the Ancient Theater*, Chichester.
Csapo, E./Slater, W.J. (1995), *The Context of Ancient Drama*, Ann Arbor.
Cunningham, M.P. (1954), 'Medea ἀπὸ μηχανῆς', *CPh* 49, 151–60.
Currie, M. (2013), *The Unexpected: Narrative, Temporality and the Philosophy of Surprise*, Edinburgh.
Dale, A.M. (1957), 'An Interpretation of Ar. *Vesp.* 136–210 and Its Consequences for the Stage of Aristophanes', *JHS* 77, 205–11.
Dale, A.M. (1968), *The Lyric Metres of Greek Drama*, 2nd edn., Cambridge.
Dale, A.M. (1969), *Collected Papers*, Cambridge.

Dawe, R.D. (2006), *Sophocles: Oedipus Rex*, Cambridge.
Dearden, C.W. (1976), *The Stage of Aristophanes*, London.
Dearden, C.W. (1999), 'Plays for Export', *Phoenix* 53, 222–48.
Desmet, C./Iyengar, S. (2015), 'Adaptation, Appropriation, or What You Will', *Shakespeare* 11, 10–19.
Diamantakou, K. (2007), *Στην αρχαία κωμική ενδοχώρα: Εισαγωγή στη σημειολογία του χώρου και του χρόνου στο θέατρο του Αριστοφάνη*, Athens.
Dijk, G.J.V. (1997), *Αἶνοι Λόγοι Μῦθοι. Fables in Archaic, Classical, and Hellenistic Greek Literature*, Leiden.
Dixon, D.W. (2014), 'Reconsidering Euripides' *Bellerophon*', *CQ* 64, 493–506.
Dobrov, G.W. (2001), *Figures of Play: Greek Drama and Metafictional Poetics*, Oxford/New York.
Dobson, M. (2013), 'Aristophanes' Myth of Eros and Contemporary Psychologies of the Self', in: V. Zajko/E. O'Gorman (eds.), *Classical Myth and Psychoanalysis: Ancient and Modern Stories of the Self*, Oxford, 283–96.
Dover, K.J. (1966), 'Aristophanes' Speech in Plato's *Symposium*', *JHS* 86, 41–50.
Dover, K.J. (1967), 'Portrait-Masks in Aristophanes', in: R E.H. Westendorp Boerma (ed.), *Κωμῳδοτραγήματα*, Amsterdam, 16–28.
Dover, K.J. (1968), *Aristophanes: Clouds*, Oxford.
Dover, K.J. (1972), *Aristophanic Comedy*, London.
Dover, K.J. (1987), *Greek and the Greeks: Language, Poetry, Drama*, Oxford.
Dover, K.J. (1993), *Aristophanes: Frogs*, Oxford.
Duckworth, G. (1994), *The nature of Roman Comedy*, 2nd edn., Norman, OK.
Dunbar, N.V. (1995), *Aristophanes: Birds*, Oxford.
Eco, U. (1976), *Il superuomo di massa*, Milano.
Edwards, A.T. (1991), 'Aristophanes' Comic Poetics: Τρύξ, Scatology, Σκῶμμα', *TAPhA* 121, 157–79.
Eisner, R. (1979), 'A Case of Poetic Justice. Aristophanes' Speech in the *Symposium*', *CW* 72, 417–8.
Ekman, P. (1972), 'Universal and Cultural Differences in Facial Expressions of Emotion', in: J. Cole (ed.), *Nebraska Symposium of Motivation*, vol. 19, Lincoln, NE, 207–83.
Ekman, P. (1980), *The Face of Man*, New York.
Ekman, P. (1983), 'Autonomic Nervous System Activity Distinguishes among Emotions', *Science* 221, 1208–10.
Ekman, P. (2016), 'What Scientists Who Study Emotion Agree About', *Perspectives on Psychological Science* 11, 31–4.
Elam, K. (2002), *The Semiotics of Theatre and Drama*, 2nd edn., London/New York.
English, M.C. (1999), 'The Stage Properties of Aristophanic Comedy: A Descriptive Lexicon', Ph.D. thesis, Boston University.
English, M.C. (2000), 'The Diminishing Role of Stage Properties in Aristophanic Comedy', *Helios* 27, 149–62.
English, M.C. (2007), 'Reconstructing Aristophanic Performance: Stage Properties in *Acharnians*', *CW* 100, 199–227.
Ermida, I. (2018), *The Language of Comic Narratives*, Berlin/New York.
Farmer, M.C. (2017), *Tragedy on the Comic Stage*, Oxford.
Farnell, L. (1933), 'The Paradox of the *Prometheus Vinctus*', *JHS* 53, 40–50.
Feeney, D. (2009), 'Catullus and the Roman Paradox Epigram', *MD* 61, 29–39.
Filippo, A. (2001–2002), 'L'aprosdoketon in Aristofane', *Rudiae* 13/14, 59–143.

Finglass, P. (2016), 'A New Fragment of Sophocles' *Tereus*', *ZPE* 200, 61–85.
Fischer-Lichte, E. (1992), *The Semiotics of Theater*, Indiana.
Fitzpatrick, D. (2001), 'Sophocles' *Tereus*', *CQ* 51, 90–101.
Fletcher, J. (2012), 'The Women's Decree: Law and Its Other in *Ecclesiazusae*', in: C.W. Marshall/
 G. Kovacs (eds.), *No Laughing Matter: Studies in Athenian Comedy*, London, 127–40.
Foley, H.P. (1988), 'Tragedy and Politics in Aristophanes' *Acharnians*', *JHS* 108, 33–47.
Fontaine, M. (2010), *Funny Words in Plautine Comedy*, Oxford.
Fornara, C.W. (1971), 'Evidence for the Date of Herodotus' Publication', *JHS* 91, 25–34.
Forster, E.S. (1941), 'Dogs in Ancient Warfare', *G&R* 10, 114–7.
Foster, M./Keane, M. (2013), 'Surprise! You've Got Some Explaining to Do', in: M. Knauff/
 M. Pauen/N. Sebanz/I. Wachsmuth (eds.), *Proceedings of the 35th Annual Conference of the Cognitive Science Society*, Berlin, 2321–6.
Foster, M./Keane, M. (2015), 'Surprise as an Ideal Case for the Interplay of Cognition and Emotion', *Behavioral and Brain Sciences* 38, E74.
Fraenkel, E. (1950), *Aeschylus: Agamemnon*, 3 vols., Oxford.
Frazer, J.G. (ed.) (1921), *Apollodorus: The Library* (Loeb), vol. 2, Cambridge, MA.
Freud, S. (1905), *Der Witz und seine Beziehung zum Unbewussten*, Leipzig/Vienna.
Fries, A. (2014), *Pseudo-Euripides: Rhesus*, Berlin.
Garson, R.W. (1974), 'Amphitheos and Anthropos in Aristophanes', *Hermes* 102, 367–9.
Garson, R.W. (1980), 'Paradox in the Greek Sepulchral Epigram', *AClass* 23, 110–4.
Garson, R.W. (1981), 'The Use of Paradox in the Amatory Epigrams in the Greek Anthology', *AClass* 24, 160–2.
Gelzer, T. (1996), 'Some Aspects of Aristophanes' Dramatic Art in the *Birds*', in: E. Segal (ed.), *Oxford Readings in Aristophanes*, Oxford/New York, 194–215.
Gerö, E.C./Johnsson, H.R. (2002), 'A Comment on the Lekythion-Scene in Aristophanes' *Frogs*', *Eranos* 100, 38–50.
Gilula, D. (1983), 'Four Deadly Sins? (Arist. *Wasps* 74-84)', *CQ* 33, 358–62.
Giora, R. (1991), 'On the Cognitive Aspects of the Joke', *Journal of Pragmatics* 16, 465–85.
Gironzetti, E. (2017), 'Prosodic and Multimodal Markers of Humor', in: Attardo 2017, 400–13.
Green, J.R. (2014), 'Zeus on a See-Saw. A Comic Scene from Paestum', *Logeion* 4, 1–27.
Gregorio, L. (1983), 'Il *Bellerofonte* di Euripide I: Dati per una ricostruzione' and 'Il *Bellerofonte* di Euripide II: Tentativo di ricostruzione', *CCC* 4, 159–213, 365–82.
Greimas, A.J. (1983), *Structural Semantics. An Attempt at a Method*, Lincoln, NE [French original: 1966].
Griffith, J.G. (1970), 'Ληκύθιον ἀπώλεσεν. A Postscript', *HSPh* 74, 43–4.
Griffith, M. (2013), *Aristophanes' Frogs*, Oxford.
Griffith, R.D. (1987), 'The Hoopoe's Name (A Note on *Birds* 48)', *QUCC* 55, 59–63.
Grossman, J.B. (2007), 'Forever Young: An Investigation of the Depictions of Children on Classical Attic Funerary Monuments', in: A. Cohen/J. Rutter (eds.), *Constructions of Childhood in Ancient Greece and Italy*, Princeton, 309–22.
Guido, R./Filippo, A. (1981), 'Ληκύθιον ἀπώλεσεν (Ar. *Ranae* 1208 sgg.)', *GB* 10, 83–93.
Habash, M. (2002), 'Dionysos' Roles in Aristophanes' *Frogs*', *Mnemosyne* 55, 1–17.
Hackforth, R. (1938), 'Aristophanes, *Clouds* 534–6', *CR* 52, 5–7.
Haigh, A.E. (1907), *The Attic Theatre: A Description of the Stage and Theatre of the Athenians, and of the Dramatic Performances at Athens*, 3rd edn. revised by A.W. Pickard-Cambridge, Oxford.

Hall, E. (2000), 'The Singing Actors of Antiquity', in: P.E. Easterling/E. Hall (eds.), *Greek and Roman Actors: Aspects of an Ancient Profession*, Cambridge, 3–38.
Hall, E. (2013), 'The Aesopic in Aristophanes', in: E. Bakola/L. Prauscello/M. Telò (eds.), *Greek Comedy and the Discourse of Genres*, Cambridge, 227–97.
Halliwell, S. (1991), 'Comic Satire and Freedom of Speech in Classical Athens', *JHS* 111, 48–70.
Halliwell, S. (2014), 'Laughter', in: M. Revermann (ed.), *The Cambridge Companion to Greek Comedy*, Cambridge, 189–205.
Hamilton, R. (1984), 'Sources for the Athenian Amphidromia', *GRBS* 25, 243–51.
Handley, E.W./Rea, J. (1957), *The Telephus of Euripides*, *BICS* Suppl. 5, London.
Harrison, E. (1972), 'The South Frieze of the Nike Temple and the Marathon Painting in the Painted Stoa', *AJA* 76, 353–78.
Haury, A. (1960), 'Le chant du rossignol ou Buffon mystifié par Aristophane', *BAGB* 3, 373–6.
Hawkins, T. (2001), 'Seducing a Misanthrope: Timon the Philogynist in Aristophanes' *Lysistrata*', *GRBS* 42, 143–62.
Heath, M. (1987), 'Euripides' *Telephus*', *CQ* 37, 272–80.
Heath, M./Okell, E. (2007), 'Sophocles' *Ajax*: Expect the Unexpected', *CQ* 57, 363–80.
Heiden, B. (1991), 'Tragedy and Comedy in the *Frogs* of Aristophanes', *Ramus* 20, 95–111.
Henderson, J. (1972), 'The Lekythos and *Frogs* 1200–1248', *HSPh* 76, 133–44.
Henderson, J. (1980), '*Lysistrate*: The Play and Its Themes', in: J. Henderson (ed.), *Aristophanes: Essays in Interpretation*, Cambridge, 153–218.
Henderson, J. (1987), *Aristophanes: Lysistrata*, Oxford.
Henderson, J. (1991), *The Maculate Muse: Obscene Language in Attic Comedy*, 2nd edn., New York/Oxford.
Henderson, J. (2000), 'Pherekrates and the Women of Old Comedy', in: F.D. Harvey/J. Wilkins (eds.), *The Rivals of Aristophanes*, London/Swansea, 135–50.
Higgins, W.E. (1977), 'A Passage to Hades: The *Frogs* of Aristophanes', *Ramus* 6, 60–81.
Hill, S.E. (2011), *Eating to Excess: The Meaning of Gluttony and the Fat Body in the Ancient World*, Santa Barbara.
Hodges, F.M. (2001), 'The Ideal Prepuce in Ancient Greece and Rome: Male Genital Aesthetics and Their Relation to *Lipodermos*, Circumcision, Foreskin Restoration, and the *Kynodesme*', *BHM* 75, 376–405.
Hofmann, H. (1976), *Mythos und Komödie: Untersuchungen zu den Vögeln des Aristophanes*, Hildesheim/New York.
Hofmann, H. (2006), 'Kritische Nachlese zur Hypothesis des Sophokleischen *Tereus* (P. Oxy. 3013)', in: S. Eklund (ed.), *Syncharmata: Studies in Honour of J.F. Kindstrand*, Uppsala, 87–112.
Holden, H. (ed.) (1868), *Aristophanis Comoediae*, vol. 1, Cambridge.
Holmes, D. (2011), 'Re-Eroticizing the Hoopoe: Tereus in Aristophanes' *Birds*', *SyllClass* 22, 1–20.
Holzinger, K. (1940), *Kritisch-exegetischer Kommentar zu Aristophanes' Plutos*, Vienna.
Hordern, J.H. (1999), 'The Cyclops of Philoxenus', *CQ* 49, 445–55.
Horowski, J. (1966), 'De vocibus, quae dicuntur onomatopoeia in Aristophanis fabulis occurrentibus', *Eos* 56, 227–37.
Hourmouziades, N. (1965), *Production and Imagination in Euripides*, Athens.
Hourmouziades, N. (1986), 'Sophocles' *Tereus*', in: J.H. Betts/J.T. Hooker/J.R. Green (eds.), *Studies in Honour of T.B.L. Webster*, Bristol, 134–42.
Huang, A./Rivlin, E. (eds.) (2014), *Shakespeare and the Ethics of Appropriation*, New York.

Hubbard, T.K. (1991), *The Mask of Comedy: Aristophanes and the Intertextual Parabasis*, Ithaca/London.
Hughes, A. (2012), *Performing Greek Comedy*, Cambridge.
Hughes, P. (1984), *More on Oxymoron*, London.
Hutcheon, L. (2006), *A Theory of Adaptation*, New York.
Janko, R. (1984), *Aristotle on Comedy*, London.
Jocelyn, H.D. (1980), 'A Greek Indecency and Its Students: λαικάζειν', *PCPhS* 206, 12–66.
Kakridis, F.I. (1982), *Αριστοφάνους Όρνιθες*, Giannena.
Kanavou, N. (2011), 'Political Myth in Aristophanes: Another Form of Comic Satire?', *GRBS* 51, 382–400.
Kanavou, N. (2011a), *Aristophanes' Comedy of Names: A Study of Speaking Names in Aristophanes*, Berlin/New York.
Kanellakis, D. (2017), 'Myth and Paradox in Aristophanes: The Poetics of Appropriation', *Logeion* 7, 170–215.
Kanellakis, D. (2017-2018), 'Paracomedy in Euripides' *Bacchae*', *Παρουσία* 21, 63–82.
Kanellakis, D. (2018), 'Aristophanes in Greek Shadow Theatre: Codification and Adaptation of *Peace* and *Frogs* Performed by Evgenios Spatharis', *BMGS* 42, 151–71.
Kant, I. (1987), *Critique of Judgment*, Indianapolis [German original: 1790].
Kapogianni, E. (2013), 'Irony and the Literal Versus Nonliteral Distinction: A Typological Approach with Focus on Ironic Implicature Strength', Ph.D. thesis, University of Cambridge.
Kapp, E. (1928), 'Πισθέταιρος', *Philologus* 84, 259–61.
Katz, J. (1972), *Semantic Theory*, New York.
Kazantzidis, G. (2016), 'Empathy and the Limits of Disgust in the Hippocratic Corpus', in: D. Lateiner/D. Spatharas (eds.), *The Ancient Emotion of Disgust*, Oxford, 45–68.
Kennedy, G. (2005), *Invention and Method: Two Rhetorical Treatises from the Hermogenic Corpus*, Atlanta, GA.
Keuls, E.C. (1993), *The Reign of the Phallus: Sexual Politics in Ancient Athens*, London.
Kilmer, M. (1990), 'Sexual Violence: Archaic Athens and the Recent Past', in: E.M. Craik (ed.), *Owls to Athens*, Oxford, 261–77.
Kilmer, M. (1993), *Greek Erotica on Attic Red-Figure Vases*, London.
Kirk, G.S. (1981), 'Some Methodological Pitfalls in the Study of Ancient Greek Sacrifice', in: J. Rudhardt/O. Reverdin (eds.), *Le sacrifice dans l'antiquité*, Geneva, 41–90.
Kloosterman, N./Meindertsma, T./van Loon, A./Lamme, V./Bonneh, Y./Donner, T. (2015), 'Pupil Size Tracks Perceptual Content and Surprise', *European Journal of Neuroscience* 41, 1068–78.
Koenen, L. (1959), 'Tereus in den *Vögeln* des Aristophanes', in: H. Dahlmann/R. Merkelbach (eds.), *Studien zu Textgeschichte und Textkritik*, Cologne, 83–7.
Koestler, A. (1964), *The Act of Creation*, London.
Komornicka, A.M. (1964), *Métaphores, personnifications et comparaisons dans l'oeuvre d'Aristophane*, Wrocław.
Konstan, D. (2013), 'Propping up Greek Tragedy: The Right Use of *Opsis*', in: G. Harrison/V. Liapis (eds.), *Performance in Greek and Roman Theatre*, Leiden, 63–75.
Konstantakos, I.M. (2014), 'Comedy in the Fourth Century I: Mythological Burlesques', in: M. Fontaine/A.C. Scafuro (eds.), *The Oxford Handbook of Greek and Roman Comedy*, Oxford, 160–80.
Konstantakos, I.M. (2015), 'On the Early History of the Braggart Soldier: Archilochus and Epicharmus', *Logeion* 5, 41–84.

Konstantakos, I.M. (2016), 'On the Early History of the Braggart Soldier: Aristophanes' Lamachus and the Politicization of the Comic Type', *Logeion* 6, 112–63.
Kossatz-Deissmann, A. (1980), 'Telephus Transvetitus', in: H.A. Cahn/E. Simon (eds.), *Tainia: Festschrift für Roland Hampe*, Mainz, 281–90.
Kouremenos, T./Parássoglou, G.M./Tsantsanoglou, K. (eds.) (2006), *The Derveni Papyrus*, Firenze.
Kovacs, D. (1997), 'Gods and Men in Euripides' *Trojan Trilogy*', *ColbyQ* 33, 162–76.
Kronauer, U. (1954), 'Der formale Witz in den Komödien des Aristophanes', Ph.D. thesis, University of Zurich.
Ku, L.C./Feng, Y.J./Chan, Y.C./Wu, C.L./Chen, H.C. (2017), 'A Re-Visit of Three-Stage Humor Processing with Readers' Surprise, Comprehension, and Funniness Ratings: An ERP Study', *Journal of Neurolinguistics* 42, 49–62.
Lada-Richards, I. (1999), *Initiating Dionysus: Ritual and Theatre in Aristophanes' Frogs*, Oxford.
Lamari, A. (2010), *Narrative, Intertext, and Space in Euripides' Phoenissae*, Berlin.
Landfester, M. (1967), *Die Ritter des Aristophanes*, Amsterdam.
Lattimore, R. (1959), *Hesiod: The Works and Days, The Shield of Heracles*, Ann Arbor.
Lauriola, R. (2004), 'Aristofane, Eracle e Cleone: sulla duplicità di un'immagine aristofanea', *Eikasmos* 15, 85–99.
Lederer, R. (1990), 'Oxymoronology', *Word Ways: The Journal of Recreational Linguistics* 23, 102–6.
Lee, K.H. (1982), 'The Iris-Lyssa scene in Euripides' *Heracles*', *Antichthon* 16, 44–53.
Lee, M. (2015), *Body, Dress, and Identity in Ancient Greece*, Cambridge.
Lever, K. (1952–1953), 'Poetic Metaphor and Allegory in Aristophanes', *CW* 46, 220–3.
Ley, G. (1988), 'A Scenic Plot of Sophocles' *Ajax* and *Philoctetes*', *Eranos* 86, 85–115.
Lianeri, A. (2016), 'Introduction: The Futures of Greek Historiography', in: A. Lianeri (ed.), *Knowing Future Time in and through Greek Historiography*, Berlin, 1–56.
Lind, H. (1990), *Der Gerber Kleon in den Rittern des Aristophanes: Studien zur Demagogenkomödie*, Frankfurt.
Loomis, W.T. (1998), *Wages, Welfare Costs, and Inflation in Classical Athens*, Ann Arbor.
López Eire, A. (1996), *La lengua coloquial de la comedia aristofánica*, Murcia.
Lowe, N. (2006), 'Aristophanic Spacecraft', in: L. Kozak/J. Rich (eds.), *Playing around Aristophanes: Essays in Honour of Alan Sommerstein*, Oxford, 48–64.
Lowe, N. (2008), *Comedy*, Cambridge.
Ludden, G./Kudrowitz, B./Schifferstein, H./Hekkert, P. (2012) 'Surprise and Humor in Product Design', *Humor* 25, 285–310.
Lullies, R. (1960), 'Βάτραχοι', in: F. Eckstein (ed.), *Θεωρία: Festschrift für W.H. Schuchhardt*, Baden-Baden, 139–49.
Luppe, W. (1972), 'Die Zahl der Konkurrenten an den komischen Agonen zur Zeit des peloponnischen Krieges', *Philologus* 116, 53–75.
Luppe, W. (1990), 'Die *Bellerophontes*: Hypothesis P. Oxy. 3651', *Eikasmos* 1, 171–7.
Luppe, W. (2007), 'Die *Tereus*: Hypothesis P. Oxy. XLII 3013', *APF* 53, 1–5.
MacCary, W.T. (1979), 'Philocleon Ithyphallos: Dance, Costume and Character in the *Wasps*', *TAPhA* 109, 137–47.
MacDowell, D.M. (1971), *Aristophanes: Wasps*, Oxford.
MacDowell, D.M. (1972), 'The *Frogs*' Chorus', *CR* 22, 3–5.
MacDowell, D.M. (1978), *The Law in Classical Athens*, London.
Macquarie Dictionary (2013), 6th edn., Sydney.

Maguire, L. (2009), *Helen of Troy: From Homer to Hollywood*, Chichester.
Major, W.E. (2013), 'Staging *Andromeda* in Aristophanes and Euripides', *CJ* 108, 385–403.
Mariscal, R./Presentación, L. (2007), 'El prólogo del *Palamedes* de Eurípides', *Lexis* 25, 229–40.
Marsden, J. (ed.) (1991), *The Appropriation of Shakespeare: Post-Renaissance Reconstructions of The Works and the Myth*, New York.
Marshall, C.W. (1997), 'Comic Technique and the Fourth Actor', *CQ* 47, 77–84.
Marshall, C.W. (1999), 'Some Fifth-Century Masking Conventions', *G&R* 46, 188–202.
Marshall, C.W. (2000), 'Female Performers on Stage? (*PhV* 96 [*RVP* 2/33])', *T&P* 21, 13–25.
Marshall, C.W./van Willigenburg, S. (2004), 'Judging Athenian Dramatic Competitions', *JHS* 124, 90–107.
Marston, V. (1973), 'Aristophanes' Use of Obscenity', Ph.D. thesis, Ohio State University.
Martin, R.P. (1987), 'Fire on the Mountain: *Lysistrata* and the Lemnian Women', *ClAnt* 6, 77–105.
Marzullo, B. (1953), 'Strepsiade', *Maia* 6, 99–124.
Mastromarco, G. (1983), 'Due casi di aprosdoketon scenico in Aristofane (*Acarnesi* 393–413, *Vespe* 526–538)', *Vichiana* 12, 249–54.
Mastromarco, G. (1989), 'L'eroe e il mostro (Aristofane, *Vespe* 1029–1044)', *RFIC* 117, 410–23.
Mastromarco, G. (1998), 'La degradazione del mostro: La maschera del Ciclope nella commedia e nel dramma satiresco del quinto secolo a.C.', in: A.M. Belardinelli/O. Imperio/ G. Mastromarco/M. Pellegrino/P. Totaro (eds.), *Tessere. Frammenti della commedia greca: studi e commenti*, Bari, 9–42.
Mastromarco, G. (2008), 'La parodia dell' *Andromeda* euripidea nelle *Tesmoforiazuse* di Aristofane', *CFC(G)* 18, 177–88.
Mastronarde, D.J. (1990), 'Actors on High: The Skene Roof, the Crane, and the Gods in Attic Drama', *ClAnt* 9, 247–94.
May, J./Wisse, J. (2001), *Cicero: On the Ideal Orator* (De Oratore), Oxford.
McDermott, E.A. (1991), 'Double Meaning and Mythic Novelty in Euripides' Plays', *TAPhA* 121, 123–32.
McGing, B.C. (2013), 'Youthfulness in Polybius: The Case of Philip V of Macedon', in: B. Gibson/T. Harrison (eds.), *Polybius and His World*, Oxford, 181–200.
McLeish, K. (1980), *The Theatre of Aristophanes*, London.
McNeil, L. (2005), 'Bridal Cloths, Cover-ups, and Kharis: The 'Carpet Scene' in Aeschylus' *Agamemnon*', *G&R* 52, 1–17.
Méautis, G. (1932), 'L'épisode d'Amphithéos dans les *Acharniens* d'Aristophane', *REA* 34, 241–4.
Meluzzi, C. (2017), 'Diminutives in Ancient Greek. Intensification and Subjectivity', in: M. Napoli/M. Ravetto (eds.), *Exploring Intensification: Synchronic, Diachronic and Cross-Linguistic Perspectives*, Amsterdam/Philadelphia, 127–46.
Meyer, G. (1923), *Die stilistische Verwendung der Nominalkomposition im Griechischen: Ein Beitrag zur Geschichte der διπλᾶ ὀνόματα*, Leipzig.
Michael, C. (1981), 'Ο κωμικός λόγος του Αριστοφάνους', Ph.D. thesis, University of Athens.
Mikolajczyk, R. (1979), 'Formy deminutywne imion własnych w komediach Arystofanesa', *Eos* 67, 221–31.
Miller, C. (2012), *Surprise: The Poetics of the Unexpected from Milton to Austen*, Ithaca, NY.
Miller, H.W. (1948), 'Euripides' *Telephus* and the *Thesmophoriazusae* of Aristophanes', *CPh* 43, 174–83.
Mitchell, A.G. (2009), *Greek Vase-Painting and the Origins of Visual Humour*, Cambridge.

Mitchell, T. (1835), *The Knights of Aristophanes*, London.
Mitchell, T. (1839), *The Frogs of Aristophanes*, London.
Moessner, O. (1907), 'Die Mythologie in der dorischen und altattischen Komodie', Ph.D. thesis, University of Erlangen.
Moulton, C. (1979), 'The Lyric of Insult and Abuse in Aristophanes', *MH* 36, 23–47.
Moulton, C. (1996), 'Comic Myth-Making and Aristophanes' Originality', in: E. Segal (ed.), *Oxford Readings in Aristophanes*, Oxford, 216–28.
Mueller, M. (2016), *Objects as Actors: Props and the Poetics of Performance in Greek Tragedy*, Chicago.
Mukařovský, J. (1982), 'An Attempt at a Structural Analysis of a Dramatic Figure', in: P. Steiner (ed.), *The Prague School: Selected Writings 1929–1946*, Austin, 171–77 [Czech original: 1931].
Müller, A. (1913), 'Die Schimpfwörter in der griechischen Komödie', *Philologus* 72, 321–37.
Müller, D. (1974), 'Die Verspottung der metaphorischen Ausdrucksweise durch Aristophanes', in: U. Reinhardt/K. Sallmann (eds.), *Musa iocosa: Arbeiten uber Humor und Witz, Komik und Komödie der Antike*, Hildesheim, 29–41.
Murray, G. (1940), *Aeschylus, the Creator of Tragedy*, Oxford.
Myres, J.L. (1938), 'Persephone and the Pomegranate (*H. Dem.* 372–4)', *CR* 52, 51–2.
Napolitano, M. (2007), 'L'aprosdoketon in Aristofane: alcune riflessioni', in: A. Camerotto (ed.), *Diafonie. Esercizi sul comico*, Padova, 45–72.
Navarre, O. (1933), 'Ληκύθιον ἀπώλεσεν', *REA* 35, 278–80.
Nesselrath, H.G. (1990), *Die attische mittlere Komödie*, Berlin.
Nesselrath, H.G. (1995), 'Myth, Parody, and Comic Plots: The Birth of Gods and Middle Comedy', in: G.W. Dobrov (ed.), *Beyond Aristophanes: Transition and Diversity in Greek Comedy*, Atlanta, 1–28.
Newiger, H.J. (1957), *Metapher und Allegorie: Studien zu Aristophanes*, Munich.
Newiger, H.J. (1961), 'Elektra in Aristophanes' *Wolken*', *Hermes* 89, 422–30.
Newiger, H.J. (1965), 'Retraktationen zu Aristophanes' *Frieden*', *RhM* 108, 229–54.
Newiger, H.J. (1989), 'Ekkyklema e mechané nella messa in scena del dramma greco', *Dioniso* 59, 173–85.
Nida, E.A. (1975), *Componential Analysis of Meaning: An Introduction to Semantic Structures*, Hague.
O'Regan, D.E. (1992), *Rhetoric, Comedy, and the Violence of Language in Aristophanes' Clouds*, New York.
Olson, D.S. (1998), *Aristophanes: Peace*, Oxford.
Olson, D.S. (2002), *Aristophanes: Acharnians*, Oxford.
Olson, D.S. (1992), 'Names and Naming in Aristophanic Comedy', *CQ* 42, 304–19.
Olson, D.S. (1999), 'Kleon's Eyebrows (Cratin. fr. 228 K–A) and Late 5th-Century Comic Portrait-Masks', *CQ* 49, 320–1.
Padilla, M. (1992), 'The Heraclean Dionysus: Theatrical and Social Renewal in Aristophanes' *Frogs*', *Arethusa* 25, 359–84.
Paganelli, L. (1978-1979), 'Blepyros nome parlante (Aristoph. *Eccl.* 327)', *MCr* 13/14, 231–5.
Paley, F.A. (1873), *The Peace of Aristophanes*, Cambridge.
Palm, G. (2012), *Novelty, Information, and Surprise*, Berlin.
Panagl, O. (1983), 'Pheidippides: Etymologische Überlegungen zu einem aristophanischen Personennamen', in: P. Händel/W. Meid (eds.), *Festschrift für Robert Muth*, Innsbruck, 297–306.
Parker, L.P.E. (1997), *The Songs of Aristophanes*, Oxford.

Parker, R. (1996), *Athenian Religion: A History*, Oxford.
Patch, D.C. (ed.) (2011), *Dawn of Egyptian Art*, New York.
Pearson, A.C. (1917), *The Fragments of Sophocles*, vol. 2, Cambridge.
Peigney, J. (2009), 'La mythologie d'Aristophane: les monstres de la comédie, parodie et création', in: J.P. Aygon/C. Bonnet/C. Noacco (eds.), *La mythologie de l'antiquité à la modernité: appropriation, adaptation, détournement*, Rennes, 61–71.
Penella, R.J. (1973), 'Κῳδάριον in Aristophanes' *Frogs*', *Mnemosyne* 26, 337–41.
Peppler, C.W. (1910), 'The Termination -κός, as Used by Aristophanes for Comic Effect', *AJPh* 31, 428–44.
Pfister, M. (1988), *The Theory and Analysis of Drama*, Cambridge.
Phillips, A. (2001), 'The Dogs of the Classical World', in: D.J. Brewer/T. Clark/A. Phillips (eds.), *Dogs in Antiquity: Anubis to Cerberus*, Warminster, 83–106.
Pickard-Cambridge, A.W. (1962), *Dithyramb: Tragedy and Comedy*. 2nd edn. revised by T.B.L. Webster, Oxford.
Pickard-Cambridge, A.W. (1988), *The Dramatic Festivals of Athens*, 2nd edn. revised by J. Gould/D.M. Lewis, Oxford.
Plass, P. (1988), *Wit and the Writing of History: The Rhetoric of Historiography in Imperial Rome*, Madison.
Platnauer, M. (1964), *Aristophanes: Peace*, Oxford.
Platter, C. (2007), *Aristophanes and the Carnival of Genres*, Baltimore.
Plutchik, R. (1980), 'A General Psychoevolutionary Theory of Emotion', in: R. Plutchik/H. Kellerman (eds.), *Emotion: Theory, Research, and* Experience, vol. 1, New York, 3–33.
Poe, J.P. (1999), 'Entrances, Exits, and the Structure of Aristophanic Comedy', *Hermes* 127, 189–207.
Poe, J.P. (2000), 'Multiplicity, Discontinuity, and Visual Meaning in Aristophanic Comedy', *RhM* 143, 256–95.
Politis, N. (1914), *Ἐκλογαί ἀπό τά τραγούδια τοῦ ἑλληνικοῦ λαοῦ*, Athens.
Pope, M. (1986), 'Athenian Festival Judges: Seven, Five, or However Many', *CQ* 36, 322–6.
Prato, C. (2001), *Aristofane: Le Donne alle Tesmoforie*, Milan.
Preiser, C. (2000), *Euripides' Telephos: Einleitung, Text, Kommentar*, Hildesheim.
Propp, V. (2009), *On the Comic and Laughter*, Toronto [Russian original: 1976].
Raeburn, D. (2000), 'The Significance of Stage Properties in Euripides' *Electra*', *G&R* 47, 149–68.
Raeburn, D./Thomas, O. (2011), *The Agamemnon of Aeschylus*, Oxford.
Ramalho, A. C. (1952), 'Διπλᾶ ὀνόματα no estilo de Aristófanes', Ph.D. thesis, University of Coimbra.
Raskin, V. (1985), *Semantic Mechanisms of Humor*, Dordrecht.
Rau, P. (1967), *Paratragodia: Untersuchungen einer komischen Form des Aristophanes*, Munich.
Reckford, K.J. (1991), 'Strepsiades as a Comic Ixion', *ICS* 16, 125–36.
Rennie, W.A. (1909), *The Acharnians of Aristophanes*, London.
Revermann, M. (2006), *Comic Business: Theatricality, Dramatic Technique, and Performance Contexts of Aristophanic Comedy*, Oxford.
Revermann, M. (2013), 'Generalizing about Props: Greek Drama, Comparator Traditions, and the Analysis of Stage Objects', in: G. Harrison/V. Liapis (eds.), *Performance in Greek and Roman Theatre*, Leiden, 77–88.

Revermann, M. (2013a), 'Paraepic Comedy: Point(s) and Practices', in: E. Bakola/L. Prauscello/ M. Telò (eds.), *Greek Comedy and the Discourse of Genres*, Cambridge, 101–28.
Riu, X. (1999), *Dionysism and Comedy*, Lanham, Md.
Robertson, M. (1982), 'Ληκύθιον and αὐτολήκυθος', *JHS* 102, 234.
Robinson, E.G. (2004), 'Reception of Comic Theatre amongst the Indigenous South Italians', *MedArch* 17, 193–212.
Robson, J. (2006), *Humour, Obscenity and Aristophanes*, Tübingen.
Rogers, B.B. (1904), *The Thesmophoriazusae of Aristophanes*, London
Rogers, B.B. (1907), *The Plutus of Aristophanes*, London.
Rogers, B.B. (1910), *The Acharnians of Aristophanes*, London.
Rogers, B.B. (1913), *The Peace of Aristophanes*, London.
Romer, F.E. (1983), 'When Is a Bird Not a Bird?', *TAPhA* 113, 135–42.
Roselli, D.K. (2009), 'Theorika in Fifth-Century Athens', *GRBS* 49, 5–30.
Rosen, R. (1988), *Old Comedy and the Iambographic Tradition*, Atlanta.
Rosen, R. (2007), *Making Mockery: The Poetics of Ancient Satire*, Oxford.
Rosen, R. (2014), 'The Greek "Comic Hero"', in: M. Revermann (ed.), *The Cambridge Companion to Greek Comedy*, Cambridge, 222–40.
Ross, A. (1998), *The Language of Humour*, London/New York.
Rothfield, T. (1999), *Classical Comedy: Armoury of Laughter, Democracy's Bastion of Defence*, Lanham, MD.
Rothwell, K.S. (1990), *Politics and Persuasion in Aristophanes' Ecclesiazusae*, Leiden.
Roy-Charland, A./Perron, M./Beaudry, O/Eady, K. (2014), 'Confusion of Fear and Surprise: A Test of the Perceptual-Attentional Limitation Hypothesis with Eye Movement Monitoring', *Cognition and Emotion* 28, 1214–22.
Ruck, C. (1975), 'Euripides' Mother: Vegetables and the Phallos in Aristophanes', *Arion* 2, 13–57.
Ruffell, I. (2011), *Politics and Anti-Realism in Athenian Old Comedy: The Art of the Impossible*, Oxford.
Ruffell, I. (2014), 'Utopianism', in: M. Revermann (ed.), *The Cambridge Companion to Greek Comedy*, Cambridge, 206–21.
Russo, C.F. (1994), *Aristophanes: An Author for the Stage*, London.
Rutherford, I. (2001), *Pindar's Paeans: A Reading of the Fragments with a Survey of the Genre*, Oxford.
Rutherford, W. (1905), *A Chapter in the History of Annotation: Scholia Aristophanica*, vol. 3, London.
Sanders, J. (2006), *Adaptation and Appropriation*, London/New York.
Sanz, M./Laka, I./Tanenhaus, M.K. (eds.) (2013), *Language Down the Garden Path*, Oxford.
Saxonhouse, A.W. (1985), 'The Net of Hephaestus: Aristophanes' Speech in the *Symposium*', *Interpretation* 8, 15–32.
Schank, R./Abelson, R. (1977), *Scripts, Plans, Goals and Understanding: An Inquiry into Human Knowledge Structures*, Hillsdale, NJ.
Schirru, S. (2009), *La favola in Aristofane*, Berlin.
Schmid, F. (1954), 'Die Deminutiva auf -ιον im Vokativ bei Aristophanes', Ph.D. thesis, University of Zurich.
Schmid, W. (1920), 'Zwei Bemerkungen zu Aristophanes' Fröschen', *Philologus* 76, 222–5.

Schützwohl, A. (2018), 'Approach and Avoidance during Routine Behavior and during Surprise in a Non-Evaluative Task: Surprise Matters and So Does the Valence of the Surprising Event', *Frontiers in Psychology* 9, 826.
Scodel, R. (1980), *The Trojan Trilogy of Euripides*, Gottingen.
Seaford, R. (1982), 'The Date of Euripides' *Cyclops*', *JHS* 102, 161–72.
Seaford, R. (1984), *Euripides: Cyclops*, Oxford.
Segal, C. (1961), 'The Character and Cults of Dionysus and the Unity of the *Frogs*', *HSPh* 65, 207–42.
Sfyroeras, P. (2008), 'Πόθος Εὐριπίδου: Reading *Andromeda* in Aristophanes' *Frogs*', *AJPh* 129, 299–317.
Shackle, G.L.S. (1938), *Expectations, Investment and Income*, Oxford.
Shackle, G.L.S. (1949), *Expectation in Economics*, Cambridge.
Shackle, G.L.S. (1970), *Expectation, Enterprise and Profit: The Theory of the Firm*, London.
Sharpley, H. (1905), *The Peace of Aristophanes*, Edinburgh/London.
Shen, Y. (1987), 'On the Structure and Understanding of Poetic Oxymoron', *Poetics Today* 8, 105–22.
Sider, D. (1992), 'Ληκύθιον ἀπώλεσεν: Aristophanes' Limp Phallic Joke?', *Mnemosyne* 45, 359–64.
Sidwell, K.C. (2009), *Aristophanes the Democrat: The Politics of Satirical Comedy During the Peloponnesian War*, Cambridge/New York.
Sifakis, G.M. (1971), *Parabasis and Animal Choruses*, London.
Silk, M.S. (1990), 'The People of Aristophanes', in: C. Pelling (ed.), *Characterization and Individuality in Greek Literature*, Oxford, 150–73.
Silk, M.S. (2000), *Aristophanes and the Definition of Comedy*, Oxford.
Silk, M.S. (2013), 'The Greek Dramatic Genres: Theoretical Perspectives', in: E. Bakola/L. Prauscello/M. Telò (eds.), *Greek Comedy and the Discourse of Genres*, Cambridge/New York, 15–39.
Slater, N.W. (1997), 'Waiting in the Wings: Aristophanes' *Ecclesiazusae*', *Arion* 5, 97–129.
Slater, N.W. (2002), *Spectator Politics: Metatheatre and Performance in Aristophanes*, Philadelphia.
Slings, S.R. (2002), 'Figures of Speech in Aristophanes', in: Willi 2002, 99–109.
Snell, B. (1979), 'Lekythion', *Hermes* 107, 129–33.
Sommerstein, A.H. (1980), 'Notes on Aristophanes' *Knights*', *CQ* 30, 46–56.
Sommerstein, A.H. (1980a), 'βινεῖν', *LCM* 5, 47.
Sommerstein, A.H. (1981), *The Comedies of Aristophanes: Knights*, Warminster.
Sommerstein, A.H. (1982), *The Comedies of Aristophanes: Clouds*, Warminster.
Sommerstein, A.H. (1983), *The Comedies of Aristophanes: Wasps*, Warminster.
Sommerstein, A.H. (1984), 'Act Division in Old Comedy', *BICS* 31, 139–52.
Sommerstein, A.H. (1985), *The Comedies of Aristophanes: Peace*, Warminster.
Sommerstein, A.H. (1989), *Aeschylus: Eumenides*, Cambridge.
Sommerstein, A.H. (1990) *The Comedies of Aristophanes: Lysistrata*, Warminster.
Sommerstein, A.H. (1994), *The Comedies of Aristophanes: Thesmophoriazusae*, Warminster.
Sommerstein, A.H. (1996), *The Comedies of Aristophanes: Frogs*, Warminster.
Sommerstein, A.H. (1998), *The Comedies of Aristophanes: Ecclesiazusae*, Warminster.
Sommerstein, A.H. (2001), *The Comedies of Aristophanes: Wealth*, Warminster.
Sommerstein, A.H. (2005), 'Tragedy and Myth', in: R. Bushnell (ed.), *A Companion to Tragedy*, Oxford, 163–80.

Sommerstein, A.H. (2009), *Talking about Laughter and Other Studies in Greek Comedy*, Oxford/New York.
Sommerstein, A.H. (2010), *Aeschylean Tragedy*, 2nd edn., London.
Sommerstein, A.H. (2019), 'Para Prosdokian' in: *idem* (ed.), *The Encyclopedia of Greek Comedy*, Hoboken, NJ, 653–4.
Spyropoulos, E.S. (1974), *L'accumulation verbale chez Aristophane*, Thessaloniki.
Squires, N.K./Squires, K.C./Hillyard, S.A. (1975), 'Two Varieties of Long-Latency Positive Waves Evoked by Unpredictable Auditory Stimuli in Man', *Electroencephalography and Clinical Neurophysiology* 38, 387–401.
Stafford, E. (2000), *Worshipping Virtues: Personification and the Divine in Ancient Greece*, London.
Stähler, K. (2000), 'Prokne: eine Mythosgestalt in Drama und Skulptur klassischer Zeit', in: S. Gödde/T. Heinze (eds.), *Skenika: Beiträge zum antiken Theater und seiner Rezeption*, Darmstadt, 175–88.
Stanford, W.B. (1957), 'Notes on Aristophanes' *Frogs*', *Hermathena* 89, 65–72.
Stanford, W.B. (1958), *Aristophanes: Frogs*, London.
Stanford, W.B. (1963), *Aristophanes: The Frogs*, 2nd edn., London.
Starkie, W.J.M. (1909), *The* Acharnians *of Aristophanes*, London.
Starkie, W.J.M. (1911), *The* Clouds *of Aristophanes*, London.
Stephen, C. (1999), *Dialect in Aristophanes and the Politics of Language in Ancient Greek Literature*, Oxford.
Stevens, P.T. (1971), *Euripides: Andromache*, Oxford.
Stevens, S. (1991), 'Charon's Obol and Other Coins in Ancient Funerary Practice', *Phoenix* 45, 215–29.
Stone, L.M. (1981), *Costume in Aristophanic Comedy*, New York.
Storey, I. (2002), 'Cutting Comedies', in: J. Barsby (ed.), *Greek and Roman Drama: Translation and Performance*, Stuttgart, 146–67.
Storey, I. (2007), Review of Robson (2006) in *BMCRev* 2007.12.38.
Storey, I. (2013), Review of Griffith (2013) in *BMCRev* 2013.08.48.
Sutton, D. (1983), 'Aeschylus and the Mysteries: A Suggestion', *Hermes* 111, 249–51.
Sutton, D. (1983a), 'Dithyramb as Δρᾶμα: Philoxenus of Cythera' *Cyclops* or *Galatea*', *QUCC* 13, 37–43.
Synodinou, K. (1978), 'Some Cases of Oxymoron in Euripides', *Dodone* 7, 351–8.
Taaffe, L.K. (1991), 'The Illusion of Gender Disguise in Aristophanes' *Ecclesiazusae*', *Helios* 18, 91–112.
Taillardat, I. (1965), *Les images d'Aristophane: études de langue et de style*, 2nd edn., Paris.
Taplin, O. (1977), *The Stagecraft of Aeschylus*, Oxford.
Taplin, O. (1983), 'Tragedy and Trugedy', *CQ* 33, 331–4.
Taplin, O. (1986), 'Fifth-Century Tragedy and Comedy: A Synkrisis', *JHS* 106, 163–74.
Taplin, O. (1987), 'Classical Phallology, Iconographic Parody and Potted Aristophanes', *Dioniso* 57, 95–109.
Taplin, O. (1993), *Comic Angels and Other Approaches to Greek Drama through Vase-Painting*, Oxford.
Taplin, O. (2003), *Greek Tragedy in Action*, 2nd edn., London.
Taplin, O. (2007), *Pots and Plays: Interactions between Tragedy and Greek Vase-Painting of the Fourth Century BC*, LA.

Taplin, O. (2014), 'Epiphany of a Serious Dionysus in a Comedy?', in: S.D. Olson (ed.), *Ancient Comedy and Reception: Essays in Honor of Jeffrey Henderson*, Berlin/Boston, 62–8.
Tarrant, H. (1991), '*Clouds* I: Steps towards Reconstruction', *Arctos* 25, 157–81.
Telò, M. (2010), 'Embodying the Tragic Father(s): Autobiography and Intertextuality in Aristophanes', *ClAnt* 29, 278–326.
Telò, M. (2016), *Aristophanes and the Cloak of Comedy: Affect, Aesthetics, and the Canon*, Chicago/London.
Tetlow, E.M. (2005), *Women, Crime and Punishment in Ancient Law and Society: Ancient Greece*, London.
Tobin, V. (2018), *Elements of Surprise: Our Mental Limits and the Satisfactions of Plot*, Cambridge, MA.
Todd, S.C. (2007), *A Commentary on Lysias: Speeches 1–11*, Oxford.
Tordoff, R. (2013), 'Actors' Properties in Ancient Greek Drama: An Overview', in: G. Harrison/ V. Liapis (eds.), *Performance in Greek and Roman Theatre*, Leiden, 89–110.
Tsitsiridis, S. (2010), 'On Aristophanic Parody: The Parodic Techniques', in: S. Tsitsiridis (ed.), *Parachoregema. Studies on Ancient Theatre in Honour of Prof. Gregory M. Sifakis*, Herakleion, 359–82.
Ussher, R.G. (1973), *Aristophanes: Ecclesiazusae*, Oxford.
Ussher, R.G. (1978), *Euripides: Cyclops*, Rome.
Vaio, J. (1985), 'On the Thematic Structure of Aristophanes' *Frogs*', in: W.M. Calder/U.K. Goldsmith/P.B. Kevevan (eds.), *Hypatia: Essays in Classics, Comparative Literature, and Philosophy*, Boulder, CO, 91–102.
Van Steen, G. (2000), *Venom in Verse. Aristophanes in Modern Greece*, Princeton.
Vanhamme, J. (2000), 'The Link between Surprise and Satisfaction: An Exploratory Research on how Best to Measure Surprise', *Journal of Marketing Management* 16, 565–82.
Varakis, A. (2010), 'Body and Mask in Aristophanic Performance', *BICS* 53, 17–38.
Vickers, M.J. (2004), 'Aspasia on Stage: Aristophanes' *Ecclesiazusae*', *Athenaeum* 92, 431–50.
Vrticka, P./Black, J.M./Reiss, A.L. (2013), 'The Neural Basis of Humour Processing', *Nature Reviews Neuroscience* 14, 860–8.
Wagner, G. (1975), *The Novel and the Cinema*, Rutherford, NJ.
Webster, T.B.L. (1956), *Greek Theatre Production*, London.
Webster, T.B.L. (1967), *The Tragedies of Euripides*, London.
Wessel, J.R./Jenkinson, N./Brittain, J.S./Voets, S./Aziz, T./Aron, A.R. (2016), 'Surprise Disrupts Cognition via a Fronto-Basal Ganglia Suppressive Mechanism', *Nature Communications* 7, 11195.
West, M.L. (1984), *The Orphic Poems*, Oxford.
West, M.L. (1987), *Euripides: Orestes*, Warminster.
West, S. (2017), '*Philogelos*: An Anti-Intellectual Joke-Book', in: M. Alexiou/D. Cairns (eds.), *Greek Laughter and Tears: Antiquity and After*, Edinburgh, 104–21.
Whitman, C.H. (1964), *Aristophanes and the Comic Hero*, Cambridge, MA.
Whitman, C.H. (1969), 'Ληκύθιον ἀπώλεσεν', *HSPh* 73, 109–12.
Whitman, C.H. (1982), *The Heroic Paradox: Essays on Homer, Sophocles, and Aristophanes*, Ithaca, NY.
Wilkins, J. (2000), *The Boastful Chef: The Discourse of Food in Ancient Greek Comedy*, Oxford.
Willi, A. (ed.) (2002), *The Language of Greek Comedy*, Oxford.
Wills, G. (1969), 'Why Are the Frogs in the *Frogs*', *Hermes* 97, 306–17.

Wilner, O.L. (1931), 'The Character Treatment of Inorganic Roles in Roman comedy', *CPh* 26, 264–83.
Wilson, P. (2000), *The Athenian Institution of the Khoregia: The Chorus, the City and the Stage*, Cambridge.
Wit-Tak, T.M. de (1968), 'The Function of Obscenity in Aristophanes' *Thesmophoriazusae* and *Ecclesiazusae*', *Mnemosyne* 21, 357–65.
Worman, N. (2017), 'Euripides, Aristophanes, and the Reception of "Sophistic" Styles', in: L.K. McClure (ed.), *A Companion to Euripides*, Malden/Oxford, 515–32.
Wright, M. (2005), *Euripides' Escape-Tragedies: A Study of Helen, Andromeda, and Iphigenia among the Taurians*, Oxford/New York.
Wright, M. (2006), 'Cyclops and the Euripidean Tetralogy', *PCPhS* 52, 23–48.
Wright, M. (2007), 'Comedy and the Trojan War', *CQ* 57, 412–31.
Wright, M. (2012), *The Comedian as Critic: Greek Old Comedy and Poetics*, London.
Wrigley, A. (2007), 'Aristophanes Revitalized! Music and Spectacle on the Academic Stage', in: E. Hall/A. Wrigley (eds.), *Aristophanes in Performance, 421 BC–AD 2007: Peace, Birds and Frogs*, London, 136–54.
Zeitlin, F.I. (1999), 'Utopia and Myth in Aristophanes' *Ecclesiazousae*', in: T.M. Falkner/N. Felson/D. Kostan (eds.), *Contextualizing Classics: Ideology, Performance, Dialogue*, Lanham, MD, 69–87.
Zelnick-Abramovitz, R. (2012), 'Slaves and Role Reversal in Ancient Greek Cults', in: S. Hodkinson/D. Geary (eds), *Slaves and Religions in Graeco-Roman Antiquity and Modern Brazil*, Newcastle upon Tyne, 96–132.
Zhao, K./Zhao, J./Zhang, M./Cui, Q./Fu, X. (2017), 'Neural Responses to Rapid Facial Expressions of Fear and Surprise', *Frontiers in Psychology* 8, 761.
Zimmermann, B. (1984), *Untersuchungen zur Form und dramatischen Technik der Aristophanischen Komödien I: Parodos und Amoibaion*, Rudolstadt.
Zimmermann, B. (2011), *Handbuch der griechischen Literatur der Antike*, vol. 1, Munich.
Zimmermann, B. (2014), 'Aristophanes', in: M. Fontaine/A. Scafuro (eds.), *The Oxford Handbook of Greek and Roman Comedy*, Oxford, 132–59.
Zweig, B. (1992), 'The Mute Nude Female Characters in Aristophanes' Plays', in: A. Richlin (ed.), *Pornography and Representation in Greece and Rome*, Oxford, 73–89.

Video-recorded performances online
Accessed on 1 November 2019

Chronopoulos, D. (dir.) (1997), *Lysistrata*, Greek National Theatre. Available at <www.nt-archive.gr/viewvideos.aspx?playID=607&videoFile=0422-01-00>.
Eastman, H. (dir.) (2013), *Frogs*, Cambridge Arts Theatre. Available at <www.youtube.com/watch?v=yYYQIn_sC-4>.
Evangelatos, S. (dir.) (1998), *Ecclesiazusae*, S. Evangelatos' Amphi-Theatre. Available at <www.youtube.com/watch?v=nTNfLrPnf10> and <www.youtube.com/watch?v=msXUyMxmz2E>.
Giannopoulos, N. (dir.) (1977), *Wasps*, National Theatre of Northern Greece. Available at <www.youtube.com/watch?v=sX2IP4N3hwA> (part 1) <www.youtube.com/watch?v=eukfGpxPwmk> (part 2) <www.youtube.com/watch?v=TCKgwa2Y37w> (part 3) <www.youtube.com/watch?v=ASSOGeHDxlw> (part 4).

Solomos, A. (dir.) (1972), *Lysistrata*, Greek National Theatre. Available at
  <www.youtube.com/watch?v=4e7PfdI8muw>.
Tsianos, K. (dir.) (1998), *Frogs*, Greek National Theatre. Available at <www.youtube.com/
  watch?v=-wT_fIMBtG4>.
Tsianos, K. (dir.) (2004), *Lysistrata*, Greek National Theatre. Available at <www.nt-archive.gr/
  viewvideos.aspx?playID=240&videoFile=0564-01-00> and
  <www.youtube.com/watch?v=HxD0LG41gZs>.
Voutsinas, A. (dir.) (1996), *Ecclesiazusae*, Greek National Theatre. Available at
  <www.youtube.com/watch?v=zsxgGH0MkuI>.

Index Locorum

Only the passages which are commented upon – i.e. not simply cited or quoted – are indexed. An asterisk (*) marks the Aristophanic passages which are (also) approached through modern performances in Chapters 3 and 4.

Aeschylus
Ag. 4	138
PV 298–9	143 n. 428
PV 747–51	181
Supp. 712	32

Archilochus
5 W	173
122 W	5, 19 n. 61
128 W	63
187 W	59
191 W	76

Aristophanes
Acharnians
17–18	41
68–75	70–2, 78, 82
80–2	73–4, 85
81–3	41–2
88–9	50
113–14	135 n. 402
118	54
119–20	23, 58–9, 78, 83
121	43
175–7	136
255–6	72, 78, 80–1
336	69
396	59, 72, 86
410–11	146
427	102 n. 287, 149 n. 451
464	59–60, 72, 84
480	25, 63, 71, 82, 120
500	43–4, 96
524–9	93
582	71, 82
615	48, 63
664	21 n. 65, 100 n. 278
684	44
732–3	60, 63, 71, 78
751	69–70
756	54
889	50
904	78
909	64, 72
950	44
967	48, 63
974	48
984–5	51
1002	50
1021	50
1026	38, 71

Knights
169–75	150
197–201	94
498–9	138 n. 410
551–63	95 n. 251, 113
581–4	113
1226	25
1249	141, 145
1321–34	129

Wasps
15–9	98–9
21–3	99
73–84	3
*143–4	156
*169–91 (donkey scene)	101, 156
379	142
397	142
*548	156
*907–30 (dog in court)	157–9
*936–9	158
*955	173
*963–6	158
1030–5	79, 100
1352–9	6

Clouds
2–4	138
149	28
179	28
181–2	142, 148

191–4	147	868	49
218	141	874	56–7
227–34	196	898	64, 73
534–44	125, 139	1017–22	135
1061–70	97, 125	1022	40
1145	136–7	1065	62–3
Peace		1116	24, 35
7	66	1186	52–3
34	51	1270–87	173
47–8	104	1298–1301	173
82	104	1315	129
95	42	*Birds*	
97	103	61–8	106
123	74–5	86–91	187
127–34	103	100 f. (Tereus)	104–5
150–2	104	174–7	150
153	33 n. 96, 51	264	129, 150 n. 454
154	104	466–521 (genealogy)	106–7, 125
169–7	104	771–5	104
173	141	482	106
181	104	667–84	108
182–3	186	688–702 (cosmogony)	107–8, 125
199	51	696	108
235	45	769–84	182
249	52	771	182
279	45	783	182
300	37	*863–94 (priest scene)	132
308	69	974–89	192
327	135	995	34
363	66, 72	1198	141
378	36	1255–6	138 n. 409
425	79	1336–1410	140
473–4	83	1477	35
505	54	1678–9	135
517	142	*Lysistrata*	
554	56	23	180
557	69	78–81	170
571–9	56	106	25
627	52	*127	164
669	52	*152–4	164
708	38–9	155–6	90–1
711	38–9	*212–37 (women's oath)	154–5
728	42	215–16	154
756	79	551–4	109
795	55	563–4	111
823	67, 72	691–5	112
864	45, 63, 77	782	113

805	113	37	180
*861–2	163	48–50	180
*879	159	*52–5	50, 66, 180
915–40 (Myrrhine scene) 160–1, 164		112–5	24
Thesmophoriazusae		140–2	119
4–6	117	*117–35	180–1
13–8	116	177	181
24	45–6	182	142
50	75, 83	*199–237 (the frogs' song) 182–4	
53–7	53	*288–92 (Empousa) 184–5	
96	141	314	186
130–3	71, 75–6, 78	338	186
158	42	419–20	25
242	47	462	186
254	76	465–7	186
276	142	479	38 n. 113, 186
288–90	48	531	188
335–7	46	582–3	188
346	46	586–8	188
509	75	612–7	188
515–6	49–50	637–9	188
530	64	*641–64 (thrashing scene) 189	
531–2	64–5	670–1	189
643–8	164	757 f. (second episode) 189–90	
694	114	765	142 n. 421
733–4	114	797–8	190
761	114	830 f. (the *agōn*)	142
769–78	115, 135, 164	860	190
804	55	866–9	190
829	80	885–94	190
857	60–1	907–8	190
862–3	116	944	191
888	116	947	192
935	61	971–91 (*pnigos*)	192
937	78–9	1008–10	190
1014	116	1030–6	190
1022–38	116	1082	86
1025	42–3	*1198–247 (*lēkythion*) 192–5	
1051	46–7	1331–64	120
1099	141	*1365–410 (weighing scales) 195–6	
1111–2	116	1427 f. (political advice) 196	
1114–24	116	1477	86
1226	47	1491–9	196
Frogs		*Ecclesiazusae*	
*1–20 (fart jokes)	177–8	60–7	169
22	90	74–5	169
*21–32 (donkey)	178–9	206–8	172

268–79	169	**Cicero**	
493–513	169	*De or.* 263	31
*539	170	*De or.* 270	31
578–80	120–1		
1041–2	121, 125	**Demetrius Rhet.**	
*1169–75	172	*Eloc.* 152	28–9
Wealth			
17	48	**Demosthenes**	
27	71	18130	28
87–92	124	18262	162
152	77		
165	72, 85	**Euripides**	
180	39–40, 85	*Alc.* 141	86
210	50 n. 139	*Andr.* 628–30	110
219	55–6	*Hel.* 1–3	61
266–7	140	*Med.* 145–7	181
277–8	36, 85	*Phoen.* 272–3	62
290–301	101 n. 284	*Tro.* 1049–50	17–18
302–15	123		
372	67	**Hermogenes**	
600	62, 86	*Meth.* 34	28–9
635	124		
693	80	**Herodotus**	
706	67–8, 72, 83	11–15	93
737	65		
765	37–8	**Homer**	
818	74	*Il.* 12200–9	94
963	40, 72	*Od.* 9430–2	102
972	36 n. 107	*Od.* 11489–91	182
976–7	48	*Od.* 17302–4	32
1032–7	24–5	*Od.* 19211	32
1097–101	134		
		Philogelos	
Aristotle		244	20
Nik. Eth. 1111a	132 n. 394		
Poet. 1448a	122 n. 360	**Plato**	
Poet. 1452a	29	*Apol.* 19c	168
Poet. 1453a	128	*Phdr.* 253e	58
Poet. 1454b	143	*Symp.* 189c–193e	117
Poet. 1460a–b	5–6		
Rhet. 21379a	30	**Plutarch**	
Rhet. 31412a	29	*De tranq. anim.* 475a 32	
Callimachus		**Rufinus**	
AP 1251	19	*AP* 519	19

Semonides
7 W   80

Sophocles
Aj. 44   127
Aj. 648   17
Ant. 463–4   182
OT 371   37 n. 109

Thucydides
7301   5

Tiberius
Fig. Demosth. 16   28–9

Index Nominum et Rerum

abuse 7, 21, 23, 62, 79–80, 85, 98–9, 111–12, 125, 172 n. 487, 186, 199
accident 5, 162–5, 198
accumulation 10, 13, 22–3, 25, 39–40, 44, 53, 64, 72, 78, 85, 145, 151, 175, 187, 189, 192, 197
adaptation 89–90, 101, 106, 111, 119, 124–5, 133, 164 n. 472, 171, 191, 194
Aeschylus (the real one) 17, 51, 91, 95, 115 n. 331, 126, 132 n. 394, 168, 178 n. 491, 190–1; (in *Ran*.) 120, 142, 146 n. 447, 165, 176, 189, 191–2, 194–7
Aesop 43, 59, 89, 103–4, 106, 112, 122, 125, 198
Agathon 42, 53, 75–6, 83, 117, 141–2, 146–7, 165, 180
agōn 62, 113, 142, 190
alazōn/impostor 81–4
alliteration 13, 23, 37 n. 109, 72, 85, 108 n. 311, 151, 177, 192
ambiguity 7, 17, 21, 25, 44, 50 n. 140, 51, 111, 135, 138, 146, 170, 173
anadiplosis 59, 151
Andersen, Hans Christian 182
animals 1, 35, 63 n. 169, 73, 78, 80–1, 85, 94, 97, 99–100, 102, 105, 112, 116, 118 n. 346, 127, 145, 156–9, 162, 177–9 (the donkey in *Ran*.), 194, 196 n. 536, 198
antilabē 36, 39, 53, 61 n. 164, 72, 135, 173–4, 191
antithesis 12–13, 25, 43, 53–4, 69
appropriation 5, 17, 21–2, 33, 36 n. 107, 45, 57, 59–60, 63–4, 76, Ch 2 *passim* (esp. 89–91 for a theoretical definition), 138, 167–8, 171–3, 175, 181, 187, 199
aprosdokēton 6 n 20, 19, 32, 73
Apulian pottery 114 n. 329, 178–9, 193
Archilochus 5, 59, 63, 76, 111, 173–4
Aristotle 1, 5, 26, 29–33, 57, 81, 89, 128, 143, 198
Aroni, Mary 155 Fig. 6a–b

aside (joke/action) 15 n. 53, 24, 53, 79, 133–4, 179, 189, 191
Aspasia 93, 166, 168
asyndeton 23
augmentatives 23

Bergson, Henri 10
bōmolochos/buffoon 81–4, 118, 176
Boulē 7, 56, 64
braggart soldier 187–8

Cameron, David 185
Cavafy, Constantine P 181
Cerberus 100–1, 118, 186, 188
characterisation 6–7, 17, 26, 78, 81–4, 126, 176, 199
chiasmus 25 n. 77, 71, 150
Chronopoulos, Diagoras 153, 155, 160–1, 163–5
Cicero 30–1, 33
Circe 13, 123–4
City Dionysia 56, 62 n. 166, 122, 126 n. 372, 131–2, 177 n. 498
Clegg, Nick 185
Cleon 20–1, 52, 79, 99–100, 103, 138 n. 410, 165
Cleonymus 35, 50, 98–9, 173–4
climax (crescendo)/anti-climax 19, 46–7, 133, 147, 156, 189, 173, 176–7, 199
cognition/cognitive linguistics 2, 4, 5, 30, 70, 78, 86 (see also: Neuroscience)
componential analysis 21, 34, 57
compounds 5, 23, 61, 94, 151, 172
contradiction 4, 21, 25, 34–6, 38, 40, 43, 48, 53–4, 58, 61–2 n. 169, 69–72, 85, 94, 130–1, 133–8, 154–5, 174, 199
crane/*mēchanē* 21, 116, 129, 131, 138, 141–5, 148–9, 163, 198
Cratinus 18, 118

dance 45, 77, 108, 124, 129, 135–6, 139, 184–5
Dandoulaki, Katia 155
Darwin, Charles 1

deixis 15, 38, 92, 113–14, 141
Demetrius Rhet. 27–9, 31, 33
Demosthenes 28, 31 n. 91, 123 n. 363, 162, 191 n. 522
Descartes, René 1
dialect 25, 94, 198–9
Di-Caprio, Leonardo 183
diminutives 23, 49, 65, 74, 76
Diodorus Siculus 31
dithyramb 122–4
door-scenes 101, 106, 134, 136–7, 145, 148, 156, 180, 186

Eastman, Helen 176, 184–5
eirōn 80–4
ekkyklēma (see: platform)
Ekman, Paul 1–2
Electra 95 – 6, 125, 126 n. 372, 151, 169 n. 483
elegy 62, 174
emotions/emotion theory 1–2, 4–5, 18, 32, 56, 70 n. 182, 120, 147
emphasis 35–6, 51, 56, 59, 67, 72, 77, 85, 127, 134, 152, 169, 186, 189
Empousa 15 n. 54, 22, 117, 184–5
epic 25, 62–3, 73, 89, 94, 110, 123, 128, 173
Epicharmus 18, 31 n. 91, 101 n. 284
epigram, Hellenistic 18–19
erōs/Eros 108–9
euphemism 24, 45, 52, 112
Eupolis 18, 118
Euripides (the real one) 17–18, 31 n. 91, 46, 59–61, 81, 86–7, 102, 104, 126–7, 165, 168, 190–2, 196; (in *Ach.*) 59–60, 63, 69, 84, 91–2, 129, 141, 146–7, 180; (in *Ran.*) 86, 120, 142, 146 n. 447, 176, 180, 189, 191, 194–5, 197; (in *Thesm.*) 42, 45–7, 53, 61–2, 75, 114–17, 141, 146, 164–5
Evangelatos, Spyros 153, 157, 171–3
exaggeration/*hyperbolē* 18, 50, 55, 57, 66, 89, 92–3, 116, 120, 154, 190–1
Expectancy Violations Theory (EVT) 3–4
extratextual/extradramatic/extratheatrical/ extradiegetic 4, 29, 33, 40, 152, 162 n. 470, 165, 169, 176, 199

face 1, 59, 74, 123 n. 365, 133, 154, 160, 173, 189–90
failure/unsuccessful 34, 75, 98, 101–2, 115–16, 133, 147, 162, 165 n. 473, 168, 172, 175, 182, 184 n. 509, 188, 196
Farage, Nigel 185
fear 1, 2 n. 3, 5, 29, 55–6, 148 n. 450, 151, 198
Freud, Sigmund 10, 12

garden-path sentences 33, 51
General Theory of Verbal Humour (GTVH) 11
Gerasimidou, Eleni 155
Giannopoulos, Ntinos 153, 156–9
grammar 14, 25, 56–7, 68, 71–2, 135, 138, 198–9
Greimas, Algirdas Julien 10
Grimm, Brothers 182

Hadjidakis, Manos 182, 164 n. 472 191
hapax 23, 53, 61, 70, 129, 148
hendiadys 109
Hermogenes 27–9, 31, 33
Hesiod 97, 107–8
Homer 17 n. 56, 25, 32, 94–5, 97–9, 101–2, 123 n. 366, 126, 187
homosexual/homoerotic/homophobic/gay 19, 58, 83, 100 n. 278, 103 n. 291, 116, 180
horizon of expectations 33, 130
Humour Theory/Humour Studies 8, 10–12
hyperbolē (see: exaggeration)

iambus 59, 96, 173, 187, 198
ideology 6–7, 171, 199
idiolect (poetic) 1, 120
idiom/proverb 13, 30 n. 88, 33, 35, 42, 45, 48–9, 56–7, 63–5, 74, 106, 113 n. 326
illusion (dramatic) 92, 102, 114–15, 123, 131, 158, 169
improvisation 13, 157
incongruity 2, 4, 10, 40, 70 n. 182, 128, 154–5, 158, 170–1
innovation (see: novelty)

Index Nominum et Rerum —— 245

intentionality/poetological intention/purpose 1, 3, 9, 15, 17, 21, 27, 37, 54–5, 65, 75, 78, 93, 96, 108, 114, 122, 124, 125, 131–2, 135, 137, 140, 146, 148, 152, 156, 162, 166, 169, 172 n. 486, 177–8, 186, 190, 196, 198
intertextual/interdramatic 4, 43, 46, 58, 61, 105, 112, 130, 148, 165, 183, 186, 199
intratextual/intradramatic 4, 14, 21, 124–6, 152, 199

Kant, Immanuel 1, 3
Karras, Vasilis 173
Konstantopoulou, Zoe 165–8
Koun, Karolos 132, 153 n. 457, 164, 182
Kourou, Gianna 159 Fig. 8
Kyriakou, Anna 155 Fig. 6a–b

laughter 3–4, 9–10, 22, 31–2, 70 n. 182, 78, 83, 113, 118, 129, 133, 139, 156, 158, 160, 163–4, 170, 173, 179, 180–1, 183–5, 188 n. 516, 189, 191–2, 194
lekythion (pottery) 22–3, 192–5; (metre) 182–3
Lenaea 122, 130–2, 142, 177, 186
logic 4, 11, 33–5, 53, 57–8, 89, 130, 165 n. 473, 175

masks 21, 40, 43, 76, 102, 124, 129–31, 133, 138, 150, 154, 165 n. 474, 169, 185, 189–90
mathematics 14
Mbezos, Giannis 153, 165–8, 177, 179 Fig. 16
Mbousdoukos, Nikos 163 Fig. 12a–c
mēchanē (see: crane)
meta-paratragedy 120
metaphor 24–5, 30–1, 45, 50–3, 63 n. 169, 74, 80–1, 111–12, 121, 137, 180–1, 187, 190, 192, 196
meta-surprise 97, 198
metatheatre 8, 24, 40, 102, 115, 120, 126, 143, 148, 152, 160, 162, 165, 169
metonymy 37, 39 n. 115, 41, 45, 50–2, 55, 77
Michalakopoulos, Giorgos 169–70

Middleton, Kate 185
Miliband, Ed 185
Modern Greek 5, 19 n. 61 153, 173
Molière 162 n. 469
Molon 50, 180 n. 503

narratology 11, 13–14, 20, 199
Neuroscience 1–2, 3 n. 12, 5 n. 18, 198 (see also: cognition)
New Comedy 6, 88 n. 226, 95
Nezer, Christoforos 149 Fig. 5
nonsense 12, 14, 25, 34, 59, 134 n. 397
novelty/innovation/invention 4, 8, 14, 20, 30, 65, 74, 87, 91, 104–6, 108, 120–1, 123–4, 127–8, 138, 154–5, 171, 187, 198
nudity 49 n. 137, 110 Fig. 4, 137, 163, 189

obscenity 11, 23, 25, 58, 81, 109, 191
Oedipus 37 n. 109, 50 n. 139, 117, 121, 126–7, 150
Olympia, Temple of Zeus 100–1
onomatopoeia 23, 48, 177
opposition 2 n. 3, 4, 7, 10–11, 71, 81, 86, 103, 106, 118, 131, 134, 146, 154, 178, 198
oratory/rhetoric 27, 29–33, 57, 60, 64, 78, 107, 190
Oxford, Sheldonian Theatre 15–16
oxymoron 17, 21, 25, 27, 33–5, 54, 59, 62, 85–7, 109, 118

paean 183
parabasis 55, 77, 80 n. 210, 95–6, 107, 131, 137, 139
paraskēnia 165
par' hyponoian 31, 45, 49, 52, 57
Parker, Camilla 185
PASOK 172
Pegasus 102–4, 148
Peloponnesian War 93, 132
Performance Theory 8–10
Pericles 54, 62, 93, 191 n. 522
personifications 24–5, 55, 96, 118
phallus/penis 50, 76, 81, 101, 111, 130, 137–40, 160, 163–4, 189, 192
Philippidis, Petros 177, 179 Fig. 16

Philogelos 20
Philoxenus 122–3, 198
phonology 23, 25, 36, 69–70, 108
Phrynichus 177
platform/*ekkyklēma* 21, 105, 129, 131, 141–8, 156, 184, 198
Plato 58, 117, 121, 141, 168
Platonius 18
pleonasm 121
Plutarch 31–2
pnigos 192
Polybius 31–2
polysyndeton 23, 53
praeter exspectationem 30–1
pragmatics 7, 10–12, 24, 35, 199
priamel 177
proagōn 124, 130, 168, 196 n. 536, 197
Propp, Vladimir 3
props 4, 116, 129, 140–2, 148, 160, 163–5, 189, 193–5
prōthysteron 67
proverb (see: idiom)
proxemics 3–4
psychology 1–2, 9
pun 11, 36, 56, 70, 74–5, 83, 105, 108

rape 5 n. 17, 7, 56–7, 88, 93, 97, 102, 104, 111–12, 154–5
realism/dramatic reality/unrealism 3, 12, 24, 34, 38, 46, 59, 67, 79, 88, 109, 114, 130, 136, 147, 149, 163, 178, 181, 188, 196
reception 1, 3, 9, 33, 83, 89, 94, 120, 132, 163 n. 471, 166, 188 n. 516
reform/revolution 128
replacement 34–6, 39 n. 115, 45, 59, 65, 69, 73, 86, 89, 91, 93–4, 102, 104, 105 n. 300, 114–15, 172 n. 486, 182–3, 195
reversal 4, 7, 18, 33, 35, 47, 57, 63–4, 88–9, 96, 100, 102, 104–6, 116, 118, 131, 133, 134 n. 400, 145, 146 n. 446, 163, 178, 180–1, 187–8
rhetoric (see: oratory)
rhyme 13, 23, 53, 72–3, 194
Rural Dionysia 88, 162 n. 468

sarcasm 69, 80, 84, 136, 166, 169
satire 20, 25, 80, 86, 94, 107 n. 306, 119, 122–3, 165, 173
satyr play 42, 62, 101 n. 284, 117 n. 342, 125, 126 n. 372, 198
scatology 7, 15, 23, 42, 73–4, 81–4, 103 n. 291, 123, 177, 186, 196
Schwarzenegger, Arnold 180
semantics 7, 10–12, 24–5, 33 n. 96, 34, 36, 38, 40, 43, 46–8, 50–1, 54, 58–9, 61, 63 n. 169, 68, 70, 75, 84, 86
Semantic-Script Theory of Humour (SSTH) 10–11
sex/sexual humour 6, 20–1, 23, 39, 50, 54–5, 58–9, 64, 75–7, 81, 84, 108–9, 111–12, 117, 121, 123 n. 364, 125–6, 146, 154–5, 160, 163–4, 171, 191 (see also: homosexual)
Shakespeare 90, 187 n. 514
similes 50–1
Socrates 4 n. 16, 20 n. 64, 28, 107, 112 n. 324, 129, 136–7, 139, 141, 147–8, 165, 167–8, 196
Solomos, Alexis 149 Fig. 5, 153, 155 Fig. 6a–b, 160–2
Sophocles 17, 31 n. 91, 91, 104–5, 115 n. 331, 126–7, 162, 176–7, 198
stimulus 1 n. 1, 2, 4–5, 10, 70 n. 182
Stoa Poikilē 190 n. 520
sudden 3–5, 14, 19, 33, 43, 61, 67, 92, 148, 160, 196, 199
superlatives 23, 70
surrealism 11, 35 n. 103, 59, 134, 175, 196–7
suspense 17 n. 56, 104, 152, 168, 196
synecdochē 52, 59, 136 n. 107, 183

Telephus 62, 69, 91–3, 114–16, 126, 165 n. 473, 198
Theatre Semiotics 9
Theodorakis, Mikis 191
Thucydides 5, 31 n. 91
Tiberius 27–9, 31
Titanic 183
Tractatus Coislinianus 29–30
Tsianos, Kostas 175, 177–80, 183, 185, 189, 194

Tsipras, Alexis 166
typology 1, 8, 21–2, 27, 37, 68–77, 89, 198–9

unexpected 3–5, 17–20, 25, 28–33, 35–6, 41–2, 44, 48, 69–71, 114, 129, 133, 144, 148, 158, 169, 171, 182, 195

Voutsinas, Andreas 153, 169–70

Wilde, Oscar 191

www.ingramcontent.com/pod-product-compliance
Lightning Source LLC
Chambersburg PA
CBHW061936220426
43662CB00012B/1931